Wilmette at 150

Wilmette at 150

★——————≈——————★

by

John Jacoby

AMIKA PRESS

First Edition   ISBN 13: 978-1-937484-91-0

AMIKA PRESS
466 Central Ave #23 Northfield IL 60093
847 920 8084   info@amikapress.com
Available for purchase on amikapress.com

Edited by Jay Amberg.

Front cover photography by Tim Perry, © National Spiritual Assembly of the Bahá'ís of the United States. Back cover logo courtesy of the Wilmette Historical Museum.

Book designed and typeset by Sarah Koz. Body and subtitles in ITC Slimbach, designed by Robert Slimbach in 1987. Titles in Americana, designed by Richard Isbell and Whedon Davis in 1965; digitized by Linotype in 1988.

Thanks to Nathan Matteson.

CONTENTS

Wilmette at 150

INTRODUCTION

In September 2010, the *Wilmette Beacon* came into being, and soon afterwards, I volunteered to be a contributing columnist. Over the ensuing nine-plus years, I wrote 500 weekly columns, stopping only when the pandemic forced the *Beacon* to close down in March 2020.

At the beginning, I had no idea what I'd write about, but in the spirit of the publication, I vowed that every column would have a Wilmette connection. As of 2010, I had lived in the village for more than three decades, and my wife and I had been active in the civic and social life of the village. Our four kids grew up here and thrived in the community and public schools. Surely, I believed, I could find something local to write about, drawing from this experience and current events.

It turned out not to be easy to find a current topic to write about every week, but my time on the village board had taught me the importance of historical context and had made me aware of some fascinating stories from Wilmette's past. These stories often became the subjects of my columns, and as I researched one, I came across others.

The *Wilmette Beacon*'s demise and stay-at-home directives, occurring simultaneously, left me with little to do and nowhere to go. I fell back on an idea that had been suggested by a few *Beacon* readers before the coronavirus suddenly changed my routine: Write a book based on these stories. For the next few months, I passed the days largely engaged in this project. A special impetus was the fact that the village will be celebrating its Sesquicentennial in 2022. I reasoned that folks will be thinking about Wilmette's history, and a book of stories about Wilmette's past might be of special interest now.

Wilmette at 150 is not intended to be a comprehensive history of the village. If that's what you want, try George Bushnell's *Wilmette: A History* (2nd ed., 1984). Unlike the Bushnell book, this book presents discrete stories, divided into 19 categories, each category with its own chapter. The stories impart historical context, but they aren't intended to present all of the significant people and events of Wilmette's 150-year existence.

The stories reveal Wilmette as a place of achievement and failure, joy and sorrow, kindness and callousness, hope and despondency, service and apathy, love and prejudice—all of humanity's virtues and frailties. While researching and writing these stories, I was touched emotionally—saddened by some, inspired by others, and amused by still more. Together, they give Wilmette a unique character.

A small sampling of subjects: Dr. Martin Luther King's inspirational visit to the North Shore, the German POW camp in Harms Woods, the colorful history of No Man's Land, an honor roll of exceptional Wilmette women, the Palm Sunday tornado that heavily damaged the Village Center, the remarkable perseverance of world pushup champion Chick Lister, and Judge Kolman's tree memorial on Glenview Road. Also, the times when Wilmette's schools almost went broke, eleven-year-old Stevie Baltz united the nation in hope and grief, and Baby Face Nelson met his maker on Walnut Avenue.

In a few stories, the subject speaks in the first person. These stories are based on facts, but most of the words and attitudes attributed to the subjects are mine. I used this and other devices in an attempt to explain Wilmette's history in an interesting, informal, and sometimes amusing way.

I also sprinkled in some opinions throughout the stories. For example, my choices of local government's best and worst decisions are purely my opinion. However, as a person who has been involved in village affairs for many years and who has spent many hours researching and writing about Wilmette's past, I believe it's appropriate and even important that I share a few insights and opinions. In that sense, the book is a little bit about me.

Many chapters end with News Flashes that are relevant to the content of the chapter. They're written as if the event just happened. I learned about these events from newspapers and other sources, but I did extensive additional research to present them fully: the exact date of the event, the ages and addresses of the people involved, background information, and future outcomes. Except for the words within quotation marks, these News Flashes are my words, not something lifted from a newspaper.

It's my hope that this book will promote unity among Wilmette residents. We who live here now need to build on the past with knowledge of the village's successes, failures, and unique experiences. No one knows what challenges will arise in the future, but I'm confident that the village will meet them successfully if unity is an underlying principle, as it has been for most of our history. Unity doesn't require the absence of disagreement, but it does require listening, empathy, and civility.

In the spirit of unity, I selected two images for the cover of this book. The first is the beautiful image of the Bahá'í House of Worship on the front cover. It's not only the most recognizable landmark in the village—one that's a source of tremendous community pride—but it's also the symbol of a religious movement that stands for the oneness of all humankind. I gratefully acknowledge the photo by Tim Perry, copyright National Spiritual Assembly of the Bahá'ís of the United States.

The second image, on the back cover, is the 1996 logo of the Wilmette Human Relations Commission. It symbolizes the Village's official commitment to the goal of equality and unity among all people, and it asks the community to honor this goal in their daily lives.

My thanks go to the officials of local government and residents who've been helpful and supportive as I've compiled these stories over the years. I'm most grateful to the Wilmette Historical Museum and also to the Wilmette Public Library for being excellent sources of historical information. Through these institutions and various websites, I found literally thousands of newspaper articles, census records, old directories, military records, birth certificates, death records, cemetery records, photographs, and other historical records that became the basis for these stories.

And finally, my deep gratitude goes to the team of advisers who helped me find a better and more accurate way to tell the stories in this book: Alan P. Henry, Elaine Fandell, Kathy Hussey-Arntson, Lisa Roberts, James Petrie, Vernon Squires, and the folks at Amika Press.

A minor technical note: Many Wilmette street names have changed over the years, which complicates the telling of these stories. Green Bay Road, often referred to in these chapters, began as West Railroad Avenue. In 1922 it became Main Street, and in 1936 it became Green Bay Road. I'm using the name that applied at the time of the events being described.

CHAPTER 1

★————————————★

The Shoreline

The poet William Wordsworth figured it out. A lake, he said, "carries you into recesses of feeling otherwise impenetrable." Perhaps that explains the intimate connection that Wilmette residents have always had with their lakefront.

Wilmette's Lake Michigan shoreline is 1.8 miles long. About 75 percent is publicly owned. The Metropolitan Water Reclamation District owns Wilmette Harbor and the North Shore Channel, which are part of the metropolitan-wide system of canals, tunnels, reservoirs, and pumps that prevents sewage from entering and polluting the lake. The Village owns the waterworks north of Lake Avenue and the Elmwood Dunes Preserve at the foot of Elmwood Avenue. The Wilmette Park District owns the rest of the public portion: Gillson Park's 60 acres and Langdon Park's 3.4 acres. The private shoreline consists of three areas: the magnificent home sites on Canterbury Court, east Linden Avenue, and Sheridan Road across from the Bahá'í House of Worship; the shoreline properties on Michigan Avenue and Sheridan Road between Forest Avenue and Langdon Park; and the high-rise section of No Man's Land.

The lake has been a major factor in the village's history and development. As a shimmering blue contrast to the beaches and flora, it dazzles lovers of nature and beauty and comforts seekers of peace and contemplation. It affects the climate, sometimes for the good, sometimes not. Its waters and beaches offer swimmers, sunbathers, boaters, and anglers opportunities for fun, exercise, and relaxation. Since 1892, it has supplied water to the homes of Wilmette.

There's also a dark side to the lake. People who use it for recreation must respect its dangers, including undertows and sudden storms. At least 38 people have drowned in the lake waters off Wilmette and in the harbor and channel (see Appendix 1). Swimmers and waders are the largest category of victims, followed by boaters, victims of falls, and heroes who attempted to rescue others. Two people have drowned at the Park District's guarded beach.

The U.S. Coast Guard left Evanston in 1931 and established a new station
at Wilmette Harbor. Courtesy of the Wilmette Historical Museum.

Two drowning victims were guardsmen stationed at the U.S. Coast Guard
Station at Wilmette Harbor, which is credited with saving countless lives over
the years. On October 28, 1951 guardsmen Robert Sawyer and Max Wage risked
their lives by searching in rough waters for three missing duck hunters. The
guardsmen themselves disappeared, and only a few scraps of boat wreckage
were ever found.

Another challenging feature of Lake Michigan is the constantly changing
water level. Measurement data goes back to 1860, when the lake was near its
historic high. In more recent years, highs were seen in 1952, 1974, 1986, 1997,
and 2019–2020, while lows occurred in 1934, 1964, and 2013. The difference
between the record high (1986) and the record low (2013) is an astounding six
feet. The highs can cause significant beach and bluff erosion and damage to
structures near the shoreline, especially during wind storms producing high
waves. Langdon Park in particular has suffered greatly.

The Gates Estate

With this background, let's take an imaginary stroll along Wilmette's Lake
Michigan shoreline, beginning just north of the Evanston border at the Gates
Estate, 336 Sheridan Road. In the mid-1880s Philetus Gates purchased a five-

acre wooded expanse at this location, fronting on Sheridan Road and extending east to the lake. For the next two decades, the property remained undeveloped.

Gates was the son of a wealthy Chicago manufacturer of industrial equipment and owner of the Gault House, a hotel at the corner of Madison and Clinton streets in Chicago. He began his career as manager of the hotel, and after his father's death in 1888 he took over the manufacturing business as well. In 1901 Allis-Chalmers Co. bought the business and made him an officer of the company. He ran its manufacturing plants until 1904 when he resigned. He ended his career as president and director of Hanna Engineering Works (1908–1922).

In 1908 Gates decided to turn his Wilmette property into a luxurious estate for himself and his wife Phimelia. The main building was an elegant three-story brick mansion with a tile roof and interior decor of mahogany, oak, and white enamel. The estate included a two-story coach house where the chauffeur and his wife lived. The grounds were attractively landscaped from Sheridan Road to the lake. The project cost $35,000, not including the land. Fifteen years later, in 1923, Gates sold the estate to Albert and Fannie Cross for $200,000.

Albert Cross also was a successful businessman. He began his career as a stenographer and teacher of a shorthand system invented by his father. In 1893 he became a grain and provisions merchant. He was a member and officer of the Chicago Board of Trade, and he was associated with a string of brokerage firms bearing his name. He was also a trustee of Northwestern University and first vice-president of Chicago's YMCA.

In 1927 Cross subdivided the five-acre estate and sold nine lots while retaining two lots for the existing mansion and coach house on Sheridan Road. He marketed "Canterbury Court" to wealthy buyers able to pay $30,000 to $90,000 for a lot and a minimum of $30,000 to $50,000 for a house. Each lot had 100 feet of frontage on an ornamentally lighted private drive and "a pleasing view of the lake." Homeowners were required to have incinerators and were prohibited from burning coal. All utilities were underground. An impressive "English gate" at the Sheridan Road entrance welcomed visitors.

Canterbury Court attracted a Who's Who of prominent Chicagoans: Charles Wrigley, president of an advertising agency and brother of William Wrigley, Jr., the chewing gum magnate; Craig Hazlewood, chairman of Lake Shore Trust and Savings Bank, executive vice-president of the First National Bank of Chicago, and president of the American Bankers Association; and Halsey Poronto, president of United States Cold Storage Co. and trustee of the Central Manufacturing District. Other notables followed: Frederick Croll, treasurer, vice-president and director of Amour & Co.; James Kraft, founder of Kraft Foods;

Carl Wickman, founder of Greyhound Bus Lines; Albert Dale, editor of the *Chicago American* and other newspapers; William Engel, grain company executive; Robert Crown, manager of the Crown family's industrial empire; and Andrew McNally IV, head of Rand McNally & Co. and great-great-grandson of its founder.

In 1930 the Crosses built and moved to their "dream home", just two blocks south at 2837 Sheridan Place, Evanston. Legend says that the movers left several crates of books in the driveway, and Albert suffered a fatal heart attack carrying the books inside.

In 1907 Philetus Gates created this five-acre estate at 336 Sheridan Road. Courtesy of the Evanston History Center.

The Marshall Mansion

On the east side of Sheridan Road across from the Baháʼí House of Worship is a vacant property owned by the Baháʼís that's used as a parking lot. At one time, this property was the site of perhaps the largest and most elaborate mansion ever to grace Wilmette, although several recently constructed lakefront mansions might be worthy rivals. The only remnant of the mansion is the former entrance to the property: two stone columns and a wrought iron gate.

The 32-room mansion was built in 1921 by architect Benjamin Marshall for his own use as a residence, studio, and entertainment venue. His acclaimed works in Chicago include the Blackstone Hotel and Theatre, the Drake Hotel, the Edgewater Beach complex, and many elegant apartment buildings on the

Near North. He also designed the doomed Iroquois Theater, discussed in Chapter 11, and the Wilmette Post Office, discussed in Chapter 4.

Marshall's pink-stuccoed edifice at Wilmette Harbor was beyond elegant. It was as flamboyant as his personality. Reportedly, it cost more than $1 million to build, the equivalent of more than $14 million in 2020 dollars. While the exterior was classical Spanish, the interior was eye-popping. The centerpiece was a tropical garden, 150 feet long by 75 feet wide and three-stories tall. Palm trees, cissus vines, and gardenias surrounded a turquoise-blue tile pool. Glass walls could be rolled back in summer, opening the garden to Lake Michigan beyond.

The uppermost space in the mansion was a solarium, decorated in red and gold fabric with Egyptian furnishings. It offered a panoramic view of Wilmette Harbor, Lake Michigan, and environs. One of its features was a dining table that could be lowered to the kitchen below, set for the next course, and raised back up.

Marshall entertained lavishly. His guests included David Windsor (later King Edward VIII of England), Ethyl Barrymore, Beatrice Lillie, Ed Wynn, Walter Hagen, Noel Coward, Leopold Stokowski, and Ina Claire. On July 18, 1933 General Italo Balbo, the Italian Air Marshall and fascist leader, was his guest. Balbo arrived in Chicago days earlier leading a squadron of 24 seaplanes to celebrate the Century of Progress World's Fair. Upon seeing the Chinese pagoda, carpeted by a satin mattress, Balbo asked in Italian, "Why do you bring us here when we are but men?" Then in the living room, he lamented, "I am dismayed that we have not come to your beautiful home before the eve of our departure."

The Great Depression forced Marshall to sell his mansion in 1936 for a paltry $95,000. The purchaser was Nathan Goldblatt, one of two brothers who, in 1914, opened their first Goldblatt's department store at Chicago and Ashland avenues in a neighborhood of Polish immigrants. The store was successful, and the brothers opened more medium-size department stores that offered merchandise at low prices. By 1933 the company owned five stores in Chicago, as well as stores in Joliet and Hammond.

Nathan and his wife Frances lived in the mansion until 1944 when he died at the age of 49. In 1947 Frances Goldblatt moved out. The following year, the mansion and its furnishings were put up for auction over a six-day period. Thousands of curiosity-seekers visited the premises during the preview period. Many of the furnishings were sold, but the mansion wasn't.

These events occurred in the context of a longstanding movement in Wilmette to create a community house similar to Winnetka's. The idea of using the mansion for this purpose was publicly debated in late 1948. Mrs. Goldblatt offered the property to the Village for $125,000, payable over 15 years, with no interest on the unpaid balance. The Village declined, primarily because the prospect of visitors crossing Sheridan Road on foot seemed too dangerous. The empty mansion was scarred by teenage vandals. In 1949 Mrs. Goldblatt decided, for tax reasons, to tear it down. Built like a fortress, it tried mightily but unsuccessfully to resist the wrecker's ball. It existed for less than 30 years. In 1951 the Bahá'ís purchased the vacant property.

Benjamin Marshall's mansion at Wilmette Harbor survived for less than 30 years. Courtesy of the Wilmette Historical Museum.

Wilmette Harbor and North Shore Channel

The Marshall mansion overlooked Wilmette Harbor, created in 1909 by the Sanitary District of Chicago (later the Metropolitan Water Reclamation District of Greater Chicago). The harbor links the lake and the North Shore Channel. A pumping station beneath the Sheridan Road Bridge pumps lake water into the channel, helping to create a southerly flow through the Chicago Area Waterway System that sends the region's treated sewage toward the Mississippi River.

The harbor wasn't designed for boats. It was intended to be a settling basin for sand that would otherwise drift into and clog the channel. During its first ten years, the basin was used by a few fishermen as a haven for their boats. This changed after World War I, because a small harbor at the foot of Clark Street in

Evanston used by the Evanston Yacht Club became irreversibly filled with sand. Two separate groups of Evanston boaters decided to move to Wilmette Harbor.

One group formed the Buccaneers Club. Its clubhouse was an old lumber schooner, rebuilt by Chicago architects Clark & Walcott in the style of the pirate ships of the Spanish Main and renamed *The Port of Missing Men*. In 1920 the Buccaneers received its first permit to moor its clubhouse and members' sailing boats at Wilmette Harbor. The Buccaneers' lifespan was brief. Financial problems led to its dissolution in 1929, and the floating clubhouse was towed into the lake near Montrose Harbor and set afire.

The Buccaneers Club's home was a refurbished schooner.
Courtesy of the Wilmette Historical Museum.

The second group organized a club that was briefly called North Shore Yacht Club but soon was renamed Sheridan Shore Yacht Club. It established a clubhouse in cooperation with Benjamin Marshall. At the time, he was seeking Village approval for his mansion overlooking the harbor, but officials nixed his plan, because a new zoning ordinance didn't allow commercial uses (i.e., his studio) at that location. Sheridan Shore and Marshall united and persuaded the Village to relent, and in exchange for the club's support, Marshall allotted it clubhouse space in the lower level of his mansion for $500 annually. The club's grand opening occurred on July 4, 1922.

During the 1920s, both clubs operated at the harbor: the Buccaneers on the north side and Sheridan Shore on the south side. Each controlled the moorings near its clubhouse. Boat owners sometimes claimed the same mooring. The Sanitary District wanted nothing to do with these disputes, and when the Buccaneers folded, the district put Sheridan Shore in charge of moorings.

For the next few years, Sheridan Shore occupied the lower level of the Marshall home and operated the harbor for both members and non-members, but two crises arose in the mid-1930s. The first was caused by the harbor's success in performing its function as a settling basin. Over the years, the sand drawn into the harbor reduced its depth from ten feet to one or two feet in some places. To accommodate boats, the harbor needed to be dredged. This would be an expensive project, beyond the club's means.

Sheridan Shore Yacht Club was built in 1937. Courtesy of the Wilmette Historical Museum.

After several years of uncertainty, the state finally agreed to pay for dredging ($33,000) if a suitable place were found for the spoil. At that point, the Park District, the Sanitary District, and the club came up with a plan. The spoil would be deposited north of the harbor to create additional landfill that would enlarge Washington (now Gillson) Park. A new organization (Wilmette Harbor Association) would take over the management of the harbor. It would furnish the steel sheeting needed to hold the spoil and would raise the cost ($5,500) through mooring fees. The Park District would install the sheeting as part of a park improvement project funded by the Works Progress Administration, a Depression-era employment and public works agency. The park project also included an amphitheater (now Wallace Bowl), wading pool, and landscaping. In 1938 the dredging was completed, and the newly-created landfill includes the area in Gillson Park called Overlook Drive.

The second crisis occurred in 1936 when Marshall sold his mansion and the new owner wouldn't allow the club to remain. The club was homeless. This crisis was resolved when the club leased land on the harbor's north bank from the Sanitary District. Based on plans donated by member Walter Stockton, the club built a new clubhouse at a cost of $15,000. It opened in August 1937.

Over the years, various proposals for expanding the harbor and increasing its capacity were made and ultimately rejected because of their huge cost. Jurisdictional conflicts occasionally arose among the Park District, the Harbor Association and Sheridan Shore, but these have been resolved, at least for now. The Harbor Association and Sheridan Shore have essentially merged, and the Metropolitan Water Reclamation District has leased the harbor and the clubhouse to the merged entity for a lengthy term.

Washington Park and Louis Gillson

Without Wilmette Harbor and the North Shore Channel, Gillson Park wouldn't exist. The spoil produced by the excavation of the northerly section of the channel in 1909 was deposited in the lake north of the harbor. This created 22 acres of landfill. The Park District was established for the specific purpose of taking title to these 22 acres for a community park. The landfill was between the harbor and Washington Avenue, east of a strip of land along Michigan Avenue owned by the Sanitary District.

Originally called Washington Park, the name was changed in 1955 to honor Louis Gillson, the Park District's first president. Gillson was born in Hudson, Ohio in 1852. His parents were natives of England. His dad was a tailor. Louis's formal education ended at the eighth grade. As a young man, he lived in Cleveland and worked in jobs leading to the practice of law. In 1874 he married Ida Bartholomew. Five years later, the couple moved to Chicago, where he embarked on a career as a patent lawyer. He held leadership positions in several professional organizations.

In 1881 Louis and Ida moved to Evanston where they were active members of the Evanston Baptist Church, and he was a founder of the Evanston YMCA. The couple had five children, but two died before the beginning of the 20th century. In 1903 the family moved to 706 Forest Avenue, Louis's home for the rest of his life. In 1906 a third child died at age 13.

Louis established the goal of expanding Washington Park's original 22 acres into a huge lakefront park extending from the harbor to Forest Avenue. Because the Park District had limited taxing power, achieving this goal would require a lengthy process. One step was converting the landfill's clay into soil that would support vegetation. Another step was purchasing the nine lots on the east side of Michigan Avenue between Washington and Lake avenues and removing several structures. This wasn't totally accomplished until 1937, after Louis retired.

Louis's attention wasn't limited to the lakefront. Between 1911 and 1914 he led the Park District in purchasing West Park, now Vattmann Park. The original name reflected the fact that until 1924, when much of the former Village of Gross Point was annexed to Wilmette, the area between the C&NW tracks and Ridge Road was "the west side of town." Louis also served as a member of the New Trier High School Board of Education from 1908 to 1920. In this role, he convinced the board to purchase land adjacent to the school property. He foresaw that additional land would be needed for future buildings and athletic fields. Short-sighted opponents called one acquisition "Louis Gillson's folly."

While serving on the New Trier board, Louis met a young chemistry teacher, Margery Stewart, who joined the faculty in 1919. Needing a place to live, she boarded with Louis and Ida. They treated her like a daughter, and she called them "Father" and "Mother." In 1928 Margery left New Trier to study school administration at Columbia University. Within three years, Ida died. Louis soon went east and brought Margery back as his wife. He was 79 years old; she was 39. Louis's family and colleagues apparently took the marriage in stride. In 1955, 13 years after his death, the Park District attached his name to the crown jewel of its park system and presented a commemorative plaque to Margery.

The Czarina of Ouilmette Beach

While Gillson Park was under development, a separate lakeshore park was established between Lake and Forest avenues, directly across from what's now Michigan Shores Club. The property was partially owned by the Village and partially by the Park District. It was called Ouilmette Park, and below its bluff was the site of Wilmette's first public beach.

The beach operation began in 1916, sponsored by the Beach Improvement Association, an offshoot of the Wilmette Woman's Club. Pearl Martin was in charge of the association during the 1916 season. If she were alive today, she might tell you this story:

Hello. My name is Mrs. George L. Martin. Well, that's just one of my names. I was born Alice Pearl Butler in Ohio in 1880. Growing up in Missouri, I was called Pearl Butler. When I married in 1903, I became Mrs. George L. Martin. That's how it was back then. My name was overshadowed by my husband's. But I'm not here to complain about that. I'm here to talk about my bathing beach—the Wilmette beach below the bluff at Ouilmette Park.

At the turn of the 20th century, there was no public access to Lake Michigan except at five street stubs. While some folks recognized the lake's recreational potential, lakefront property was privately owned, and the street stubs were quite narrow. Moreover, the lake's recreational potential was limited by the Village's practice of dumping sewage directly into the lake at Elmwood Avenue. Ugh! This posed a health hazard for anyone entering the water.

In 1914 the pollution problem was solved. The Sanitary District built an "interceptor" sewer under Sheridan Road from Highland Park to the North Shore Channel. By connecting their discharge sewers to this interceptor, Wilmette and other North Shore towns stopped polluting the lake, and the sewage was sent harmlessly down the channel to who-knows-where.

Still, as of 1916, there was no municipally-operated bathing beach in Wilmette. The Village and the Park District refused to get involved. Sure, many folks, especially youngsters and out-of-towners, were using the unsupervised beach at the foot of Lake Avenue for swimming, sunning, and who-knows-what, prompting neighbors to complain about litter and "bathers divesting themselves of their clothing in full view."

This scandalous behavior led the president of the Woman's Club, Mrs. Donald M. Gallie, to stroll up Elmwood Avenue from her home to mine. Impressed by my many civic activities, she asked me to head up a new Beach Improvement Association and create a supervised bathing beach at the foot of Lake Avenue. I made the dreadful mistake of saying yes.

Under my leadership, the association succeeded. We adopted a fee structure that generated funds to pay for equipment and operations while discouraging outsiders from overrunning the beach. We also adopted rules to prevent indecent, disorderly, and unsafe behavior: rules prohibiting overexposure of the human body, rules allowing dressing and undressing only in bathhouses, rules requiring outer-clothing to be stored in baskets and not be strewn on the sand, rules prohibiting hanky-panky, and so on. Our staff, mostly volunteers, included lifeguards, sworn police officers, and chaperones—all charged with the duty of strictly enforcing the rules. I was there on a daily basis directing these forces.

Despite our good administration, the association was ridiculed for its over-bearing rules and nitpicking. I was called "mayoress" and "czarina." The stress was horrible! Overwhelming! It caused me to suffer attacks of paralysis. I died the following year at the tender age of 36.

The Park District took charge of my bathing beach in 1917 and has run it ever since. Perhaps I should take pride in having paved the way, but in truth, I'm sorry I ever got involved.

The Beach Master

After the Park District took over the public beach in 1917, it created the position of Beach Master with responsibility for all aspects of the beach operation. James Wrenshaw held this position for many years. If he could speak today, he might tell this story:

Hello Wilmette beachgoers! I'm James Wrenshaw. I was the Beach Master from 1918 to 1932.

What's that? You don't know what a Beach Master is? Well, in my day, the Beach Master was the king of the beach. I was in charge of everything: life-guards, beach house, equipment, swimming lessons, water carnivals, and most important, enforcing the beach's rules and regulations. These heavy responsi-bilities earned me the lofty salary of $800 per season. I deserved every penny.

How did I qualify for this plum job? I worked my way up from lifeguard and chief lifeguard at Wilson Beach in Chicago. I had a heroic record there. I saved hundreds of people from drowning. I was often honored at the annual reception and ball thrown by the Life Guards Association. I especially enjoyed saving young women. A *Chicago Tribune* reporter wrote that some of us he-roes "went about bearing as many as a half dozen worshipful nymphs on their muscled arms." I even met my lovely wife while saving her from drowning.

What's different about Wilmette's swimming beach today from the beach in my day? Well, the most obvious difference is the location. In my day, the beach was down the bluff at Ouilmette Park, due east from the club you folks call Michigan Shores. The water plant is there now, and as you know, the swimming beach is just to its south.

Another big difference is the rules and regulations. The rules in my day were designed to assure safety, cleanliness, orderliness, decency, and modesty.

For the sake of safety, children under eight years of age weren't allowed on the beach unless accompanied by an adult. Non-swimmers were forbidden from crossing the life line. And throwing balls and sand was verboten. For the sake of cleanliness, dogs weren't allowed, and food could be eaten only in a restricted area. For the sake of orderliness, patrons were required to check all wearing apparel in baskets provided at the beach house (except their swimming garb, of course). For the sake of decency, "profane language" and "rough conduct" were absolutely banned, and women were warned not to accept swimming instructions from strangers and were encouraged to report annoying and offensive conduct.

The modesty rules, in my opinion, were critical to the village's moral well-being. Changing clothing on the beach or in the bushes was outlawed, as was wearing swimming garb with no cover-up while walking in the park above the bluff. Swimming garb for both men and women was strictly regulated: No "all-white or flesh colored suits" were permitted, nor "suits that expose the chest lower than a line drawn on a level with the arm pits." The rules for women were especially strict, as any decent person would understand: "Blouse and bloomer suits may be worn, with or without skirts, with or without stockings, providing the blouse has one-quarter arm sleeve, or close fitting arm-holes, and providing the bloomers are full and not shorter than four inches above the knee (top of patella)."

I had a cadre of beach policemen who helped me enforce these rules and regulations, and believe me, we didn't let anyone get away with anything. I'm still befuddled by the widespread criticism that we received. Why couldn't folks understand that if we became soft and lax, the beach would quickly become an outdoor brothel attracting hordes of out-of-town troublemakers? I must say, the Wilmette beach of my day reflected the positive influence of a good old-fashioned Beach Master like me.

The Ouilmette Country Club and its Successors

Across Michigan Avenue from the former Ouilmette Park is Michigan Shores Club. Its "grandfather" was Ouilmette Country Club (OCC), founded in 1898. OCC's first clubhouse was located near Ashland Avenue and 9th Street, but in 1906 it bought the first of four lots now owned by Michigan Shores Club and built a new clubhouse there.

The view of the park and lake from the east windows of OCC's clubhouse was magnificent, and the ready access to the park and beach were attractive

Ouilmette Country Club enjoyed beautiful views of the lake across
Ouilmette Park. Courtesy of the Wilmette Historical Museum.

amenities of membership. The club provided beach-related services to its members, and the staffs of the club and the Park District worked together cooperatively. The relationship was so close that some club members assumed that Ouilmette Park was club property.

In 1927 OCC and Evanston Century Club merged to form Shawnee Country Club. OCC's clubhouse on Michigan Avenue was torn down, and an elegant new clubhouse was designed by Daniel H. Burnham and Co. in the style of an old manor house of England. The grand opening was in February 1929. The Shawnee Club assured its members, including many who weren't Wilmette residents, that despite the merger with the Evanston club, all members would be allowed to use the beach at Ouilmette Park for an annual fee of five dollars, the same fee charged to Wilmette residents.

The Shawnee Club's financial problems during the Great Depression led to a reorganization and the emergence of Michigan Shores Club in the mid-1930s.

The Pickle Pioneers

Pardon me. I'm Peter Piper. While you parade at Ouilmette Park, please permit me to present a profile of Wilmette's pickle pioneers. They picked this precise place to produce pickles. It was a premier U.S. pickle processing place of the past.

John Westerfield, Wilmette's first village president, was a pickle
pioneer. Courtesy of the Wilmette Historical Museum.

The pickle pioneers were brothers Squire and Samuel Dingee and their brother-in-law John Westerfield, all New York natives. Perhaps they never planned to part from their place of propagation, but in 1857, a pecuniary panic paralyzed the U.S. economy. That's when Westerfield purchased 200 acres of promising prairieland in the Ouilmette Reserve, previously populated by Pottawatomi.

The pickle pioneers punted their previous professions and propelled themselves to this prime pastoral property. They built a house and barn near present-day Michigan Shores Club. They plowed and planted a cucumber patch. They processed pounds and pounds of pleasing, plump pickles that were particularly popular with the public. Plus, pickles produced plentiful profits for the pioneers.

In the 1860s Westerfield became the sole proprietor of this pickle plantation. By the early 1870s he perceived the potential for ponderously prodigious profits in a new pursuit. He partnered with adjacent property owners. They packaged their properties, prepared a plat, and procured Wilmette's village charter. Westerfield packed his possessions and moved to a place on Greenleaf Avenue near present-day Poplar Drive. He passed his remaining days as a professional purveyor of petite parcels of property at premium prices. He was also a surveyor, civil engineer, and Wilmette's first village president.

Meanwhile, Squire and Samuel Dingee persevered in the pickle processing profession: Squire in Chicago and Samuel in Evanston. They persisted as partners for ten years. Then Squire started his own firm, the Squire Dingee Pickle Co. It became the nation's predominant pickle processor, with pickle plants everywhere. In 1892, at age 75, he sold his pickle interests to brothers Frank and Harry Brown, both Wilmette residents (612 Lake Avenue and 819 Ashland Avenue). They and Frank's son Orley continued the company for many years. They introduced the popular Ma Brown pickle brand, taking its name from the delicious pickles made by their beloved Grandma Brown. The firm was merged into Beatrice Foods in 1958.

As to Samuel, he founded the S.M. Dingee Pickle Co. in Evanston and purchased a pretty place for his pride at 926 Lake Avenue. When he perished in 1891, his pickle processing proprietorship passed to his progeny. By 1915 parasites and other pesky pests were preying on cucumber plants in these parts. The pests prevailed and pushed the progeny's pickle processing properties out of this province.

The Waterworks and Carbon Petroleum Dubbs

In the earliest days of the village, residents obtained their water from shallow wells and cisterns. When the wells and cisterns dried up during periods of drought, they carried water from the lake. Water was an individual responsibility, not a public service. This changed in 1892 when the Village entered into a ten-year contract with Evanston to purchase unfiltered water from its waterworks, located on the lakeshore at Lincoln Street, six blocks south of Wilmette. After finalizing the contract, the Village built its water distribution system.

In 1910 the Village purchased two lakefront lots on the corner of Lake and Michigan avenues. The lots were 100 feet wide each, and with the stub of Lake Avenue, they gave the Village a total frontage of 275 feet along Michigan Avenue. The land was purchased in anticipation of a possible need for a Wilmette waterworks if the supply contract with Evanston couldn't be renewed on favorable terms.

Over the years, the contract was renewed several times, even though Wilmette experienced occasional supply problems: low pressure, contaminated water, shortages, and stoppages caused by ice in the intake pipe. By 1930 all neighboring lakeshore villages (Kenilworth, Winnetka, Glencoe, and Highland Park) had built waterworks, and consultants hired by Wilmette had recommended several times that the Village do the same. A referendum in 1930 that would have authorized $700,000 in bonds to pay for a Wilmette waterworks was defeated overwhelmingly.

The person most responsible for building the Wilmette waterworks was Carbon Petroleum Dubbs. He was given this odd moniker by his father, who had invented a process for cracking crude oil for use in petroleum products and hoped the name Carbon Petroleum would inspire his son to pursue a career in the same field. This tactic worked. Dubbs became a chemical engineer, improved his father's cracking procedure, helped Universal Oil Products Co. develop commercially successful technologies, and earned enormous wealth.

In 1931, at age 50, Dubbs sold his shares of Universal Oil for $3.6 million, retired, and built a 20-room lakefront mansion for his family at 1004 Michigan Avenue at a cost of $200,000. It was designed by prominent architect Philip Maher, who also designed the twin mansions at 1110 and 1040 Chestnut Avenue.

Although Dubbs had lived in the village since 1915, he had never participated in civic affairs. That changed with his retirement. He ran for village president and was elected. He vigorously attacked the countless problems facing the village during the Great Depression, including widespread unemployment, declining tax receipts, and expensive and unreliable water.

Shortly after taking office, Dubbs concluded that a Wilmette waterworks could produce water at a lower cost than Evanston was charging, eliminate water dependency, and provide employment for Wilmette residents. He announced his support for a $600,000 waterworks on the Village's two lakefront lots. To compensate for the loss of parkland, the plant's flat roof, rising only a few feet above street level, was designed to serve as an attractive public gathering place. Dubbs campaigned vigorously for the proposal, and it was approved in a December 1931 referendum, 60 percent to 40 percent, despite vocal opposition.

Voter approval was only the first hurdle. The zoning ordinance had to be amended to allow a "public utility" at the site. Bonds had to be sold to pay for the facility, but when the Village sought bids, no one responded. So, Dubbs turned to the federal government and obtained a pledge from the Reconstruction Finance Corporation to buy the bonds. Opponents continued to pressure the Village—some to resume negotiations with Evanston for a new water contract and others to find a different site. Construction began in November 1932, and Shawnee Country Club promptly sued, challenging the amendment to the zoning ordinance and claiming that the value of the club's property would be unconstitutionally diminished by the obstruction of the club's view of the lake.

Dubbs pressed forward. Construction of the waterworks and prosecution of the lawsuit proceeded simultaneously. Meanwhile, Dubbs was reelected village president in 1933 without opposition. Shortly after the waterworks started pumping water to Wilmette homes in 1934, the club withdrew its lawsuit. With this, the waterworks was firmly established. Yes, it's unfortunate that some of the village's treasured lakefront property was converted from parkland to public utility, but the decision to build was one of the most farsighted ever made by the Village. The waterworks allows the village to control its water supply while sharing the cost with other municipal customers.

In 1951, long after Dubbs left office and shortly after he moved from the village, he gave Wilmette citizens another option for a community house. He offered to donate his lakefront mansion for this purpose. After three months of study, the village board said no, concluding that local organizations wouldn't make sufficient use of the facility or adequately contribute to its operating costs.

A sledder zooms down Suicide Hill in 1960. Courtesy of the Wilmette Historical Museum.

Suicide Hill

Suicide Hill was the name given to the steep incline from the bluff at the foot of Forest Avenue to the beach below. It was a favorite local sledding and tobogganing site from at least the 1940s through the 1980s. It was really fun, because the incline was steep and scary. In the early days, the Wilmette Fire Department enhanced the terror by spraying the hill and coating it with ice. Especially exciting for some brave youngsters was zooming down on ice skates or skis.

Occasionally, an out-of-control sled or toboggan collided with a person, tree, or other object. A serious accident occurred in the mid-1950s when two boys, grade-schoolers who lived nearby, went to Suicide Hill to initiate a new toboggan. As usual, the fire department had sprayed the incline, increasing the downhill speed but reducing the riders' ability to steer. At the top of the bluff, the boys flipped a coin to see who would ride up front. Then they took their positions and zoomed downhill. At the bottom, the toboggan crashed into the steel post of a barbeque grill placed there for use by summertime picnickers. The boy in front was shaken up badly. When he arrived home still dizzy, his parents summoned an ambulance. At Evanston Hospital, he was found to have suffered a broken neck. Fortunately, he recovered.

In the 1970s, the Park District took charge of Suicide Hill and in response to ongoing accidents and injuries, stopped flooding the bluff. A personal injury lawsuit finally caused the district to stop the activity entirely. Undeterred, thrill-seekers ignored the fence that was supposed to keep them away and continued to race down Suicide Hill until an insurmountable barrier was erected.

Northwestern University's Lakefront Property

Northwestern University enjoys a special legal status. Under its 1855 Illinois charter, all of its property "of whatever kind" is "forever free from taxation for any and all purposes." This exemption has long been a source of conflict between the university and the City of Evanston, because the university doesn't pay real estate tax on its substantial landholdings in Evanston, even though it receives significant municipal services.

This exemption was also a source of friction between the university and Wilmette. At one time, the university owned some of the most valuable real estate in the village—a section bounded roughly by the Wilmette border to the north, Lake Michigan to the east, Elmwood Avenue to the south, and 10th Street to the west—eleven blocks in total. Why would the university own land in Wilmette?

The answer involves Milton Wilson. He was born in Ohio in 1843. At age 18, he enlisted in the Union Army, 11th Ohio Infantry, as a private. He served for three years and advanced to the rank of Lieutenant. Following his discharge, he settled in Chicago and, with three brothers, formed Wilson Bros., a highly successful manufacturer and wholesaler of men's haberdashery. In the late 1890s he moved from Chicago to Evanston and lived at 1100 Forest Avenue. He was active in Northwestern's affairs and served as a university trustee.

Wilson also invested in real estate. In 1895 he purchased the section of Wilmette described above. At the time, the land was undeveloped forestland. Two years later he filed a plat of subdivision for Milton H. Wilson's Addition to Wilmette. It laid out the blocks, lots, and streets essentially as they exist today, including an 80-foot-wide public right-of-way extending Elmwood Avenue from Sheridan Road to the lake.

In 1904 Northwestern established a Jubilee Memorial Fund to raise $1 million and shore up its finances. Wilson came forward with a donation of all his Wilmette real estate holdings, valued at more than $200,000. Title to the land was transferred to Northwestern, and in 1906 the university started opening the streets and selling the lots.

At the time, the property amounted to 5.5 percent of Wilmette's territory. It was a significant piece of the village's real estate tax base, but once the property was transferred to Northwestern, the future of this revenue source was in doubt. The Cook County collector took the position that the university's tax exemption didn't apply to land acquired after the exemption was created and began proceedings to collect the tax. Northwestern took the position that the exemption applies to all the property it owns, regardless of the date of acquisition. It sued to enjoin the collector's attempt to collect the tax.

The case went to the Illinois Supreme Court, which ruled in the university's favor. The court observed that the purpose of the exemption, granted when institutions of higher learning were scarce in Illinois, was to encourage "the establishment of a university by granting to it perpetual freedom from taxation of its property." In other words, the exemption was intended to be a broad grant of ongoing financial assistance from the state.

Fortunately for Wilmette, Northwestern gradually sold its Wilmette property, which was then returned to the tax rolls. Wilson went on to be one of the university's largest benefactors. Upon his death in 1929, he bequeathed his $8.5 million estate to the university with directions that it be used to create "the best undergraduate school possible."

The Elmwood Dunes

In 1909 the Village authorized a private organization, the Wilmette Playground Association, to operate a "free beach" on the public right-of-way at the foot of Elmwood Avenue. Since the property to the north and south was still undeveloped, the beachgoers, as a practical matter, weren't confined to the 80-foot space. By 1930, though, there were at least eight homes on lakefront lots north of Lake Avenue, including the lots immediately north and south of the right-of-way.

For a time, the private property owners didn't assert their right to stop Elmwood beachgoers from intruding. However, the free beach became a magnet during the Great Depression, attracting not only Wilmette residents, but also throngs from Chicago. The private property owners complained that conditions were intolerable.

In July 1933 the village board passed a resolution, noting that while the Park District provided a guarded beach at Lake Avenue, Elmwood Beach had no guards. The resolution characterized Elmwood Beach as a nuisance. It directed the police chief to stop its use "as a bathing beach or picnic grounds, for sunbathing, loitering, robing, disrobing, depositing clothing and playing games."

Closing the free beach created a furor. Before air-conditioning, beach-going was immensely popular, but during the Great Depression, many residents couldn't afford the Park District's beach fee ($4 per family per year) and had chosen instead to patronize the free Elmwood Beach. At a public meeting in May 1934, 200 residents demanded that the Park District reduce its fee to $2. As the meeting progressed, attendees became highly agitated and demanded that the Park District be eliminated entirely from the beach operation. Village President Dubbs supported the crowd, heaping scorn on the district for insensitivity and mismanagement.

The conflict was resolved when cooler heads prevailed. The $4 fee for Lake Avenue Beach would continue, but the Park District would open a second guarded beach, without amenities, on property to the south called Washington Avenue Beach. There the fee would be only $1.

Over the years, the Elmwood right of way was ignored and forgotten. The bluff became overgrown, and the stairs to the beach were not only unusable, but also invisible. However, in 2010 the property returned to the public's consciousness. A debate began over whether to restore public use or sell it to adjoining property owners. Those favoring a return to public use prevailed, and the Elmwood Dunes Preserve is now a peaceful and beautiful retreat.

The Shoreline North of Forest Avenue

Two proposals floated in the 1970s would have drastically changed the character of Wilmette's beach north of Forest Avenue. One proposal was for the Park District to acquire the entire privately-owned beach between Forest and the village's northern border. This proposal found its way into the Village's 1971 comprehensive plan, but not very forcefully. The plan contained a map that simply designated this stretch as a "Potential Public Beach."

This proposal would have involved purchasing the beach portion of property belonging to 16 riparian homeowners and six high rise condominium and cooperative buildings. Both the Village and the Park District had the power to acquire the land by eminent domain if the owners wouldn't sell. Commenting in 1975, the district's president, William Lambrecht Sr., called the concept "acceptable," but said it was financially unrealistic in the near future because of the district's recent acquisition of the Wilmette Golf Course and construction of the Centennial Park ice rinks. Even today, the idea remains financially unrealistic and, additionally, politically impossible.

The second proposal was also a non-starter. In 1975 a group called the East Michigan Avenue Association petitioned the village board to rezone the riparian properties between Forest Avenue and Langdon Park (consisting of 30 to 40 acres) from "R" to "R-5." "R" zoning allowed single family homes on large lots; "R-5" zoning allowed high-rise residential buildings. This proposal would have allowed the row of high-rise condos and co-ops in No Man's Land to be extended all the way south to Forest Avenue.

The association was led by Irving Zimmerman of 1132 Michigan Avenue. Only three riparian property owners weren't part of the association, and they voiced no objection to the proposal. Zimmerman argued that rezoning would significantly increase the value of the land and the property tax revenue of local governmental units, especially Wilmette School District 39. He claimed that the future of single-family homes on large lots was "doomed," and multiple-unit housing was the wave of the future. Admitting that the property owners would "make an awful lot of money off of this," Zimmerman glibly asserted, "But that's the American way. You buy something at two cents and sell it at three cents."

Langdon Park

The lakefront property known as Langdon Park (named to honor former Park District President Lawrence Langdon) was purchased by the district in 1957. It was then a wedge-shaped five-acre parcel with frontage along Sheridan Road at Chestnut Avenue, 500 feet of shoreline, and a 300-foot beach between the bluff and the waterline. This purchase came at a time when the future of the adjacent No Man's Land was unsettled, and the idea of the district's acquiring all the lakefront property north of Langdon was still alive. (No Man's Land is the subject of Chapter 2.)

The property was previously part of a commercially-operated beach called

Sand-Lo. For many years, Sand-Lo was an integral part of the No Man's Land environment—the "Coney Island of the North Shore." Sand-Lo was popular with non-residents because the price of admission was less than the Park District's non-resident fee at the public beach.

During the 1970s, 1980s, and 1990s, Langdon Park suffered heavy damage. The high lake levels, in combination with ice and wind, caused the beach and the bluff to erode. This erosion may have been exacerbated by the sea-walls of the new high-rises built in the 1960s. According to a 1983 Army Corps of Engineers study, the seawall at the 1420 Sheridan Road high-rise "apparently creates eddies [currents flowing against the main current] which are directed at the shoreline." A 1989 report phrased it differently: "The longshore current flows south, carrying a heavy load of sediment, but this current was deflected into the deeper waters by the new building and seawall. There the sand has settled permanently. Wave action is unable to return the sediments to the beach, thus starving the downstream beaches."

The Park District took steps to protect Langdon's beach and bluff, but they didn't solve the problem. By 1980 erosion forced the district to stop using Langdon Park as a storage area and launching site for small sailboats. Low lake levels between 1998 and 2013 exposed more beach and suspended the bluff erosion. When lake levels returned to their high point in 2019–2020, more damage occurred, and the beach has disappeared.

News Flashes from the Shoreline

- August 8 1916: Village Attorney Charles Carnahan announced that the Village would take legal action against residents whose property abuts the lake and who are extending their fences across the beach to the water's edge. Carnahan explained, "It may mean a long fight, but the public should have the lakeshore. Because a man owns property along the lake gives him no right to run a fence into the water and shut off the beach from the use of the public."

- August 12, 1916: Thirteen Evanston beachgoers, led by Philip Danielson, 23, were the latest targets of Wilmette's beach rules. To assure the wholesomeness of the operation, the Beach Improvement Association enforces strict rules, one of which requires bathers to store their outer clothing in wire baskets at the beach house, for which a fee of 50 cents is charged. Mr. Danielson and his group, seeing no need for these facilities, deposited their outer clothing on the sand. The garments were confiscated by guards, who refuse to return them until the fee is paid. It's rumored that the Evanstonians plan to bring larceny charges against the guards. Mrs. George L. Martin, head of the association, is adamant in support of the guards and adds, "Besides, I don't like being called the mayoress of Wilmette."

- August 15, 1916: Philip Grau, 34, of 925 Elmwood Avenue, was prevented by Park District police from visiting the beach at Lake Avenue while wearing a raincoat over his bathing attire. Several days ago, beach guards cried foul when Grau removed the trousers he was wearing over his bathing suit and handed them to his wife for safekeeping. "What's a man to do?" asked Grau. "He can't wear trousers and he can't wear a raincoat.... Does he have to pay 50 cents for swimming in a lake that belongs to the public, but which Mrs. Martin is now czar of?" Grau, an attorney, wonders "whether Mrs. Martin is really the new 'mayoress of Wilmette' and where she gets her authority for [the clothing rule]."

- July 24, 1919: The problem of "automobile parties" at the Wilmette beach persists. Groups of Chicagoans undress in their cars and invade the park and beach, much to the annoyance of Wilmette beachgoers. In response, Village President Edward Zipf, 55, of 925 Lake Avenue, and Marion White, 44, of 1021 Central Avenue, beach chair of the Wilmette Woman's Club, have posted these rules: No undressing on the beach. No walking or lounging in the park in bathing suits. No strewing garments on the sand: they must be placed in lockers, and the locker fee must be paid.

- July 29, 1919: The Park District, in consultation with members of the Wilmette Woman's Club, issued an edict prohibiting beachgoers from eating lunch in their swimming suits on the public beach. Bathers must change into acceptable dining attire if they wish to eat. The new rule targets Chicagoans holding beach parties on the sand. The club will also station a bathing suit censor at the beach to stop the overexposure of epidermis.

- April 20, 1928: The Village rejected the offer of Shawnee Country Club to donate its old clubhouse for residents' use as a community house and recreation center. The offer would have required the Village to move the building off the club's property at Lake and Michigan avenues to a more central location. While the Village has long sought to establish a community house, the age and configuration of the old clubhouse make its relocation and reuse impractical.

- July 5, 1933: Louis Gillson, president of the Wilmette Park District, responded to a tirade by Edward Dunne, former Illinois governor, Chicago mayor, and Circuit Court judge. When Dunne's family came to the Wilmette beach on June 26, his daughter was given a parking ticket; several family members were stopped from swimming in a restricted area; and the group's clothing, strewn about the beach, was confiscated. "It's an outrage that anyone should be treated that way," Dunne blustered. "Most of the residents of Wilmette gain their livelihood in Chicago. They come to this city, get police and fire protection, and are invited to use our beaches, but when we go up there we are treated like Ishmaelites or enemies." Gillson responded that the beach rules were applied to Dunne's family the same as Wilmette residents. One resident publicly waded into the dispute, agreeing with Dunne that the rules and their enforcement are "arbitrary."

- August 16, 1953: A visitor to the Wilmette beach will notice something unusual: The entire crew of lifeguards are young women. While females were allowed to serve as lifeguards in the Chicago area during World War II, males have since displaced them at most places. But not at Wilmette. It was only six years ago when an irate group of citizens confronted the Wilmette Park Board to complain about the girl lifeguards. At that time, Park Superintendent Gordon Wallace, the father of at least one girl, responded that female life guards perform their duties more conscientiously than males and are capable of "hauling in any two of us board members."

CHAPTER 2

★──────────────★

No Man's Land

Many communities, no matter their reputable nature, have a little naughty in their past, a tint of bawdy in their history. Wilmette's quirk was No Man's Land.

No Man's Land is the 22-acre parcel bounded by Wilmette, Kenilworth, and Lake Michigan, presently home to Plaza del Lago, the Sheridan Road highrises, and the Westerfield Drive townhomes. It received this strange moniker because for decades it remained unincorporated (part of no municipality) and was essentially ungoverned, while the villages of Wilmette and Kenilworth grew up around it. Under Illinois law, neither Wilmette nor Kenilworth could annex the territory without the consent of its owners and residents.

John Gage, a New Yorker who came to Chicago in the 1830s, made a fortune in the flour milling business and purchased No Man's Land in 1857 as an investment. It remained in the hands of the Gage family for decades and was still undeveloped woodland going into the 1920s, except for a few cottages and small businesses. That's when the trouble started. The spirit of the Roaring Twenties and anti-Prohibition fervor found a friendly home as the quiet woods gave way to gasoline stations, roadhouses, fireworks stands, commercial beaches, a movie theater, a dance hall, retail shops, and private clubs. The area had no police protection, fire protection, or municipal controls on development; and unsavory activities like gambling and boozing had a free hand. Neighbors petitioned Wilmette to close 10th Street at Chestnut Avenue because the unpaved roadway to the north through No Man's Land had become a "lovers' trysting place."

None of this could have happened without the Gage family's acquiescence, particularly that of Stanley Gage, John's grandson who was managing the family's holdings. The family's goal after World War I was to maximize value. This wouldn't be accomplished by annexing to Wilmette or Kenilworth and subdividing the land into single family home sites like the adjoining neighborhoods. Instead, maximum profits would require high-density residential buildings and commercial uses. As an "orphan territory," the Gage's property had significant development potential that greatly enhanced its value.

A Park

As the prospect of undesirable development loomed, local citizens asked the Cook County Forest Preserve District to purchase some or all of the territory and preserve it as open space. In 1920 the estimated value of the entire parcel was $300,000, and just the portion east of Sheridan Road was worth an estimated $125,000. This acquisition would give the district its only lakefront property—"a splendid retreat for throngs now denied the beauties of the North Shore," according to the district's chairman. But Wilmette's village president, Edward Zipf, opposed the idea, arguing that the property was "wholly unsuitable for the use of women and children." He probably was more worried about the throngs of Chicagoans who were already clogging Sheridan Road and spilling into the lakefront neighborhoods. Ultimately, the district rejected the idea because the parcel was too expensive and too isolated from the district's other landholdings.

By the mid-1920s the Gage family was proceeding apace to develop No Man's Land into a center of commerce, entertainment, and recreation. Neighbors in Wilmette and Kenilworth became more alarmed and asked the Wilmette Park District to intervene. While the territory couldn't be annexed to either Wilmette or Kenilworth without its owners' and residents' consent, it lay within the Park District's boundaries. The neighbors' proposal was for the Park District to condemn it and levy a special assessment on all district residents to pay for it. Kenilworth would contribute in an unspecified way. Some appraisers valued it as low as $500,000, while the Gage family claimed its value was $7 million. In late 1926 the district decided not to proceed because the price was too high.

Undaunted, the neighbors turned to New Trier Township. With the endorsement of the governing boards of Wilmette, Kenilworth, Glencoe, and New Trier High School, they successfully petitioned a Cook County judge to order a referendum in April 1927 that, if approved, would allow the township to issue $500,000 in bonds to acquire ten acres of No Man's Land for a park. During a two-month campaign, supporters argued that the planned commercial ventures in the territory would be "detrimental to the home life of the North Shore villages." Opponents responded that the proposed ventures wouldn't be harmful; that the $500,000 price was prohibitive; and that the park would benefit only a few immediate neighbors. When public opinion turned against them, supporters abandoned the referendum, and it was canceled.

In 1938 the Chestnut Avenue neighbors made a last ditch effort to persuade the Wilmette Park District to purchase a southern strip of No Man's Land for a "buffer park" between their homes and the commercial properties. (The proposed park is the present site of the Westerfield Drive townhomes and the 1410 Sheridan Road condo building). The district again said no.

Vista del Lago Club

Vista del Lago Club was the brainchild of J. Stuart Blackton, a man who made a fortune as head of Vitagraph Co., a firm that produced motion pictures and employed Hollywood's biggest stars. In the mid-1920s he led a syndicate that purchased a three-acre lakefront site from the Gage family—the most northerly point of No Man's Land. The syndicate's plan was to create "a new form of club life" modeled after clubs in Southern California and Florida. The clubhouse would be a magnificent facility costing $1.5 million and offering a "year-round program of sports and arts activities" to all family members. Women would enjoy the same privileges as men.

Blackton favored the Spanish-style of architecture popularized by the 1915 Panama-California Exposition in San Diego. He chose John Reed Fugard, a Chicago architect of luxury apartment buildings on Lake Shore Drive, to design the clubhouse. It would be completed in three phases. Phase 1 would be a two-story structure on the beach below the bluff. It would include an esplanade, grill, ballroom, and locker rooms. Phase 2 would add a third-story over the western portion of the original structure. It would be visible from Sheridan Road and would provide space for new and expanded athletic and social facilities. Phase 3 would add ten floors with 300 apartments. The structure would have colorful furnishings in the Spanish style—"simple in detail, yet exotic in effect."

Why did many residents of Wilmette and Kenilworth oppose this venture? First, they were skeptical of the non-local promoters with their Hollywood connections. Second, they were opposed to high-rise buildings as a general principle and didn't want them to gain a foothold on the North Shore. And third, the club was just one piece of what they believed was a plan to overdevelop No Man's Land.

For Every Member of the Family Every Day of the Year

This rendering shows the original vision for Vista del Lago
Club. Courtesy of the Wilmette Historical Museum.

But they couldn't stop the club. It opened its beach-level facilities in 1927
and its second-floor facilities in 1928. It attracted more than 500 members from
the North Shore and beyond and seemed destined for success. Then, in October 1929, the stock market crashed and the Great Depression followed. Members had the right to resign without financial penalty, and they did. Phase 2
was canceled. The club fell into receivership in 1933. Efforts to save it failed.
The receiver leased the club to tenants who briefly operated a semi-public
dining/dancing venue.

In 1939 the receiver leased the clubhouse to a new tenant who advertised
keno games on Wednesday nights. The advertisement came to the attention
of Wilmette Police Chief Cloyd McGuire. On December 27, 1939 he "mobilized
his entire force of 24 men," deputized eight American Legionnaires, and rented
Indian Hill Country Club's bus. McGuire's raiders swooped into the building
and arrested 60 people: proprietors, employees, and mostly female patrons
from Chicago. One woman shouted, "Suburbanites! Why don't you raid the
church socials?" All arrestees were bused to the Wilmette Village Hall, charged
with illegal gambling, released on bond, and eventually fined. This raid was
the final blow. Vista del Lago fell into ruin and became an eyesore on the
lakefront.

Breakers Beach Club

Breakers Beach Club was organized in 1926. Like Vista del Lago, it was modeled after beach clubs that were popular in California and Florida. The promoters (none of whom lived in Wilmette) intended to build and operate a luxurious $1.5 million clubhouse with a wide array of facilities that would promote social intercourse and athletics among its members. They also intended to create an 18-hole golf course at an offsite location. The club would have 3,500 members, both men and women, whose immediate family members would have full privileges to use the facilities.

Like Vista del Lago, Breakers Beach Club fell into
ruins. Courtesy of the Wilmette Public Library.

The promoters leased from the Gage family, for 99 years, a site at 1600 Sheridan Road. This location was only a short distance south of the Vista del Lago clubhouse then under construction. They hired architect John Eberson to design a luxurious clubhouse in the "Hispano-Italian style." (Eberson was known nationally for designing movie theaters in the "atmospheric style.") The clubhouse would be seven, eight, ten, or even twelve stories tall, as variously reported. It would have 200 guest rooms and amenities including an indoor swimming pool, nursery, dining rooms, handball courts, bowling alleys, ballroom, billiard rooms, library, and writing rooms—"all such equipment as is usual and customary in a high class family club and hotel." The offsite golf course would include tennis courts and amenities "such as are usual and customary in golf clubs."

Not all local citizens objected to the club. Theodore Robinson, of 215 4th Street, praised the club for offering a place where families could retreat from urban congestion and enjoy swimming and other healthy activities in a beautiful natural setting. The club would provide, he said, "a means to preserve the right relation between man and his work and his play and his environment." And, he added, "The plan for the club is ideal." It will be run like a "business institution" and its "definite income guarantees continuous operation."

The club's membership quickly grew to more than 1,000. In 1927 the promoters leased 250 acres northwest of Waukegan and Dundee roads in unincorporated Northfield Township for the golf course. They began construction of both the clubhouse at the beach and the outlying golf facilities. By the summer of 1928 the foundation, first story, and upper deck of the clubhouse were completed and opened. The space consisted of only a lobby, dressing rooms, and showers. The only services offered that first year were "beach conveniences" like tables, umbrellas, and lunch service. Nevertheless, membership climbed to 2,000.

But the financial plan wasn't working well for the promoters. Unwilling to proceed, they forfeited their investment and turned the project over to the members. A plan was devised to assess each member $250, abandon the idea of a high rise building, and create from the existing structure a scaled-back clubhouse for "purely social and recreational purposes." One year later, in the summer of 1929, the club idea failed completely, and a new developer took control, planning to build either "a high class hotel or a large apartment building." This was four months before Black Tuesday, which undoubtedly accounts for the eventual abandonment of the project.

The golf course was taken over by a separate group, renamed Middlebrook Country Club, and operated initially as a private club. By 1933 it was a public course named Blackheath Golf Club. In 1945, the property became part of the Glenbrook Countryside subdivision for single family homes.

Miralago

Miralago was conceived in the late 1920s. Located on the west side of Sheridan Road 300 feet south of the Kenilworth border, the building had ten shops on the first floor and a huge ballroom above. The ballroom was described as a place that would attract "the young set of automobiling, jazz dancing nite lifers"—"a fitting place for the little modern American girl, short haired, short skirted, clean, direct, and colorful." Some residents of the two staid villages regarded Miralago as a threat to decency, despite assurances that lone males, unescorted women, and liquor wouldn't be allowed.

Like Vista del Lago and the Breakers Beach Club, Miralago owed its existence to its location in No Man's Land where zoning controls didn't apply. This location had disadvantages, though. The biggest drawback was the lack of a reliable water source. Water might be purchased from Wilmette (which purchased water from Evanston) or Kenilworth (which had its own treatment plant), and indeed both villages, at one time or another, supplied water to the territory. But the two villages weren't reliable suppliers. In the early 1920s, Wilmette cut off water service to two Gage family cottages in No Man's Land after supplying them for seven years. The Gages sued, alleging that the Village was a public utility that had a duty to continue service. The case went to the Illinois Supreme Court, which ruled that absent a binding contract, Wilmette could discontinue water service to customers outside its borders at any time. Despite the uncertainty created by this ruling, major building projects went forward in No Man's Land, with Wilmette supplying water to the territory.

Miralago's promoter was Bills Realty, Inc., a firm heavily involved in the development of Indian Hill Estates. Bills selected modernist architect George Fred Keck to design the building. At the time, Keck was also designing residences in Indian Hill Estates, including three homes for Bills family members. Keck's dazzling design for the second-floor ballroom featured "silvered ceilings, plush jade-green draperies, black marble columns, murals and a lighting system that was innovative for the time because it provided an array of changing colors."

On opening night, July 12, 1929, the Dell Coon Orchestra entertained a capacity crowd of 1,200. Reviews were positive. But the Great Depression began a few months later, and Miralago struggled financially. Some first-floor shops remained vacant. In 1931, a new manager, James Davis, took charge of the ballroom and introduced fine dining. (Davis's tenure in the restaurant industry had been interrupted in 1928 when the feds shut down his Alamo Cafe in Chicago for violating the Prohibition Act.) Shortly after Davis took charge, State's Attorney's police raided Miralago and arrested him and six others for running a gambling operation.

In the summer of 1931, Wilmette stopped providing water to No Man's Land because it was concerned that the volume of water being supplied by Evanston might be insufficient to meet even the needs of Wilmette's residents. However, Wilmette offered to provide water for fire protection for a $500 monthly fee, payable in advance. The territory's leaders refused to pay and contracted with Kenilworth for domestic water. However, the contract explicitly excluded water for fire protection because the pipes from the lake to Kenilworth's water plant were too small to assure continuous service to Kenilworth residents while fighting a fire in No Man's Land.

On March 8, 1932, at 4:45 PM, fire broke out at Miralago. Wilmette's and Winnetka's fire departments refused to respond, but Evanston firefighters arrived, attached their hoses to a nearby Kenilworth hydrant, and began to quench the flames. Then, Kenilworth police ordered the Evanston firefighters to stop. Eventually, sanity prevailed, and Evanston's firefighting efforts resumed with aid from Wilmette and Winnetka, but it was too late. Miralago was destroyed. Subsequent lawsuits by Miralago's owners against Kenilworth were dismissed.

Miralago burned down less than three years after opening.
Courtesy of the Wilmette Historical Museum.

Teatro del Lago

Adding to the distress of some Wilmette and Kenilworth residents during the mid-1920s was a three-part project west of Sheridan Road on the site now occupied by Plaza del Lago: a row of nine stores in two buildings along the north side of a 70-foot-wide private roadway (Spanish Court) that connected Sheridan Road and 10th Street; a three-story apartment building at the corner of Spanish Court and 10th Street; and a 1,400-seat movie theater (Teatro del Lago) on the south side of Spanish Court, opposite the stores. A 500-car outdoor parking lot was intended to attract and accommodate the growing number of shoppers and theater-goers who had automobiles.

All this sudden development was too much to swallow for many of the villages' residents. Yet, try as they might, they could do nothing to stop it. The worst of the three-part project in the minds of vocal residents was Teatro del Lago. Movies were a form of entertainment still viewed with moral skepticism. Showing movies on the Sabbath was strongly opposed by local churches and was prohibited in Wilmette by ordinance. In No Man's Land, Teatro wasn't subject to any prohibition of this type, and its developers planned to show Sunday movies. Thus, Teatro was seen as a threat to the moral fiber of the community.

Leading the syndicate that sponsored the three-part project were two prominent Winnetka residents, Ayres Boal and Harry Edmonds. They chose Edwin Clark, also a Winnetka resident, as architect. (His work included Brookfield Zoo and Winnetka's Village Hall.) He designed the movie theater, the shop buildings, and the apartment building in the Spanish style to coordinate with the nearby clubs and dancehall. He described the Spanish Court buildings as "designed to represent a picturesque Spanish street with rough white plaster walls in which panels of Spanish tile are inserted. The copings and cornices are brilliant blue and the railing and balconies of old wrought iron. The roofs are red Spanish tile."

One of the two shop buildings had small apartments on its second floor and a distinctive bell tower in the center. Behind the stores was a 50-car garage. The apartment building at the corner contained twelve five-room apartments.

Teatro was a gem. Its interior, designed by Winnetka resident Ernst von Ammon, maintained the Spanish style. The lobby was spacious. The auditorium's 1,400 seats were comfy and amply spaced. It had no balcony, and its floor was sloped to provide unobstructed views of the screen. It had the most modern projection equipment and sound system. Its $25,000 Kimball organ was grand. The theater would be operated by Sam Meyers of 934 Elmwood Avenue. He was a brother-in-law and business associate of Abe Balaban of Balaban & Katz, which owned and operated the grand movie and entertainment houses of Chicago. Teatro would thus be able to present the popular movies and live entertainment that Balaban & Katz offered its Chicago audiences.

None of this mattered to the New Trier Citizens Committee. In a full page open letter to the syndicate, published locally on April 29, 1927, the Committee asserted, "You are about to impose Sunday moving picture performances on a community that has always voted and legislated against them." The letter continued, "Gentlemen…how in the light of your long residence on the North Shore and the privileges you have enjoyed as its residents [can you] feel justified in soliciting the patronage of this North Shore community for your theatrical enterprise?" The syndicate wasn't swayed. Its members had their collective finger on the pulse of the community. Teatro opened on April 23, 1927 and was well received. Its success quickly forced the closing of the only movie theater operating within Wilmette's borders and led to a 1928 referendum in which residents, hoping to reestablish a Wilmette-sited theater, voted overwhelmingly to repeal the Sunday movie ban.

Teatro del Lago opened in 1927 and closed in 1965. Both images courtesy of the Wilmette Historical Museum.

The forerunner of Plaza del Lago, built in 1927, included a three-story apartment building (left), a row of stores along Spanish Court (center), and Teatro del Lago (right).

Annexation

The "Wilmette Plan," authored by the Plan Commission in 1922, was supposed to be a vision for the village's future. Yet, the Plan failed to address obvious pending issues involving future territorial expansion. Regarding No Man's Land, the plan simply expressed "the hope that through the appointing of a competent committee in conjunction with Kenilworth that ways and means may be found to annex or control the land...."

Illinois law remained unchanged. The consent of a territory's owners and residents was required before it could be annexed by a municipality. The owners and 90 residents of No Man's land had no interest in giving their consent. Neighboring villages pressured the Illinois legislature to change the law. In 1927, a proposal that would have allowed Wilmette to annex No Man's Land unilaterally was defeated in the Illinois Senate by a vote of 16 yes, 13 no, with 20 abstentions. Passage required 26 yes votes. A similar 1937 proposal passed the legislature but was vetoed by the governor.

In 1939, bowing to intense lobbying by Wilmette and Kenilworth, the legislature finally passed, and the governor signed, a law entitled "An Act to provide for the annexation of unincorporated territory which is entirely surrounded by incorporated territory." Phrased in general terms, the law allowed a village to annex adjoining territory that was less than 30 acres, had fewer than 200 voters, and was "bounded on one side by any navigable body of water and is otherwise wholly bounded" by two or more villages. The consent of the territory wasn't required. Following passage of this law, Wilmette promptly adopted an ordinance annexing No Man's Land.

This apparent solution was only temporary, though, because Stanley Gage mounted a successful court challenge. He claimed that the law violated the Illinois Constitution's requirement that the subject of a law "shall be expressed in the title" of the law. The Illinois Supreme Court agreed that the title of the 1939 law was defective, because it didn't express the requirement, specified in the law's text, that one portion of the border must be bounded by navigable water.

Gage's victory was short-lived. In 1941 the legislature corrected the defect in a new law that gave Wilmette the power to annex No Man's Land unilaterally. On January 6, 1942 Wilmette finally adopted an ordinance that made No Man's Land a part of the village and subject to the village's governance. The zoning ordinance placed most of the newly annexed territory in a commercial zone that stymied new development.

The Taming of No Man's Land

In 1959 the Village recognized the need to stimulate the redevelopment of No Man's Land. To this end, it adopted an ordinance creating three separate zoning districts in the territory. One was the land along the south side of 7th Avenue (now Westerfield Drive). Prior to 1959 it was the only portion of No Man's Land zoned for single family homes, but it remained vacant and had become an unofficial dumping ground. The new zoning allowed townhouse buildings with up to six units each. They'd serve as a buffer between the commercial area to the north and the residential area to the south. This new zoning led to the construction of 38 attractive townhouses during the 1960s. The Village enhanced this redevelopment by vacating 20 feet of right-of-way along Westerfield Drive to provide open space for landscaping.

The second zoning district was the area east of Sheridan Road between Langdon Park and the Kenilworth border. This area was home to many of the commercial activities that were regarded as objectionable. In 1952 a consultant hired by the Village had recommended that the area was "better suited for residential use, preferably of apartment or residential hotel type." The report continued, "With the natural amenities of view, exposure, beach and the proximity to shopping facilities such use would be ideal. If left in its present zoning, the haphazard and temporary uses will continue." Seven years later the 1959 zoning ordinance incorporated this recommendation and allowed "high-rise" development.

The new zoning performed as predicted. The quick transformation that followed was due to three factors: the strong demand by older residents for lakefront apartments, the opportunity for developers to make a good profit under the new zoning, and the booming economy of the 1960s. The undesirable commercial uses (except one gas station) and the derelict structures quickly disappeared and were replaced by six high-rise residential buildings, listed in order of construction. (The rentals have since been converted to condominiums.)

YEAR BUILT	ADDRESS	# OF FLOORS	# OF UNITS	TYPE
1960–62	1410 Sheridan	7	29	Co-op
1961–62	1440 Sheridan	9	46	Rental
1961–62	1616 Sheridan	11	83	Rental
1962–64	1630 Sheridan	10	104	Co-op
1966–68	1420 Sheridan	7	74	Condo
1967–69	1500 Sheridan	10	109	Condo

The 1410 building, furthest to the south, was built by its future residents, many of whom were members of the Indian Hills Golf Club looking to downsize. The 1440 building (The Sand Lo Beach Apartments) was developed by Harold Lundberg, who was a member of the Wilmette Planning Board and a Chestnut Avenue neighbor. It and the building at 1616 Sheridan (The Kenilworth Apartments) were converted to condominiums in the early 1970s.

The 1630 building (The Vista del Lago Apartments) is the furthest north. It was built by some of its future residents. The 1420 building was the first condominium building. The award-winning structure at 1500 Sheridan was built by a group led by Plato Foufas, a young Evanston attorney, and Joseph Stefan, a retired Brunswick Corp. executive. (Foufas and Stefan were simultaneously developing the Westerfield townhouses and Plaza del Lago.) The only post-1970 building is the ten-story condominium building at 1618 Sheridan, the former gas station site. Developed by Optima, Inc., it has eight units, one unit per floor except a two-story penthouse.

Unfortunately, the authors of the 1959 zoning ordinance failed to consider Lake Michigan's dynamics. They provided that a building could be positioned as close as 70 feet from the waterline, as measured at the time of construction. This meant that a building constructed when the lake level was low could be positioned farther east than a building constructed when the lake level was high. And seawalls weren't regulated at all.

The consequences of this oversight were severe. For example, the buildings at 1440 and 1410 Sheridan were built in 1962. They were conservatively positioned based on the waterline at a time when the lake level was only slightly below its long term mean level. Between these two buildings was a vacant lot, 1420 Sheridan, awaiting development.

In 1964 developer Charles Nixon started planning the building at 1420 Sheridan. By that time, the lake level had dropped dramatically to its then all-time low. Nixon took advantage of the receded waterline and positioned his building (with a protective seawall) far to the east of the adjacent buildings, giving his building fabulous views of the lake and beach while impairing the views from the buildings to the north and south. When the Village finally recognized the problem, it was too late to stop Nixon and other high-rise developers from encroaching too close to the lake with buildings and seawalls.

Neighbors vehemently protested Nixon's plan. Harold Lundberg, owner of the 1440 Sheridan building, called the proposed Nixon building "a sore thumb sticking out into the lake." He urged that "no one should be permitted to take advantage of the fact that the lake is now at a 100-year low to hog the beach, interfering with his neighbors' view and impairing the value of their properties." Despite these protests and a lawsuit brought by the 1410 Sheridan building and Wilmette Park District, Nixon's plan was approved.

Until the high-rises were built, it was possible to stroll the beach all the way from what's now Langdon Park to Mahoney Park in Kenilworth—"before the water gouged it out," as one Wilmette resident recalled in 1977. Unfortunately, the water is still gouging.

The third new zoning district in No Man's Land was the area north of Westerfield Drive and west of Sheridan Road. Its regulations allowed retail and other light commercial uses, theaters, and buildings with three or more residential units. No building could be taller than 35 feet. This new zoning reflected the uses that already existed on the property: the shops and apartment building along Spanish Court, Teatro del Lago, and a gas station and restaurant north of Spanish Court.

The new zoning didn't envision the creation of a shopping center. Credit for this goes to Plaza del Lago's developers, led by Plato Foufas and Joseph Stefan. They believed that a small upscale shopping center would be successful in the midst of a growing and prosperous suburban neighborhood. They were also involved in developing the high-rise building at 1500 Sheridan Road and the Westerfield townhouses.

Their plan for the shopping center was to preserve the row of attractive Spanish motif buildings along Spanish Court and build on this tradition. In the same architectural style, they built a new row of stores to the south of the existing row. In the area between, they eliminated the private Spanish Court roadway and created a U-shaped piazza with attractive landscaping and ample parking. They converted the old garage into an indoor arcade.

Sam Meyers had hoped to retain Teatro as part of the new Plaza del Lago, but the Village said no because the number of parking spaces would be inadequate in light of the new development. And so, the wrecker's ball brought down a theater that once employed young ushers Rock Hudson and Charles Percy, presented live concerts by Mario Lanza and Rise Stevens, and entertained thousands of devoted patrons. It was replaced by a Jewel grocery store.

Pressured by financial considerations, the Plaza's developers reluctantly allowed Howard Johnson's to build a restaurant in the southeast corner of the property. The building was subsequently occupied by the Ground Round and Convito Italiano restaurants. It was demolished in the 1980s and replaced by a Spanish motif building with three stores. Convito moved to a different location in the Plaza.

Plaza del Lago was a fully developed shopping center by 1968. Foufas and Stefan rounded out their contribution to the rebirth of No Man's Land by constructing the mixed retail/residential building north of Plaza del Lago at 1625 Sheridan Road, completed in 1971.

Breaking News From No Man's Land

- June 5, 1928: After years of debate, Wilmette's village board approved a contract to pave its section of 10th Street from Chestnut Avenue to No Man's Land. New Trier Township has agreed to pave the remaining section to Sheridan Road. Neighbors have long favored closing the unpaved area, which they call a "lovers lane" where "orgies" are "a menace to public morals." Proponents have argued that paving will create a convenient roadway between Sheridan Road and locations to the southwest.
- March 14, 1930: Two men and two women, all intoxicated, invaded the Spanish Court Apartments and created a noisy disturbance. Tenants called Wilmette and Kenilworth police, but they refused to respond since the building is outside the villages' borders. When the janitor and his brother tried to evict the invaders, one male invader brandished a pistol. The brother held one of the women as a shield and convinced the naughty group to leave.
- May 26, 1930: Two Wilmette youths, Larry Mouat, 20, and Joseph Monfort, 17, were severely beaten by five Chicago hoodlums in the parking lot of The Cottage roadhouse. The Wilmette youths' vehicle had accidentally bumped the hoodlums' car.
- July 8, 1930: The Illinois Department of Public Works ordered that all billboards and "other unsightly features" must be removed from the Sheridan Road right-of-way. The order was based on an Illinois law that prohibits all signs except official markers on State highway property.
- July 24, 1934: The proprietors of four roadhouses (Murphy's Lodge, 1420 Sheridan Road; Villa De Metre, 10th Street and Sheridan; Lakota Beach stand, 1426 Sheridan; and The Cottage, 1440 Sheridan) and one liquor store in No Man's Land were arrested by County police for illegally selling liquor in a "dry" territory and without a county license.
- August 13, 1934: The proprietors of four roadhouses were in court today. They successfully contested charges that they sold intoxicating liquor without a County license and in violation of the Township's liquor ban. Prosecutors dropped the charges because of uncertainty whether the "3.2 beer" sold by these establishments is "intoxicating liquor" under Illinois law.

- July 29, 1936: County police raided six establishments and arrested their proprietors for selling beer without a license: San Pedro Cafe, Vista del Lago, Lakota Beach stand, Board Walk Casino, Murphy's Lodge, and The Cottage.
- September 28, 1936: A county Judge canceled a referendum to decide whether No Man's Land would become a separate village called Nomansland. Some owners and residents of the territory had petitioned for the referendum, but the number of signatures became insufficient when nine signers withdrew. The campaign's organizer, John Immell, operator of a milk station in the territory, admitted that conditions along Sheridan Road "are an offense to the community." He explained that short-term leases are "responsible for the unsightly shacks which mar the thoroughfare."
- June 2, 1937: County police raided four establishments (Lakota Beach stand, Murphy's Lodge, The Cottage, and Red Candle Sweet Shop). They found gamblers, mostly high school boys and girls, happily playing "pins."
- July 2, 1939: Al Friedman's fireworks stand in No Man's Land was completely destroyed by a powerful explosion. Friedman suffered burns to his hands. County police threatened to arrest the owners of eight other stands if they fail to keep fire extinguishers and buckets of water ready.
- April 3, 1991: A historic 1928 building at Plaza del Lago, part of the original Spanish Court complex, was destroyed by fire. The fire was caused by the carelessness of workers reroofing the building and was compounded by their ineffectual attempts to extinguish the fire without calling the fire department.
- January 3, 2018: Retail Properties of America, an Oak Brook, Illinois investment firm, announced that it has purchased Plaza del Lago from the family of Joseph Moss for $48.3 million. Moss, who purchased the plaza in 1971, died at the age of 90 on March 16, 2017.

CHAPTER 3

★————————★

Ways and Means

Just as railroad barons famously laid beds of steel and timber westward across America during the 19th century to grow and energize a nation, so too have local captains of industry busily completed all manner of rail and roadway projects as a means to supercharge the growth and economic vibrancy of the Greater Chicago area. In fact, Wilmette owes its existence to the Chicago & Milwaukee Railroad (later the Chicago & North Western and now the Union Pacific) that was built through the area in 1854, and also to the train station built in 1871 by the real estate investors who founded the village. These facilities led to the development of a distinct community that was eventually incorporated as a municipality in 1872.

A small village must have ways and means to connect with commercial areas in its region. The main commercial areas that Wilmette connected to in its early years were Chicago, Milwaukee, and points between. Thus, it's no surprise that in addition to the Chicago & Milwaukee railroad, the major routes affecting Wilmette were north/south routes: two additional train routes and four highways. Originally, the primary means of regional travel were trains and horses, until horses were replaced by cars, trucks, and buses.

The immense changes in the ways and means of travel over the years are reflected in these innovations that contributed to safety and comfort:

- 1897: The first paved streets (macadam) were Forest Avenue from Sheridan Road to West Railroad Avenue, and Hill Street (now Maple Avenue) from Sheridan Road to just west of 6th Street.
- 1900: Lake Avenue between Lake Michigan and 15th Street was the first roadway paved with bricks.
- 1908: The first automobile license was issued to Howard Hitchcock, an investment banker who lived at 413 Central Avenue. His "machine" could reach the speed of 15 mph.
- 1921: The first electric street lights were installed as a demonstration at the

intersection of Washington Avenue and West Railroad Avenue, at the intersection of Lake Avenue and Wilmette Avenue, and along Maple Avenue between 4th and 5th streets.

- 1926: The first three-stage traffic signals were installed at the Lake/Sheridan, Wilmette/Ridge, and Lake/Ridge intersections.
- 1933: The first automatic gates were installed at the Chicago and Northwestern (C&NW) crossings. Some residents opposed them, believing the warning bells would be a nuisance that would lower property values.

C&NW's Left-Hand Travel

We're accustomed to right-hand travel. We drive our cars on the right side of the road. We ride our bikes on the right side of the path. We instinctively veer right when pedestrians approach us from the opposite direction on the sidewalk. We take the right-hand moving walkway at the United Airlines terminal. Why, then, do we travel on the left-hand tracks when we ride the Union Pacific train downtown and back?

Almost 90 years ago, this question was put to Earl Orner, C&NW's popular station master in Wilmette for the first 50 years of the 20th century. He was also village clerk (1906–1925) and village president (1925–1931). Orner answered, tongue in cheek, that trains operate on the left "as a measure of safety and identification." With trains operating on the left-hand tracks and engineers stationed at the cab's right side, he explained, the engineers can more easily identify the engineers of oncoming trains, and they have a more comprehensive view of the right-of-way. He concluded by disclaiming any knowledge of railroading. Judged by his bewildering explanation, Orner was well-suited for the office of village president.

The true story is lost to time. The railroad began operations between Chicago and Waukegan in 1854. For many years, it operated on a single set of tracks. C&NW, like other railroads, declined to bear the cost of constructing multiple tracks until traffic required it.

C&NW eventually found it necessary to build a second set of tracks between its Wells Street terminal (near present-day Merchandise Mart) and Clybourn Junction, where its two lines separated. The double-track layout was extended on the Chicago-Milwaukee line another 14 miles to Evanston in 1882 and further north later in the decade. It wasn't until the early 1890s, in anticipation of huge crowds coming to Chicago for the Columbian Exposition, that the second track was extended to Milwaukee.

The decision to operate trains on the left side was probably made when C&NW, on one of its various lines, constructed its first set of double tracks. What led the designers to opt for left-hand operations? When trying to find explanations for seemingly-strange decisions, it's useful to consider how money might have played a role. Many seemingly strange decisions make perfect sense when viewed in the light of money.

The explanation offered by the C&NW Historical Society is this: At the time the decision was made to build a second set of tracks, C&NW had been providing passenger service for many years. Either the railroad itself or the towns along the lines had built stations to shelter waiting inbound commuters. (Outbound commuters tended to disperse promptly upon disembarking, so they didn't need or use the stations.) By and large, these stations were on the left side of inbound trains. To avoid the huge expense of building a bunch of new stations on the right side of inbound trains to accommodate right-hand operations, C&NW found a cheaper solution: operate the inbound trains on the left-hand tracks. And once the decision was made, it became irreversible, because over the years, huge sums of money were invested in signals and other facilities based on the left-hand design.

The C&NW Historical Society rejects another explanation: that the original investors were British, and they demanded left-hand operations. The Society says that only local farmers and businessmen, not foreign investors, were willing to take the financial risk of building railroads on the "uncivilized prairie."

As a lefty myself, I'm pleased to be served by a southpaw railroad, especially when drinking fountains, revolving doors, gravy ladles, and scissors continue to be made with a right-hand bias.

The Shore Line Route

The Chicago, Milwaukee & St. Paul Railroad (the "Milwaukee Road") was the village's second steam railroad. In 1888, it extended an existing line north from Chicago through Evanston to a station in Wilmette at the northwest corner of 3rd Street and Maple Avenue. The company's intention was to continue on to Milwaukee and compete with the C&NW, but that idea fizzled, and operations in Wilmette were discontinued in the late 1890s. However, the Milwaukee Road's right-of-way became a path for two electric train lines. One was the Shore Line route of the Chicago, North Shore, and Milwaukee Railroad, commonly called the North Shore Electric. The other was the Northwestern Elevated, predecessor of the CTA's Purple Line.

Let's start with the Shore Line route of the North Shore Electric. During the 1890s, the Bluff City Electric Street Railway built an electric street car line south from Waukegan through Wilmette to Evanston. Wilmette granted Bluff City a franchise to operate its trolleys over a right-of-way just east of the C&NW's tracks between the Kenilworth border and Greenleaf Avenue. At Greenleaf, the right-of-way curved eastward and ran down the middle of the street to a point just east of 4th Street, where it curved again southward and connected to the old Milwaukee Road right-of-way and continued to Church Street in Evanston. When the Bluff City tracks were completed in 1899, passengers could transfer at Church Street and travel between Chicago and Waukegan.

At about this time, Bluff City was reorganized as the Chicago & Milwaukee Electric Railroad. The line grew quickly, reaching Milwaukee in 1907. Then financial difficulties, caused by overly aggressive expansion and exacerbated by a 1907 financial panic, forced the company into receivership. Federal Judge Kenesaw Mountain Landis (later commissioner of Major League Baseball) supervised the receivership. Besides its financial problems, the railroad also butted heads with the North Shore villages along its line. High among the villages' complaints was speeding by the trolley cars. In December 1915, following a fatal accident in Glencoe, Judge Landis directed the line to comply with local speed limits.

Excessive speed may have contributed to a Wilmette accident that occurred a few days after Judge Landis's ruling. January 6, 1916 was a typical winter day: no precipitation, but snow on the ground and temperatures in the teens. At 11:30 PM a northbound trolley car entered the curve at Greenleaf Avenue carrying 36 passengers, the conductor, and the motorman. Despite the cold weather, the car's interior was comfortable, warmed by its coal-burning stove. Suddenly, the car jumped the tracks, overturned, and knocked down a tree and a telegraph pole. Red-hot coal scattered from the overturned stove and set the car and its passengers' clothing ablaze.

One passenger, a Highland Park maid, was riding in a seat opposite the stove. "The car bumped for a moment and seemed to leave the rails, overturning and throwing us in a heap on the floor," she said. "The stove overturned and we were showered with burning coals, which set fire to our clothes. Both of my arms and legs were burned and my clothing was on fire when some man pulled me through a broken window. He put out the fire in my clothes and then I lost consciousness."

"Automobilists" returning home from a dance at the Evanston Country Club (then situated at the present-day Canal Shores Golf Course site) were the first to lend aid. Soon, firefighters from Wilmette and Evanston arrived, pulled passengers from the wreckage through windows and doors, and extinguished the fire, which would have been more severe but for the car's steel construction. Wilmette doctors Bryon Stolp and Maud Sands rendered first aid, and injured passengers were transported in private automobiles to Evanston Hospital, St. Francis Hospital, and the Kenilworth Sanitarium, where they received further medical care.

Police arrested the motorman, William Oppenheimer, 32, and charged him with criminal negligence. Several witnesses reported that the trolley was traveling too fast and suggested that the motorman appeared intoxicated. However, both Oppenheimer and the conductor insisted the car was going no faster than ten mph. Oppenheimer claimed that the air brakes failed as he approached the curve, and that his dazed appearance was due to a blow to his head. The charges against him were dismissed two days later.

No one died, but one victim was badly injured. At least four victims lived in Wilmette: Henry and Prudence Fowler, both 46, of 1404 Forest Avenue; and cousins Vinton and Thomas Mickey, both 23, of 1525 Lake Avenue and 1523 Columbus Avenue (now Walnut Avenue), respectively.

In 1916 the railroad was reorganized again as the Chicago, North Shore & Milwaukee Railroad. Its Shore Line route continued to serve North Shore travelers successfully for the next three decades, but after World War II, things changed. America fell in love with the automobile and built highways to accommodate them. Folks switched from trains to autos and from downtown retailers to outlying shopping centers. The Shore Line route suffered chronic losses and shut down in 1955. The railroad's Skokie Valley Line, described later in this chapter, continued to operate.

What would become of the Shore Line's abandoned right-of-way? A few years later the right-of-way north of Wilmette Avenue and just east of the C&NW tracks was sold off in pieces for public use. Two pieces were purchased by the Village for $41,000. One was between Wilmette and Central avenues. It's now part of the village hall property. The other was between Lake and Forest avenues. It's now the site of the Fire Department's Station No. 1. The Wilmette Park District purchased three pieces, two between Forest and Elmwood avenues for $15,000, and the other between Elmwood Avenue and the north village limits. The Park District's section of the Green Bay Trail bike path now runs through this property.

The Northwestern Elevated, Now the CTA's Purple Line

Return with me to the turn of the 20th century when the Chicago & Milwaukee Electric Railroad was just beginning to operate electric trains between Waukegan and Church Street in Evanston. While this was happening, another electric railroad, the Northwestern Elevated (which would become part of the CTA in 1947) was extending its operations towards Wilmette from Chicago. The Chicago & Milwaukee Electric and the Northwestern Elevated shared portions of the old Milwaukee Road right-of-way.

In 1908 the Northwestern Elevated reached Central Street in Evanston. It had its eye on continuing into Wilmette and establishing its rail yards and other facilities in the vicinity of Linden Avenue. Wilmette's town fathers strongly objected and refused to grant a franchise. They feared that the railroad would build workshops and storage barns that would harm the nearby residential neighborhood.

Architect Arthur Gerber designed the Northwestern Elevated's Linden Avenue station in 1913. Side wings were added a few years later. It was placed on the National Register of Historic Places in 1984. Courtesy of the Wilmette Historical Museum.

Faced with this opposition, the Northwestern Elevated took matters into its own hands on the night of April 1, 1912. The railroad sent a large crew of workmen into Wilmette. They installed a spur line off the Milwaukee Road right-of-way to a new 40-foot platform and ticket booth near 4th Street and Linden Avenue. The next day, the railroad began service at Wilmette. The Village filed a lawsuit to reverse this intrusion, but the suit was denied. Some Wilmette residents were pleased that they now had the option of traveling from Wilmette to downtown Chicago without transferring at Church Street.

The Northwestern Elevated tried to assuage Wilmette's concerns by promising to build an exquisite $20,000 station "in keeping with the high-grade improvements elsewhere in the village." It would replace the flimsy ticket booth that had been erected in the middle of the night. Instead, in 1913 the company built a small prairie-style structure and allowed "a real estate agent and fruit vender to occupy space in the cramped quarters until the space left for patrons of the line is barely wide enough to allow them to pass in and out of the depot."

In October 1913, residents circulated a petition protesting the Northwestern Elevated's failure to build the promised upscale station, but nothing significant happened until 1993, when a new facility was finally completed. The old prairie style structure was preserved because of its historic interest.

The new CTA station at 4th and Linden has proved to be an excellent facility, but it hasn't lived up to expectations in one respect. When the planning process began in the 1980s, average weekday boardings at Linden numbered about 2,750. Ridership was expected to be stable at that level. Since then, the number has gradually declined to 954 in 2019. This drop is a concern for anyone who favors public transportation in general and a viable Purple Line in particular.

The Skokie Valley Line

In 1926 the North Shore Electric, which had been running electric trains over its Shore Line route for more than a quarter century, started a new Skokie Valley Line that avoided the congestion of North Shore villages and offered high speed service between Chicago and Milwaukee. The new line followed a north/south route through undeveloped territory near the village's western border. It crossed Lake Avenue just east of Skokie Valley Material Co. and Meier's Tavern.

At the time, the village had just completed the annexation of a huge tract of undeveloped land that established a new (and the present) western border, and it was believed that the Skokie Valley Line would facilitate development of that territory. Passengers could board trains at the Glenayre station at Glenview Road (present-day Old Glenview Road) and travel south to Chicago or north to Milwaukee. Unfortunately, the Skokie Valley Line started to bleed money in the 1950s. It was shut down in January 1963, the victim of automobiles, trucks, modern highways, and changing life styles. C&NW purchased the right-of-way and, for a time, used it for freight service.

Sheridan Road

The vision was ambitious: A grand driveway through the picturesque North Shore of Lake Michigan, "the Riviera of the west," surpassing the world-famous driveways of New York, Paris, Berlin, and Vienna. The vision was conceived after the Civil War. During the 1870s and 1880s, the Lincoln Park Board (one of several park districts in Chicago) was already developing Lincoln Park and roadways serving it, including Lake Shore Drive.

In 1889 a group of Evanstonians pushed the vision forward by spearheading an organizational meeting at the offices of Burnham & Root, architects and planners. Their purpose was to form the North Shore Improvement Association to push for an extension of Lake Shore Drive north to Waukegan. This extension would open up the North Shore real estate market, just in time for the Columbian Exposition which Chicago was vying to host. The road's name would honor General Philip Sheridan, Civil War hero, who had died a few months earlier.

The meeting was attended by representatives of the communities through which the road would pass. Wilmette's representatives were Edgar Paul and Horace Drury. An Executive Committee was appointed for each community. It was responsible for convincing local officials to create the section of Sheridan Road lying within their jurisdiction using existing roads and, where necessary, new roads. Wilmette's Executive Committee consisted of Thomas Bryan, Edward Burge, and Drury.

These men were advancing their own financial interests as much as the grand driveway vision. Paul and Drury had both served as village president and were Wilmette real estate investors and developers. Bryan didn't live in Wilmette, but he was a top official of the Columbian Exposition and a major investor in Wilmette real estate. Burge was a Wilmette real estate broker who, five years earlier, had led the failed attempt to annex Wilmette to Evanston.

After the organizational meeting, the *Chicago Tribune* reported that the original vision of a straight-line driveway along the shore had to be abandoned, mainly because some of the affected property owners opposed that path. Accordingly, "there will be many curves in the road, now leading it along the lake close to the edge of the banks, now running westward and shutting the lake out from sight. Many of the natural beauties of the country will thus be preserved, and the road will have less of the artificial than if it were cut straight through." One of the opposing landowners was Daniel ("make no little plans") Burnham. His six-acre Evanston estate—bounded by Forest Avenue, Dempster

Street, Lake Michigan, and Burnham Place—would be bisected by a straight-line road. His opposition caused 90-degree turns in that area.

North of Chicago, the standard roadway width would be 50 feet with parkways on both sides. The natural grade would be preserved. The surface would be "clayed and graveled, well rolled and packed." Stone sidewalks, landscaping, electric street lights, and flood protection would be included in some areas. In Wilmette, the road would follow the old country road along the shore called State Street.

The necessary right-of-way from Lincoln Park to Fort Sheridan (24 miles) was assembled within two years. Catholic Archbishop Patrick Feehan donated a 100-foot strip at the east edge of Calvary Cemetery. Northwestern University granted a strip west of the campus. The last holdouts, George and Robert Scott of Glencoe, donated the final piece on Christmas Day 1890. Ten years later the road was completed to Lake Forest. That event was celebrated by a drive from end to end, followed by a banquet and ball at the Hotel Moraine in Highland Park. Among those attending were Philip Sheridan Jr., Illinois Governor John Tanner, Wisconsin Governor Edward Scofield, and the mayors of the towns between Chicago and Milwaukee. "On to Milwaukee" was their cry.

By 1910, though, the road was in "a condition of dilapidation," a "frightful nightmare, owing solely to neglect and indifference." North of Chicago, Sheridan Road "was much worn out macadam, poor gravel, and bad sandy and earth roads." The goal of a road reaching Milwaukee remained unfulfilled.

Without mentioning Sheridan Road by name, the 1909 "Plan of Chicago" by Daniel Burnham and Edward Bennett called for action: "A highway should be built from Wilmette along the western shore of Lake Michigan to Milwaukee; and even where this road runs through intermediate towns it should be located as close as possible to the edge of the water." (Recall that in 1887, Burnham had opposed locating Sheridan Road "as close as possible to the edge of the water" since it would bisect his six-acre Evanston estate.)

The road's poor condition was due partly to the manner in which it was governed. Each municipality, township, or park district owned the section of roadway within its jurisdiction and was responsible for locating, building and maintaining it. There was little coordination, and as originally constructed, the road wasn't capable of withstanding the wear and tear of the motor vehicles that became the road's dominant users.

The situation was critical. A new organization, the Sheridan Road Improvement Association, was created in 1911. Its mission was to persuade local officials to improve their sections of the road and to secure enactment of a state law that would encourage local governmental bodies to transfer their sections of the road to the Lincoln Park Board.

Today, the idea of Wilmette and other North Shore villages surrendering their sections of Sheridan Road to a Chicago park district seems bizarre. But not in 1911. For many years, the Lincoln Park Board had possessed the legal authority to create driveways and boulevards contiguous to its parks. Pursuant to this authority, it had established a network of roads, including the southern segment of Sheridan Road in Chicago. It had substantial expertise in roadwork.

In 1913, the state adopted legislation that facilitated the transfer process. One by one, local governmental bodies improved and transferred their sections, but progress was slow. At the time, the Metropolitan Sanitary District was building a huge intercepting sewer beneath Sheridan Road from Cook County's northern line to the North Shore Channel in Wilmette. This construction delayed the roadwork. Finally, in 1917, the stretch from Wilmette's southern border to Kenilworth's northern border was complete. Thirty to 40 feet wide, the pavement was brick through Wilmette and concrete through No Man's Land and Kenilworth. The Lincoln Park Board then took over this stretch. Wilmette even authorized the Lincoln Park police to patrol the road in the village. Other sections, especially near Fort Sheridan and between Lake Forest and Waukegan, remained in poor condition until the 1920s when the State paved the road through Lake County and incorporated it into State Route 42 from St. Louis to Milwaukee.

Then another problem emerged: too much vehicular traffic through Sheridan Road's mostly residential neighborhoods. Another organization, the North Shore Property Owners Association, sprung into action in the 1930s. Its goals were threefold: remove the State Route 42 designation and assign it to non-residential roads to the west, reduce bus and truck traffic, and stop improvements that would encourage more and faster traffic. The association was successful. It deserves a large measure of credit for making Sheridan Road what it is today: A grand driveway through the picturesque North Shore of Lake Michigan.

The Automobile Age

It wasn't that long ago when car dealers were major businesses in Wilmette, selling and servicing cars while contributing substantial tax revenue to local coffers. The last dealership, Imperial Motors, closed its Wilmette doors in 2017, more than 100 years after the first dealers opened for business.

The first businesses to sell new cars in Wilmette were Wilmette Motor Car

Works and Fosters' Garage. Of the two, Motor Car Works may have been first. Robert Waters started this firm in 1910 at his blacksmith shop at 721–723 West Railroad Avenue. (Years later this site would be part of Imperial Motors' extensive property.) Waters advertised himself as a "horseshoer," but he branched out into storing, selling (on commission), and repairing automobiles. He also offered to "build cars to order." By late 1913 he was out of business. There's no proof that he ever "built a car to order," and this lack of evidence casts doubt on his right to be called Wilmette's first new car dealer. During his brief residency in the village, he married a Wilmette woman, Martha Curley of 1243 Central Avenue. That didn't last long, either.

The other claimant to the first dealership title, Fosters' Garage, opened in 1911. One year earlier, two Wilmette brothers, George and Norton Foster, secured a franchise to sell Hudson automobiles. They went to the Wilmette Exchange State Bank for a loan to build a garage at 611 West Railroad Avenue, future site of Wil-Shore Ford. The bank's president, Seymour Wheelock, was uncertain. "How do we know that this automobile business won't be only a flash in the pan?" He ultimately approved the loan.

Fosters' Garage ended up selling not Hudsons but the Paige Car, manufactured by the Paige Co. of Detroit. The price was $1,000, less than $30,000 in 2020 dollars. Fosters' advertising tried to persuade potential customers: "The Paige is not a $2,000 car. It's just the best automobile you can buy anywhere for a thousand dollars, a well-designed, well-built car: comfortable, speedy and enduring and fully equipped. We honestly believe that you'll have to pay at least two to three hundred dollars more to get as good value in most of the other cars." Joined by Jack Shown, a prominent figure in Wilmette's auto business in subsequent years, Fosters' created a comfortable rest area within their building as a convenience for tourists passing through the village. Besides selling new Paiges, the firm also sold used cars and offered livery service. It stayed in business only five years.

The early dealerships were garages—places to store and service cars. They had no pleasing showrooms where they could proudly display their products. The first Wilmette dealer to create a show room was the Willys-Knight and Overland dealership at 1141 Greenleaf Avenue, across the street from today's Panera. The dealership, owned by Carlton Biggs of Evanston, opened in early 1924 and bragged, "The strapping big new Overland engine has everybody talking. It's all sinew and power. It'll send you zooming up the stiffest climbs as nimbly as you please. This is Overland Power Demonstration week. Come in—take an Overland out and prove to yourself that it's the most automobile in the world for the money." Customers didn't come in, and the show room was gone within months.

Wilmette's automobile business continued to be unstable until the late 1940s when the big four dealers emerged: Imperial Motors, Foley Buick, Joe Jacobs Chevrolet, and Wil-Shore Ford. They prospered for five decades. Their contribution to Wilmette in many ways can't be overstated. Now they're gone, too.

Green Bay Road

The name Green Bay Road suggests a roadway extending to Green Bay, Wisconsin. While there once was in this area an Indian trail that evolved into a post road linking Fort Dearborn in Chicago and Fort Howard in Green Bay, it no longer exists. Present-day Green Bay Road has more to do with the C&NW.

In all of the North Shore towns along the railroad's path, the train depots were the early center of activity. Commercial establishments sprang up nearby. Local roads adjacent to the tracks accommodated the traffic generated by these activities. In the early 1900s the condition of these roads varied widely. Some were barely passable, and they weren't connected from one town to another. The main north/south route through the North Shore was Sheridan Road, but by 1920 it had become severely congested.

Enter the Chicago Regional Planning Association, an advisory group with only the power of persuasion. It urged the North Shore towns from Evanston to Glencoe to create a "through highway" west of the tracks from Emerson Street to Lake County. It would serve as a northerly extension of Western Avenue and McCormick Boulevard. Cooperation by all the towns was required. Each would have to widen and straighten its section, improve the surface, and fill the gaps. Land would have to be acquired. The projects would be expensive, even with partial funding from Cook County.

In Wilmette, the major hurdle was that Main Street, located just west of the tracks, dead-ended at Elmwood Avenue. Vehicles headed north to Kenilworth had to turn left on Elmwood and right on 15th Street, then proceed to Kenilworth. To eliminate this maneuver, the Village took action to acquire the land adjacent to the tracks north of Elmwood, including two homes. Each was owned by an elderly couple: John Hoffman, a house painter, and his wife Agnes (1404 Elmwood); and Peter Morton, a railroad flagman, and his wife Delphina (1408 Elmwood). Legal proceedings, started before 1920, weren't concluded until 1931.

Then there was the matter of a name. Evanston's and Kenilworth's sections were called West Railroad Avenue. Wilmette's section shared this name until 1922 when it was changed to Main Street. Winnetka's section was called Center

Street (southern portion) and Linden Avenue (in Hubbard Woods). Glencoe's section was called Glencoe Road.

A uniform name was considered highly desirable. As early as 1925 the name Green Bay Road was suggested to honor the old trail and post road that once traversed the region. Proposals were also made to honor a Native American chief or a war hero. In 1928 Wilmette dedicated its section to the memory of John Couffer, a one-time railroad executive who served as village president from 1906 to 1915 and advocated for public improvements, but the name Main Street was retained. At first, the towns couldn't agree on a name. In 1931 Kenilworth took the bull by the horns and renamed its section Green Bay Road and urged other towns to go along. In 1936 Wilmette agreed.

Skokie Highway

Green Bay Road wasn't envisioned as a solution to the difficulties of traveling by automobile between Illinois and Wisconsin. In 1925 the main Illinois-Wisconsin routes were Sheridan and Waukegan roads: the first was described as "hilly and crooked and at present in the process of repairs" and the second as "so congested that traffic is considerably slowed up, particularly over the week-ends." Urban planners and commercial interests longed for a superhighway west of the North Shore towns that would connect Cicero Avenue to Wisconsin's Route 57 at the state line. Such a superhighway, it was hoped, would eliminate traffic congestion in the villages while providing a safe and fast travel experience.

Planning and construction lasted for almost 20 years, with completion in the late 1930s. Initially, the new superhighway was called Route 57. It was built nearly in a straight line and had few slopes. Its pavement was 40 feet, divided in Cook County by only a white line (Skokie Highway). Further north, two strips of 20-foot pavement were divided by a parkway (Skokie Boulevard). The road was intersected by the major east/west arteries along its path where traffic signals were installed. Upon completion, it was used by an estimated 12,000 to 15,000 cars and trucks daily, and double these numbers on Sundays.

The superhighway quickly earned another name, Death Highway. In 1938 and 1939, 286 accidents occurred between Gross Point Road and Lake-Cook Road, resulting in ten persons killed and 181 injured. The accidents occurred mostly at night, leading to the installation of sodium vapor lights. Excessive speed was a major factor, with most accidents occurring at traffic signals.

Edens Expressway

The face of western Wilmette changed dramatically in the 1950s, and Edens Expressway was largely responsible. The growing use of the automobile led planners in the 1930s to conceive a network of superhighways, radiating from downtown Chicago. Like Skokie Highway, the planners' objective was to relieve congestion, enhance safety, and facilitate travel. By 1940 consensus on a plan emerged.

One element of the network was a northern Cook County superhighway (now called Edens Expressway). Edens would start at a planned northwestern superhighway through Chicago (now called Kennedy Expressway) and stretch 14 miles northward to the Cook County line. It would supplant Skokie Highway as the major north-south roadway through northern Cook County.

The plan for Edens was to utilize the Skokie Highway right-of-way in some places and convert Skokie Highway into a local roadway in other places. At the county line, Edens would connect to the original Skokie Boulevard. The land for Edens was acquired during World War II, but construction was deferred because of the War. In 1947 construction finally began. Four years later Edens was completed at a cost of $23 million.

The grand opening occurred during a snowstorm in December 1951. A motorcade traversing the new superhighway was led by a dozen snowplows. Among the dignitaries present was William Edens, the 88-year-old retired banker and civic leader honored by the expressway's name. An early advocate of paved roads, he's said to have "taken Illinois out of the mud" by promoting the state's first highway bond issue in 1918.

Spurred by the expressway and pent up post-war housing demand, the truck farms that dominated the area were rapidly subdivided and filled with homes. Wilmette's population jumped from 18,162 in 1950 to 28,268 in 1960, and the village became an almost-fully-developed residential community. The expressway led to the creation of Edens Plaza (described in Chapter 7) and contributed to Loyola Academy's and Regina Dominican High School's decisions to locate in Wilmette. Westlake Plaza was also established at Lake Avenue and Skokie Highway, across from Eden's Plaza, during the 1950s.

Hunter Road

If you drive in Wilmette, you probably use Hunter Road, if not regularly, at least occasionally. It intersects the village's important east-west roadways: Lake Avenue, Illinois Road, Wilmette Avenue, Glenview Road, Old Glenview Road, and Crawford Avenue. It takes you to two of the village's important destinations: Highcrest School and Centennial Park. It's a logical route for a roadway.

But Hunter had a difficult ten-year gestation period. In the 1940s it was called 23rd Street, and it ran only between Beechwood Avenue and Lake Avenue. South of Lake, it wasn't an official street. Instead, it was a dirt path "full of chuckholes, deep ditches, and trash and garbage," ending north of Highcrest School.

In 1951 the opening of Edens Expressway foreshadowed big changes for west Wilmette. The Expressway blocked all east-west traffic except at two overpasses: one at Lake Avenue and a second at Glenview Road. However, the second overpass didn't connect Glenview Road in Glenview to Glenview Road in Wilmette. Instead, it extended Glenview Road in Glenview eastward to a "T" intersection at Hibbard Road in Wilmette. To continue east into Wilmette, motorists had to take Hibbard north to Wilmette Avenue or south to Glenview Road (now Old Glenview Road).

In 1955 village fathers devised a three-point plan that would reconfigure the village's west side roadways to eliminate this detour and facilitate residential development. First, Crawford Avenue would be extended north from "old" Glenview Road past Wilmette Avenue to Illinois Road. Second, Hunter Road, south of Lake Avenue, would be paved and connected to Crawford at Illinois. Third, a "new" Glenview Road would be built from a point just west of the Crawford/Wilmette Avenue intersection to the Glenview Road overpass.

This three-point plan is essentially what exists today. But in 1955 it was shot down. Why? Because everyone associated with Highcrest School—District 39's Board of Education, the PTA, and parents—strongly opposed extending Crawford to Illinois. They were certain that the extension would create a high volume roadway adjacent to the school, jeopardizing the safety of children. The village board bowed to their pressure and dropped the idea of extending Crawford beyond Wilmette Avenue. The board even urged the owner of the vacant land south of Highcrest School to build houses that would forever prevent the connection of Crawford and Hunter.

In 1962 the portion of the plan extending Crawford north to Wilmette Avenue and creating New Glenview Road was implemented. By 1967 villagers had a change of heart about connecting Hunter to Crawford. Almost everyone

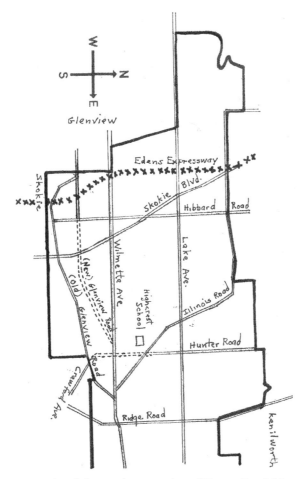

New Glenview Road and the southern portion of Hunter Road (the two dotted roadways) were built in the 1960s to facilitate west side traffic after Edens Expressway blocked Illinois Road, Wilmette Avenue, and Old Glenview Road.

agreed it was a good idea. But a new obstacle arose. The Village had to acquire the necessary land. This wasn't a problem, except for the stretch in front of Highcrest School. Title to this land was held by the New Trier school trustees.

Who were these trustees? They comprised an archaic unit of government that supposedly served as financial manager and watchdog over the township's public schools. They held title to the real estate of all township school districts and were the only body empowered to transfer it. They were elected, but without much public attention. (Years later township residents voted overwhelmingly to abolish the office.)

In early 1967 District 39 asked the school trustees to donate the necessary land to the Village. For a year, the trustees procrastinated. The Village lacked the power to force the transfer. Finally, a deal was struck. The Village owned a dedicated but unopened street (Central Avenue) that ran straight through the middle of McKenzie School. Theoretically, the Village could build a road there. The school trustees agreed to a swap: Central Avenue for Hunter Road. And so, Hunter Road, as we know it today, finally became a reality.

Hibbard Road, the Skokie Lagoons, and Camp Skokie

Hibbard Road runs 3.5 miles between Old Glenview Road in Wilmette and Tower Road in Winnetka. It's a convenient route for folks traveling between the west sides of Wilmette and Winnetka. It was named to honor William Gold Hibbard, Jr.

Born in 1870, Hibbard was the son of a wealthy Chicago hardware merchant. Following his graduation from Harvard College, he worked in his father's business. In 1908 he moved to Winnetka near the Skokie Valley marsh, which became the center of his attention. At the time, the marsh was a mosquito-infested, peat-smoldering, flood-spilling swamp. Hibbard's goal was to reclaim the land and convert it into a nature preserve for public enjoyment. He labored tirelessly to achieve this goal for twelve years until his death in 1920.

Hibbard was largely responsible for inspiring the Cook County Forest Preserve District to acquire the marsh in the 1920s. In 1933, the federal government, through its Depression-era Civil Conservation Corps (CCC), embarked on a huge project that would accomplish Hibbard's goal. For eight years, thousands of members of the CCC moved millions of cubic feet of dirt, much of it by arduous manual labor using picks, shovels, and wheel barrows. They converted the marsh into a recreational area consisting of seven lagoons connected by canals and regulated by dams. The system was designed to eliminate the evils of the marsh: flooding, peat fires, and mosquitoes. The project was the largest performed by the CCC in its nine-year history. The workers, numbering up to 1,000 at the peak, lived in wooden barracks at Camp Skokie Valley, a 30-acre military-style encampment in Harms Woods.

The CCC was phased out in 1942, and Camp Skokie Valley was taken over by the Army's 740th Military Police Battalion for the duration of World War II. The 800 MPs at the camp performed multiple functions. Maintaining citizens' morale at a high level was an important wartime goal, and the MPs appeared at moral-building events like parades and ceremonies in the Chicago area. In 1944, when Sewell Avery, head of Montgomery Ward & Co., defied President Roosevelt's seizure of the company during a labor dispute, MPs from the camp forcibly removed him from his office.

In March 1945 Camp Skokie Valley became a Prisoner of War (POW) camp. For seven months, the camp held as many as 400 German POWs, all privates. The U.S. experienced a dire labor shortage during World War II, and the Army put able-bodied POWs to work, subject to the terms of the Geneva Convention. The records disclose little about their work, but at least one was hired out as a tailor, and several worked in the laundry at Vaughn General Hospital, an Army hospital opened in 1945 at the Hines Hospital complex in Maywood. Important to Wilmette, many POWs labored on the truck farms still functioning on the village's west side. By the end of 1945 the war had ended, the prisoners were repatriated, and the camp was closed.

Breaking Travel News

- January 30, 1895: Dr. William Rittenhouse of Chicago was injured by a flying mail sack while standing on Wilmette's C&NW platform. Rittenhouse had visited a local patient and was waiting for a commuter train back to Chicago. Before it arrived, a mail train roared through, and the clerk on board threw a large sack toward the platform, striking the doctor below the knee. This incident follows a similar one in which a small girl was struck in the face and disfigured for life.

- July 31, 1906: Frank Collier, 49, of 601 Lake Avenue, an automobile enthusiast, is using his substantial wealth to bring village government to its knees. Collier is angry about Wilmette's speed-limit ordinance and the speed traps being used to catch "scorchers." On recent Sundays, he positioned himself at the entrance to the speed trap on Sheridan Road and flagged down unsuspecting motorists to warn them. Police retaliated by setting up a speed trap that ended at Collier's gate post. Collier was snared and fined $35. He says he'll appeal and spend whatever it costs to recoup the fine. "I'm going to fight them until they're sick."

- June 28, 1909: Dr. William Tomlinson, 81, of 1028 Greenleaf Avenue, was struck and killed by a C&NW express train as he crossed the tracks at Wilmette Avenue. The train was traveling at a high speed, and the physician's body was carried on the cow catcher to Central Street in Evanston where the train was brought to a stop.

- March 10, 1914: A Northwestern Elevated train rear-ended a North Shore Electric train at Hill Street (now Maple Avenue). Between Evanston and Linden Avenue, the two train lines share tracks. The Elevated train apparently missed a switch that would have sent it to its terminal at Linden Avenue. Its motorman claimed that he suffered an electric shock rendering him unable to stop his train in time to avoid the collision, but he could not explain why he was following so close behind the North Shore Electric train. Several passengers on the North Shore Electric, riding on the rear platform, were injured. Four passengers were hospitalized, including two Wilmette residents: Wallace Arneson, 19, and James Sullivan, 60. Sullivan may be permanently disabled.

- August 3, 1922: William Bingham, the chauffeur employed by Lake Forest's power-couple, John Mitchell, Jr. and Lolita Armour Mitchell, was found not guilty of speeding on Sheridan Road in Wilmette. Prior to the trial, Police Chief Edward Sieber resisted tremendous pressure to settle the case out of court. "I don't care whom my officers arrest," he said. "If they arrest a man for speeding he has to go on trial. I'll back my officers to the limit." At the trial, the arresting officer testified that he followed the Mitchell car for more than a mile, and its average speed was 32 mph. The Mitchells and their chauffeur testified that the car's speed never exceeded the limit, 25 mph. The jury deliberated for one minute before returning the not-guilty verdict.

- November 6, 1922: Bernice Cook, twelve, the daughter of Thomas and Helen Cook, who recently moved to 912 12th Street, was arrested in Milwaukee today, along with Wallace Coffey, 18, son of Michael and Nellie Coffey of 603 Central Avenue. The pair had "borrowed" Nellie Coffey's new car and had run away. Matrimony wasn't their motive. Rather, Bernice feared parental punishment for an earlier transgression, and Wallace was angry over discipline administered by his father. "We can sleep in the car and stay away for a week," Bernice reasoned. "When we come back, everybody will have forgotten about it. I can pretend I am 16 and get a job in a restaurant."

- May 19, 1929: Mary Gray, 24, traveling from Fort Sheridan to Wilmette, was killed when she jumped from the rear platform of a moving North Shore Electric train near Lake Avenue. She had fallen asleep en route and awoke as the train was moving from the station. Her body struck a fence alongside the tracks and fell back against the train. A native of Richland Center, Wisconsin, she had recently relocated to Wilmette to work as a maid in the home of George and Helen Stewart, both 35, at 1033 Greenwood Avenue.

- June 30, 1930: Old Charley left town. In 1915 Charley started working in Wilmette's fire department. He performed well, responding promptly to alarms and traveling quickly to fires to prevent the frequent outcome: total conflagration. Three years later the department acquired a gasoline-powered hose cart, and Charley was transferred to the public works department. Despite circulatory problems, he pulled his load without complaint for twelve more years. Recently, the Village decided it could no longer afford him and didn't need his wagon. Fortunately, the Wisconsin farmer who bought the wagon was willing to take Charley, too. With the retirement of this dedicated public servant with a dapple gray face, Wilmette is no longer a one-horse-town.

- November 12, 1931: James Hunter and Loren Wilson were stopped by an Evanston motorcycle policeman for driving 50 mph on Main Street. Hunter gave this explanation: "We were racing that railroad train running on the track beside the highway. The Village of Wilmette hires us to race trains. They think the trains go too fast across unprotected grade crossings. We time the trains and tell the village council. If you don't mind, there's another train coming, and we ought to race it, too." The policeman let them go with orders to stay within Wilmette's village limits.

- February 4, 1932: Wilmette's local newspaper made a laughable prediction. Commenting on a recent automotive innovation (the key-operated ignition switch), the author predicted, "Time is not far distant when we'll probably see automatic gear shifting and, who can tell, perhaps someday an automation will drive our cars for us."

- July 18, 1933: The village board is billing the North Shore Electric $100,425.72. The railroad has operated its trains over Greenleaf Avenue and Electric Place for 35 years—from January 5, 1898 to July 8, 1933—without compensating the Village. The railroad is now in receivership, and the U.S. District Court has ordered that all claims of creditors be presented to the receiver by the end of the month. The railroad's "free" use of the streets has been a long-standing controversy.

- May 12, 1936: Chief McGuire announced that two radio motorcycles costing $1,000 have been placed in service. They're the first cycles in this region to be equipped with short-wave radios, allowing instant communication between the cycles and police headquarters. Loudspeakers are mounted on the handlebars, and the receivers are fastened behind the seat.

- December 29, 1936: Frank Kunz, 171 Prairie Avenue, has died at the age of 81. He was one of Wilmette's first blacksmiths, if not the first. He opened his shop in 1879. Besides shoeing horses, he manufactured light wagons. When automobiles supplanted wagons, he transitioned from blacksmithing and wagon-building to automobile-painting, his occupation until his death.

- August 12, 1937: Chief McGuire announced that a phone box has been installed at the intersection of Lake Avenue and Skokie Boulevard. Motorists and others will now be able to report emergencies directly to police headquarters and obtain fast responses.

- October 21, 1947: The village board voted to oppose the North Shore Bus Co.'s proposal to establish bus service between Chicago and Waukegan. The proposal is pending before the Illinois Commerce Commission. The board objects to the proposed route through the village, namely, Green Bay Road from the Kenilworth line to Central Avenue, east on Central to Sheridan Road, and south on Sheridan to the Evanston line. The board was most concerned about bus traffic on Central Avenue. East of 11th Street, it's a narrow residential street with multiple schools in the vicinity.

- March 31, 1948: Road rage ended with Irving Beitzel, 1328 Wilmette Avenue, in police custody and a Highwood resident, Ole Haugland, hospitalized in serious condition. The incident began at Sheridan Road and Greenwood Avenue when Beitzel made a left-hand turn from the right lane in front of Haugland's car. Haugland pursued Beitzel to 13th Street and Lake Avenue and forced him to the curb. During the ensuing argument, Haugland struck Beitzel with a tire chain. Beitzel then procured a knife from his car, stabbed Haugland in the abdomen, and drove to the police station to surrender.

- December 1, 1965: Wilmette shoppers will no longer be required to feed parking meters in the Village Center (one cent for twelve minutes). These annoying devices, 316 of them, were installed in 1954 to prevent extended parking and to raise money for off-street parking lots. The Chamber of Commerce has long objected to the meters, claiming they drive shoppers to Edens Plaza and Old Orchard where ample free parking is provided. A two-hour parking limit will replace the meters.

CHAPTER 4

★————————————★

The Village Center

A village's downtown is often the setting of lasting memories. It's where dad frequented the hardware store and the bank, mom dropped off the dry cleaning and bought the groceries, and the family enjoyed a movie or a meal together. It's where the kids ate their first ice cream cone and saw their first parade. It's where, years later, those same kids might bring their own children back to the homestead and entertain them with memories of the way things were.

A village's downtown, properly respected and nurtured, is a testament to its responsible stewardship and a promise of stability. Over time, the shops may be different, but the feel is the same. Wilmette's downtown has been blessed with all of that.

I always thought of the Village Center as the area of Wilmette, east of the C&NW tracks and west of 11th Street, mainly along Wilmette, Central, and Greenleaf avenues, but the 2010 "Village Center Master Plan" has a broader definition. It adds the area west of the tracks along Green Bay Road between Linden and Lake avenues, including the post office and library sites on Park Avenue. I'm sticking with the narrower definition. The area east of the tracks has a much different feel than the more heavily trafficked Green Bay Road corridor.

Planners of the past believed that preserving the Village Center's "small town ambience," "traditional hometown character," and "pedestrian scale" is a worthy goal. I agree, as is preserving architecturally and historically significant structures. These goals aren't necessarily incompatible with the pro-redevelopment goals of the "Village Center Master Plan," but in my opinion, additional controls are needed to protect designated areas of the Village Center, including the sites of heritage buildings, from four- and more-story redevelopment, as is now possible.

Some folks complain that the buildings in the Village Center are "unattractive" or a "hodgepodge," but next time you're there, look at the buildings individually with a critical eye. I think you'll see that the vintage buildings don't deserve the label "unattractive," especially if the owners would restore ornamental features that once existed but have deteriorated. It's true that there's no coordinated design plan, but the Village Center, like other older suburban downtowns, developed over many years under the auspices of multiple property owners, and design variety is a natural and interesting consequence of that process. Not long ago, the Village Center lacked "a sense of vibrancy," as noted in the Master Plan, but today a sense of vibrancy has emerged, thanks to the recent restaurant-based resurgence.

It's hard to imagine but it's true: The Village Center was once a residential neighborhood with single family homes and no commercial structures. This was the early pattern of development along Wilmette, Central and Greenleaf avenues east of the railroad tracks from 1870 to the 1890s. Wilmette's commercial activity first developed west of the railroad tracks along West Railroad Avenue.

After 1900 all of the single family homes in the Village Center were gradually demolished or relocated to make way for commercial activity. Some of the commercial buildings that replaced these homes were one-story structures with one or more stores. Others were two or three-story story structures with stores on the first floor and apartments or offices above. Most were owned and developed by local investors who had the village's interest at heart (and of course their own financial interest as well). They hired prominent architects to design buildings of quality. Several of these architects were also Wilmette residents.

Nineteen commercial structures built during this era, 1890–1930, are still standing. Eleven are more than 100 years old. There are only four post-1970 buildings in the heart of the Village Center (Wilmette and Central avenues). One is the Chase Bank. It was built by the Wilmette State Bank in 1972 and was the third bank building on the site. Another is the building at 1199 Wilmette Avenue that's partially occupied by Panera Bread. It and the adjacent parking lot were built in 1995. The site was previously occupied by a small florist shop called Flowers By Collette and an IHOP restaurant. A third is the Optima Building on Central Avenue, a mixed commercial-residential structure built in 1997. It replaced a supermarket called Meat-N-Shoppe. The North Shore Community Bank complex at 1145 Wilmette Avenue was built in 1995 and 2006. It replaced three small retail buildings.

The Village Center will be a unique and highly attractive feature of Wilmette's future if its historic buildings are preserved and, in some cases, restored. Appendix 2 identifies 20 old buildings in the Village Center and nine more along the Green Bay Road corridor between Washington and Wilmette avenues. A few of the most significant buildings are described in detail on the following pages.

Second C&NW Depot, 1873

Ironically, the oldest commercial building in the Village Center wasn't originally located in the Village Center. It's the Chicago & North Western's second depot, built in 1874 on the west side of the tracks when the first depot burned down. The third depot was built in 1897, and the second depot was moved north and used by the railroad as a storage facility. In 1974, when the railroad planned to demolish it, local preservationists came to its rescue. Opponents urged that it wasn't worth saving and couldn't be put to any good use, but the preservationist won. The building was moved to 1139 Wilmette Avenue, a Village-owned property that had been acquired for a parking lot. The depot became a village-owned building available for renovation and reuse. A restaurant planned for the building never got off the ground, but soon the village's new cable TV franchisee agreed to lease the building, renovate it, and use it as its headquarters. A few years later, the cable company vacated the building, and it was converted into a restaurant.

The C&NW's second depot was replaced in 1897. Courtesy of the Wilmette Historical Museum.

The original facade of the Shultz Building (shown here) was changed substantially after the building was heavily damaged in a 1920 tornado. Courtesy of the Wilmette Historical Museum.

The Schultz Building, c. 1898

The Schultz building at the northeast corner of Central Avenue and 12th Street (1152–1156 Central) is probably the oldest surviving commercial building at its original site in the Village Center. It was built before 1898, but the exact date is unknown. There were two stores on the ground floor and apartments above. For many years, grocery stores occupied the west side of the building, King & Schultz being the first.

In 1911 Emil Nord and Henry Schultz formed a cleaning, dyeing, and tailoring partnership and soon moved into the store on the east side of the building. This business, which recently closed, is described in Chapter 7.

The Shoe Store Building, c. 1900

The Shoe Store Building, next door to the Schultz Building, was built in about 1900. It was home to a bicycle shop and hardware store in its earliest days, but for decades it was a shoe store. In 1920, it was called the Wilmette Shoe Store and was operated by Zygmund Rafalski.

Wilmette police investigate a fender-bender across from the Shoe Store Building (center) c. 1930. Courtesy of the Wilmette Historical Museum.

In 1922 the Wilmette Plan Commission recommended that future buildings in the Village Center should "have a rural French type of architecture." That same year, Rafalski remodeled the building in that style. He also moved the front façade several feet toward the street and increased the building height. His architect was Edgar O. Blake, a Wilmette resident. Blake worked on the World's Columbian Exposition of 1893 before establishing his own architectural practice in Evanston. Most of his work was single-family homes, but he also designed office buildings, churches, and apartment houses.

John Schneider purchased the shoe business from Rafalski in 1926 and continued it at this location for 60 years.

The McGuire & Orr Block, 1905

The McGuire & Orr Block at 1138–1148 Central Avenue and 1160–1168 Wilmette Avenue was built in 1905. Decades ago, the word "block" was used to describe a large building subdivided into several stores, offices or other units. For example, on stonework above the marquee of the Wilmette Theater on Central Avenue is inscribed "Metropolitan Block," a reminder that the building originally contained stores and offices besides the theater.

The McGuire & Orr Block was built by a Chicago-based real estate firm named, not surprisingly, McGuire & Orr. J. Fred McGuire and Willard Orr worked separately in real estate for several years before they formed a partnership in 1896. Their firm engaged in many facets of the real estate business in Chicago and on the North Shore from Evanston to Lake Forest: investing in land, laying out subdivisions, building homes and commercial buildings, and brokering transactions. Nearly every North Shore suburb had at least one McGuire & Orr subdivision, and the firm's branch offices were conveniently located near railroad terminals in Evanston, Wilmette (one near the C&NW station and the other near the Northwestern Elevated station), Kenilworth, Winnetka, Glencoe, and Highland Park. At one time, the firm owned or controlled more than half the vacant lakefront property between the Great Lakes Naval Station and Evanston.

The firm's homebuilding projects included one in Wilmette on Greenleaf Avenue between 4th and 6th streets. This development was advertised in 1910 as "pretty new homes just being completed…; modern and up to date in every particular; large lots, 200 feet deep; beautiful trees. Prices $6,500 to $7,500." In the 1920s, the firm purchased and subdivided 31 acres along Sheridan Road in southwest Kenilworth (formerly the Mahoney farm). Lots were offered for sale at prices ranging from $25,000 to $50,000 but only to carefully selected buyers who pledged to build their own homes.

The McGuire & Orr Block was the third commercial building on Central Avenue east of 12th Street. Courtesy of the Wilmette Historical Museum.

The McGuire & Orr Block was designed by architect Howard Hodgkins, a onetime resident at 602 Maple Avenue. He's most remembered for two buildings in Chicago's Motor Row Historic District on South Michigan Avenue, now designated as a Chicago Landmark and listed on the National Register of Historic Places. Before construction, his McGuire & Orr Block was described as a one-story building with "pressed brick, iron and plate glass fronts, composition roofs, maple floors, and cost $15,000." Some attractive stonework at the top of the building has been removed, including an inscription at the corner reading "McGuire & Orr Block."

The original tenants included the Gathercoal Pharmacy in the prime corner location. The proprietor and pharmacist, Edmund Gathercoal, left Wilmette a few years later to teach at the University of Illinois College of Pharmacy, turning the location over to a succession of other drug stores. Another original tenant was the U.S. Post Office, located at the north end of the building.

McGuire & Orr ceased to exist as a separate entity in 1970 when it merged with three other firms to form Continental Real Estate. The firm is now only a memory, but its impact on North Shore real estate for more than seven decades is undeniable.

The Cox Building, 1909

The Cox Building at 1167 Wilmette Avenue was built in 1909. It was designed by Arthur Foster, a prominent Chicago architect. He designed many Chicago apartment buildings, including the Julius Blain Apartments at 3967 S. Drexel Boulevard, cited by the Chicago Commission on Landmarks as one of the "significant surviving structures in the Oakland community." His other projects include the clubhouse of the Ridgemoor Country Club and Hackman Hall (music conservatory) at the Academy of Our Lady.

The Cox Building was the largest of the structures built east of the railroad tracks in the first decade of the 20th century. When completed, it provided space for five retail shops on the first floor and ten medical offices on the second floor. Its builder and original owner was Wilmette resident Albert Cox.

Cox was a native of Indiana and a veteran of the Civil War. After the war, he was a dealer in patent rights, a stove dealer, and a real estate investor. He and his wife Ellen moved to Wilmette in the early 1900s when they were both in their sixties. They joined several family members living in the village, including their adult daughters, Mary Yeazel Greiner and Lueva Test.

The Coxes retired to Texas a few years after the building was completed,

Diagonally across the intersection from the Cox Building was a drinking fountain for horses and humans. It appears here at the right foreground. It was donated to the village by the Woman's Club. Courtesy of the Wilmette Historical Museum.

leaving its management in the hands of their son-in-law, Dr. Frederick Test. On February 27, 1920 a major fire broke out in the basement of the pharmacy located in the building's corner space. Wilmette and Evanston firefighters fought the blaze for more than three hours. Most of the damage was suffered by the pharmacy and an adjacent dry goods store. Total damage was estimated to be $30,000, the equivalent of more than $350,000 today, not counting the entire inventory of the stores. The doctors and dentists on the second floor were displaced, but the damage to their offices was miraculously repaired within two weeks.

One of the displaced doctors was Rufus Stolp. He and his father, Dr. Byron Stolp, had moved their practice from the Brethold Building (located west of the railroad tracks and described later in this chapter) to the Cox building when it first opened. Byron was a dearly beloved family doctor, always available at times of need. He practiced in Wilmette for 43 years until 1917 when he was killed in an automobile accident while en route to care for a patient. In 1918 School District 39 renamed the school at 10th Street and Central Avenue the Byron C. Stolp School in his memory. Byron's son Rufus was also a popular family doctor. When the fire at the Cox Building threatened to destroy Rufus's personal belongings, a group of citizens rushed in and saved them.

The Brown Building, 1912

The Brown Building at 1155–1163 Wilmette Avenue was developed by long-time resident J. Melville Brown in 1912. Melville was born in Nova Scotia in 1863. When he was age four, his parents and four siblings moved to Wilmette, then an unnamed settlement with fewer than a dozen homes. His father, a carpenter, built a house for the family at 1010 Central Avenue where the Masonic Temple was later built.

During Melville's childhood, his father was blinded in an accident, and family members had to contribute whatever they could to the family's support. Melville ran errands, did chores at Central School, and tended the village's oil street lamps. As he reached adulthood, he worked as a messenger for the C&NW and then as an aid to Oliver Norton, co-owner of Norton Bros., the biggest can manufacturer in the U.S. Like Melville's father, Oliver was blind, and Melville's sensitivity to this disability contributed to the close relationship that existed between the two men. Later in his career, Melville worked as a Chicago restaurant manager.

In 1900 Melville married a Wilmette woman, Lillian Crocker, and the couple began family life in the village. Four years later Melville built a house at 738 11th Street that he and Lillian occupied for decades except for a brief interlude in Kenilworth. By the time he reached age 48 in 1911, he had accumulated sufficient wealth to invest in commercial real estate.

The Brown Building's third floor included a widely used assembly hall. Courtesy of the Wilmette Historical Museum.

His first big project was the Brown Building, a three-story structure with stores on the first floor, offices on the second floor, and an assembly hall on the third floor. The basement housed two bowling alleys, later expanded to four. Completed in 1912, the building was a commercial success. The third-floor assembly hall has particular historical significance. It was one of the few facilities in the village that could accommodate large meetings and events. Rent was usually charged, but sometimes the civic-minded Melville donated the space. The Masonic Lodge met there for several years before building its Temple on Central Avenue. The Baptist Church (now the Community Church) worshiped there before building on Forest Avenue. Members of Ye Old Town Folk (a history and social club) and local political organizations held events there. During World War I, a local group called the War Camp Community Service Committee hosted dinners and dances there on Saturday evenings for recruits from Fort Sheridan and Great Lakes. The Exemption Board (draft board) had offices in the building, and registrants underwent their physical exams in the hall.

Melville wasn't done with his real estate projects. He would start another major project in the Village Center four years later, the Boulevard Building, described shortly. In the meantime, the two movie theaters, described in Chapter 11, continued the inexorable course of commercial development along Central and Wilmette avenues, with single family homes giving way.

The Harding Building, 1913

George Harding built the Harding Building at the southeast corner or Greenleaf Avenue and Poplar Drive (then called East Railroad Avenue) in about 1913. Harding was an important South Side Chicago politician, office holder, and real estate investor. He was also a major collector of paintings, sculptures, and old weapons and armor. His collection was donated to the Art Institute of Chicago, and it's an important part of the Institute's holdings.

Greenleaf and Poplar may seem somewhat out-of-the-way for Village Center visitors today, but in 1913 and for many years afterwards, the property was at the heart of village life because it was adjacent to the North Shore Electric railroad, and one of the railroad's Wilmette depots was nearby. Harding may have developed the building in collaboration with the railroad.

The building was originally part of a two-structure complex, one facing Greenleaf and the other facing Poplar. However, on January 14, 1923, a fire destroyed the portion along Poplar. Seven store spaces were destroyed, and six families who resided in the building (proprietors of the stores) were rendered homeless.

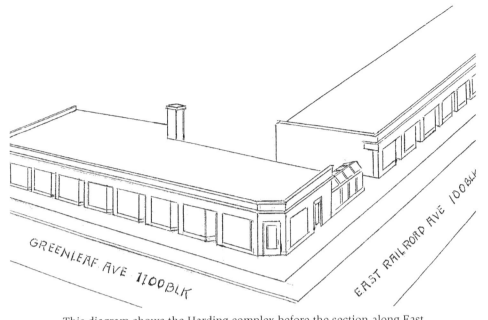

This diagram shows the Harding complex before the section along East
Railroad Avenue burned down in 1923. The diagram was drawn by Jackson
Rettke, who grew up in the 1100 block of Greenleaf.

The Boulevard Building provided temporary space for school classrooms in 1923.
See page 78. Both images courtesy of the Wilmette Historical Museum.

The Boulevard Building, 1916

Melville Brown's second building, the two-story Boulevard Building at 1101–1107 Central Avenue, was built around 1916. It had stores on the first floor and apartments above. During World War I, Melville donated store space to Wilmette's branch of the Red Cross. The space was used for making bandages, knitting, and preparing packages for the soldiers. A three-story addition with eight apartments was built to the south in 1923. One of the early tenants was Welch's Cafeteria, but by 1923 it had moved elsewhere, and School District 39 converted Welch's former space into 4th and 5th grade classrooms to accommodate the overflow of students at Central School .

It's likely that the original Boulevard Building was designed by Howard Sturges and its 1923 addition by John Pridmore. Both were prominent Chicago architects, especially Pridmore, who designed many theaters and apartment buildings.

The 1921 Post Office Building

Frank Rockhold was the developer of the 1921 Post Office Building. At the time, the post office had outgrown its space in the McGuire & Orr Block. Frank proposed to build a suitable building and lease part of it to the post office. He procured a site at 1144–1146 Wilmette Avenue, and the project was approved by the government.

The architect's identity is uncertain, but Alfred Alschuler, an experienced post office designer, is the likely choice. Frank used Alschuler on another project two years later (described next). The building was a one-story brick and terra cotta structure with 4,000 square feet of space. The eastern portion was for the post office, and the western portion was occupied by the McAllister-Worthen Dry Goods store. The new post office was said to be adequate in size for many years to come. That turned out to be less than 15 years.

In the mid-1930s, the federal government decided that Wilmette needed a new post office. The idea of replacing the 1921 Post Office with a new post office was highly controversial. You might think that during the depths of the Great Depression, villagers would warmly welcome the idea of a brand new post office, paid for by the federal government and offering the prospect of jobs for some of the village's 1,000 unemployed residents, but that's not what happened. In 1931, Democrats took control of the U.S. House of Representatives and elected John Nance Garner as Speaker. (Republican President

Herbert Hoover would remain in office for two more years.) In 1932 Garner decided that Hoover's program for relieving unemployment was too limited. He proposed a billion dollar public works program that would include new post office buildings throughout the country. One would be in Wilmette.

When the conservative directors of the Wilmette Civic League heard about Garner's proposal, they were furious. The federal government shouldn't be spending money and raising taxes when it was having a hard time meeting ordinary expenses, they asserted. Moreover, it would be "illogical to build now when so much improved real estate is lying idle in Wilmette." The League launched a postcard survey of its members that showed unanimous opposition to Garner's "pork barrel" program. The village board joined the opposition. In the existing economic climate, said the board, only "revenue producing projects" should be considered, and anyway, the present post office facilities are "ample." The local newspaper added its voice, calling Garner's proposal "reprehensible" and praising the opposition of local communities.

Garner successfully pushed his program through Congress, but Hoover vetoed it. Then a compromise was reached on a significantly reduced program. Congressman Carl Chindblom, whose 10th District covered heavily-Republican Wilmette, urged village officials to drop their opposition to a new post office, pointing out that the money would be spent elsewhere if Wilmette rejected it. The village board softened its position and responded that the village would welcome a new building "if it is cheaper for the government to build a post office in Wilmette than to rent space for one."

Civic groups and residents urged the federal government to acquire and remodel the shuttered First National Bank Building (now the Baker Building), which might otherwise remain unoccupied indefinitely. Sale of the building to the government, they argued, would hasten payouts to depositors, most of whom were Wilmette residents. Ignoring these pleas, the government purchased, for $40,000, the current post office site at the southeast corner of Central and Park Avenues and hired the prominent Chicago architect, Benjamin Marshall, to design a building in the early colonial style.

The project was off-again, on-again. In March 1934, the government decided, without explanation, to extend the existing 1921 Post Office Building lease and modernize the space. Two months later it reversed course and ordered full steam ahead on construction at Central and Park avenues. By the end of 1935 the new post office, largest on the North Shore between Evanston and Waukegan, was completed and operational.

The original 1921 Post Office Building was beautiful, with its white ceramic facade. When Encyclopedia Britannica Films acquired the property in the 1940s, the company decided to modernized it rather than restore it. The ceramic tile was stripped off, and the building became a non-descript brick box. The newest occupant, Sophia steakhouse, has given the building's facade some needed character.

The Rockhold Building, 1923

The one- and two-story Rockhold Building at the southeast corner of Central and Wilmette avenues, across from the village hall, was completed in 1923. Its addresses are 1137–1141 Central Avenue and 1177–1199 Wilmette Avenue.

Previously, a single family home occupied the entire site. The home initially belonged to Alexander McDaniel, the village's first postmaster, and later to Dr. Asahel Childs, a physician. The home fronted on Central Avenue, and its rear yard extended west along Wilmette Avenue. Dr. Childs recognized the commercial potential of the property and intended to erect four buildings along the Wilmette Avenue frontage, but labor troubles delayed the project, and his death in 1915 derailed it.

In 1922, the Wilmette Plan Commission published a "Plan of Wilmette" that was intended to guide the village's future development. One of its recommendations was to preserve open space in the Village Center. It noted, in particular, that "Wilmette still has the opportunity of acquiring for civic purposes the [Childs property], which might appropriately be named the 'Village Green.'"

Walgreen Drugs moved into the corner store of the Rockhold Building in 1933. Courtesy of the Wilmette Historical Museum.

One of the plan commissioners was Frank Rockhold, who had recently acquired the Childs property. (Conflicts of interest were viewed less strictly then.) Rockhold and his family came to Wilmette in 1905 and lived at 1014 Elmwood Avenue. He was a successful Chicago attorney and served for a time as Russian consul. He was also a real estate investor.

The village board didn't follow the plan commission's recommendation, so Rockhold proceeded to redevelop the property in 1923. He hired architect Alfred Alschuler to design a commercial block. Today, Alschuler's large body of work is highly respected. Perhaps his most famous existing structure is the London Guaranty Building at 360 N. Michigan Avenue, Chicago.

The Rockhold Building's initial roster of tenants reflected life in Wilmette during the 1920s. The most prominent space (at the corner) was taken by Public Service Company and was used partly as a showroom for new-fangled gas and electric appliances. That space was later occupied for many years by Walgreen Drugs. Other tenants were two grocery stores, a meat market, a restaurant, a bakery, a hardware store, a 5-10-cent store, a record (music) store, a cigar store, a bird store (parrots etc.), a roofing company, a real estate firm, and several doctors' offices.

The Nelson Building, 1923

The Nelson Building at 1129–1135 Central Avenue was developed in 1923 by David Nelson, who lived at 821 Elmwood Avenue from about 1913 until his death in 1955.

Nelson was born in Sweden in 1868. He came to the U.S. as a young man, settled on the North Shore, worked as a coachman for a wealthy family, and in 1893 bought a small laundry in Evanston. In 1897, he married Elizabeth Lundgren, also a Swedish immigrant, who worked as a domestic servant in Evanston. His highly successful laundry business came to be known as the Nelson Bros. Laundry Co., with facilities in Evanston, Wilmette, and Glencoe. His Wilmette laundry plant, established in 1900 and greatly expanded over the years, was located at the northwest corner of West Railroad and Central avenues. (It was demolished in the 1950s and replaced by a building occupied by First Federal Savings and Loan and a parade of other financial institutions.) That 1950s building, in turn, is now slated to be replaced by a mixed use commercial and residential building.

Nelson was heavily involved in Wilmette's business, religious, and civic affairs. For many years he was a director of the First National Bank (which went belly-up during the Great Depression). He was a charter member of the Baptist Church (now the Community Church), the Chamber of Commerce, and the Rotary Club; and he was a member of the Masonic Lodge. During the Great Depression, he donated office space at his laundry plant for the emergency relief work of the Wilmette Welfare Board.

Nelson selected Swedish-native Andrew Sandegren as his architect. Sandegren was a prominent Chicago architect who specialized in luxury apartment buildings when the term "luxury apartment" actually meant something. Among his commissions was the Swedish Old People's Home in Evanston (now Three Crowns). His design for the Nelson Building included a restaurant and four stores on the first floor, and 16 three-bedroom apartments on the second and third floors. Initial tenants included Welch's Cafeteria (which moved from the Boulevard Building down the street) and Lulias Brothers fruit and vegetable store. Lulias Brothers also operated a store on Green Bay Road.

The Nelson Building is center-right, on the south side of Central Avenue and adjacent to the Rockhold Building. Courtesy of the Wilmette Historical Museum.

The Wolff-Griffis Building, 1928

The Wolff-Griffis Building at 1119–1121 Wilmette Avenue was built in 1928 to accommodate the growing general hardware business of Alfred Wolff and Ernest Griffis. The two men had previously operated independently: Wolff in the Rockhold Building and Griffis at 1124 Greenleaf Avenue. They merged their hardware and sheet metal businesses in 1924.

They purchased the Wilmette Avenue property from Fred Clampitt, the grandfather of Kendall Clampitt, who left bequests to the Village and the Wilmette Historical Society that were used in 1990 to purchase the old Gross Point Village Hall. The Clampitt family had lived in a house on the property for at least 20 years. Wolff and Griffis moved the house to another location and built a three story building with eight apartments on the two upper floors. The first floor and basement were for their hardware store.

The building was designed by Howard Bowen, a prominent North Shore architect and resident of Wilmette. He served as Wilmette's Building Commissioner and designed the Wilmette Storm Water Pumping Station. His commissions included the Wilmette Baptist Church and the Chimney Apartments of Winnetka.

DeGiulio Kitchen Design remodeled the interior of the Wolff-Griffis Building and now occupies the first floor and basement.

The Public Service Building, 1929

The Public Service Building is the Spanish-style building at 1220 Washington Court, just east of the Wilmette Metra station. It was designed by Herman von Holst and was built in 1929 as a substation for Public Service Co. of Northern Illinois (now part of Commonwealth Edison). Von Holst is well known for overseeing Frank Lloyd Wright's architectural practice during Wright's travels in Europe (1909–1911), but he was an accomplished architect in his own right. Among his commissions were designs for the enterprises of Samuel Insull. Von Holst and Insull liked the Spanish-style which was popular at the time. Regrettably, the appearance of the Public Service Building has been neglected, and it's now difficult to appreciate Von Holst's vision.

The Brethold Building was the most impressive structure on West Railroad Avenue at the turn of the 20th Century. To the west was Jones Hall with retail shops on the first floor and a popular meeting room on the second floor. See page 85. Courtesy of the Wilmette Historical Museum.

John Millen moved his hardware store from 605 West Railroad Avenue to his new building in 1923. See page 85.

The Brethold Building, c. 1895

The Brethold Building at 1209 Wilmette Avenue contained the village's first pharmacy. It was built by Charles Brethold for druggist Samuel Sexauer in about 1895. The pharmacy occupied the first floor, and doctors' offices were on the second floor. The building also housed the village's first telephone exchange.

Sexauer's pharmacy business wasn't successful. In 1900 he declared bankruptcy and briefly worked as a deliveryman for an ice company before returning to his profession as a druggist in Chicago. After Sexauer, the first floor of the building continued as a pharmacy for many years. Henry Snider was there from about 1903 to 1909, followed by John Wilming.

Jones Hall and Millen Hardware, 1901 and 1923

To the west of The Brethold Building on Wilmette Avenue are two vintage buildings: Jones Hall and Millen Hardware. Jones Hall, at 1211–1217 Wilmette Avenue, was also known by three other names over the years: The Wilmette, Jones Building, and Lodge Hall. It was built in 1901 by Edward P. Jones. He was a Civil War veteran, an executive of the United States Broom and Brush Co., and a Wilmette resident at 1323 Central Avenue. The building had stores on the ground floor and a large hall on the upper floor that hosted a wide variety of meetings, events, and activities. In 1922 Wilmette's Odd Fellows Lodge No. 892, which had rented the hall for its meetings and events, purchased the building for $50,000. John Millen, discussed in Chapter 7, built the adjoining building at 1219 Wilmette Avenue for his hardware business in 1923. The two buildings now have common ownership.

Four Small Buildings in the 600 Block of Green Bay Road

North of the Brethold Building on Green Bay Road, across Wilmette Avenue, are four other vintage structures. The two-story brick building at 601 Green Bay Road (now Mona Lisa Stone and Tile) was built about 1887 and was originally Max Mueller's general store. The two-story frame structure at 605 Green Bay Road (now the Wilmette Bicycle Shop) dates back to at least 1890 when it was the Hansen & Hubbell hardware store. In 1908 John Millen purchased Hansen & Hubbell and operated the business under his name until 1923 when he moved to his new store on Wilmette Avenue. The small grey structure between these two buildings was a separate store in the early 20th century: a florist and later a shoe store.

Further to the north, the one-story brick building at 619 Green Bay Road, now West End Antiques, was built in 1929 by George Rasmussen and his grocery chain, National Tea Co., which at the time was the region's largest operator of grocery stores. Its architect, like that of many other National Tea stores, was Jean B. Rohm & Son.

The Heffron Building at 629 Green Bay Road originally housed the Central Hotel on the second floor. Courtesy of the Wilmette Historical Museum.

The Heffron Building, 1912

The two-story building at the southwest corner of Green Bay Road and Central Avenue is a prime target for redevelopment. When it was built in 1912, it was called the Heffron Building. Its developer was Patrick Heffron, an Irish native who came to the U.S. as a small child.

Following his marriage in 1886, Patrick and his wife Emily (Mahon) lived in Chicago. They moved up the city's social ladder as Patrick succeeded in the liquor business: importer, wholesaler, saloon operator, and wine company president. In the early 1900s they moved to Wilmette with their daughter Elizabeth. Emily had connections to the village, because her sister (Blanche Mahon) married a member of the Westerfield family, one of the village's pioneering families. The Heffrons lived at 610 Forest Avenue, described in a Chicago newspaper as "the finest and best appointed home in Wilmette." Emily was active in raising funds to build the original St. Francis Xavier Church. The couple remained in Wilmette until 1915, when they moved to Evanston.

The Heffron Building was only four years old when, on August 2, 1916, a suspicious fire engulfed the second floor, causing damage to the business establishments at ground level, including the fledgling First National Bank of Wilmette. With amazing speed, Patrick brought in the resources needed to restore the first floor businesses.

For many years the second floor was occupied by the Central Hotel which operated more like an SRO than a hotel with transitory guests. The rooms were spartan. Each apartment had cooking facilities, but tenants shared communal men's and women's bathrooms. The apartments provided housing to folks of modest means like laborers, drivers, painters, and store clerks.

The Krauss Building, 1919

It's interesting to ponder physical remnants of yesteryear that dot the local landscape. Ride your bike along the Green Bay Trail and see the concrete foundations of the North Shore Electric railroad. Until 1955 its trains rumbled along the right-of-way. Step cautiously into 11th Street near Chestnut Avenue or into Forest Avenue near Ridge Road and see a concrete marker crediting the Works Progress Administration for repaving the brick streets during the Great Depression.

Another example is the smokestack (now a cell tower) looming over the three-story building at 1215 Washington Avenue (just west of Green Bay Road). Viewing the smokestack from a distance, you'll see five letters formed by white bricks inserted into the stack's predominantly red-brick structure. From top to bottom, the letters are "R-A-U-S-S." What's the explanation for these letters?

The letters are the last five letters of the name "Krauss." When the smokestack was readapted for use as a cell tower in the 1980s, the top portion displaying the letter "K" was removed. This leads to the next question: Who was "Krauss"?

Joseph Krauss was born in Bohemia in 1880. Seven years later the family (including Joseph's sister Jennie and brother Max) immigrated to the U.S. Family members went on to become important figures in Chicago's cleaning and dyeing industry. Joseph was part-owner of Clifton Cleaners and Dyers on Chicago's North Side. Max was an attorney whose clients included the cleaners and dyers association. Their brother-in-law, Fred Salzman (Jennie's husband), owned and operated another cleaning and dyeing plant in Chicago.

In those days, this was a tough business, to say the least. The association published minimum prices for services. It "strongly encouraged" all cleaners and dyers to join, charge the minimum prices, and follow the terms of labor contracts that it negotiated with the unions. Firms that refused might face strikes, picketing, bombings, or other means of "persuasion."

In November 1924 Joseph decided to expand into the northern suburbs by opening a cleaning and dyeing plant at 1215 Washington. There was already a two-story structure, built by Frank Gathercoal as a shop and office for his construction and real estate business in 1919. Joseph converted this building into "one of the most modernly equipped cleaning and dyeing concerns in the Middle West." His advertisements boasted, "This plant is the last word of perfection in the dry cleaning and dyeing industry, with its naphtha softening process and cleansing, drying and finishing equipment, all steam and electrically operated, in a daylight fireproof building." The plant was capable of cleaning 750 to 1,000 garments daily, as well as other items like hats and tapestries. A fleet of trucks stood ready to pick up and deliver.

Joseph's Wilmette venture initially succeeded. In 1927–1928 he remodeled and expanded the original two-story building by adding a boiler house with a chimney and a third floor. (If you look closely, you'll see a similar but plainer white stone facade above the second floor.) But new competitors cast their shadow on the future. Schultz & Nord, the cleaner at 1152 Central Avenue, won zoning approval for a new cleaning and dyeing plant, despite opposition stirred up anonymously by Joseph. Another firm announced plans for a new cleaning plant at 439 Main Street. Meanwhile, a price war broke out among Chicago area cleaners and dyers. It forced all cleaners to lower their prices and ultimately led to a lockout of union employees.

Joseph decided to sell out in July 1929. He and his wife Marie moved from their Wilmette apartment at 510 5th Street to their farm in Wisconsin. The successor firm, Shore Line Cleaners, survived Black Tuesday (October 29, 1929) and operated the plant for 20 more years. Joseph returned to the family cleaning and dyeing business in Chicago, leaving only five letters on a smokestack as evidence of his five-year run in Wilmette.

After the laundry businesses departed, the building was used during the 1950s by the U.S. Army as a research facility, studying cold temperature conditions. The activity was called SIPRE: the Snow, Ice and Permafrost Research Establishment. That's the official line, anyway.

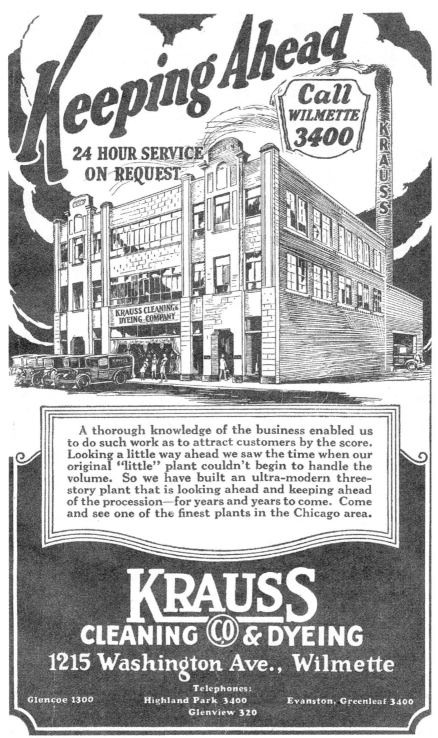

Joseph Krauss's expanded cleaning and dyeing plant was pictured in this 1928 advertisement. In the 1990s, the top of the smokestack (including the letter "K") was removed. Courtesy of the Wilmette Historical Museum.

CHAPTER 5

★——————————★

Local Government

Sport has been made forever of governmental bodies and the people that run them. W.C. Field's musing, "I never vote for anybody, I always vote against," encapsulates the general disdain. I have a different view, at least when it comes to the local governance of Wilmette over its 150 year history.

Yes, there have been plenty of miscalculations, bonehead decisions, and short-sighted judgments. But the long view reveals a steady continuum of responsible growth, adherence to democratic principles of stewardship, and an overarching focus on the advancement of the community good.

September 19 is Charter Day in Wilmette. It's the date when in 1872 the village was formally empowered to function as a municipal government. This birthday wasn't chiseled in granite at the time. There were several other options, including the date when citizens voted to incorporate the Village (August 15, 1872) and the date when the village board first met and elected John Westerfield as the first village president (November 8, 1872). It took a formal legal opinion by William James, the village attorney, to determine the "correct" date of the village's founding.

For its first 74 years, Wilmette didn't recognize the anniversary of its founding, but that changed in 1947 when the 75th anniversary inspired a Wilmette History Project for the purpose of gathering and preserving historical documents and photos. This project led immediately to the creation of the Wilmette Historical Commission (1948) and eventually to the founding of the Wilmette Historical Museum (1951) and the Wilmette Historical Society (1966). In 1972 the village's centennial celebration was planned by a commission that sponsored events throughout the year, beginning with a parade and culminating with a street fair in the Village Center attended by 20,000 people. In 1997 the 125th anniversary (quasquicentennial) celebration followed the same pattern, with a committee sponsoring year-long events that ended with a community picnic and fireworks display at Gillson Park and the 25th annual village fair.

Folks gathered at the village hall on September 24, 1972 to celebrate
Wilmette's centennial. Courtesy of the Wilmette Historical Museum.

I hope that the citizens of Wilmette will enthusiastically celebrate the village's 150th anniversary in 2022. It's a unique opportunity to bring everyone together in a shared experience that's unifying, educational, and fun.

The Form of Government

The original form of Wilmette's government was the "village form." The legislative body consisted of six trustees and a president. All were elected at large. Elections were held every spring, and officials were elected for overlapping two-year terms. The president was also the chief executive, responsible for enforcing laws and supervising administrative staff.

The village form worked satisfactorily in small towns where governmental affairs required little attention. But as populations grew, the need for public facilities and services also increased, and financial management became more complicated. A part-time elected board wasn't up to this task. And an elected board that also ran day-to-day operations was subject to the criticism that politics unduly influenced their decisions.

Two reform concepts emerged in Illinois: One was the commission form of government; the other was the council-manager form. The commission form was authorized by a 1910 Illinois law, subject to residents' approval in a referendum. Serving as models for the law were Des Moines and Houston, where this form had been implemented with success. Under the Illinois version, commission government consisted of a mayor and four commissioners elected at-large. Each official independently managed one of these five departments: Public Affairs (headed up by the mayor), Accounts and Finances, Public Health and Safety, Streets and Public Improvements, and Public Property. The commissioners together comprised a council that adopted ordinances and elected other officials. The mayor and commissioners were paid salaries prescribed by law. By petition, citizens could initiate proceedings to rescind ordinances, to enact ordinances that the council declined to enact, or to recall a commissioner. The commission form was designed to create greater accountability for efficient administration and greater control over government by the electorate, but it didn't address the need for professional, non-political management.

The council-manager form was born in Staunton, Virginia in 1908. Glencoe was the first Illinois community to adopt it in 1914, and other Illinois towns soon followed. This form wasn't specifically authorized by Illinois law for villages with populations exceeding 5,000 residents until 1951, although the General Assembly seriously considered the idea in 1929 and 1938. At its core was the employment of a professional manager to administer operations. The manager's authority varied from one village to another, depending on the provisions of local enabling ordinances. In concept, the president and trustees (or the mayor and commissioners) left day-to-day operations to the manager, and the elected officials served as the legislative, policy-making body with ultimate control over administration through their power to appoint and remove the manager and department heads and to approve budgets. Council-manager supporters argued that administration by professionals was more efficient than administration by elected officials, who often lacked the necessary training and experience to perform this role. The cost of the manager, they argued, was more than offset by the efficiencies achieved, and politics would play less of a role in administrative decision-making.

Between 1914 and 1918 Wilmette's key employee was the public works superintendent, Frank Forrester. During this period, Forrester was sometimes called village manager. His successor in 1918 was Carl Schultz, a local merchant who previously served as a village trustee. At the time of Schultz's appointment, the village board adopted a resolution formally granting him the title village manager and defining his duties as "general supervision, management and charge of the fire and police departments, and all employees of said Village."

Late in Schultz's tenure (1918–1930), the need for a technically trained manager became a political issue. In 1930 the rival political factions reached an agreement and adopted a new ordinance that made the village manager "the business officer of the Village" with "responsibility for supervising all Village departments, handling all Village purchases, and preparing the annual budget." Following this action, the board conducted a search and hired Clare Osborn, a manager with extensive experience in other municipalities. Schultz was demoted to his former position.

The Great Depression was a period of extreme stress in the village. The two village presidents of that era, Carbon Dubbs and Harry Kinne, were strong-willed men who probably ignored the distinction between the board's policy-making role and the manager's supervisory and budgeting role in dealing with that era's problems. Osborne lasted for only four years, and Boyne Platt, his successor, only two. With Platt's departure, President Kinne dropped the pretense of the council-manager form and assumed the dual roles of president and manager.

In 1938 citizen groups pressured the village board to restore the council-manager form. Following a search, Alfred Koenig, a man educated and experienced in municipal administration in Michigan and Wisconsin, was appointed. A few months later, President Kinne, running for reelection, campaigned to abolish the manager position. The question was put to voters in a referendum, and by a small margin, the council-manager form was retained. The following year, Koenig was reappointed manager over Kinne's objection, but he soon resigned.

The next two managers, William Wolff and Armon Lund, together served more than three decades (1940–1974). Originally hired as engineers, they were both longtime Village employees when they were promoted. During Lund's tenure, Wilmette citizens voted in a referendum to grant the manager enhanced authority and security under a 1951 Illinois law applicable to municipalities with populations under 250,000.

WILMETTE'S VILLAGE MANAGERS

MANAGER	TENURE	BACKGROUND
Frank Forrester	1914–1918	Forrester was officially the superintendent of public works but was unofficially the village manager.
Carl Schultz	1918–1930	A former village trustee, Schultz was the first person to be formally appointed manager.
Clare Osborn	1930–1934	Osborn was the first "professional manager" hired from outside the village.
Boyne Platt	1934–1936	Platt was promoted from an engineering position.
Harry Kinne	1936–1938	As village president, Kinne appointed himself manager and served without compensation.
Alfred Koenig	1938–1940	Koenig, a professional manager hired from outside the village, survived a campaign to eliminate the position.
William Wolff	1940–1964	Wolff was promoted from an engineering position and is the Village's longest serving manager.
Armon Lund	1965–1974	Lund was promoted from superintendent of the water plant.
Stan Kennedy	1974–1990	Kennedy, a professional manager, had previously served as city manager of Highland Park.
Heidi Voorhees	1990–2001	Voorhees, a professional manager, was promoted from assistant manager. She's the Village's first woman manager.
Mike Earl	2001–2009	Earl, a professional manager, was promoted from assistant manager.
Tim Frenzer	2009–2020	Frenzer was promoted from corporation counsel and is the only lawyer ever to hold the manager position.
Michael Braiman	2020–	Braiman, a professional manager, was promoted from assistant manager.

Many Wilmette residents may not realize how critically important the village manager is to Wilmette's municipal government. The job requires expertise in government finance and working knowledge of other aspects of the operation like public works, the water plant, zoning regulations, public health and safety, information technology, human resources, and more.

Term limits magnify the importance of the manager's job. Under an ordinance adopted in 1967, members of the village board serve a maximum of two four-year terms. Afterwards, their knowledge and experience are lost to the organization unless they continue serving in another capacity. The manager, by contrast, serves indefinitely. The five most recent managers have averaged eleven years in the job, but four of the five spent many additional years in important staff positions before becoming manager. As a result, the manager and his or her subordinates, not the elected officials, are the major repository of institutional knowledge, and as Sir Francis Bacon said, "Knowledge is power."

Municipal Elections

From its earliest days, Wilmette's municipal elections have been governed by the "partisan format" under Illinois law. The partisan format assumes that political parties are presenting opposing slates. Ballots in partisan elections list candidates with their party affiliation shown next to their name. If they have no party affiliation, the word "Independent" appears next to their name. During the period from at least 1913 to 1933, Wilmette elections were dominated by local parties. Candidates were identified by party affiliation, like "Community Party" and "Home Party." Over the years, numerous parties came and went. Sometimes, a party's candidates were unopposed. More often, two or more parties battled it out in nasty and divisive campaigns. Independent candidates were rare.

In 1932 a caucus system called the Harmony Convention emerged. Its purpose was "to eliminate the strife and contention of the present system." The Convention was intended to be a widely representative body that slated highly qualified candidates under the Harmony Party banner. For 40 years, the caucus slates were usually unopposed. Even when challenged by a party or an independent candidate, the caucus candidates usually won. However, the caucus system started to lose its grip in 1969 when some residents accused it of being undemocratic and unrepresentative. In 1975 the caucus era ended, replaced by the current tradition of independent candidates.

The current tradition seems to be working well, or at least better than the party and caucus systems of the past. Capable independent candidates have stepped forward. The problems and concerns of the community have been debated openly. The public has judged the candidates' qualifications and policy positions and has chosen wisely. No independent-minded person has been discouraged from running because of his or her reluctance to affiliate with a party. Residents are pleased, in my opinion, that no party or caucus is dominating the election process.

There's an alternative to the partisan format, appropriately called the "non-partisan" format. If residents want to reduce the possibility of parties returning and dominating Wilmette elections, they can petition for a referendum to switch to the non-partisan format, which exists in many Illinois municipalities and many of the nation's largest cities. The village board could also initiate such a referendum. If it passes, future ballots would list candidates by name only, i.e., without any party affiliation shown on the ballot. While parties wouldn't be precluded from participating in the process, their potential role in civic affairs would be somewhat deemphasized.

Even during the more peaceful period since 1932 there have been several elections that have taken interesting twists and turns. Here are four examples:

- Election Fraud: In the 1949 election a newly-formed Citizens Party challenged the Harmony caucus candidates. The Citizens Party's initially won all contested offices except village president. It sued for a recount of the votes for village president, prompting the Harmony group to ask for a recount of the votes for the other offices. The recount confirmed the original tally for village president, but it also showed that the Citizens Party had lost, not won, the other offices. In one precinct, 90 votes credited to the Citizens Party were actually cast for the Harmony slate. The judge who conducted the recount blasted Wilmette election officials: "I'm surprised that all this wrangling occurred in a district like Wilmette. It might be expected in some blighted area or the Madison Street flophouse district, but certainly not in such an enlightened community." The state's attorney investigated the counting errors which, he said, were "too large to be mere accidents." Eventually, the investigation was dropped.

- Write-In Upset: In the 1959 election John Sanderson, the popular incumbent village president, was denied the Harmony Convention's nomination for village president by a caucus vote of 50–46. A quiet write-in movement on his behalf began two weeks before the election. He didn't campaign. A big turnout brought him a solid victory, 1,399–1,001. His reaction? "I'm astounded."

- Voter Disenfranchisement: In the 1969 election the Harmony Convention's slate was challenged by a political party for the first time since 1949. A group dissatisfied with the "liberal leaning" of the caucus broke away and formed the United Party. The election campaign was bitter. In those days the Village, not the county, ran local elections. Based on past turnout, Village officials figured that about 2,500 residents would vote and only six polling places were needed. This was a gross underestimate. On election day, 10,000 voters showed up, overwhelming the polling places. Folks who didn't give up and go home had to wait for hours to vote, and some were still waiting when the polls closed. The vote tally favored the United Party, but Harmony supporters filed lawsuits in both state and federal courts, claiming that hundreds of residents had been disenfranchised. The federal court ruled that voters had been deprived of their right to vote and ordered a new election. The rerun produced another victory for the United Party's candidates, but one of four referenda originally approved was defeated. It would have authorized the issuance of bonds in the amount of $4 million to pay for 2,700 cobra-style street lights (pink granite poles with bracket arms and mercury vapor lights) throughout the village. The original referendum had passed by a vote of 4,052 yes to 3,559 no. In the re-run, voters rejected the proposed streetlights by a vote of 7,310 no to 5,199 yes.

- Flawed Nominating Petitions: In the 1993 election, six candidates filed nominating petitions for three vacancies in the office of village trustee. Two residents reviewed the petitions and found that the pages of three candidates' petitions weren't numbered and bound, as election rules required. The residents objected to the petitions and urged that the candidates be disqualified. The Wilmette Election Board—consisting of the village president, village manager, and senior trustee—overruled the objection, finding that the petitions "substantially complied" with the rules. The objectors took the matter to court and won. The candidates were disqualified and stricken from the ballot. Undeterred, they ran as write-in candidates. Energized by the whole affair, voters turned out in record numbers. Two of the three disqualified candidates won.

Village Hall

Though some say "you can't fight city hall," you can definitely *find* city hall in Wilmette. That's because it's been located at the same prominent site for more than 130 years: the triangular parcel in the Village Center bounded by Wilmette and Central avenues and the railroad tracks. While the site hasn't changed, it has hosted three different village halls, one of which was significantly expanded only ten years after it was built.

The first village hall was built in 1890 when the village's population was a mere 1,458. It was a small two-story wooden structure with an arched front portico entrance facing the railroad tracks. It was poorly insulated, allowing the winds of winter and the noise of rumbling steam locomotives to intrude. It was positioned very close to the intersection of Wilmette and Central avenues on the current village hall's front yard, leaving considerable open space between the building and the railroad tracks. In 1897 C&NW built a new commuter depot in a portion of this open space, just east of the tracks.

By 1910 the village's population had more than tripled. Wilmette was transitioning from little more than a flag station to a bustling suburb. In the two decades since the first hall was built, some streets and sidewalks were paved, and sewers were installed. New homes featured electric lights and telephones. Horse-drawn carriages were giving way to automobiles. A second railroad (the North Shore Electric) began serving the Village Center in 1899. Its tracks also ran behind the village hall, parallel to the C&NW's. The commercial district was creeping east from West Railroad Avenue across the tracks to Wilmette, Central, and Greenleaf avenues. All of this development caused the work of village government to expand. The amount of public business overwhelmed the old village hall which, in any event, presented an unimpressive image to prospective homebuyers when compared to the more substantial edifices of neighboring communities, including Gross Point to the west.

In 1910 Wilmette voters approved a proposition to build a new village hall. The old village hall was purchased by local hardware merchant Alfred Wolff, moved to 625 Park Avenue, and converted into a house that's still there. The new village hall was designed by Henry Schlacks, a prominent Chicago architect and Wilmette resident (730 Linden Avenue). He was known primarily for designing significant ecclesiastical buildings and for starting Notre Dame University's Department of Architecture. This second village hall was an imposing one-story peristyle building with Grecian columns, sure to impress prospective homebuyers. Like its predecessor, it was built at the point of the triangle close to the street intersection. The western portion of the triangle was still occupied by two sets of railroad tracks, the C&NW depot, and parking spaces.

The first village hall was built in 1890. Courtesy of the Wilmette Historical Museum.

This impressive structure replaced the first village hall
in 1910. Courtesy of the Wilmette Historical Museum.

Only ten years later, on Palm Sunday 1920, a destructive tornado smacked
the village. It swept northeasterly along Wilmette Avenue, tore off the village
hall's roof, and deposited it at Ashland Avenue and 7th Street. This disaster
created an opportunity. The village's population was growing rapidly, and
the 1910 village hall was already inadequate. Architect Schlacks had designed
the building to support a second floor, and the village board decided that this
was the time to cash in on the architect's foresight. Their plan was to repair,
remodel, and expand by reconfiguring offices on the first floor and adding a
"beautiful and dignified" council chamber on the second. Work was completed
in 1922. The expanded village hall was expected to satisfy the village's needs
"for many years to come." Many years turned out to be 50.

The current village hall provoked one of Wilmette's most contentious issues
ever. The controversy came to a head in 1973. Should the 1910 village hall be
restored and expanded? Or, should it be torn down and replaced? Should the
issue be decided by voters in a referendum?

The 1910 village hall with its 32 Grecian columns had a monumental presence that many residents admired. It exuded strength and elegance. But it was
structurally unsound. Pencils placed on tabletops rolled onto the floor, and
chairs with casters transported their occupants to the walls. It was also too
small. The second-floor council chambers had been converted into offices

for the growing staff, and village board meetings were held at the village hall annex, the unattractive and neglected building at 825 Green Bay Road that had served as Wilmette's police and fire stations until the late 1960s.

A plan was devised by the Village and the C&NW. The railroad owned the property between the village hall and the railroad tracks where its depot was then located. It also owned the property east of the tracks between Central and Lake avenues that it leased to Hoffmann Bros., a popular firm that operated a lumber yard there for many years. Under the plan, C&NW would sell the depot property to the Village. It would also evict Hoffmann Bros. and build a new depot and commuter parking lot at the former Hoffmann Bros. site. The Village would then build a new village hall and parking lot on the former depot property. Then it would tear down the 1910 village hall and create a fountain and green space in its place. If you think this sounds like the current configuration, you're correct.

The plan was strongly opposed by preservationists and folks who wanted Hoffmann Bros. to remain in business. Nevertheless, the village board moved forward. It rejected the idea of a referendum, hired Coder Taylor Associates of Kenilworth as architects, and sold $1.9 million in general obligation bonds to pay for the project. Meanwhile, the plan became the major issue in the local election of 1973. A political party called the Village Party was formed to field opposition candidates. These candidates argued that the board was an arrogant old guard, as evidenced especially by its refusal to hold a referendum to resolve the controversy. At its last meeting before the election, the outgoing village board approved a contract with C&NW to purchase the depot property.

The Village Party prevailed in the election and tried to stop the project, but C&NW was anxious to build a new depot surrounded by ample parking and refused to rescind the contract to sell the depot site to the Village. Moreover, the Village's sale of bonds for the project was already a done deal. The newly elected village board was left with no choice but to proceed.

Only the final design of the new hall remained an open issue, and the main question was whether the building would have space to accommodate the Park District's administrative offices. At the time, the district's offices were housed at the old Laurel School at Laurel Avenue and 7th Street. The school had been closed by School District 39 in 1971. The arguments favoring a shared building were persuasive: It would achieve efficiencies, improve intergovernmental communications, and draw more citizens to the Village Center. After several months of jousting, the Village and the Park District agreed to share space in the new village hall.

The new village hall was completed in 1976. It serves the village well, and the fountain, war memorial, and green space in front are important and attractive features of the Village Center.

Police and Fire Protection

Perhaps the most important services that the Village provides are police protection, fire protection, and emergency medical care. The Fire Department dates back to 1893. Initially, it consisted of two companies of volunteers, one for the territory east of the C&NW tracks, the other for the western territory. Their hand-pulled hose carts were stored in barns at 1035 Lake Avenue (east side) and present-day Vattmann Park (west side).

Wilmette's first fire station, 1233 Central Avenue, was on the current Post Office site. See page 102. Courtesy of the Wilmette Historical Museum.

Wilmette's second fire station and first police station were located at 829 Green Bay Road, just south of Lake Avenue. Courtesy of the Wilmette Historical Museum.

In 1899 the Village built its first fire station, a two-story structure at 1233 Central Avenue. All fire-fighting operations were centralized at this location. In 1905–1906 the Village bought a fire wagon and a team of horses. A 20-year-old milkman, Walter Zibble, was hired to tend the horses and drive the wagon. (Zibble would eventually become the Fire Department's longtime Chief.) The Zibble family lived in an apartment on the second floor of the station.

In 1916, as the department began to convert from horse-power to gasoline-power, it moved to a new station at 829 West Railroad Avenue. By 1935 full-time firefighters fully replaced the volunteer force. After World War II the village's far western territory developed rapidly. This led to the establishment of a second station at Lake Avenue and Illinois Road (1958). Soon, the station on Green Bay Road was outgrown and replaced by the current station on Lake Avenue east of the railroad tracks (1964). (This site was previously part of the North Shore Electric's right-of-way.) The paramedic program was introduced in 1974, and today all firefighters are also certified emergency medical technicians.

The Police Department was created by ordinance in 1886. Its members were the village president, the village trustees, and other persons appointed by the village board. In 1896, Edward Sieber was the first appointed police officer. He became the first chief when a second officer was appointed in 1910.

For many years the Police Department was based at the village hall. By the 1930s, though, space had become tight, and the need for separate police quarters was acute. The plan was to build an addition to the fire station on Green Bay Road. It was hoped that the federal government would provide funding through a Depression-era recovery program, but that didn't happen, and the project was postponed until after World War II.

Once the addition was completed, the Fire and Police Departments shared the enlarged building on Green Bay Road for 15 years. This arrangement ended when the Fire Department moved to its new station in 1964. Four years later the Police Department moved to its new station at 710 Ridge Road. The new police facility was built on a portion of what was then called the Village Green, a Village-owned park where the Village's recreation department conducted recreational programming. The vacated Green Bay Road building continued to be used for meetings until the present village hall was completed in 1976. Then it was sold and demolished, and the property was redeveloped as a private office building.

As of 2021 the Fire Department has 44 sworn firefighters, plus a handful of non-sworn employees. All firefighters are certified paramedics. The Police Department has 44 sworn officers, plus other personnel in various capacities like telecommunicators and a social worker. All police officers are college graduates. Both departments have been honored by accrediting agencies. The 2021 Village budget estimates that taxpayers will pay more than $23 million for the public safety and law enforcement services of these two departments (55.5 percent of the Village's general fund budget).

Water and Sewer Service

Wilmette took giant steps toward becoming a modern suburb in 1892 and 1893, but not without controversy, violence, and scandal. These were the years when the village's "modern" water distribution and sewer systems were built. No longer would residents be required to fetch water from wells, cisterns, or Lake Michigan; and no longer would residents be required to visit the smelly outhouses at the rear of their property.

This modernization project required Wilmette to find a water supply, and the obvious source was the City of Evanston's water filtration plant at Lake Michigan and Lincoln Street. Residents of both towns anticipated that Wilmette would eventually be annexed by Evanston, so Wilmette's connecting to the Evanston system was logical. The two municipalities successfully negotiated a contract that guaranteed Wilmette a long-term supply at a reasonable rate. Wilmette's system would be connected to the Evanston system at two locations: one at Sheridan Road and the other at West Railroad Avenue. The considerable cost of Wilmette's new water and sewer systems, more than $400,000, would be raised by special assessments.

Construction began in late 1892. As the village election of April 1893 approached, critics severely attacked the village board's management of the project. Dr. Byron Stolp, the village's most influential resident, was quoted as saying, "I think there can be no doubt that the village affairs are poorly managed and that a great deal of money is wasted." Village Trustee Samuel Dingee, a candidate for president, was quoted as saying that "members of the village board could be bought for $5 each." Both men denied making these statements, and harmony was restored, but then another controversy arose.

The Chicago press reported in March 1893 that hundreds of sewer and water laborers were working in the village, and many had been around long enough to be eligible to vote in the village's upcoming election. These laborers far outnumbered the 400 voters who were permanent residents. Rumors spread that these workers planned to vote and elect candidates favorable to the contractors and themselves.

Then, ten days before the election, violence erupted. The contractor building the water system was paying its laborers $1.65 for a ten-hour-day, while a different contractor building the sewer system was paying its employees $1.75 for an eight-hour-day. The water employees went on strike for equal treatment. When the sewer employees refused to join them, fights broke out, and several workers were injured, one seriously. In the end, the dispute was resolved, and the laborers didn't vote in the election, although one was arrested and jailed for shouting his displeasure with the election results and telling the policeman on duty to "shut up."

The project led to a crisis for the Rufus Jordan family. In 1885 Rufus and Ellen Jordan emigrated from England and settled in Wilmette. In 1893 they lived on Henry Street (now 9th Street) between Lake and Central avenues with their three children (two boys and an infant daughter) and a boarder, George Millbank. George was employed by one of the construction contractors as a special policeman. On March 7 Ellen and George disappeared. It quickly became apparent that their disappearances weren't coincidental: Ellen had cashed out some family assets, packed her clothes, sent two large satchels to the train depot, and arranged for a neighborhood girl to care for the baby. George had left his police uniform with a note to return it to one of the village trustees. Villagers, scandalized by the affair, knowingly recalled seeing the pair socializing at various events. _____

Chicago newspapers reported the "elopement" extensively but never reported the outcome. Years later, Rufus and Ellen were living at 505 Maple Avenue with four more kids (and a new male boarder). George was long gone.

Best Decisions

Wilmette's a great place to live because its officials and citizens have made forward-thinking decisions over the years. Here's a list of Wilmette's Best Decisions, in no particular order. The first two items have been explained in other chapters:

- Building the water plant.
- Annexing No Man's Land.
- Rejecting annexation to Evanston. During the early 1890s a movement to annex Wilmette to Evanston gained steam. The supposed advantages for Wilmette included better municipal services and access to Evanston High School. (New Trier High School didn't exist yet.) Two referenda were held on the issue in 1894. Evanston residents favored annexation, but Wilmette residents rejected it, once by only three votes. Wilmette went it alone and developed its own distinctive small-town character.
- Establishing a free public library. In 1900 residents approved a referendum to establish a free public library and authorize a tax for its operation. The library was initially an arm of village government, but in 1975 Wilmette voters approved a referendum to create a separate library district, with the idea of including Kenilworth, but Kenilworth voters decided not to join the new district.
- Creating the Wilmette Park District. The district was created in 1908 to take title to the landfill created when the spoil produced by digging the North Shore Channel was deposited in Lake Michigan north of Wilmette Harbor. In 1973 the Village's recreation department was merged into the Park District, which then became responsible for both maintaining the parks and offering recreational programming to the populace. Over the years, the district has taken bold steps, usually with voters' approval in referenda, to increase open space and add new recreational facilities, thereby creating ample parkland and a wide array of recreational opportunities for residents.
- Annexing Gross Point. Incorporated in 1874 and dissolved in 1919 for financial reasons, Gross Point bordered Wilmette at Ridge Road and extended west to Locust Road. Most of its territory was annexed to Wilmette in 1924 and 1926 (along with other western territory). These annexations greatly

increased the village's size, allowed municipal services to be offered more efficiently, and protected the area east of Ridge Road from undesirable development to the west. They also established the village's western border at the North Branch of the Chicago River, enabling the Village to create a storm sewer system that empties into the river without any regulation or interference by another municipality.

- Expanding the Park District to the west: While the annexations of 1924 and 1926 had moved the village's border to the west, the Park District's western border continued to be Ridge Road, and west-siders had no parks or park district. In 1946 west-siders initiated a referendum on expanding the district west to Hibbard Road. Voters on both sides of town approved. The district soon began adding parkland in west Wilmette, beginning with Thornwood Park and Community Playfield. In 1956 the village's and the Park District's borders became identical as the result of a State law that allowed the district to take the territory between Hibbard Road and the western village border from Glenview Park District. The Wilmette Park District was required to pay $44,000 for the territory's pro-rata share of Glenview Park District's debt, but this was a small price to pay for the expanded tax base (like Edens Plaza), the opportunity for more park facilities (like West Park and Wilmette Golf Club), and an increased sense of community unity.

- Approving the "Plan for a Better Wilmette." After World War II, the village turned its attention to the future needs of a community on the brink of tremendous growth. The Wilmette Planning Board came up with a $3.8 million plan involving new and expanded schools, municipal facilities and infrastructure; a new library building; additional parkland; and a community center on Green Bay Road between Wilmette and Central avenues. In a 1948 referendum, voters approved two-thirds of the package while rejecting the community center, some of the additional parkland, and the remodeling of the village hall. As predicted, the village's population skyrocketed from 18,162 in 1950 to 28,268 in 1960.

- Adopting Term Limits for Village officials. In 1967 the village board passed an ordinance imposing a two-term limit on elected members of the village board and appointed members of its boards and commissions. The rationale was that Wilmette's growing village population included many qualified residents who, if given a chance, would bring new and vibrant thinking to village government.

- Keeping Highcrest School. In the 1970s student enrollment in School District 39 declined dramatically, creating excess capacity. Among other actions, District 39 closed Highcrest in 1977 but retained ownership in case enrollment increased in the future. The building was leased to the Park District. By 1994 District 39's enrollment had increased and additional space was needed. Because of District 39's foresight, Highcrest was available. Contrast this with the ill-advised decision of New Trier High School to sell its west campus following closure in 1985. Fortunately, the attempt to sell the campus failed, and the west campus was still available when needed.

- Dealing humanely with an AIDS victim. In January 1987 Central School principal Paul Nilsen learned that seven-year-old student John Graziano had AIDS. An adoptee, John had contracted the disease from his heroin-addicted natural mother. Despite the widespread fear of AIDS at the time, Nilsen courageously decided that John would be allowed to continue in school. Nilsen won the support of the Central School community by calmly communicating about the negligible risk of transmission. John continued in school until he died two years later.

- Purchasing the former Bell School. In 1994–95 the Park District faced the loss of Highcrest School as its recreation center because D39 needed to repossess the building to accommodate the growing enrollment. The Park District proposed to purchase the old Bell School as a replacement facility. It had been closed in 1977 and sold to the Alter Group for its corporate headquarters, but in 1994 the Alter Group was moving away and selling the property. Neighborhood opposition to the Park District's proposal was fierce. According to opponents, a recreation center at this location would generate too much traffic, offer too little parking, cost too much money, contain too much space for recreational needs, and be too far west. The district had the vision and courage to proceed in the face of this opposition. It asked the Village for a "special use permit" to allow the project to go forward. After lengthy zoning hearings, the village board voted 4–3 to grant the permit.

Biggest Mistakes

A strong candidate for Wilmette's biggest mistake is the 1938 decision not to elevate the C&NW railroad tracks to create a grade separation where the main east-west roadways cross the tracks. Grade separation became a recognized need in Wilmette at the beginning of the 20th century. In the early years it was primarily a safety issue, because numerous accidents and fatalities occurred where roadways crossed railroad tracks at the same grade. Evanston took the initiative and forced the railroad companies, at their expense, to elevate their tracks early in the 20th century, but Wilmette and towns to the north deferred action.

The 1922 "Plan of Wilmette" stated that "there is no inhabitant of serious mind in the village who would recommend the continuation of the railway tracks at grade, for the necessity of eliminating grade crossings over railway tracks is so obvious from the standpoint of safety, that regardless of the enormous expenditures required of railroad companies, such work must be done." The plan recognized that the only feasible way to create a grade separation was by elevating the tracks. Depressing them wouldn't work, mainly because of the elevation that had already occurred in Evanston. While the 1922 planners favored elevation, they weren't proposing the high concrete walls and blind underpasses that Evanston had built. They recommended a more aesthetically pleasing design with low curbs, terraces, landscaping, and broad underpasses.

The power of municipalities to force railroads to foot the bill for grade separation evaporated in the 1920s. The newly-created Illinois Commerce Commission had the power to approve or disapprove grade separation projects and to apportion the cost between railroads and municipalities. Since most of the benefits of grade separation inured to the municipalities, said the ICC, most of the cost should be borne by them. And so, while Wilmette's officials continued to support grade separation and joined with towns to the north in planning, financing was a major obstacle, especially as the Great Depression arrived, the railroads struggled financially, and tax revenues dried up.

But then a potential savior was born unto Wilmette, in the form of the federal government's Public Works Administration. In 1938 Congress adopted legislation that made PWA funds available for public works projects: up to 45 percent of the cost in grants and up to 55 percent in loans bearing a 4 percent interest rate. Winnetka promptly applied for funds to pay the cost of elevating the tracks south of Willow Road and depressing them north of Willow.

At the time, the grade crossing danger was fresh in the minds of Wilmette officials. Within the past year, a near tragedy occurred when Ralph Brown, 55, of 1315 Chestnut Avenue, was crossing the tracks at Forest Avenue. His car stalled, just as a speeding passenger train bore down from the north. Unable to push the car off the tracks, Brown grabbed one of two canine passengers and raced for safety. The train smashed the car to smithereens. Flying wreckage injured Brown and one dog. The other dog was killed.

It was therefore no surprise that Wilmette applied for funds to elevate its tracks. The plan was to use the material removed in depressing Winnetka's tracks to elevate the roadbed in Wilmette. Then Wilmette became cautious. Making no recommendation, the village board conducted a "postcard referendum." Citizens were asked to vote yes or no. Village President Harry Kinne committed that the village wouldn't proceed "unless a majority of the citizens of Wilmette who reply to this questionnaire are in favor of it." Only one-third of the postcards were returned, and the votes were 2–1 opposed. Opponents contended that the village's share of the cost ($570,000) would limit its ability to borrow for future needs. And despite the 1922 plan's promise of a pleasing design, opponents also feared that a "Chinese Wall" would divide the village at the tracks and depress property values in the area. Bowing to the outcome of the survey, the village board acquiesced and withdrew its application. Winnetka proceeded alone.

Although officials continued to support the idea of grade separation for another decade or two, the project became increasingly unaffordable. Wilmette's last chance had been rejected, and future generations of motorists were consigned to long waits at the crossings as the trains come, stop, and go. Perhaps those who are annoyed by the long waits can find solace knowing that that safety concerns have been largely solved by modern signals and gates at the crossings, and there's no "Chinese Wall" dividing the village's downtown.

Here are some other big mistakes, again in no particular order.

- Dealing with Storm Water. Over the years, the Village contributed to the problem of basement and street flooding during heavy rainstorms by allowing too much land to be covered by impervious surfaces and by not requiring storm water detention and/or sewer system improvements as part of new construction projects. This has resulted in rainwater runoff that exceeds the capacity of the sewer systems and has no place to go other than basements, yards, and streets. West of Ridge Road, the Village allowed homebuilders to install storm sewer laterals and sanitary sewer laterals too close to one another, enabling storm water that leaks from the storm sewer laterals to enter the sanitary system and overwhelm it. Climate change also contributes to the flooding problem. The Village and its residents are now paying dearly for solutions.

- Controlling subdivisions. In 1924 and 1926 the Village annexed vast territory west of Ridge Road, mostly farmland and swampland at the time. Annexation gave the Village control over this vast territory's future development. Over the years, developers came to the Village with plans for subdivisions. The Village had the authority to set development standards and require developers to pay for public improvements, but the absence of sidewalks, streetlights, adequate sewers, storm water detention, and interface with neighboring subdivisions indicates that the controls were lax. The real estate investors and developers were very influential throughout the village's history.

- Hosting the Curling Center. In 1966 the Village accepted the proposal of Darwin Curtis, a Winnetka curling enthusiast, to build a curling center on Village-owned parkland at Ridge Road and Schiller Avenue. Curtis put up $400,000, and the Village agreed that its Recreation Board (later merged into the Wilmette Park District) would operate the center. A perennial money loser, the center was closed in 1978 and sold for affordable senior housing. The parkland was gone. The senior housing, called the Village Green Atrium, is the bright side of this story.

- Resisting zoning controls. The relationship between the Village and Wilmette Park District reached a low point in the 1980s because of zoning. The Village's zoning ordinance treated new and expanded parks as a "special use" subject to review for impacts on the surrounding neighborhood, but the Park District claimed that its land wasn't subject to zoning. The dispute reached a crescendo when the district installed lights at Howard Park's softball fields without undergoing zoning review. At the end of a costly and contentious lawsuit, the Illinois Supreme Court unanimously rejected the district's claim of zoning immunity.

- Spiking Salaries. Wilmette's school districts have contributed to the state's horrendous pension funding crisis. They engage in the practice of spiking educators' end-of-career salaries to inflate their pension benefits. Under the Teachers Retirement System, the state pays the cost of these inflated pensions. In other words, the school districts blithely pass the cost of inflated pensions onto the state. I disagree with the arguments advanced in favor of this practice: that "everyone does it"; that encouraging retirement and replacing highly paid senior staff with new hires is financially advantageous; and that state law authorizes it (even though it doesn't require it.) This practice is especially annoying in light of the state's overall failure to control pension costs. In my opinion, the state shouldn't allow it, and local school boards shouldn't do it.

- Supporting the Balefill. In the 1980s, experts predicted that landfills were about to reach capacity. In response, Wilmette joined a consortium of 23 suburbs that purchased a 500-acre site near Bartlett, Illinois, where they planned to bury their baled solid waste. Not surprisingly, Bartlett folks didn't cotton to the idea of remote suburbs dumping garbage in their backyard and possibly damaging the environment. They mounted a fierce legal and political battle in opposition. Meanwhile, the need for a new landfill subsided as recycling programs proved effective. After spending millions of dollars, the 23 suburbs eventually dropped the Balefill proposal.

Breaking News from Local Government

- February 1, 1913: Police Chief Edward Sieber announced that he'll no longer bury dead cats unless they're found on public roadways. This announcement comes on the heels of the deaths of 30 Wilmette cats over the past two weeks. It's believed that the rash of cat fatalities is due to recent rains that filled empty salmon cans with rancid water that the cats unwittingly drank. Sieber commented, "I've been the official undertaker for the last dead cat. Hereafter, Wilmette people will bury their own cats."

- March 4, 1913: The village board approved the purchase, for $15, of an old set of bobsleds. Joseph Steiner, 38, a plumber who resides at 1451 Wilmette Avenue and serves as the Village's fire commissioner, made the purchase because of the unprecedented snowfall causing travel on roadways to be dangerous, except with sleds. Steiner removed the wheels from the horse-drawn hose cart and installed the apparatus on the sleds. Walter Zibble, 26, who lives above the fire station at 1233 Central Avenue and serves as the cart's driver, placed two strings of sleigh bells on the harness to complete the happy wintertime scene, but the horses were frightened by the sound and ran away.

- October 1, 1936: Police Chief Cloyd McGuire is training 14 volunteers, all members of American Legion Post No. 46, to serve as auxiliary police officers. When they complete their training, they'll serve at the call of the chief without pay.

- February 4, 1939: A rash of home burglaries led Chief McGuire to "spread a dragnet" of 18 automobiles manned by his entire force of regular and auxiliary officers. When a burglary-in-progress was reported at 100 Woodbine Avenue, two squads quickly responded and captured a hardened criminal, Joseph Mackay, 26, as he was breaking through the rear door with a screwdriver. Mackay confessed to five other Wilmette burglaries.

- August 10, 1939: John Marten, 19, of 536 Roslyn Road, Kenilworth, was shot in the arm by Wilmette police officer Edward Phillips, 32, of 2508 Thornwood Avenue. Phillips was attempting to arrest Marten and Stafford Drake, 20, of 1011 Greenwood Avenue. Neighbors had complained to police that the pair were breaking streetlights. Phillips discharged his gun when the pair resisted arrest. They've been charged with disorderly conduct. (Sadly, Drake, a First Lieutenant in the Marine Corps, was killed in action on Midway Island in November 1943. Marten was an Army captain during World War II and afterwards was a highly respected businessman and citizen.)

- August 17, 1960: Theodore Vassar, 17, escaped from detention at the Wilmette Police Department on Green Bay Road. He was being held in Wilmette pending transfer to Northfield to face burglary charges there. He escaped by prying open a window screen. His next mistake was returning to the scene of the original burglary and breaking in again. Police were still there, investigating the first crime, and they arrested him a second time. Vassar, a native of Texas, admitted that he had been "banished from Abilene for two years after he got into trouble there."

- August 11, 1966: A historically significant house at 1136 Greenleaf Avenue is about to be demolished and replaced by an apartment building. The house was once owned by Andrew Sherman, whose business career and civic life displayed many admirable virtues and accomplishments. He moved from Evanston to Wilmette in 1871, leaving behind Sherman Avenue as his marker. His Wilmette house is of particular significance to Wilmette residents, because it's the site where the village government was organized at a meeting in 1872 with Sherman serving as temporary chairman. The first village president, John Westerfield, was elected at this meeting. Sherman also served as a village trustee and village president.

CHAPTER 6

★————————★

Public Schools

Folks choose to live in Wilmette for many reasons, but for most parents with kids, a huge factor is the quality of the schools. Without good schools, they wouldn't even consider the village as a place to live. District 37 (Avoca), District 39 (Wilmette), and District 203 (New Trier) have deservedly gained a reputation for excellence.

The Feeder Districts

Why are there two elementary school districts serving Wilmette? (Actually, there are three: Kenilworth District 38 includes a tiny section of northeast Wilmette.) Most folks know that Wilmette District 39 covers most of Wilmette and a small section of east Glenview, and Avoca District 37 covers the northwestern section of Wilmette plus sections of Winnetka, Glenview, Northfield, and unincorporated territory west of Kenilworth and Winnetka.

But why? Wouldn't it make more sense for the boundaries of elementary school districts to match municipal boundaries? Or for the New Trier area to have a unified elementary school district whose boundaries match the high school district's boundaries? Or even for the New Trier area to have a unified elementary and high school district, kindergarten through grade 12? To understand what makes little obvious sense, you need to know how the elementary school districts developed.

Public schools in Illinois were authorized by law in the mid-19th century. By the 1860s, before any village in New Trier Township was founded, there were already five elementary school districts in the township, each serving a small population center. In other words, the school districts were established before the municipalities. Roughly speaking, the five school districts covered these five areas: Glencoe, Winnetka, Wilmette, the former Village of Gross

Point, and the western territory now known as Avoca. These school districts gained importance in 1883 when Illinois passed its first compulsory school attendance law.

By 1900 the villages of Glencoe, Winnetka, Wilmette, Gross Point and Kenilworth were established. (Northfield wasn't incorporated until 1926.) At this time, Cook County assigned each elementary school district a number: Glencoe became D35, Winnetka D36, Avoca D37, Wilmette D39, and Gross Point D40. A separate new Kenilworth district was also created, D38, carved out of the Wilmette and Gross Point districts. All district boundaries roughly corresponded to municipal boundaries except Avoca D37, which consisted of unincorporated land west of the villages.

The Gross Point Standard School was the home of Huerter Post 669, later Post 46, from 1945 to 2015 when it was sold to Housing Opportunity Development Corp. HODC has demolished the building and is constructing an affordable housing facility on the site. Courtesy of the Wilmette Historical Museum.

These were all elementary school districts. When New Trier Township High School District 203 was created in 1899, its boundaries included all the territory covered by these elementary school districts, plus a section in east Northfield Township that was encompassed within no school district at the time.

Several adjustments in the elementary school districts' boundaries occurred in the 20th century. The major changes were the transfer of Mahoney farm in Kenilworth from Wilmette D39 to Kenilworth D38 (1923), the transfer of Indian

Hill Estates from Avoca D37 to Wilmette D39 (1925), and the merger of Wilmette D39 and Gross Point D40 (1932). In addition, Sunset Ridge (Northfield) D29 was established in 1924.

The merger of Wilmette D39 and Gross Point D40 occurred eight years after Wilmette annexed most of the former Village of Gross Point. At the time, Highcrest School, D40's school building, was new. Built in 1931, it replaced a two-room school at 1925 Wilmette Avenue that was built in 1895 and called the Gross Point Standard School. Grades 1–4 were taught by one teacher on the first floor, and grades 5–8 were taught above by a second teacher. This small building met D40's space needs before 1930, because most Gross Point kids attended St. Joseph School.

The builder of the Gross Point Standard School was Joseph Heinzen, a leading citizen of Gross Point and later Wilmette. He was a carpenter and stone mason who built many commercial and residential buildings in the area, including the Gross Point Village Hall (now home of the Wilmette Historical Museum). He served as Gross Point's village president (1905–1907) and was one of Wilmette's longest-serving village trustees (1913–1921 and 1931–1935).

The Standard School became the property of Wilmette D39 when it merged with Gross Point D40 in 1932. It was used as a community center, storehouse for the library's surplus books, and meeting place for Huerter Post 669 of the American Legion. Post 669 (renamed Huerter Post 46 following a merger) purchased the building in 1945.

Declining enrollments during the 1970s placed financial stress on school districts, prompting cautious conversations about consolidation. This was soon after a state commission recommended drawing elementary school district boundaries to achieve minimum enrollments of 1,000 pupils. Avoca D37 and Sunset Ridge D29 seriously discussed consolidation in 1975, but D29 backed away because of concerns over differences "both in philosophical direction and in structure," possible loss of "educational attributes," and opposition by teachers. Subsequent merger talks between Wilmette D39 and Avoca D37 went nowhere.

History is a big reason why six separate elementary school districts now feed into New Trier D203, but other powerful forces are also at work: Each district takes pride in its achievements; residents of each district wish to maintain control over educational policies; and officials and teachers have concerns about the effects of consolidation on them personally. So the status quo prevails: six elementary school districts, each with its own board, superintendent, and administrative structure. The 1922 "Plan of Wilmette" made the following observation regarding the multiplicity of districts: "Undoubtedly such diversified control as we have in this township does not secure the best school system. Probably sometime in the distant future the schools in the township will all be under one system and one board of education. Such changes come slowly. On the other hand the local pride that each community here on the North Shore has in the local system serves to keep it up to a very high standard."

The Founding of New Trier

Public elementary schools were well-established in Wilmette and Gross Point by the 1880s, but there was no high school. Most students who wished to pursue secondary education attended Evanston High School, established in 1883. They paid a non-resident tuition.

By the mid-1890s, Wilmette District 39 was offering two years of high school courses. This enabled students to enter high school elsewhere with advanced standing. During the debates of 1894 over the question whether Wilmette should be annexed to Evanston, the proponents of annexation made the argument that annexation would bring Wilmette children the advantage of access to a public high school. This argument didn't prevail, but the issue of a high school for Wilmette and other New Trier Township children remained alive. In 1894 a referendum to start a township high school failed by a narrow vote, but two years later a similar proposition was overwhelmingly approved.

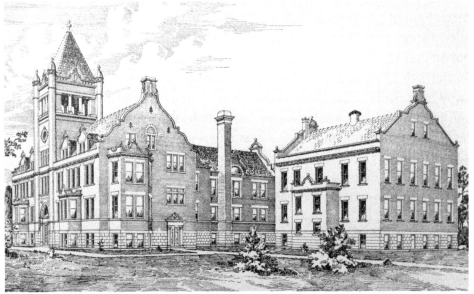

The Tower Building (left) was opened in 1901, and the Manual Arts Building (right) was added in 1907. See page 117. Courtesy of New Trier Township High School District 203.

(Despite having similar names, New Trier Township High School and New Trier Township are totally separate units of government. In this chapter, the term "New Trier" refers to the high school; the terms "East Campus" and "East" refer to New Trier's facilities in Winnetka; and the terms "West Campus" and "West" refer to the facilities in Northfield.)

The first New Trier Board of Education included three men from Wilmette: Rev. William Netstraeter, pastor of St. Joseph Church; Dr. Byron Stolp, beloved family doctor; and James Johnson, Chicago businessman. One of their first tasks was to select a site for the new school. The board offered two choices, and voters selected a six-acre site on Winnetka Avenue, part of the current East Campus. The cost was $14,400. The following year, Norman Patten was chosen as architect; a construction contract was let; and by year end the Tower Building was nearly complete and furnished at a cost of $86,000. February 4, 1901 was the first day of school, bringing together 40 girls and 36 boys under the tutelage of a seven-member faculty.

Growth and Success

By 1907 enrollment had climbed to 300 students, and the Manual Arts Building was added for instruction in the use of hands and tools for tasks like cooking and woodworking. Over the next five years, enrollment doubled to 600 students.

By 1923 multiple buildings made up the campus. Courtesy of New Trier Township High School District 203.

Nine more acres were added to the campus, and more facilities were built, including an auditorium, a dining hall, boys' and girls' gymnasiums, and the first indoor swimming pool in a U.S. public high school. Summer school was instituted in 1917.

Through the 1920s New Trier kept growing its student body, its faculty, its facilities, and its reputation for excellence. The Advisery System began in 1923. In 1925 a boiler plant was added, followed in 1926 by a gymnasium (later named Gates Gymnasium). By October of 1929 enrollment had swelled to 1,800 students, and the student body was increasing at the rate of 100 students per year. The school was running out of space, and the board of education was on the verge of building new facilities to increase the capacity to 2,500, the likely enrollment within a few more years.

The Great Depression

At first the Great Depression did nothing to slow the building plans of New Trier officials. After all, the existing space was inadequate, and new space was desperately needed regardless of the financial disaster that had befallen the nation and the community. Then reality sank in. Many residents had stopped paying their property taxes, and investors wouldn't buy the construction bonds because they lacked confidence that New Trier would be able to pay the interest and principal.

The school's problems went far beyond its inability to proceed with the building project. Drastic financial measures were required to keep the school open: layoffs, salary cuts, and program cuts. New Trier was forced to sell tax anticipation warrants to finance its operations. Warrants are simply loans that are repaid from future property tax receipts. New Trier paid its teachers partly in cash and partly in warrants and sold warrants to local banks and the public to pay other operating expenses. In March 1932 New Trier announced that it had only $5,000 on hand, and it might be forced to close on April 1 for the balance of the term and for the entire 1932–33 school year. Students' who wanted to continue their education would have to attend another school and pay its non-resident tuition. Sale of additional tax warrants was the only hope for avoiding these consequences. A last minute sales effort, strongly supported by the student body, saved the day.

Although the enrollment continued to grow at the rate of 100 students per year, reaching 2,300 in September 1934, the financial crisis abated because the municipal bond market improved. New Trier was able to sell long term bonds to Harris Bank at a favorable interest rate. Moreover, the Works Progress Administration (WPA) stepped in to help finance the building plans that had been deferred. The new addition included science laboratories, classrooms, and domestic science rooms; and the capacity of the school increased to 3,000 students. In 1936 a second WPA project added a natatorium with a swimming pool 75 feet long and 60 feet wide, three times the dimensions of the original pool.

Post World War II

The war years saw enrollment continue to grow without any corresponding increase in the land and building space needed to provide a high quality educational experience. By 1953 enrollment had reached 3,100 students. The most immediate need was more building space. This need was addressed when voters approved a $5.9 million bond issue to demolish the Tower Building and replace it with a 42-classroom building and a 1,500-seat auditorium. The expanded facility could comfortably accommodate 3,500 students.

The next problem was outdoor space. Landholdings consisted entirely of today's 27-acre East Campus. Because this site was too small to accommodate the physical education program of a 3,000-plus student body, the program had been cut significantly. While searching for an off-site location for interscholastic athletics, officials decided to acquire a seven-acre site immediately west of the Winnetka campus for gym classes and intramurals. They scheduled a referendum in June 1957 to authorize $900,000 in bonds to pay for the site. They announced that even if voters rejected the bonds, they'd purchase the site anyway, using future tax revenue.

The site was adjacent to Indian Hill Park. It encompassed 30 single family homes with 150 occupants on both sides of Bertling Lane and on the west side of Woodland Avenue. The plan was to use the existing parkland and the newly acquired property on a shared basis with the Winnetka Park District.

The referendum was vigorously opposed. Objectors claimed that the cost was "outlandish"; that demolishing homes was un-neighborly; that the need for more playfields was overstated; and that the seven-acre addition wouldn't solve the long-term problem posed by a rapidly growing student body. These objections resonated with voters. The bond issue was rejected by a resounding 80–20 percent margin.

New Trier officials accepted this strong message and abandoned the plan. Instead, they turned their attention to a site owned by the Village of Winnetka at Hibbard and Willow roads. New Trier and Winnetka agreed to a deal that was approved by Winnetka voters in October 1959. New Trier would purchase ten acres southwest of the Hibbard-Willow intersection, then part of a 30-acre sanitary landfill and storage area, for $80,000. In addition, New Trier would lease a 17-acre parcel northwest of the intersection (encompassing what's now Duke Childs Field) for $162,000 per year for 18 years. New Trier would use the land as playfields.

A Second High School?

New Trier's enrollment continued to grow, exceeding the school's recommended capacity of 3,500 students in 1958 and projected to go much higher. Officials saw another approaching crisis. A second school, capable of housing 2,500 students, was needed. They selected a 43-acre site at Happ Road and Winnetka Avenue in Northfield (current site of the West Campus) and asked voters to approve $975,000 in bonds to purchase it.

Some opponents were dead set against two schools, believing that a second school would inevitably be inferior to the highly-rated Winnetka school. Others opposed the proposed boundary line. Still others argued that a new school should be in Wilmette to serve Wilmette students, who comprised 40 percent of the student body. Northfield residents were especially opposed, claiming that the cost of additional police, fire and other municipal services would overwhelm the small village's budget.

Knowing that the West Campus now occupies the Northfield site, you'd probably guess that voters approved the bonds, but you'd be wrong. In May 1961 voters rejected the proposal 56 percent to 44 percent margin. The space problem became more urgent.

The East Campus could house 3,500 students comfortably, but in 1960 the enrollment reached 3,902, and by 1963 it would reach 4,475, on its way to peaking at 6,540 in 1972. Mobile classrooms would be needed immediately, and double shifts might be required if more space wasn't provided soon. Following voters' rejection of the 1961 referendum, officials formed a citizens' committee to re-study the problem.

Later that year the committee unanimously recommended "that a second four-year high school be built to house approximately 2,500 students." The recommended location was a 40-acre site at the southwest corner of Hibbard and Willow roads in Winnetka. This site consisted of the ten acres that New Trier had already acquired from the Village of Winnetka in 1959, plus another

20 acres owned by Winnetka and used as a sanitary landfill and storage area, plus ten acres owned by the Cook County Forest Preserve District.

Thirteen other sites were considered, including a 17-acre site at Crawford and Wilmette avenues (now Wilmette Park District's Centennial Park); Northwestern University's 107-acre golf course on Lake Avenue (now the Wilmette Park District's golf course); the 44-acre Mallinckrodt property on Ridge Road (now senior housing and parkland); and the Northfield site previously rejected.

The Winnetka site recommended by the committee was doomed from the start. Many Winnetka residents opposed it, based mainly on concerns about traffic congestion and the burden of hosting two high schools in the village. Winnetka's village board decided that the requested village-owned land was needed for municipal purposes and nixed a sale. The Forest Preserve District sealed the outcome by announcing that it wouldn't deviate from its policy not to sell, lease, or trade its land to anyone for any reason.

New Trier officials reacted quickly. In early 1962 they revived the Northfield site and presented it to voters again. Shortly after the previous referendum, Northfield had changed the site's zoning from residential to light industrial, causing its value to nearly double (to $1.8 million). Despite the higher price, voters approved bonds to purchase the site by a comfortable 67 percent to 33 percent margin. Voters were reassured by promises that the facilities, faculty, and programs of the two schools would be equal; that New Trier's vaunted Advisery System would be adopted at the new school; and that extracurricular activities would be encouraged and supported equally at both schools. Using a boundary line to be drawn later, the student body of each school would include children from each of the district's major communities.

One year later voters approved $8.7 million in bonds to construct a six-building complex in Northfield. The overwhelming margin was 78–22 percent. Designed by Perkins & Will, the architecturally-acclaimed New Trier West opened for freshmen and sophomores in 1965 at a fully equipped cost of $12 million, and its first senior class graduated in 1968.

What Goes Up Sometimes Comes Down

If you lived in District 203 during the 1970s and 1980s, you know that this "solution" to New Trier's growing pains wasn't the final word. It turned out that the rapid enrollment increase after World War II was a baby boom blip. From the 1972 peak of 6,550, enrollment steadily dropped to 3,858 in 1985. Demographer

John Kasarda predicted it would drop further to 3,000 in 1990 and would eventually stabilize at about 3,300.

New Trier West served as a four-year school only until 1981. By then, District 203's total enrollment had declined from its 1972 peak by almost 2,000 students. This prompted officials to convert West, the smaller of the two schools, into a freshman-only campus. Four years later, in 1985, the district's enrollment was down to 3,858, and West was closed entirely. New Trier East, the sentimental favorite of many of the school's graduates living in the area, once again became the district's only high school.

The next problem was what to do with the surplus facility. A high-ranking New Trier official, citing data provided by Kasarda, stated publicly, "We'll be down to approximately 3,000 students in 1990. Then we'll increase gradually to 3,300 and stay there...with very slight ups and downs." The official explained that Kasarda "analyzed the societal factors and the broader demographics of the population and concluded that even though it gets pretty iffy when you go out [beyond 2001], he doesn't think enrollment will ever exceed the projected 3,300." Even unforeseen demographic changes, he added, would increase enrollment only to "an absolute high" of 3,800, a number that can be comfortably housed at the East Campus.

In other words, the mindset of New Trier's officialdom in the mid-1980s was that the West Campus would never be needed again, and future needs would be satisfied by one four-year school at the East Campus. With this mindset, officials took up the options of either leasing or selling the West Campus. They initially followed a conservative approach and tried to lease, but the market for leased office space was poor, and these efforts failed. In early 1987, with mothballing costs at $440,000 per year and growing, they decided to entertain offers to purchase. National College of Education, located on Sheridan Road at the Wilmette-Evanston border, indicated a willingness to purchase the West Campus for $22 million. New Trier officials were enthusiastic.

But the Village of Northfield wasn't anxious to host a tax exempt entity like National College. It amended its zoning ordinance to provide that any tax-exempt college or university must pay an impact fee to compensate the village for police, fire, and other municipal services. This new regulation would cost National College an estimated $305,000 per year, and the college said it wasn't interested in purchasing the West Campus if the property was subject to this fee. New Trier responded by suing Northfield, claiming that the new regulation was illegal and void.

Meanwhile, the decision to sell the West Campus met with stiff community resistance. A citizens' group argued that the athletic facilities were still needed, a portion of the building space could be used for administrative of-fices and specialty programs, and the entire facility might be needed in the future if enrollment exceeded projections. The opponents also argued that, even if New Trier was destined to be a one-campus school forever, the West Campus was the preferable location, because the site was much larger, and the buildings were newer.

Officials believed that selling the West Campus rather than the East Campus would be financially preferable. Selling East would generate only $12 million, not enough to pay the $16 million cost of enlarging West to accommodate the district's projected long-term enrollment of 3,300. By contrast, the $22 million that National College was offering was twice the amount needed to finance the renovation of East to accommodate 3,300–3,500 students comfortably in a modern facility.

The ongoing legal skirmish between New Trier and Northfield tabled the sale to National College and gave District 203 residents a chance to weigh in on the question of selling. In December 1987 they conducted a successful peti-tion drive to force an advisory referendum on the question of whether New Trier should sell the West Campus. In March 1988 a large majority of District 203 residents (62–38 percent) voted not to sell.

Officials didn't embrace this advice. Shortly after the referendum, they de-cided to continue the lawsuit against Northfield. Referring to the referendum results, the president of the board said, "The only thing I have new is that they [opponents of the sale] were able to influence 10,000 people through a heavy campaign. I don't know the reason behind all those votes." The school's super-intendent said, "Our first priority has always been to find a favorable long-term lease. Maybe the efforts should be intensified."

The lawsuit dragged on. In May 1988 the Circuit Court of Cook County ruled that the impact fee was invalid. Northfield appealed and won at the appel-late court. New Trier tried to appeal to the Illinois Supreme Court, but in late 1989 the court refused to hear the case. National College then withdrew from negotiations.

Meanwhile, the West Campus started to attract some tenants. It served as a movie set for the popular movies *Uncle Buck* and *Home Alone,* generating $120,000. In 1990 National College rented one building for administrative of-fices and adult classes for $132,000 per year for two years, and Stepan Co. rented another building for offices and a computer center for about $200,000 per year for 20 years. Additional tenants soon joined the mix. The idea of sell-ing faded away.

As leasing efforts started to bear fruit, New Trier's enrollment sank to its modern-day low of 2,710 in 1990. Then enrollment started back up. It moved above its once-predicted long-term level of 3,300 in 1998, and crashed through its once-predicted "absolute high" of 3,800 in 2002, on its way to 4,047.

The West Campus Reopens

By 1997 New Trier officials realized that the East Campus wouldn't be able to house the growing student body. Four options emerged: Return to two separate four-year schools, one at the East Campus with 55 percent of the student body and the other at the West Campus with 45 percent; open West as a smaller "lab school" for 650 students; open West as a freshman-only campus; and enlarge East to accommodate the entire student population.

In 1998 New Trier surveyed District 203 residents regarding these options. The survey disclosed no clear favorite, with the two-school option and an enlarged East both at the top with about the same level of support. The option of opening West as a freshman-only campus had little support. As between the two favored options, an enlarged East was more costly and might overload its east Winnetka neighborhood. "Education experts" advised that smaller schools in the 1,500–2,000 range provide the optimal educational experience. The elephant in the room was the boundary line that would divide the district if the two-school option were selected. As everyone knew from New Trier's prior two-school experience, the boundary line is a hugely controversial subject with political, social, and religious overtones.

So which option was selected? Like the district's residents, the Board of Education was divided, with three members supporting two four-year schools, three supporting an enlarged East, and one supporting a freshman-only West. In an admirable demonstration of flexibility and compromise, the board united in support of opening West, initially as a freshman-only campus, but perhaps in the future as a separate four-year school attended voluntarily by students who preferred a small-school environment.

District 203 residents supported this compromise. In November 1998 they approved, by a 57–43 percent margin, an $11 million bond issue to offset the $23.7 million cost of renovating and repairing the East and West campuses to accommodate the "1–3" model. The balance was paid from reserves.

As New Trier was preparing to open the West Campus for freshmen in 2001, it supplemented its landholdings by joining with Northfield Park District to purchase a 9.8 acre site at the southeast corner of Willow and Waukegan roads for additional athletic fields. New Trier paid two-thirds of the $4.2 million cost,

The West Campus, built in 1965, is pictured here in 2020. Both
images courtesy of New Trier Township High School District 203.

The most recent addition to the East Campus (right side of
photograph), opened in 2017. It was designed by Wight & Co.

and Northfield Park District paid the rest. New Trier also paid $687,000 for site
improvements. One board member said, "This land is crucial for the freshmen next year at New Trier West Campus to have more athletic opportunities."

West opened with an enrollment of 960 freshmen. The experiment revealed
no major problems with the 1–3 model. Indeed, it drew praise. But the option
of a four-year school at West, attended on a voluntary basis, remained on the
table for another year. Finally, in mid-2002, the voluntary school idea was rejected by a 5–2 vote of the Board of Education. This idea was also opposed by
faculty and staff, most of whom feared that the small voluntary school would

become "New Trier Least" when compared to East. The superintendent joined the opposition. A major factor was the estimated $6.5 million cost of converting West to a four-year school at a time when New Trier was operating in the red and was about to ask taxpayers to increase the district's tax rate.

In 2010 a massive $174 million re-building plan for the East Campus was rejected by voters overwhelmingly. In 2014 a scaled-back $100 million plan to replace three outmoded buildings at East with a single, larger building was approved.

New Trier officials have done a good job over the years providing the facilities needed for the district to maintain its well-deserved reputation for educational excellence. But taxpayers deserve credit, too, not only for being willing to pay for the facilities, but also for stopping missteps. The proposed purchase and demolition of 30 homes adjacent to the East Campus in 1957 does indeed seem to be "un-neighborly" and heavy-handed, as opponents argued at the time. The proposed sale of the West Campus in 1987 would have left the district with no reasonable option for dealing with the second enrollment surge which forced the re-use of West in 2001. And the massive re-building plan for the East Campus in 2010 was asking too much of taxpayers.

What's in store for New Trier's facilities in the future? History shows that change is inevitable and that the best decisions are made when officials consult with the community throughout the planning process and don't overreach. Remote teaching during the pandemic may also show that technology, while not a replacement for in-person give and take, can be used effectively to offset the need for additional classroom space if enrollment spikes again.

CHAPTER 7

★————————————★

Business Talk

In 1942 economist Joseph Schumpeter described capitalism as "the perennial gale of creative destruction." By that he meant that businesses succeed and fail based on their ability to compete, adapt, and innovate in an open and free market, and the end result, though often messy, is progress and economic vitality.

Wilmette's ever changing business community, replete over the decades with winners and losers, is certainly evidence of messy progress. Long gone are the blacksmith shops, the horse-powered liveries, the small grocery stores, the candy shops, the cigar stores, and the corner drugstores with their soda fountains. Long gone are the businesses that delivered ice, coal, fuel oil, and milk to homes. Once there were several hardware stores; now there's one. Once there were truly local newspapers; now there's none. Once there were four major automobile dealerships; now they've closed or moved to locations outside the village with more space for modern showrooms and service departments and a wide array of brands. In the territory that once was Gross Point, gone are the saloons and florists along Ridge Road and the fruit and vegetable stands that sold produce from the area's truck farms.

Edens Plaza and Plaza del Lago were developed in the 1950s and 1960s. They challenged the established retail businesses in the village's downtown and neighborhood shopping areas. Now the shopping centers are being challenged by Amazon and other online retailers. Recently, much of the space in the Village Center has been taken over by restaurants, a business with little online competition, but the neighborhood shopping areas continue to struggle.

Meanwhile, many distinguished leaders of major business enterprises have made Wilmette their home over the years, and seven of them will be profiled later in this chapter. Others include Benjamin Affleck, president, Universal Portland Cement Co.; Mark Brown, president, Harris Bank; Kenneth Zwiener, chairman and CEO, Harris Bank; Howard Reeder, chairman, CNA; Lester Crown, multiple enterprises; Gordon Segal, founder of Crate & Barrel; Christie

Hefner, chairman and CEO of Playboy Enterprises; John Donahoe, CEO of eBay and Nike, Inc.; Charles Knight, CEO of Emerson Electric; Dennis Chookaszian, chairman and CEO of CNA; Philip Purcell, chairman and CEO of Morgan Stanley; and Andrew McNally IV, chairman and CEO of Rand McNally & Co.

The Oldest Businesses

Fourteen businesses founded locally before or during the Great Depression are still operating today. Surviving that economic calamity and overcoming other challenges for eight or more decades is remarkable. In some cases the business names have changed. In other cases the locations have changed. In still others the ownership has passed from the founding family to entirely new ownership. Nevertheless, they can all legitimately claim to be in continuous operation from the date of their original founding.

- Millen Hardware (1219 Wilmette Avenue) was established in 1908. John Millen, its proprietor, had worked at an Evanston hardware store for 15 years before purchasing the Hansen & Hubbell hardware store at 605 Green Bay Road, the present site of the Wilmette Bicycle Shop. He operated at this location for 15 years. His motto was "If it's hardware, Millen has it." In 1923 he moved to the current location, now enlarged. Among many hardware stores that once operated in Wilmette, Millen is the only one to survive.

Wm. H. Scott Funeral Home moved into the Westerfield house in 1930.
See page 129. Courtesy of the Wilmette Historical Museum.

- Sweet's Heating and Air Conditioning (736 12th Street) was founded by tin-smith John Sweet, but the date is uncertain. It's known that John moved to Wilmette and started a furnace repair business before 1910 and expanded into hardware retailing by 1916. His first business location may have been his residence at 611 Elmwood Avenue. In 1920 he discontinued the hardware line and opened a sheet metal shop (furnaces, gutters, and downspouts) at 1209 Washington Avenue. In 1929 he built Sweet's Tin Shop at the present location. There, besides traditional sheet metal work, he made molds for Girl Scout cookies. Frank Beitzel, a former employee, bought the business in 1945 when John retired. Frank's grandsons, Robert and Roger Beitzel, are the current proprietors.

- Mid-Central Printing & Mailing (1211 Wilmette Avenue) was founded in 1910 at 302 Park Avenue as Acme Addressers and Acme Udell Printers. Its founder was an outspoken and controversial character, Bertram Udell. The firm performed printing and mailing services and, until 1933, published the *Wilmette Announcements,* a weekly newspaper. Udell and his sons moved the printing and mailing business to 1225 Central in the 1950s. Steve Cramer bought the firm in 1968 and renamed it Mid-Central, based on its location in the middle of the 1200 block of Central Avenue. In 1973 John Korzak, Sr. bought the business. His son, John Korzak, Jr., moved the business to its current location in 2016.

- Kashian Brothers (1107 Greenleaf Avenue) was established in 1910 by two young brothers, Haig and Melikoff Kashian. Haig immigrated from Turkey in 1908 with only 25 cents and a few small oriental rugs. Melikoff followed two years later. The business was originally called Eastern Rug Cleaning Co. Located in the same Greenleaf Avenue block as now, the Kashians cleaned and repaired oriental rugs and carpets and also sold rugs and carpets. Jim Allans bought the business in 1949 and added new products and services over his 50 years of ownership. It's now owned by Doug Stein.

- Wm. H. Scott Funeral Home (1100 Greenleaf Avenue) was founded, not surprisingly, by William H. Scott. He came to Wilmette in 1914 as manager and part-owner of Western Casket and Undertaking Co.'s new branch at 1123 Central Avenue. Seven years later, in 1921, he left Western and opened his own undertaking firm, first at 1124 Central and then at 1109 Central. In 1930 he relocated to a house at 1118 Greenleaf Avenue that once belonged to Wilmette's first village president, John Westerfield. In 1956 the house was razed, and the current funeral home was built. After William's death in the mid-1930s, the business was continued by his son Norman F. Scott and later by his grandson Norman H. Scott. In 1979 the business was sold to Service

Corporation International, a huge corporate owner of funeral homes, crematories, and cemeteries.

- Shawnee Service Center (332 Linden Avenue) traces its roots to 1916 when Wilmette Motor Sales was established in the 700 block of West Railroad Avenue as a repair garage and Paige auto dealership. The proprietors were brothers, Peter and George Schaefer. Within a few years, they relocated to 515 4th Street and changed the name to Shawnee. In the early 1930s Peter left the firm, and George took on a new partner, Sam Marvin. At the time, two other repair garages operated in Linden Square. In 1934 the three firms merged, and Al Rodenkirk became a third partner. Shawnee moved to 322 Linden in the 1950s, and its proprietor now is Sam Marvin's son, Peter.

- Lucke Plumbing (736 12th Street) was launched when William Lucke received his Chicago master plumber's license in 1916. William established a place of business at 7 Electric Place. (Electric Place ran between Lake and Central avenues east of the C&NW railroad tracks.) He soon moved to 1101 Linden Avenue and finally settled at 514 Poplar Avenue for many years. Plumbing may not be thought of as a particularly innovative business, but William received plaudits for inventing a much-used device that prevented bathtubs from settling and pulling away from the wall. His son and grandson carried on the business until the firm was sold to its present owner, Scott Stieber.

- Skokie Valley Material Co. (3640 Lake Avenue) was established in 1926 by a young Wilmette couple, Marcus and Lillian Mick. Lillian was the daughter of Philip Hoffmann, one of two Hoffmann brothers who operated a coal and lumber yard near the railroad tracks in the Village Center where Marcus had worked as a clerk. The young couple purchased three acres of land on the west side of town, adjacent to Skokie Valley Line of the North Shore Electric railroad. There, they sold coal and building materials and excavation and hauling services. During the 1930s and 1940s Skokie Valley was involved in the construction of St. Joseph Church as an excavator and the Bahá'í Temple as a supplier. In 2019 the firm was sold by Mick family descendants to a buyer that continues to operate it at the same location.

- Wilmette Bowling Center (1903 Schiller Avenue) was created by Paul Bleser in 1927 when he built a bowling alley with ten lanes next to his Ridge Road barber shop. Decades earlier, Paul's father John had offered bowling to patrons of his saloon at 615 Ridge Road, but in 1927 the regulatory environment for a bowling alley on the west side of Ridge Road was more hostile. Wilmette annexed the area in 1924, and Wilmette officials looked askance at bowling and banned it on Sundays. Paul resisted the ban until he finally

In 1948, the Wilmette Bicycle & Sport Shop occupied both 605 Green Bay
Road (current location) and the building to the north (607 Green Bay Road).
Courtesy of the Wilmette Historical Museum.

convinced the village board to repeal it in 1931. His son Philip took over and
operated Bleser's Bowling Academy for many years until it was sold to the
current owner, Jeff Strange, in 1998

- Lapels of Wilmette (819 Ridge Road) was founded in 1931 by Larry and Madeline Schaefer as Wilmette Tailors & Cleaners. Previously, Larry had been a North Shore mail carrier and had briefly tried his hand at insurance brokerage. Neither he nor Madeline had any experience in the cleaning business. After occupying two other Ridge Road storefronts, they purchased land and built the current cleaning plant in 1946. Three years later, they bought adjacent land for customer parking and the village's first drive-through window. Their son Peter took over in 1970 and managed to survive the financial challenge posed by wash-and-wear clothing. Peter's stepson, Kurt Raggi, joined the firm in 1978. He and his wife Rita bought it in 1983. They operated it for 35 years and sold it to Lapels of Wilmette in 2019.

- Wilmette Bicycle & Sport Shop (605 Green Bay Road) was founded in 1932 by 18-year-old John Versino. Four years earlier, the Versino family (including John and his younger brother Jim) had emigrated from Italy and settled in Wilmette. John began with a bicycle repair business in a barn behind the family home. By 1935 he opened a shop at 607 Main Street, where he sold, rented and repaired bikes; sold sporting goods; strung tennis rackets; and even sharpened lawnmowers. By 1936, brother Jim joined the business, and in the late 1940s they moved to the current location. Now, the proprietors are John and Jim's sons: Al, Larry, and Jim. For decades, the Versino family has actively supported local youth sports.

- Karl G. Knobel, Inc. (1150 Wilmette Avenue) was established in 1933 by the company's namesake. When the Great Depression struck, Karl was recently married and was working as a carpenter for his father, who was the carpentry foreman of a homebuilding firm. As the Depression dragged on, the father was forced to tell his son that he could no longer provide work. That's when Karl started his own carpentry firm, working out of his garage at 1431 Central Avenue. After serving in the Navy during World War II, he resumed the business and moved it to 1218 Washington Avenue, its location for many years. Its focus gradually became kitchen and bathroom design and remodeling. Now, the proprietors are Karl's sons, Peter and Paul, and the business recently moved to the Wilmette Avenue location.

- Homer's Ice Cream (1237 Green Bay Road) opened in 1935, but its founders were no strangers to the ice cream business. Three brothers—James, Gus, and Peter Poulos—emigrated from Greece in 1916, 1918, and 1920, respectively. Many years before opening Homer's, they operated the Winnetka Sweet Shop at 749 Elm Street, where they served up delicious ice cream and confectionaries. Homer's was an expansion of that business, with Gus in charge. It took its name Homer's from one or more of these sources: Gus's middle name, the Greek poet, or a baseball round-tripper. In 1964 Gus was shot in the abdomen during a robbery at the store. He recovered, and ten years later doubled the store's size. His sons took over following his death in 1979.

- On December 4, 2020, Schultz & Odhner's Dry Cleaners (1152 Central Avenue), the village's oldest business, closed its doors for good, a victim of the coronavirus pandemic. The business dates back to 1901 when Henry Schultz opened a cleaning, dyeing, and tailoring establishment in the 600 block of West Railroad Avenue. In 1911 Emil Nord joined Schultz to form Schultz & Nord. The firm soon moved to 1152 Central and remained in the Schultz family until the 1960s when it was acquired by Odhner's Tailor and Cleaner, a Winnetka family firm that also dates back to 1901. In recent years, the business continued under proprietors Dennis Golden and Cory Schipfer.

The Chalet

At the northeast corner of Skokie Boulevard and Lake Avenue, there's an un-usual building that looks like a Swiss chalet. Its original location, from 1937 to 1947, was elsewhere: on the east side of Skokie Boulevard between Tower and Dundee roads. Back then, Skokie Boulevard was this area's most heavily traveled north-south roadway. Edens Expressway didn't exist.

The building originally housed a restaurant and tavern called The Chalet Inn. It was owned and managed by Anton Kerscher and Max Baetz. Anton and Max were related: Anton's wife was Max's sister. Both had immigrated to the U.S. from Germany in the 1920s as young men. Early on, before part-nering as restaurateurs, Anton worked as a gardener for a wealthy Winnetka family, and Max worked as a tire salesman in Chicago.

The Chalet Inn was popular and successful but short-lived. The Cook County Forest Preserve District wanted the site to expand the Skokie Lagoons preserve. In a proceeding that went all the way to the Illinois Supreme Court in 1946, the district acquired the property through eminent domain.

As the new owner, the district had no use for the building and requested bids from anyone who wanted to buy and relocate it. That's when an enterpris-ing Wilmette man, Lawrence Thalmann, Sr., entered the picture. Lawrence's great grandparents came to New Trier Township from Prussia in 1847. They purchased considerable land in what's now west Wilmette and engaged in farming for many years. They had many descendants. Hibbard Road was once called Thalmann Road because of the family's prominence in the area.

Lawrence grew up during the early 1900s at 2311 Lake Avenue, then located in the Village of Gross Point. The home of his youth was surrounded by the homes of many Thalmann relatives. At age 18, he was employed as a clerk for the C&NW, but he started a landscaping business on the side, tending the lawns and gardens of North Shore homes.

Before long Lawrence left the railroad, studied landscape architecture at Northwestern University, and concentrated on his landscaping business. He married Elaine Brown in 1927, and they established both their home and business headquarters for L.J. Thalmann Architectural Landscaping at 2323 Lake Avenue. The business expanded to a second location, 2134 Schiller Ave-nue. The Schiller property was used as a nursery and for storing landscaping equipment and supplies. By 1946 the Thalmann landscaping business served 500 clients on the North Shore and employed 50–60 employees during its peak months.

That's when Lawrence made two bold moves. First, he purchased seven acres of vacant farmland at the northeast corner of Skokie Boulevard and Lake Avenue for about $3,600 per acre. The surrounding land was vacant except for a few scattered houses. The entire area was zoned exclusively for single family homes. Second, he also purchased the Chalet Inn building from the Forest Preserve District for $751. He cut it in three pieces and moved it down Skokie Boulevard to its current site. His overall plan was to use the building as his home and garden shop, and the remaining land as his nursery.

The Village fought Lawrence tooth and nail for two decades. It initially tried to prevent him from engaging in any commercial activities whatsoever at the site, and even after Edens Plaza was developed across the roadway, it tried to limit his commercial activities. Lawrence plowed ahead anyway. From the beginning, folks called his garden shop The Chalet, and the name stuck.

Carried on by Lawrence Sr.'s descendants, The Chalet is now one of the village's most successful and respected businesses enterprises and one of its biggest taxpayers.

The Chalet Inn was originally located between Tower and Dundee roads on Skokie Boulevard. Courtesy of The Chalet.

Edens Plaza

Postwar planning for the new superhighways didn't go unnoticed by giant retailers Marshall Field & Co. and Carson Pirie Scott & Co. While both had already branched out from their State Street flagship stores, the superhighways created new opportunities. Both retailers recognized the potential of regional shopping centers with a variety of shopping attractions, plentiful parking, and easy access from a superhighway.

In 1948, Carson's quietly purchased the 20-acre site in Wilmette bounded by Skokie Highway, Lake Avenue, and the proposed Edens Expressway. Two years later, Field's announced plans for a huge shopping center on an 80-acre site at Skokie Highway between Golf and Old Orchard roads, just east of Edens. Field's claimed that numerous retailers, including Carson's, were interested in joining the center.

Field's and Carson's never got together, and Field's went forward without its main competitor. In 1953 Carson's submitted its proposal for Edens Plaza to Wilmette. The property was zoned residential, so a zoning change was needed. The proposal was controversial. Neighbors complained that the Plaza would generate too much traffic. Supporters argued that it would raise tax revenue for local government. After a year-long debate, the Village finally changed the zoning to retail.

Edens Plaza opened in May 1956, beating Old Orchard by five months. Following a festive dedication ceremony, the first customers were ushered into Carson's new store by eight-year-old flower girls from area communities. William Edens, 92, the man honored by the Expressway's name, was present. Early tenants included John T. Shayne (women's specialty), National Tea (supermarket), Terminal Hardware, Kenneth Fogelberg (children's goods), Schmitt's Bakery, Shore Line Cleaners, Allen's Stationers, Lester D. Parker (gifts), Fannie May, Thomas J. Cullen (jewelry), Bellringer's (grill), Steinway Drugs, Woolworth's, Phillip's Shoe Repair, and Schaul's Poultry. Today, neither Carson's nor any of the original tenants is there.

Fred Salerno

"Mommy, I want a Salerno butter cookie!" For decades, these words were etched into the brains of radio-listeners and TV-watchers. They were screamed by a kid with an annoying voice as part of a commercial that made Salerno Butter Cookies the best-selling product of the Salerno-Megowen Biscuit Co. They usher in the story of Fred Salerno, who lived at 501 Lake Avenue for 40 years, along with his wife Frances and their three children.

Fred was born at San Fili, Italy, near the toe of the boot, in 1877. Twelve years later, he left Italy, traveling on his own to Chicago. He started working in the biscuit business (crackers, cookies) as a pan greaser for Kennedy Biscuit Works, later part of Nabisco.

Fred's career was interrupted when he returned to Italy for a visit in the mid-1890s and was drafted into the Italian Army, which had just been defeated in a war against Ethiopia. He served for two years. While in Italy, he met his future wife, Frances Noto. He returned to Chicago and married Frances by proxy five years later, with his brother standing in. Frances arrived in Chicago in early 1906, and they were promptly remarried.

Lacking formal education, Fred succeeded in the biscuit business for four main reasons: he worked hard and through practical experience became a master baker; he was a mechanical genius who invented and held 87 patents on industry-revolutionizing equipment; he demanded perfection in all products and services; and he had a mentor who helped him along.

His mentor was Roger Sullivan, the longtime leader of the Illinois Democratic Party and a successful Chicago businessman and investor. Sullivan High School is named in his honor. Sullivan and his brothers, along with Charles Sawyer, organized Sawyer Biscuit Co. in 1901. Fred joined the company as one of its first employees and, with Sullivan's support, rose through the ranks, becoming its president after Sullivan died in 1920. Sawyer merged with other bakeries in 1927 under the umbrella of the United Biscuit Co. of America (known today as Keebler Co.). Fred remained president of Sawyer and also became vice-president of United.

In 1927 the Salerno family moved from Chicago to Wilmette. Fred purchased the vacant lot at 501 Lake Avenue from the owner of the adjacent Frank Lloyd Wright-designed house at 507 Lake and built a home that stayed in the family for almost 60 years.

As an executive of Sawyer and United, Fred worked for outside investors. He yearned for a biscuit company of his own. In 1933 he and several colleagues left Sawyer and United. They opened the Salerno-Megowen Biscuit Co. at 4500 Division Street, Chicago. This was a risky undertaking in the depths of the Great Depression, but the new company was immediately successful and eventually became a dominant baker in the Chicago region. Besides Butter Cookies, it manufactured more than 50 other products.

In 1960 Salerno-Megowen moved to a new 350,000-square-foot plant at 7777 N. Caldwell Avenue, Niles. It was a model baking operation replicated by other biscuit manufacturers throughout the U.S. Unfortunately, in 2004, long after the Salerno Co. was sold by the family, Kraft Foods (the final owner) closed the plant for good and hundreds of employees lost their jobs.

Fred died in 1968. One of his granddaughters fondly remembered family gatherings at a Barrington farm that Fred owned and used as a retreat. She described him as a generous and gregarious man who had a "cute sense of humor." He spoke with a heavy Italian accent. Towards the end, he became crippled by arthritis and was confined to a wheel chair, but his physical difficulties didn't diminish his playfulness with and enjoyment of children.

James Kraft

James Kraft, born in Canada on December 11, 1874, was the founder of the food products company that bears his famous surname. He lived at 17 Canterbury Court with his wife Pauline and daughter Edith from the late 1930s until his death at age 78 in 1953.

Kraft grew up on a farm in Ontario, along with seven brothers and three sisters. He moved to Buffalo, New York as a young man and invested in a cheese company. In 1903 he came to Chicago to manage the company's Chicago branch. His partners forced him out of the business and stranded him in Chicago. With only $65 in his pocket, he started a new company. He hired a horse and wagon, bought cheese from wholesalers at Chicago's South Water Street Market, and delivered it to retail grocers in the Austin District. This venture was successful, and he soon brought four of his brothers into the business, originally named J.L. Kraft & Bros. Co.

James Kraft founded the food company that bears his name. Courtesy of Kraft Foods.

Cheese was nowhere near as popular in the early 20th century (less than one pound per capita annually) as it is now (almost 40.4 pounds per capita in 2019), mainly because it spoiled quickly and couldn't be transported long distances. Kraft overcame this obstacle by developing and patenting a revolutionary pasteurizing process that greatly extended its shelf life. Applying this process, he was able to supply tins of cheese to soldiers in World War I and rapidly expand his company's market throughout the U.S. and beyond.

Although the company merged with Phenix Cheese Corp. in 1928 and was acquired by National Dairy Products Corp. in 1930, Kraft remained at the helm of the business he founded. During his lifetime, the company successfully introduced Velveeta (1928), Miracle Whip (1933), macaroni and cheese dinner (1936), Parkay margarine (1937), sliced cheese (1949), and Cheez Whiz (1952).

Kraft was a genius in promoting his company's products and associating quality with its brand. In 1933 the company began to sponsor the long-running and popular radio variety show called the *Kraft Music Hall*. It featured the top entertainers of the day. From 1947 to 1958, the company sponsored the prestigious *Kraft Television Theatre*, a drama series.

Kraft, a generous philanthropist as well as a businessman, gave primarily to religious organizations. "The only investment I ever made which has paid consistently increasing dividends," he said, "is the money I have given to the Lord."

Henry Cutler

Henry Cutler, a founding member of one of Chicago's most distinguished law firms, Chapman & Cutler, lived at 407 Central Avenue with his wife Henrietta and six children from 1921 until his death in 1959.

Chapman & Cutler is nationally known for its work in the field of public finance: advising public officials, underwriters, and investors regarding bond and tax issues. After joining Theodore Chapman's law office in 1913, Cutler took over the municipal bond practice, and Chapman & Cutler became the region's go-to municipal bond law firm.

Cutler was born in 1879 and raised on a northwest Indiana farm. He began his working life as a schoolteacher and newspaper reporter before studying law at Valparaiso University and apprenticing with lawyers in Valparaiso and Crown Point. In 1905, after three years clerking for the Indiana legislature, he came to Chicago and joined the legal staff at Chicago Title & Trust Co. Eight years later he was hired by Chapman.

Cutler is a shining example of the many professionals who freely give their talents to help their communities. In the mid-1920s he was elected to the Wilmette District 39 school board. He served for eleven years, the last eight as president. These years encompassed most of the Great Depression when D39's property tax receipts withered as folks lost their jobs and savings.

In the early 1930s D39's financial condition became dire. The board cut teachers' salaries and reduced staff. It issued tax anticipation warrants (notes to be repaid from future tax receipts) and used them to pay teachers. The district tried to sell additional warrants to banks, but they declined. It turned to local residents, but their response was lukewarm. When the school year ended in June 1934, D39 was out of money with $50,000 of overdue debts.

Cutler appealed to the public. After noting that $100,000 in warrants were still unsold, he asked, "We boast of over 15,000 population, numerous fine churches, comfortable homes, fine cars, modern public improvements, imposing clubhouses, a proud and intelligent people with over 1700 school children. Shall these 1700 school children romp the streets?" Then he laid it on the line: The schools won't reopen in the fall unless the warrants are sold. "Whether Wilmette shall suffer such a calamity and proclaim to the world such utter disregard of public duty is a matter for serious consideration by every citizen." In the end, residents came through.

When Cutler retired as D39 president in 1937, his colleagues credited him with restoring "the gratifying financial condition of the schools" and mentioned the contribution of his law firm: "During these years Mr. Cutler has not only given freely of his own time but the legal services of the firm of Chapman and Cutler have been at the call of the schools and without any cost for service rendered."

A Chapman & Cutler in-house history contrasts the two men who led the firm during its early years: They "were very different people but they hit it off. Cutler was a meticulous and sober lawyer with a warm heart, liked by most everybody both in and out of the firm. TS [the initials by which Chapman was known] was a dynamo, albeit careful and conservative, and his personality did not suit everyone. TS acknowledged that there were tasks for which Cutler was better suited than he—indeed, TS never had a problem working with personalities different from his so long as everyone recognized that he was the boss."

Today, Chapman & Cutler employs more than 230 attorneys in six U.S. cities, serving clients in the financial services sector.

Arthur Andersen was the paragon of integrity in the accounting profession. Courtesy of North-western Libraries, McCormick Library of Special Collections and University Archives.

Arthur Andersen

Arthur Andersen, founder of one of America's premier accounting firms, was born in Plano, Illinois on May 30, 1885. He was the son of parents who had recently immigrated from Norway. From 1924 to the mid-1930s he lived at 930 Chestnut Avenue with his wife Emma and three children.

Andersen knew from a young age that he wanted to be a CPA, but he was orphaned at age 16 and had to get there on his own. He worked as a bookkeeper while attending classes at the University of Illinois where he received, in 1908, a certificate to be a CPA, the youngest in Illinois (age 23) at the time. Over the next four years, he was associated with Price Waterhouse, Allis-Chalmers, and the Uhlein family of Milwaukee. In 1913 he and Clarence DeLaney, a colleague at Price Waterhouse, bought an accounting firm and changed its name to Andersen, DeLaney & Co. When DeLaney left in 1918, the name was changed again to Arthur Andersen & Co. Andersen was the senior partner until his death in 1947, when the firm was one of the nation's Big 5 accounting firms with offices in 16 U.S. cities, plus London, Paris, and Mexico City.

Besides leading his firm, Andersen taught accounting at Northwestern University from 1909 to 1922. He received a bachelor's degree in business administration from Northwestern in 1917, and he later served on its board of trustees and was president of the board in 1930. He was a paragon of honesty and high ethical standards in the accounting profession, and he introduced practices and procedures to assure that his high standards were observed throughout the firm. His mother, who died when he was only 14, had impressed on him a Norwegian axiom that translates, "Think straight and talk straight." He would have never tolerated the practices that led to the firm's demise in 2002.

Carl Wickman

Carl Wickman, founder and president of Greyhound bus lines, lived in Wilmette with his wife Olga and their two children at 16 Canterbury Court from 1938 to 1954. He was born in Sweden with the name Martis Jerk on August 7, 1887. After immigrating to the U.S. from Sweden in 1905, he adopted a more "American" moniker.

Wickman initially settled in Hibbing, Minnesota, a town in the heart of the Mesabi Iron Ore Range, and worked in the mining industry. He boarded with a family of Swedish immigrants that included a young girl (Olga Roden) who, ten years later, would become his wife. They would have two children, Carl and Jean. His first few years in Hibbing did little to foretell the successful business career that was coming.

The Greyhound logo traces its origin to Fageol Motor Co. "safety buses" (circa 1921). Courtesy of Citizen Auto Stage Co.

In 1914, when he was laid off from his last mining job as a drill operator, he started down a new highway. He and two other Swedes, Andrew Anderson and Carl Heed, purchased a seven-passenger Hupmobile and formed Wickman & Anderson, a "first class auto livery," to transport miners between their homes and the mines for 15 cents a ride. In those early days they carried up to 18 passengers per trip, with some passengers riding on the running boards and fenders.

The livery business was highly competitive at the time, with many owners offering their cars for hire. By 1925, there were 6,500 bus companies in the U.S. The average company operated two vehicles. Long-term success would require expanding into new territories, eliminating competitors, establishing inter-city routes with reliable scheduled service, upgrading equipment, and offering fares that appealed to potential travelers.

From the start, Wickman and his partners were aggressive. They invested their profits in new bus-type vehicles and established scheduled runs. They soon merged with a young competitor and mechanic, Ralph Bogan, to form Hibbing Transportation Co. Two more partners joined the business in late 1915, forming the Mesaba Transportation Co. By 1917, 14 buses were regularly carrying passengers and freight as far north as Bear River and as far south as Grand Rapids, MN. In 1919 the partners created a subsidiary, the Mesaba Motor Co., to manufacture and repair auto and bus bodies.

In 1922, the ownership of the two Mesaba companies split. Wickman and Heed took sole ownership of the Motor Co. and moved to Duluth, while the Transportation Co. remained in Hibbing in the hands of the others. At this point, Wickman's tremendous business acumen emerged. Through a highly complicated series of acquisitions, mergers, and financial arrangements, he created a bus empire consisting of multiple regional lines, all united under the Greyhound brand. Perhaps the most notable transaction occurred in 1925 when the Great Northern Railway, the dominant railroad in Minnesota, decided not to compete with Wickman's bus operations but instead to become an investor and coordinate rail and bus operations. The Great Northern's infusion of capital funded Wickman's ongoing expansion and success.

How did Wickman's enterprise become known as Greyhound bus lines? During the 1920s he acquired a Wisconsin line that operated "safety coaches" manufactured by the Fageol Motor Co. The low, sleek appearance of these grey-painted Fageol buses caused them to be nicknamed "greyhounds." In 1929 Wickman adopted the name for his entire enterprise and made the sprinting dog one of the most time-honored logos in American history.

Greyhound's headquarters moved from Duluth to Chicago in 1930. That's when the Wickman family moved to Evanston and in 1938 to Wilmette. Their daughter Jean married Ralph Bogan Jr., the son of his early partner. Wickman served as president of Greyhound until 1946 and then became chairman. He retired in 1951 and died in 1954 while vacationing in Florida.

Dining at Charlie Trotter's Armitage Avenue restaurant was a truly unique experience. Courtesy of the Trotter family.

The Great Restaurateurs: Berghoff and Trotter

Herman Berghoff opened his cafe in Chicago in 1898 as a place to sell the beer he brewed in Ft. Wayne, Indiana. At the beginning, he sold a stein of beer for five cents and included a free sandwich. In 1913 he moved the café to its current location at 17 West Adams Street. During prohibition, the cafe survived by expanding its menu and serving its own line of soft drinks.

Clement and Lewis Berghoff, who both lived in Wilmette, were Herman's youngest sons. Clement lived at 727 Laurel Avenue (1932–1937) and 640 Gregory Avenue (1937–1981). Lewis lived at 1128 Greenwood Avenue (1936–1969). Clement joined his father's business in 1929 at age 35, and Lewis joined in 1935 at age 44. Over the next 30 years, they expanded the café by creating a two-room restaurant on the first floor and a more casual restaurant downstairs. Clement managed the staff at the front, and Lewis took care of the menu and the finances in the back. Patrons liked the classic German cuisine, the reasonable prices, the convenient location, and the old world atmosphere. Berghoff's became a Chicago institution.

Charlie Trotter might consider it an insult to include him in a chapter about business, because he was truly a creative artist. He was born in 1959 and was raised at 2822 Blackhawk Road. He learned his craft mainly by reading cookbooks, practicing in his own kitchen, eating at fine restaurants, and working under great chefs.

Charlie opened his own restaurant at 816 Armitage Avenue in Chicago at age 28 and was soon recognized as one of the top chefs in the world. Among the keys to his success were his creative recipes, quality ingredients, tasty cuisine, ever-changing menus, elegant service, and intense and constant search for perfection. He introduced one of the first multi-course tasting menus, replacing the typical three-course approach to dining. Charlie closed his restaurant in 2012 and died the following year.

News Flashes from the Business Community

- February 2, 1898: The Village of Gross Point faced destruction from a wind-driven fire that originated at the Felke & Miller greenhouses at Ridge Road and Washington Avenue. The greenhouse complex was destroyed, and neighboring buildings were in grave jeopardy. The only sources of water were neighborhood wells and a pipe supplying water to the greenhouses from the Evanston water system. Wilmette firefighters were called to the scene with their hose cart, but when they connected the hose to the pipe, the pressure was insufficient to create a stream. Firefighters responded by placing blankets on the roofs of endangered buildings and forming bucket brigades. Water was passed from the wells to the buildings, and the rooftop blankets were kept saturated so that flying embers wouldn't spread the flames. After several hours, the fire burnt out, and the danger passed. Five persons were injured, and property damage was $35,000.

- December 22, 1899: Richard Dalton, 44, of 1148 Isabella Street, is demonstrating the capability of his revolutionary trenching machine while performing a 10,000-foot trenching job for the City of Evanston. The machine, powered by steam, is digging a trench three feet wide and six feet deep at the rate of one foot per minute and, so far, it has done 55 times the work that men with shovels could do in the same time. Dalton, who has no training in mechanical engineering, spent years creating his invention, which is now receiving nationwide acclaim.

This illustration of Richard Dalton's trenching machine
appeared in the *Pittsburgh Daily Post,* September 2, 1900.

- July 22, 1906: A huge fire at Hoffmann Brothers Coal and Lumber Co., 1208 Central Avenue, consumed buildings, wagons, harnesses, coal, and lumber. Three horses died in the blaze. Also destroyed were four lumber-filled box cars, owned by C&NW, that were parked on a siding some distance away. The combined efforts of Wilmette and Evanston firefighters were needed to prevent an even more widespread conflagration. The fire was clearly arson, as were two other small fires at the same location within the past two months. Proprietor John Hoffmann pointed his finger at labor unions, who he claimed are angry that he's selling building materials to non-union home builders. Total damages amounted to $38,000.

- August 19, 1906: Gross Point farmers and Wilmette businessmen united to form a "vigilance committee" to prevent more cases of arson. Since the Hoffman Bros. fire almost one month ago, eight more fires of an incendiary nature have destroyed homes and business property in the area. Committee members, operating in coordination with the police department, will patrol the streets at night and challenge every stranger at the point of a shotgun. Hubert Schwall, one of the house-fire victims, warned, "There may be some shooting, and somebody may be badly hurt, but in the end we're going to have this part of Cook County safe to live in. I don't know who has been lighting these fires, but when we find out it will be very bad for the person, whoever he may prove to be."

- February 16, 1907: Wilmette complained to the Chicago City Council about the tolls being charged by the City's telephone franchisee for calls from Wilmette to the City. Village Trustee Henry Gardiner, 34, of 720 Lake Avenue, is chair of the village board's public service committee. He argues that the current rate for a call to Chicago—10 cents for one minute, 15 cents for two or three minutes, and 5 cents for each additional minute—is too high for Wilmette's 600 phone customers, many of whom are Chicago businessmen. He's requesting that the rate be lowered to 5 cents for a three-minute conversation.

- June 10, 1911: Wilmette's justice of the peace, attorney Joseph Arns, 53, of 325 Park Avenue, was caught soliciting "marriage business" in the County Building in Chicago's Loop. Until recently, Evanston's justice of the peace, William Stacey, 68, had enjoyed the exclusive right to perform marriages at the county clerk's office. He charged $3.50 per wedding and reportedly earned $12,000 to $15,000 per year. Stacey was ousted from this "marriage mill" when numerous underage marriages came to light. Arns sought to exploit the situation by camping at the County Building and passing out cards announcing his availability to perform marriages, even after the county clerk, having been burned by the Stacey scandal, banned this type of solicitation in the building.

- October 20, 1913: John Fielding, 51, of 425 Washington Avenue, was found guilty of embezzling $4,900 from his former employer, the Northwestern Gas Light and Coke Co., and was sentenced to one to ten years in the Joliet penitentiary. Fielding disappeared with the funds more than three years ago. His colleagues, friends, and wife were baffled. For 16 months, he spent the money while traveling in Canada and Europe. On Christmas Day, 1911, he surrendered to New York police. "My conscience drove me to come back to America and give myself up," he explained.

- November 3, 1914: Two burglars broke into the office of Edinger & Speidel (dealers in coal, coke, and building materials at 1301 Lake Avenue) at 2:00 AM. They wrecked the safe and stole $800. Two men working as house movers in the area noticed the broken door, became suspicious, went to investigate, and confronted the burglars inside. The burglars pretended to be watchmen. One casually lit a cigar, while the other calmly explained, "The burglars made a good haul and they got away before we discovered the broken door. I think they got about $600 or $700. It's all right boys; just go on with your house moving job." The two house movers left, but one remained suspicious and contacted the police. By the time police arrived, the burglars were gone.

- July 21, 1914: A proposal to build and operate an osteopathic sanitarium at the southwest corner of Linden Avenue and Sheridan Road was rejected by the village board. This plan, presented by Dr. Lawrence Clarence H. Zeigler, 44, of Chicago, was doomed from the start. Wilmette has an ordinance that prohibits the establishment of a hospital or similar institution without the village board's consent, and the plan stirred grave and insurmountable opposition from homeowners in the residential neighborhood.

- April 3, 1917: John Schaefer, reputedly the first white child born in New Trier Township (on October 23, 1844) died today. He built a two-story hotel, one of the area's first such establishments, at the corner of Ridge Road and Schiller Avenue in Gross Point and operated it for 26 years before turning it over to his son George. "His place was noted for its hospitality, and he became a favorite with all who went his way."

- January 12, 1918: A second paralyzing storm (eight inches of snow, winds of 30 mph, and temperatures of 14 below) struck the Chicago metropolitan area. Less than one week ago, on January 8, when there was already 4.5 inches of snow on the ground, the area's worst blizzard in recorded history brought 14.8 inches of snow and winds peaking at 70 mph. This triple whammy caused roads and rails to be blocked by drifts up to eight feet high. The most critical problems are the curtailment of coal and milk deliveries to homes and the danger of fires that are inaccessible to firefighters.

- April 26, 1918: Wilmette and Kenilworth residents are agitated by a proposal that would "industrialize" their residential neighborhood and diminish their property values. The proposal involves a parcel of 15 acres, more or less, immediately west of the C&NW tracks and south of Kenilworth. The parcel was annexed by Wilmette in 1912, and for several years the neighbors have successfully fought off a proposal to extend a railroad siding into the area to accommodate factory uses. The current proposal by an Evanston teaming company is to stable 40 horses in a building on the property to service a three-year grading project in Winnetka.

- November 18, 1921: Two days ago, Wilmette's Zoning Commission held the final meeting to hear public comment on the proposed zoning ordinance. The most divisive issue—whether the territory west of the C&NW tracks would be zoned residential or industrial—was seemingly resolved to the satisfaction of west-siders, who fought indignantly against industrial zoning. Yesterday, the *Chicago Tribune* poured salt on the healing wound when reporting on the meeting's outcome: "The village is divided by the North Western railroad tracks, the east half being a residence section and the west a factory district." Reacting to the wrath of west-side residents, the *Tribune* today issued a correction: "There is no factory district in either the west or east part of the village."

- November 16, 1922: Muriel Dalton, of 1006 Michigan Avenue, is quoted in a nationwide advertising campaign on behalf of English Beauty Clay, a facial cream. The ads cite an outlandish assertion by the popular women's magazine, *Ladies' Home Journal,* that "the healthy woman who looks her age is either stupid or lazy." Mrs. Dalton claims to have been outraged by this assertion until she tried English Beauty Clay. The product "took ten years off my age in 40 minutes," she claims. One problem: There's no Muriel Dalton living at 1006 Michigan or any other place in Wilmette. The house at 1006 Michigan is occupied by the Robert Ricksen family. He's in the advertising business.

- July 20, 1926: Milton Reed Barker, 74, a physician who lives at 730 Central Avenue and practices in the Village Center, reports that the Village's recent annexation of the vast territory west of Illinois Road has derailed his plan to build a hospital on Locust Road. In the early 1920s Dr. Barker purchased a site on the east side of Locust Road, midway between Lake and Wilmette avenues, intending to build a hospital. At that time, the property was beyond Wilmette's western boundary. The recent annexation has made the site subject to Wilmette's zoning controls which don't allow hospitals in residential areas.

- November 15, 1931: Catherine O'Brien, 51, of 336 Greenleaf Avenue, was again featured in a *Chicago Tribune* ad endorsing Rinso, the granulated soap used by millions of Americans "in tub, washer and dishpan." O'Brien praised the product: "Rinso suds are so quick and active, they're almost alive. How they make the dirt let go! Clothes come out so white, I never even think about boiling them." However, O'Brien may have had reservations about her endorsement: She signed it using her maiden name (O'Brien), not her married name (Tracey) that she's used exclusively for the past 23 years. Tracey is president of St. Francis Xavier's PTA.

- October 7, 1934: One hundred Wilmette business and professional men were deputized as police officers, supplied with badges, equipped with firearms, trained in police tactics, and placed "on call" in case of trouble. This action was taken in response to recent acts of violence and intimidation by a Chicago labor union trying to organize truck drivers employed by North Shore florists and dry cleaning plants. The men were placed in three divisions corresponding to the business districts of the village: 4th and Linden, Village Center, and Ridge Road. A Chicago police official called Wilmette's deputies "a vigilante group worthy of duplication in other suburbs."

- December 12, 1935: Allan Lundberg, 17, of 515 5th Street, claiming to be the son of Police Chief Cloyd McGuire, ordered 19 hamburgers at the Wilmette restaurant of Nicholas Allans, 41, and told the restaurateur to charge them to "his father's account." Allans filled the order but called the police to confirm "the son's" identity. Lundberg was arrested and charged with obtaining property under false pretenses. He explained, "I was hungry."
- February 8, 1938: An enormous blast rocked the Aero Motor Co., a Chrysler and Plymouth dealership at 721 Green Bay Road. The heating plant in the basement exploded, causing three automobiles on the first floor to slam into the ceiling above before crashing in a heap in the basement below. The manager, a salesman, and two mechanics were dazed but not seriously injured. A manhole cover in front of the building was shot 40 feet into the air and narrowly missed a passing automobile when it landed.
- September 12, 1940: Rudolph Bergeson, 37, is asking the Cook County Zoning Board to let him establish a small amusement park at the northwest corner of Illinois Road and Skokie Boulevard. This location is within no municipality, so the county's lax zoning rules are the only obstacle to this enterprise. Bergeson previously operated the little railroad in No Man's Land on the lakeshore, where he also operates a Wimpy's hamburger stand at 1501 Sheridan Road. The amusement park proposal caused residents of Indian Hill Estates to "quake a bit," so Wilmette's village board instructed the village attorney to oppose the request. He told the zoning board that if the county grants the request, "property values all around the area would be cut in half."
- May 22, 1947: Late-night burglars made a clean getaway from the A&P grocery store at 811 Green Bay Road with the contents of the store's safe. They were able to blow the safe open without attracting attention by moving it into the store's freezer where the sound of the explosion was muffled. How were they able to move a safe weighing hundreds of pounds? They placed it on a dozen bars of soap, dampened the floor, and slid the safe into the freezer. Police called it "one of the slickest jobs they had ever seen."

CHAPTER 8

★────────────★

Churches, Temples, and Clergy

In his classic work, *Democracy in America,* published in 1835, Alexis de Tocqueville stressed the importance of religion in a free society: "The safeguard of morality is religion, and morality is the best security of law as well as the surest pledge of freedom." Since its founding, Wilmette has been blessed by the presence of welcoming religious institutions that have promoted values essential for living in a harmonious community and nation.

Today, fewer Americans are turning to churches and synagogues for moral direction. Long-term declines in membership and attendance, particularly among younger generations, have emerged both nationally and among Wilmette's 15 active congregations. This trend is especially worrisome at a time when long-standing and generally-accepted notions of right and wrong are being overwhelmed by the forces of power, profit, and pleasure.

This chapter doesn't attempt to describe the rich history of religion and religious institutions in Wilmette. What follows are just a few stories that you may find of interest.

Rev. William Netstraeter, Religious and Civic Leader

In the late 19th century, William Netstraeter, a Catholic priest serving the German-American community of Gross Point, became president of the largely Protestant village of Wilmette. Voters elected him to the office of village trustee from 1882 to 1888 and from 1889 to 1891. On three occasions, his colleagues on the village board chose him to fill a vacancy in the office of village president.

Wilmette during this period was much smaller. Its western boundary was Ridge Road. Its population was about 1,500. Most residents were Protestants. Many commuted to places of business in Chicago. The Village of Gross Point lay to the west of Ridge Road. Its population was under 500. Most residents were German immigrants or their descendants. Many were Roman Catholic farmers who spoke German as a first or second language.

William was born in Westphalia, Germany in 1843. His education pointed him toward the Catholic priesthood. In 1867 he immigrated to America, completed his studies at St. Francis de Sales Seminary in Milwaukee, and was ordained in 1868. William's first mass was celebrated at St. Joseph Church. Although the church was located in Wilmette, it served mainly the German-American population of Gross Point. He spent four years in downstate Illinois and then returned to St. Joseph as pastor for 52 years.

William earned the respect of Wilmette residents by courageously opposing the saloons along Ridge Road in Gross Point. Wilmette and neighboring North Shore communities were "dry," and their residents thought the saloons were offensive or worse. William believed that these establishments degraded Gross Point and threatened the youth of the parish. His stand was unpopular with many of his parishioners.

A major issue in the 1880s and 1890s was public education. In 1883 Illinois adopted a law making school attendance compulsory for children from age eight to 14. Both Wilmette and Gross Point built public elementary schools in the 1880s and 1890s. William was a strong supporter of education. Under his leadership, St. Joseph built a school in 1873 and enlarged it in 1876 and again in 1892. By 1894 St. Joseph School had 350 pupils.

The New Trier villages had no high school, a situation that William decried. He was a leader of the Annexation Club, which pushed for the annexation of Wilmette to Evanston, partly to gain access to Evanston High School. On two occasions in the mid-1890s annexation propositions were defeated by Wilmette voters, once by only three votes. Undeterred, William successfully pushed for the creation of New Trier Township High School, accomplished in 1899. He served on its board for eight years.

Wilmette residents also knew William as a businessman. He bought, subdivided, sold, and financed real estate. Some sales were made to newly-arrived German immigrants destined to be St. Joseph parishioners. In his business dealings, he was regarded as both shrewd and a straight-shooter.

William had positive personal qualities: He was distinguished-looking—well dressed and well-groomed—an impressive figure as he walked along Ridge Road and Lake Avenue in his frock coat and top hat. He was a proper gentleman, a life-long scholar, and a good speaker and writer. At a gathering, he commanded attention. While he was said to be autocratic and set in his ways, he was also said to be witty, practical, humble, and kind. He never turned a beggar away and never foreclosed on a defaulted mortgage. One source reported, "If shrewdness was his vice, generosity was his virtue."

William died on April 7, 1924, at the age of 81. His estate was valued at more than $300,000, the equivalent of more than $4 million today. Of course, he had no children. He was his father's only child. His mother had been married previously and had two children by that marriage. In other words, William had two half-siblings. William's mother died when he was eight years old, and his father (Franz) never remarried. Franz immigrated to America and lived with William until his death in 1910. William's half-siblings remained in Germany, had children, and also died before William. His only living heirs were the descendants of his half-siblings in Germany.

William left his entire estate to George Mundelein, Cardinal of Chicago, to be used for the construction of a new St. Joseph Church. He stipulated that this bequest would be effective only if St. Joseph's members raised the additional money required within five years after his death. The will, if valid, meant that William's heirs would take nothing.

Rev. William Netstraeter was pastor and president.
Courtesy of the Wilmette Historical Museum.

St. Joseph's parishioners satisfied the condition. They raised $180,000 within the five year period. However, William's heirs challenged the will. In three proceedings, they claimed that the will was invalid because the language of the bequest was "vague, indefinite, and uncertain" and because William wasn't of sound mind when he executed the will. The latter contention was ridiculous. Witness Peter Wagner testified, "Why, the week before he died, I took him down to the election; we talked about the election and he was as good as anybody could expect. I had no idea he was sick at all."

One legend says that German Chancellor Adolf Hitler prompted these will challenges. Supposedly, Hitler was angered over a widely-publicized speech given by Chicago's Cardinal Mundelein, the son of German immigrants. Hitler, in his early years, was an aspiring Austrian artist, and the cardinal publicly revealed his contempt for the Führer by twisting this fact and mocking him. The cardinal said, "Perhaps you will ask how it is that a nation of 60 million intelligent people will submit in fear and servitude to an alien, an Austrian paper hanger, and a poor one at that, and a few associates like Goebbels and Goring, who dictate every move of the people's lives." Hitler is said to have sent agents to Chicago to find a way to embarrass the cardinal. They supposedly hatched the scheme to challenge the will.

The facts don't support this legend. The last of the three challenges to William's will was filed in 1928, long before both Hitler's ascension to chancellor in 1933 and Cardinal Mundelein's speech in 1937. More likely, the challenges were motivated by the heirs' cupidity. Two challenges were dismissed, but the third went forward. It raised the issue whether the bequest was sufficiently clear and definite. There was enough doubt that William's executor and Cardinal Mundelein decided to settle. In 1931 the heirs were paid $30,000 to withdraw their challenge. The balance of William's estate went to the cardinal to fulfill William's wish. Construction of the new St. Joseph Church began in 1938 and was completed in 1939.

It's difficult to look back more than 100 years and understand why a community chose a specific individual to be a civic leader. Nonetheless, I think that William must have been an exceptional man to have overcome religious prejudices of his day and earned the confidence of Wilmette's mostly Protestant residents.

Rev. William Walker, the Undiplomatic Preacher

"Never bite the hand that feeds you." This old expression has no Biblical origin, but perhaps Rev. William Walker would have been wise to consider it during his extensive studies for the ministry.

Walker was born in 1864 and raised in Flint, Michigan. He graduated from the University of Michigan (1887), Andover Theological Seminary (1892), and the University of Strasbourg (1894). He was ordained as a Congregational minister (1894) and began his career as a pastor. He served at churches in Chelsea, Michigan (1895–1896) and Emporia, Kansas (1896–1898), and then he was called to Wilmette's First Congregational Church.

Rev. Walker's career might have bypassed Wilmette if his references had been checked more carefully. The church was undoubtedly impressed by the young man's educational credentials and brief pastorates at two other churches, but it probably didn't know about a big problem he had in Chelsea with the area's large German-American population. On March 5, 1895, he delivered a lecture entitled "The Germans at Home." It was a "general tirade against the country, people and customs." He characterized German society as "rotten" and its people as "hogs." He accused the German military of "social impurity," asserting that "every military officer had his mistress and didn't care if everybody knew it." He said there was "scarcely a virtuous servant girl in the empire." Several Germans in the audience walked out, and "every prominent German in the city" condemned the lecture's "wholesale denunciation" of Germans. This ended Rev. Walker's pastorate in Chelsea.

The lesson of Chelsea went unlearned. Rev. Walker was already "skating on thin ice" in Wilmette by 1902. He characterized the congregation as "unprogressive" and, by implication, himself as "progressive." He asserted that the women didn't like his "appearance," especially his hair brushed in the "pompadour style" which, he said, was adopted to please his mother-in-law. He confessed, "I have never been led to believe that I am a handsome man. Many people would rather see a good looking man than hear a good sermon."

The straws that broke the camel's back were two sermons condemning "speculation." Widely quoted in the national press, they were delivered in February 1902 to his Wilmette congregation that included brokers and their families and friends. He explained, "The man who makes a cent on the Board of Trade or elsewhere through someone's loss is a robber. Wealth so gained is only wealth stolen. Some fortunes are made by thrift. There are men who are worth a fortune to society and succeed in collecting the debt. Thomas A. Edison, for instance, collected the debt. But many fortunes have been made, in whole or

Rev. William Walker cited his "appearance" as a reason for his troubles as pastor.
This illustration appeared in the *Detroit Free Press*, February 1, 1895.

in part, through speculation. If the speculator does not get his return out of the expenditure of his own brain and brawn, where does he get it? Evidently out of other people's brain and brawn."

The big shots at the Board of Trade shot back. Alonzo Curry said he would remember the minister's words the next time a church committee came begging for a subscription. Luther Bodman said, "There's little satisfaction in criticizing the statements of a man who clearly doesn't know what he's talking about." Sam Scotten opined, "Surely, as a matter of business, I fail to see wherein Board of Trade work is not fully as legitimate as preaching." Warren Lamson responded, "There's what might be called a legitimate speculative element in everything. The minister's statements are absurd."

Rev. Walker left Wilmette. He served a pastorate at the Congregational Church in South Haven, Michigan (1903–1912), and then was a professor at a string of colleges, ending his career at Berea College in 1937. Perhaps he was more suited to higher education, a safer haven for provocative thinking.

Rev. Edward Vattmann, Army Chaplain, Roosevelt Friend

A couple of years ago, I came across a photograph on the Wilmette Public Library's website. It was supposedly taken in about 1918 by longtime Wilmette resident Nathaniel Webb. It shows a crowd standing on the west platform of the C&NW depot in Wilmette. The caption describes the scene as "residents waiting along the railroad tracks for Theodore Roosevelt's train to pass." It continues, "Roosevelt was on his way to the Great Lakes Naval Station to visit Father Edward J. Vattmann, Army chaplain during World War I."

A German-born Catholic priest, Vattmann became a chaplain during the Indian campaigns of the late 1800s, and for many years he was chaplain at Fort Sheridan. He and Colonel Roosevelt became acquainted in Cuba during the Spanish–American War. In 1902 he was sent by President Roosevelt to the Philippines to investigate alleged misconduct by the Spanish friars toward the native Filipinos, and he helped the U.S. government and the church resolve that problem. Following his retirement from the Army in 1904 with the rank of major, he settled in Wilmette at 1733 Lake Avenue and was attached to St. Joseph's Church. From that point forward, he became an active participant in Wilmette's civic life. At the outbreak of World War I, he went to Washington, D.C., secured his reappointment as Fort Sheridan's chaplain, and returned to active duty. He died in 1919.

While I admire Father Vattmann's service to country and community, I had doubts about the photo. Father Vattmann wasn't assigned to the Great Lakes Naval Station, and as an Army chaplain, he had no obvious reason for being there. I could find only one record of a Roosevelt visit to this area in 1918, the last full year of his life, and he merely changed trains in downtown Chicago.

And then a random mouse click removed my doubts. It revealed a photograph of Roosevelt seated on a reviewing stand at Fort Sheridan as 4,000 troops paraded by. The date was September 27, 1917. Seated with the former president were four men, including Father Vattmann. A second photograph showed Roosevelt disembarking from a C&NW train upon his arrival at Fort Sheridan that day. Behind him in the train's vestibule was Father Vattmann.

Further research revealed that Roosevelt arrived in Chicago on September 26, 1917. That evening, he spoke to a large and enthusiastic crowd in Dexter Pavilion at the stock yards to appeal for national unity as World War I dragged on. Following an invocation by Father Vattmann, Roosevelt opened his speech by gesturing toward the priest and saying, "If I had been allowed to raise a division to go to the other side, I should have had as my divisional chaplain at headquarters Father Vattmann. Father Vattmann's creed is not my creed, but I strive with stumblings and shortcomings to act in the spirit of his preachings and his practice. Father Vattmann was born on the other side of the ocean, in Germany, and he is just exactly as good an American as I am."

The following morning, Roosevelt and Father Vattmann boarded a C&NW train and travelled to Fort Sheridan. The crowd on the Wilmette platform waited patiently to view their two heroes pass by, and Nathaniel Webb snapped the photo that eventually found its way to the Wilmette Library's files, albeit with an inexact caption.

Was there more evidence of a close friendship between Father Vattmann and Theodore Roosevelt? Indeed there was, dating back to Roosevelt's failed presidential campaign of 1912. Roosevelt had succeeded William McKinley as president following McKinley's assassination in 1901. In 1904, as a candidate for president, he pledged that he wouldn't seek another term. In 1912 he changed his mind and tried to unseat his hand-picked successor, William Howard Taft. Roosevelt was disenchanted by Taft's conservatism and challenged him for the Republican Party's presidential nomination. Failing that, he deserted the party and ran on the Progressive (Bull Moose) ticket.

The 1912 campaign brought Roosevelt to Milwaukee on October 14 for a speech. Shortly before 8:00 PM he left the Gilpatrick Hotel and entered a car waiting to take him to the Auditorium. Just then, a deranged man, John Schrank, shot him in the right breast with a .38 Colt revolver from a distance of seven feet. The bullet, slowed by Roosevelt's heavy clothing and items in his breast pocket, penetrated no vital organ. Roosevelt insisted, "I will make this speech or die." He went on to the Auditorium and spoke for almost an hour while becoming weak from loss of blood.

Afterwards, he was transported by special train to Chicago's Mercy Hospital. There he asked for Father Vattmann. He explained, "I'm not much alarmed about my spiritual condition, but I would like to see Vattmann and talk to him just the same. I've known him for a long time. We were in the Army together."

When Father Vattmann received the summons, he feared that Roosevelt was dying. He called Dr. George Butler, a physician and surgeon who lived at 1011 Lake Avenue. Together, the two men rushed to Mercy Hospital, arriving shortly after 7:00 AM. Father Vattmann and Roosevelt spoke for about 25 minutes. Upon departing, the priest reported that "the colonel" would survive: there was little danger he would die. Dr. Butler was then admitted. Roosevelt, looking as if nothing were wrong, thrust his hand out to grasp the doctor's. He smiled and enthused, "I'm glad to meet a friend of Father Vattmann." The doctor replied, "Mr. President, you were elected last night. It was the turning of the tide in your favor."

Nathaniel Webb's photo shows Wilmette residents waiting for the C&NW train carrying Theodore Roosevelt and Father Vattmann from Chicago to Fort Sheridan on September 27, 1917. Courtesy of the Wilmette Historical Museum.

Dr. Butler learned a lesson that morning: Stick to medical prognoses. Roosevelt defeated Taft but lost to Woodrow Wilson. During the years that followed, though, he remained an enthusiastic booster of "Americanism" and friend of Father Vattmann. In the midst of World War I he spoke the following words at Wittenberg College:

"I accepted the invitation to come here, from the president of Wittenberg College, who informed me he wished me because Wittenberg College, founded by Lutherans of German blood, was American and nothing else, and that he wanted me to preach the straightest and stiffest doctrine of Americanism, exactly such doctrine as I have been preaching all of my life, and most of all during the past four years. To emphasize the quality of true Americanism, President Heckert, the president of this Lutheran college, has asked my old and deeply valued friend, Monsignor Vattmann to come, so that it is a Lutheran preacher and a Catholic ecclesiastic who give the invocation and the benediction of this meeting. Both alike are of German blood, and both of them are as straight and good Americans as are to be found in the whole United States, bone of our bone and flesh of our flesh, Americans in body and in spirit, standing like all other good Americans, for America and the allies of America, and against the Prussianized Germany of today and all her allies and vassal states."

The two friends died in the same year, 1919. The priest's obituary, published in the *Chicago Tribune* on September 20, 1919, contained this statement: "Roosevelt never passed through Chicago without paying a visit to Father Vattmann in Wilmette." Wow! I was impressed. How interesting that one of America's most fascinating presidents was not only a friend of a Wilmette resident, but was also a regular visitor to Wilmette. I wanted to learn more. I assumed that these regular visits by a famous man from faraway Oyster Bay, New York would be well documented and that newspaper articles, photographs, and reminiscences would abound.

Alas, the evidence is meager. One newspaper article alluded to a visit by Roosevelt. It was written decades after the event it described. It quotes Esther Hoffman, a longtime resident born in 1898, saying that she was present at the Wilmette depot when a double line of Boy Scouts from Troop 1 greeted Roosevelt as he arrived to visit Father Vattmann. The time frame thus would be late 1910 (when Troop 1 was established) to early 1919 (when Roosevelt died).

A second article, in the *Chicago Tribune* of Monday, May 1, 1916, contains detailed evidence of a visit by Roosevelt. At the time, Europe was mired in World War I. The article reported that on the prior Saturday evening, Roosevelt addressed 1,500 members of the Chicago Bar Association at the LaSalle Hotel to advocate for U.S. military preparedness, universal military service, and national unity. On Sunday morning, he attended services at Chicago's

On the reviewing stand at Fort Sheridan on September 27, 1917 are (from left) Father Vattmann, businessman Samuel Insull, Colonel James Ryan (the Fort's commanding officer), Theodore Roosevelt, and Captain Georges Etienne Bertrand (a Frenchman who instructed Army trainees in trench warfare). Courtesy of the Glenview Public Library.

new Fourth Presbyterian Church. Before the services ended, he slipped out a side door, piled into an automobile, and was whisked to the Hubbard Woods home of Harold Ickes, who was then a progressive Republican but later Secretary of the Interior under FDR. At the Ickes home, Roosevelt dined with more than two dozen prominent supporters. During the dinner, he was honored by a group of Boy Scouts standing at attention on the lawn. He left the Ickes home in ample time to catch a train back to the City, but first he stopped at Father Vattmann's home in Wilmette. As reported, "He had a few minutes chat with the 'fine old priest' who was one of the army chaplains closely associated with the Roosevelt and Taft regimes."

Despite the dearth of additional evidence, Roosevelt likely visited Father Vattmann more than once. The two men clearly had a close relationship, as confirmed once again by this note that Roosevelt sent the priest shortly before his death:

"No Christmas greeting that I have received—not even that from Cardinal Gibbons [archbishop of Baltimore]—has touched and pleased me more than yours. You have been a good soldier and a good priest; a most useful citizen and one of the staunchest of American patriots—and in addition a true and loyal friend. What higher praise can be given any man? May many happy years come to you, old friend."

The Bahá'í House of Worship

Visit the Bahá'í House of Worship. Take some time to absorb its awesome beauty. It's a stunning architectural achievement and an inspired embodiment of the beliefs of a religious movement. It's the most significant building in Wilmette—one that's proudly pictured on virtually all literature describing the village.

The temple traces its U.S. roots to Chicago's Columbian Exhibition of 1893. The World Parliament of Religions was held in conjunction with the Exhibition. It was the world's first ecumenical gathering and the first exposure that the Bahá'í movement received in America. By 1907 Chicago's growing Bahá'í community numbered 500 adherents.

A 1910 *Chicago Tribune* article was headlined "FREAK RELIGIONS FROM ALL OVER THE WORLD FIND HOME IN ONE CHICAGO SKYSCRAPER." The article reported that space in Chicago's Masonic Temple was being used by "exponents of strange creeds and cults." Bahá'í was the first example cited in the article. (So much for religious tolerance and open-mindedness in 1910.)

The Bahá'ís' dream of a North American temple drew them to the idyllic seven-acre lakeside setting at Sheridan Road and Linden Avenue. They started purchasing the lots in 1908. The total cost of the property, including a 293-foot lakefront tract on the east side of Sheridan Road, was $51,500. Corrine Knight True, who lived at 418 Forest Avenue from 1928 until her death in 1961, was called "the mother of the Bahá'í Temple". She and a colleague selected the site for the temple, and until 1920 she served as treasurer of the construction funds donated from around the world.

By 1920 the Bahá'ís had raised $300,000, and they applied for a building permit to construct the temple's foundation. At the time, building permits required village board approval. The approval process gave citizens a chance to wade in. The proposed temple was the subject of intense community debate. The opponents came out in force and presented these arguments:

- Wilmette is a residential community. The temple would disrupt the peace and quiet that attracted residents here.
- Wilmette doesn't need the temple, because few if any Bahá'ís live in the village. The temple should be built where most of its members live.
- The temple's visitors, being non-residents, will have to use automobiles to travel there. Because the site offers little parking, they'll have to park on the public streets. This will cause traffic jams, especially on Sheridan Road, the area's major north-south thoroughfare.
- Bahá'ís have neither the organizational structure nor sufficient members to raise the additional $1.2 million needed for the project. The temple will never be completed, and Wilmette "will have to endure for years the unsightliness of a pile of brick and tile upon our beautiful drive at the entrance of our village." The village board should issue no permit unless and until sufficient funds are on hand to complete the entire project.
- If the Bahá'ís are successful in recruiting Wilmette residents as members, they'll draw them away from the village's existing churches and harm those institutions.
- The Bahá'ís won't say exactly how the temple will be used. They say it's up to their leader, 'Abdu'l-Bahá. The village board shouldn't issue a permit for a building whose use "is to be directed by a non-resident alien living in Asia."
- The Bahá'ís say the temple will be a place of prayer for people of all religions, but there's nothing to commend non-Christian religions, which pale in the light of "the teachings of Jesus, the founder of the only religion that brings forth fruit that has no bitterness."

Voices were also raised in support of issuing the building permit. One resident pleaded not to "allow the fear of blocking our driveways, the risk of a structure not being completed for lack of funds, or the possibility of losing members of our congregations to be our motives for refusing a permit for the construction of an edifice which, if carried out according to present architectural plans, would be a credit to Wilmette from an artistic standpoint, not only, but an honor as being the first to cooperate in a movement seeking to unite all men as brothers and children of one Father."

In the end, the Bahá'ís submitted detailed plans that complied with the village's building ordinance and assured the village board that construction would be completed, without interruption, within two years. On March 15, 1921, the board issued the building permit.

A symbolic cornerstone was laid several years before construction began. It was a discarded limestone block salvaged from a construction site and donated by a Chicago Bahá'í unable to contribute money. When the interpreter and exemplar of the faith, 'Abdu'l-Bahá, visited Wilmette in 1912 for a ceremonial groundbreaking, he directed the placement of the block and answered the question, "Why build a temple?": "The purpose of places of worship and edifices for adoration is simply that of unity, in order that various nations, divergent races, varying souls may gather there and among them amity, love and accord may be realized."

The temple's architect was Louis Bourgeois. A Bahá'í himself, he submitted a design concept that was chosen by delegates to the Bahá'í national convention in 1920. During construction, he lived and worked at a studio and home at the Bahá'í lakefront property at 536 Sheridan Road. Bourgeois died in 1930, before the temple was completed.

Work started on the foundation in 1921. To support the temple structure, nine concrete caissons, six feet in diameter, were sunk 120 feet to bedrock. The work was marred by a tragedy in 1922. William Gorman, 26, a recently married electrician employed by a contractor, fell into the North Shore Channel while troubleshooting the lighting system that allowed nighttime work. He called for help, but coworkers couldn't find him in the darkness, and he drowned.

The temple's foundation was completed later that year. It was more than a foundation; it was a base enclosure that looked like a huge mushroom from above. Called Foundation Hall, the enclosure was used for meetings until the rest of the temple was completed years later.

Construction stopped in 1922 because of dwindling funds. It didn't resume until 1930 when a contract for the superstructure was let, followed in 1932 by a contract for the exterior ornamentation. A 1931 fire in the superstructure was extinguished by Wilmette and Evanston firefighters, but not until $50,000 in damage was suffered.

The Temple's superstructure was under construction in April 1931.
Courtesy of the Wilmette Historical Museum.

The Bahá'í Temple is Wilmette's most recognized landmark today. Courtesy of
Tim Perry © National Spiritual Assembly of the Bahá'ís of the United States.

The exterior work was completed in 1943. Interior work began in 1947. The temple was completed in 1953. In a ceremony attended by 3,500 people, it was dedicated to the world community. The cost of construction rose from the original estimate of $1.5 million to more than $2.6 million. All funds were raised from Bahá'ís. No outside contributions were accepted.

In 1978 the House of Worship was listed on the National Register of Historic Places, and in 2007 the Illinois Bureau of Tourism named it one of the "Seven Wonders of Illinois." A visit to the temple and its gardens is an awesome experience that the Bahá'ís are eager to share. Before the coronavirus pandemic, they welcomed about 250,000 visitors annually.

Breaking News from the World of Religion

- July 16, 1876: Members of Wilmette's churches are engaged in a lively debate over the Fourth Commandment: "Remember the Sabbath day, to keep it holy." The debate began when one member of the Methodist Church criticized another for reading the Sunday newspaper. The issue grabbed the attention of churchgoers throughout the village. The *Chicago Tribune* reported that despite the controversy, "not one reader of the *Tribune* has ordered his subscription discontinued, and it is fair to presume that such narrow and bigoted views as are advanced against reading Sunday papers will not be accepted by the majority of the citizens of the village."
- June 17, 1902: Bad blood between neighbors—John Welter, a brick mason, and Rev. Christopher Jorgensen, assistant pastor of Wilmette's First Congregational Church—erupted in violence. The feud began when Welter refused to send his children to the preacher's Sunday school. It escalated when the two men argued over Welter's right to cut weeds on three vacant lots separating their houses. It culminated when Welter started cutting, ignoring Jorgensen's demands to stop. Jorgensen responded by casting the first stone at Welter, causing Welter to brandish his scythe and chase Jorgensen into his house. Jorgensen, in turn, armed himself with a pistol and resumed the argument from a window. Enraged by the drift of the discussion, Jorgensen discharged his pistol. The bullet struck and wounded Welter. Hundreds of angry neighbors gathered at Jorgenson's house, shouting "Lynch him!" The riot ended with Jorgenson's arrest on a charge of shooting with intent to commit murder.
- March 21, 1908: Prominent citizens of Gross Point, including John Schaeffer, 63, and Markus Mick, 70, sounded an alarm that the 350 students of St.

Joseph School, located on Lake Avenue just east of Ridge Road, are in grave danger. The warning comes just two weeks after a disastrous school fire in Collinwood, Ohio that took the lives of 161 children. Conditions in the three-story St. Joseph School are similar to conditions that led to the Collinwood tragedy: a narrow obstructed stairway that provides the sole means of egress from the upper floors. Schaefer and Mick are confident that Pastor William Netstraeter will take quick action to widen the stairway and add fire escapes.

- May 7, 1911: Relations between the well-established Congregational Church of Wilmette and the embryonic Presbyterian Church of Wilmette were strained this week. Rev. Julius Armstrong, 70, Superintendent of the Congregationalists' Missionary Society, publicly expressed his opinion that "there is no room in Wilmette at present for another church organization." Local Congregationalists publicly called on residents to attend Congregational services and "hear reasons why a new denomination should not enter the field of [the Congregationalists'] endeavors to furnish the community with churchly ministrations." (The *Chicago Tribune* erroneously reported that Wilmette has 8,000 residents and only two Protestant churches, the Congregational Church and the Methodist Church, but actually the population is significantly less than 8,000, and the *Tribune* overlooked four existing church organizations: St. Augustine's Episcopal Church, St. John's Lutheran Church, Wilmette Baptist Church, and the Church of Christ, Science.

- January 27, 1913: The Wilmette Federation of Churches, consisting of four Protestant churches and one Catholic church, marshaled 149 members of their congregations to canvas the village. Their goal is to increase church membership. At present, one-third of the village's residents have no church affiliation. Organizers estimate that 1,500 families were visited.

- December 29, 1929: The Presbyterian Church at 9th Street and Greenleaf Avenue was destroyed by fire during a heavy blizzard. The Church will conduct services at the Wilmette Woman's Club pending the construction of a new edifice.

- January 25, 1959: The National Spiritual Assembly of the Bahá'ís held an open house today to show off its new Home for the Aged, 401–413 Greenleaf Avenue. The one-story facility cost upwards of $250,000. It has 16 one-room and four two-room residences, each with its own bath. It includes amenities designed to offer a pleasant, stimulating, and safe environment for 20 residents, age 65 and older, selected without regard to creed, class, or race. Residents will pay for their room and board based on their financial ability. Construction of the facility was delayed for over one year when nearby townhouse associations and homeowners filed suit, claiming that the Village improperly granted zoning changes to allow the project without requiring the Bahá'ís to show a public necessity for the changes. The Circuit Court of Cook County recently rejected this claim.

- May 6, 1962: The Church of Jesus Christ of Latter Day Saints will dedicate the new center of its Chicago Stake tomorrow. Built at a cost of $750,000 in the 2700 block of Lake Avenue, the facility includes places for worship, recreation, meetings, and education. The center is the church's largest construction project in Illinois since 1846 when the temple at Nauvoo was completed. At that time, the Mormons were being forced to flee from Nauvoo.

- January 5, 1963: Beth Hillel congregation conducted the first service at its new temple at 3220 Big Tree Lane in the auditorium, as the sanctuary is yet to be built. The congregation has made rapid progress since February 1958 when a small steering committee met to plan for the future of a new Jewish congregation that now includes 560 families. The facilities completed to date include, in addition to the auditorium, eleven classrooms for instruction of children. Beth Hillel is the village's first Jewish congregation, reflecting the movement of many young Jewish families to Wilmette since the mid-1950s.

CHAPTER 9

★────────────────★

A Mixed Civil Rights Record

"We must now learn to live together as brothers, or we will perish together as fools," Dr. Martin Luther King said during his 90-minute civil rights address before 10,000 area residents at the Village Green in Winnetka on July 25, 1965. It was a warning 100 years in the making. As the Civil War came to a close, the U.S. adopted laws promising due process and equal protection to African-Americans throughout the nation. For decades, the promise of these laws was undermined by the prejudice of the white majority: a belief that African-Americans are intellectually and culturally inferior and should be excluded from white society. True equality requires a fundamental change in white thinking.

Attitudes have gradually changed. Today, most Wilmette residents understand the grave injustice that African-Americans have suffered. They want it to end. They're willing to do their part. They'd welcome African-American families to their neighborhoods, for example. So why do so few African-Americans live in Wilmette?

The Exclusion of African-Americans

As of July 1, 2019, the African-American population of Wilmette is estimated to be only 190 of 27,089, or 0.7 percent of the total. You might hear an explanation that the dearth of African-Americans is due to economic and social factors, not racial discrimination. Specifically, when African-Americans came north during the Great Migration, they settled on the South Side of Chicago where the steel mills, stock yards, and railroads offered employment. The unavailability of employment north of the city was a major obstacle to settling here. Anyway, birds of a feather flock together, and once the African-American communities were established in Chicago, few wanted to relocate to the North Shore, even if they had the means.

Is this a valid explanation for the statistic cited above? Or, is there a contributing factor: a history of racial intolerance that discourages African-Americans from considering Wilmette as a place to live?

The village's African-American population probably never exceeded 225, the number reported in the 1940 U.S. Census. During the village's early years, it consisted mainly of domestic employees like maids, cooks, and chauffeurs, although many Wilmette families refused to employ non-white domestic employees. The first of Wilmette's numerous "white only" help-wanted ads was published in 1912 and the last in 1961. Only two African-American families (Smiths at 1428 Wilmette Avenue and Mitchells at 1822 Walnut Avenue) lived in the village for an extended period.

In 1904 the *Chicago Tribune* reported that the towns of the North Shore—Evanston, Wilmette, Winnetka, and Glencoe—were "aroused" and "alarmed" over the "influx of Negroes." Evanston citizens proposed a "solution": create "a town for Negroes, to be located near Niles Center" (now Skokie). "To this it is proposed to deport objectionable characters."

In August 1913 a seven-room house on Elmwood Avenue near Ridge Road in Wilmette was sold to "a small colony of Negroes" (actually, two families). Residents of the area paraded through town and petitioned the village board to provide relief "from unsanitary conditions in an overcrowded house." The petition added, "We respectfully request that each citizen use his influence to prevent further bringing into the village of Negroes, particularly with the real estate dealers handling property in Wilmette, to induce them to cease selling or renting to undesirable people." The village board referred the petition to a committee.

The dealer who sold the Elmwood property was threatened with a boycott, and a white-only citizens group, the Wilmette Civic Association, was formed for the purpose of keeping African-Americans from residing or working in the village and eliminating "nuisances." Real estate dealer Milton Barker was identified as the culprit. He admitted selling two houses to African-Americans, but only as investments, not as residences. He promised not to transgress again.

The following year, an African-American janitor at a building in the Village Center received a death threat for "bringing Negroes to this village to work." The note demanded that he leave within two weeks. The unwanted employee lived in Evanston, where he was "the first Negro scoutmaster named in the Boy Scout movement and is in charge of a troop of more than 30 colored boys in Evanston."

In 1918 a white resident, intending to strike fear in his neighbors' hearts, publicly threatened to sell his Sheridan Road lakefront property to African-Americans if whites wouldn't pay his price. Ten years later, when a house on Locust Road was sold to an African-American family, neighbors denounced the real estate firm thought to be responsible. The firm defended itself, not by standing on the principle that race should be irrelevant in real estate transactions, but by insisting that it sold the house to a white flipper who quickly resold it to the African-American family. In other words, "Bad, but not my fault."

The law at that time didn't prohibit housing discrimination. Instead, it recognized the right of property owners not to sell to African-Americans. Restrictive covenants in some deeds, enforceable until 1948, prohibited home owners from selling to African-Americans (and others), but even without these covenants, a gentlemen's agreement among homeowners and real estate brokers had the same effect. Real estate brokers acknowledged that they wouldn't show properties to African-Americans because of an owner's explicit instructions, or because they assumed this was the owner's desire, or because they believed that the neighbors and community opposed integrated housing. Or maybe, because of their own bias and fear of rocking the boat.

In 1951 a prominent Wilmette broker was hired to sell the house at 1424 Wilmette Avenue, next door to one of the few Wilmette homes occupied by African-Americans. The white owner and broker assured neighbors that the house wouldn't be sold to "colored people," but neighbors were dubious. After the sale to a white purchaser, the broker wrote to her client: "Well, I guess, by now, the folks in the neighborhood of '1424' are convinced that we were not going to sell to colored people.... We feel so happy about it and know you do, too." As late as the mid-1960s, local brokers aggressively defended the right to discriminate.

Even the community's good works were tainted. During the first half of the 20th century, Arden Shore was a prominent North Shore charity that provided summer respite to the Chicago area's poor women and their children at a lakeside camp in Lake Bluff. Its supporters included many leading Wilmette citizens. A 1936 article about the camp bragged that it admitted "all races with the exception of Negroes."

Minstrel shows portrayed African-Americans as stupid, lazy, and comical. One of the first local minstrel shows was staged in 1909 by the Ouilmette Country Club, predecessor of Michigan Shores Club. Later shows, sponsored by leading civic, social, and religious organizations, were a popular form of entertainment. They featured prominent citizens and children as blackface actors. In 1950 two women in blackface were pictured on the cover of the local newspaper, promoting the American Legion's upcoming minstrel show at the Wilmette Woman's Club.

In 1938 the Wilmette Public Library presented a puppet show in the children's room. Intended to teach children about "Negroes," it was set in a cotton patch and featured Dina, "dressed in a red calico dress, a head cloth, and a white apron," with a "basket of clean wash on her head," and Mammy, who "cradles a white baby on her arm." The event also promoted several children's books dealing with "Negroes" that would be seen today as blatant reinforcements of racial stereotypes.

Crime reports in the local newspaper typically identified African-American perpetrators (unlike white perpetrators) by race. A 1914 item reported, "The Negro, who was armed with the usual weapon used by that race, a razor, slashed [a Wilmette victim] around the head and body, inflicting serious but not fatal wounds." African-Americans who achieved success were also identified by race, as if to suggest that their achievements were somehow especially remarkable and rare. In 1935 two performers at upcoming concerts were described by the local newspaper: "Marian Anderson, Negro contralto," and "Albert Spalding, American violinist." Anderson, born in Philadelphia, was one of America's most acclaimed singers of the 20th century. Wasn't she, like Spalding, "American"?

John Erwin's "Business Approach" to Racial Equity

Wilmette resident John Erwin attracted national attention twice: first for his "progressive" views on the post-bellum plight of African-Americans in the South, and later on account of the strange circumstances of his death.

John was born near the end of the Civil War on a plantation in Greenwood, Florida. His father was a colonel in the Confederate Army, a prominent citizen of Greenwood, and probably a slave owner. John observed firsthand the injustices suffered by African-Americans in the post-bellum South. He watched his father, in the presence of a corrupt U.S. marshal, stuff ballot boxes to assure that the votes of African-Americans wouldn't matter. Despite his southern background, John was considered "progressive" regarding the treatment of African-Americans at the turn of the 20th century.

John came to Chicago as a young man. In 1893 he married Sarah Bennett, daughter of Charles Bennett, a prominent Mattoon attorney, county judge, and Union Army veteran. John worked in Chicago as western agent for a New York firm that made baling twine. With the backing of investors in New York and

St. Louis, he also invested in thousands of acres of unimproved woodland in Louisiana and Mississippi. The couple's daughter, Susan, was born in 1902, and the family moved to 817 Central Avenue.

In November 1901 John wrote an article for *New Outlook*, a weekly publication edited by Al Smith, who later was New York's Governor and the Democratic Party's 1928 presidential candidate. The article was widely quoted in the national press. John described the post-bellum condition of African-Americans who worked as tenants or share croppers for plantation owners: "On many of the plantations South the Negro is an industrial serf. He is not improving as a citizen.... The landlord keeps the books and controls the cotton at settlement time. The Negro takes what is allotted to him.... [T]here is a widespread belief that the Negro can be controlled better if he is kept poor.... [O]n many plantations the Negro is in worse condition today than he was as a slave."

John urged a "business approach" to the "Negro problem"—an approach that he believed would be beneficial to African-Americans and profitable to investors. It was an approach that he himself was employing on the lands he bought in the South—selling and leasing small tracts to African-Americans at fair prices with liberal payment terms. He explained, "The mass of Negroes need cooperation, not charity. Give the Negro an alliance with the cold, hard, practical businessman. Give him a chance to substitute for himself industrial self-government in place of the industrial imperialism that prevails on the large plantation. Put him on 40 acres of land on a decent basis, and go away and let him alone. He will do the rest, and in doing it he will learn something that no school can teach.... He becomes a citizen in fact. The sons and daughters from those independent little homes will soon get for themselves educational, political, and other advantages that others cannot give them, and they will deserve those advantages."

On the night of October 25, 1909 John boarded the steamer *Puritan* at Chicago for a trip to Holland, Michigan to close a land deal. When the boat arrived the following morning, John was missing. His coat, hat, satchel, and other personal items were strewn on the floor of his locked stateroom. At the time, his health was good, his financial condition was sound, and his family-life was "ideal." The mystery of his disappearance would never be solved. Nor will America's racial problems, so long as progressive thinking about race relations, like John's, continues to drown in a sea of ignorance, fear, bigotry, complacency, and politics.

The Seeds of Unrest

In May 1919, as the World War drew to an end, civil rights leader W.E.B. Du Bois foresaw a bigger fight at home: "By the God of Heaven, we are cowards and jackasses if now that the war is over, we do not marshal every ounce of our brain and brawn to fight a sterner, longer, more unbending battle against the forces of hell in our own land." African-American soldiers had fought in Europe to protect the American values of liberty, equality, and justice. They returned home to find persistent inequality, injustice, and lack of opportunity. The war had strengthened their resolve. Within weeks of Du Bois' warning, Chicago's Red Summer riots broke out.

Rioting began on July 27 when an African-American boy, Eugene Williams, swam to a raft in the white-only area of Chicago's beach near 29th Street. White males threw rocks at Williams, causing him to fall from the raft and drown. Police refused to arrest the rock-throwers, and three days of rioting erupted. Fifteen whites and 23 African-Americans were killed, hundreds were injured, and many homes of African-Americans were burned.

A Wilmette resident, Arthur Kenning, 39, of 714 Elmwood Avenue, was an important figure in the aftermath of the riots. He was a manager at the International Tag Co. in Chicago and was one of 23 men appointed to the blue ribbon grand jury that heard evidence of crimes committed during the riots. On the very first day of deliberations, August 4, the grand jury swiftly indicted 17 African-Americans for murder and other offenses. As of August 6, though, the state's attorney had presented no cases against white rioters, and the grand jury refused to proceed based on this apparent discrimination. Finally, on August 7, the first white cases were presented, resulting in the first indictments of whites on August 12. In the end the criminal justice system disproportionately held African-Americans accountable.

Dr. Martin Bickham, Early Civil Rights Leader

During a lifetime spanning 95 years, Dr. Martin Bickham, a Methodist lay minister, sociologist, and longtime Wilmette resident at 429 9th Street, worked tirelessly on behalf of the needy, including those suffering from racial discrimination. He held important leadership positions with the Church Federation of Chicago, YMCA, United Charities of Chicago, and the Illinois WPA. In the 1930s he founded the North Shore Human Relations Council and the West Suburban Human Relations Council. In 1943 Governor Dwight Green appointed him chairman of the newly-created Illinois Interracial Commission charged with studying the growing racial conflict and making recommendations. He wrote and spoke extensively on social issues, always advancing progressive ideas. He served on the ACLU's board for many years. In the 1960s he helped organize the Wilmette Human Relations Committee (WHRC) and served as a WHRC advisor.

In 1960 the Deerfield Park Board exercised its power of eminent domain to acquire a site where a private developer was building a racially-integrated housing project. Some folks saw this action as racially motivated. Dr. Bickham and the Church Federation issued this statement: "The issues of open or integrated housing and freedom of movement and residence are ones…which ultimately must be resolved with justice to all according to sound Christian principles. No community can segregate itself from the march of historical processes which are now moving with seeming irresistible force toward justice for all and especially for those who in the past have consistently been discriminated against."

Dr. Martin Bickham was WHRC's co-founder and advisor. Courtesy of the Bickham family.

It turns out that the Church Federation's prophesy was a bit optimistic. The march toward racial justice hasn't been irresistible, but Dr. Bickham deserves recognition and honor as a local and regional leader of the effort to move past the era of racial injustice. He was honored by Wilmette's Bahá'í community in 1966 as Illinois' "Father of Human Rights." A few months later the Alumni Association of the University of Chicago recognized him for his unselfish service to the community, nation, and humanity.

The Local Civil Rights Movement Gains Steam

During the 1950s the issue of civil rights was moving to the forefront in American society. The Supreme Court ended segregation in public schools and tossed out the "separate but equal" doctrine (1954). Rosa Parks was arrested for refusing to vacate her seat on a Montgomery bus, and a long boycott began (1954). Emmett Till was lynched in Mississippi (1955), and the murderers were acquitted by an all-white male jury. President Eisenhower federalized the Arkansas National Guard and ordered the troops to support the integration of Little Rock's Central High School (1957). The widely-acclaimed play *Raisin in the Sun* premiered on Broadway (1959).

Raisin in the Sun depicted an African-American family's struggle against racism while pursuing their American Dream. The play was set in Chicago, where in real life the burgeoning African-American population was unable to find jobs, decent affordable housing, and quality schools in segregated neighborhoods. These conditions gave rise to poverty, crime, protests, race riots, and white flight.

The North Shore attitude toward the racial unrest of the 1950s probably ranged from compassion to fear to apathy. By 1960, the national civil rights movement was well underway. It was led by a charismatic African-American preacher who exposed racial injustice through inspirational speeches and peaceful demonstrations that sometimes elicited violent responses. Federal and state governments took up legislation to prohibit racial discrimination in employment, public accommodations, voting, and housing. Against this background, Wilmette and other North Shore communities began to awaken. In the spring of 1963 WHRC was formed by private citizens.

Pat and Patty Crowley were WHRC's first co-chairs. Courtesy of the Crowley family.

Pat And Patty Crowley, Leaders Of WHRC

Patrick Crowley (a business lawyer) and his wife, Patricia Caron Crowley, both devout Catholics, were the first co-chairs of WHRC. They moved to 2304 Elmwood Avenue in 1941 and lived there until 1969. During the 1940s, their search for life's meaning led them to join with other couples in small groups to discuss issues affecting marriage and family. They utilized the "inquire technique" developed by Cardinal Joseph Cardijn of Belgium: observe conditions, judge them in light of Christian teachings, and act to bring conditions into harmony with the teachings. This led, in 1949, to the founding of the Christian Family Movement (CFM). The Crowleys served as the executive secretary couple for two decades, and the organization's membership grew to over 100,000 couples in America and abroad.

Besides raising five children and leading CFM, the Crowleys hosted numerous foster children and foreign students from diverse backgrounds in their Wilmette home. They gave valuable service and financial support to many humanitarian organizations, including organizations whose mission was to promote racial justice.

They were members of a 72-person commission (the only American couple) appointed by Pope Paul VI to study the Catholic Church's position on population and birth control. Citing real-life examples of the harm to couples and families caused by the church's strict ban on all forms of birth control other than the rhythm method, they helped convince the overwhelming majority of commissioners to recommend change. They were terribly disappointed when the pope rejected the commission's recommendations, but they remained loyal Catholics.

Like Dr. Bickham, the Crowleys are inspiring local examples of lives devoted to justice for all. Their goals were worthy, but some worthy goals can't be fully achieved in a lifetime of work, despite heroic efforts.

From Planning to Action

After one year of planning and organizing, WHRC's membership exceeded 300 families. It gained the cooperation of the Bahá'í, Lutheran, Baptist, Congregational, Presbyterian, Catholic, and Jewish congregations of the village. Its first public action, in the spring of 1964, was to publish a petition in the local newspaper. Signed by more than 1,000 residents, the petition declared: "[WHRC] wants to make known that the following residents of Wilmette do not want persons excluded from living in this community on the basis of their race, color or creed."

Acting in concert with similar committees in other North Shore villages, WHRC sponsored marches, informational meetings, and petition drives in support of open housing. In the spring of 1965 WHRC and Winnetka's commission presented the play *In White America* at Howard School. Winner of a New York Drama Critics' award, the play recounts the history of African-Americans' quest for racial equality.

During the summer of 1965 WHRC joined civil rights and religious groups from eleven North Shore towns to sponsor the North Shore Summer Project. The project's goal was to end racial and religious housing discrimination on the North Shore. It targeted real estate brokers who claimed the right not to show homes to African-Americans based on the stated or presumed preferences of the homeowners and their neighbors. It began with a petition drive in which residents were asked to sign a petition supporting open housing and calling on brokers to show and sell listings on a non-discriminatory basis. More than 10,000 residents signed. The project's organizers also recruited 85 college students to survey 2,000 current home sellers regarding their willingness to sell to minorities. The students also tried to persuade these home sellers to offer their homes on a non-discriminatory basis. The survey showed that a large majority of residents would welcome or accept African-Americans as neighbors, that most home-sellers impose no racial or religious conditions on their listings, and that brokers are the main source of these restrictions. Their report urged realty firms "to establish a new policy of equal opportunity in housing for all."

Dr. Martin Luther King's Endorsement

The highlight of the North Shore Summer Project was a visit to the North Shore by Dr. Martin Luther King on Sunday evening, July 25, 1965. He spoke to an audience of 8,000–10,000 at Winnetka's Village Green. The speech occurred in the context of the national voting rights campaign. Earlier in the year, civil rights marchers on their way to Montgomery, Alabama were violently accosted outside of Selma by state and local police. The event aroused public indignation and prompted President Lyndon Johnson to use all his power and influence to push voting rights legislation through Congress. In early August, just a few days after the King speech in Winnetka, Congress passed and the president signed the Voting Rights Act of 1965.

Dr. King was in Chicago for three days (July 24–26) to support civil rights groups campaigning in the city against de facto segregation of schools, neighborhoods, and places of employment. His schedule was brutal: eight speeches on Saturday; five more before his Winnetka speech on Sunday; and a speech, luncheon, rally, and march to Chicago's City Hall on Monday.

The Winnetka event was peaceful. The crowd was mostly supportive. The weather was ideal. While waiting for Dr. King, folks picnicked and listened to folk music. The only hostile incident was the appearance of four young Chicagoans wearing Nazi-style uniforms and carrying anti-King and anti-integration signs, but they left (at the suggestion of police) before Dr. King arrived.

The speech lasted for an hour and a half. It wasn't recorded, but these excerpts, taken from press reports, are probably the crux of his message, one that's still relevant today: "History has presented us with a cosmic challenge. We must now learn to live together as brothers, or we will perish together as fools. The shape of the world today does not permit our nation the luxury of an anemic democracy. The price America must pay for continuing its oppression of the Negroes and other minority groups is the price of its own destruction."

He praised the work of the project. "We must go all out to end segregation in housing. Every white person does great injury to his child if he allows that child to grow up in a world that is two-thirds colored and yet live in conditions where that child does not come into person-to-person contact with colored people. Racism in housing will not be removed until there is an assault on the structure of power that reaps huge profits from the divisions in our society. What is profitable to a realtor is not always profitable to a city.

"You will hear the arguments that the Negro isn't culturally ready, that integration will pull the white race back a generation, that the Negro is a criminal. Individuals who use these arguments never go on to say that if there are lagging standards in the Negro communities—and there certainly are—they lag because of segregation, discrimination, poverty and ignorance. Criminal responses are environmental, not racial, and it is tortuous logic to use the tragic results of segregation as an argument for the continuation of it. We also must rid ourselves of the belief that only time can solve the problem. Be nice and patient, some say, and wait 100 or 200 years and the problem will work itself out. But time is neutral. It can be used constructively or destructively, and the forces of evil have used time much more effectively than the forces of good will. It may well be that we will have to repent in this generation not merely for the vitriolic words and violent actions of the bad people, but for the appalling silence of the good people. "

WHRC's Work after the Summer Project

The efforts of the Wilmette Human Relations Committee continued after the King speech and after the North Shore Summer Project. In 1966 and 1967 WHRC sponsored Operation Host, bringing kids from other areas to live in Wilmette homes with same-age kids and attend School District 39's summer enrichment program. In 1968 and 1969 it sponsored Come Live in Wilmette, bringing members of minority groups to the village for tours with dinner afterwards. It pushed the village board for open housing, an effort that ended with the adoption of an ordinance by a vote of 4–2 in July 1968. One negative vote was cast by a trustee who was president of a real estate firm and former president of the Evanston-North Shore Board of Realtors. At the time, the number of African-American families in the village was estimated to be three.

The work of many committed Wilmette activists during the 1960s changed attitudes and laws. While it would be naive to believe that racial prejudice has been eliminated here or anywhere else, the vast majority of Wilmette residents welcome new families regardless of their race, national origin, or religion, and any discriminatory behavior would be loudly condemned. Yet, the work that began in the 1960s hasn't brought change in African-Americans' presence among the village's population, despite the superior amenities (schools, parks, etc.) that the village has to offer.

Why? It's not because African-Americans can't afford to live in the village, an explanation sometimes offered. Plenty of African-Americans can afford Wilmette; they simply choose to live elsewhere. Again, why? Is it because Wilmette is seen as an unwelcoming community with no established African-American presence to reassure? If so, is there a way to counter this image?

John and Ellen Smith, among the first African-Americans to live in Wilmette, operated a grocery store and restaurant at 1428 Wilmette Ave. The building still stands but was significantly renovated in 2016. Courtesy of the Wilmette Historical Museum.

Breaking News about African-Americans in Wilmette

- August 18, 1879: The 16th Battalion, one of the earliest African-American military units in Illinois, held an outing at the picnic grounds in Wilmette today. More than 1,000 guests arrived in the village on a 16-car train and enjoyed an afternoon of military parades, games, and picnicking. The 16th Battalion was founded in 1877, reflecting the fact that Chicago's growing African-American community is becoming more influential in the city's civic affairs.
- December 24, 1917: John Stewart Smith, one of Wilmette's first African-American residents, died today. He's survived by his wife, Ellen, also African-American. He was born in Maryland in 1848, and she in Canada in 1866.

Their families had gone to Canada to escape slavery. In the mid-1880s the couple was married and moved to Wilmette. They opened a grocery store and restaurant at 1428 Wilmette Avenue, where they and several relatives lived on the upper floors.

- July 8, 1921: The Ku Klux Klan is conducting a membership drive on the North Shore. The leaders of the movement claim that the purpose of the new Klan is to oppose the lawlessness that has arisen since the end of the World War, and that they desire "only that right and justice should prevail."

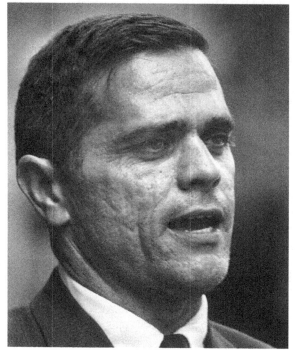

Rev. Buckner Coe went all-in fighting discrimination, poverty, and war. See page 181. Courtesy of the Coe family.

- October 17, 1921: A gathering of Wilmette men heard former Illinois Governor Edward Dunne excoriate the Ku Klux Klan at a meeting of the Xaverian Club of St. Francis Xavier Church held at the Wilmette Woman's Club. Dunne pointed out that the Klan's definition of "100 percent American"—persons eligible for Klan membership—excludes 95,700,000 Americans. Pastor Francis Kelley said that democracy requires "the intelligent cooperation of an intelligent and well-educated people" and cannot "be sustained by secret organizations."
- May 31, 1924: Several North Shore residents report that they observed a ceremony conducted by the Ku Klux Klan in the forest preserve on Milwaukee

Avenue two miles north of Glenview Road. According to the reports, about 15,000 Klansmen were present, and the ceremony included the burning of a huge cross.

- September 12, 1924: The Ku Klux Klan announced that the organization will hold a large open air ceremony, complete with a burning cross, somewhere on the outskirts of the North Shore, on Saturday, September 20.
- May 30, 1939: Chief McGuire led a contingent of Wilmette police officers to the Civilian Conservation Corps camp at Harms Woods to stop "an incipient riot" with racial overtones. The incident occurred during a baseball game between a CCC team comprised of African-American players and a Glenview team. "Tempers were cooled" and the game went forward.

The CCC segregated the workers at Camp Skokie Valley by race. The members of Company 605, one of two African-American companies, are pictured here in 1939. Published in "Pictorial Review: Sparta District, Company 605, Camp Skokie Valley, SP-15" (Glenview, IL: Civilian Conservation Corps, 1939).

- June 26, 1966: Members of the First Congregational Church of Wilmette voted 246–220 to ask their recently-resigned pastor, Rev. Buckner Coe, to stay on the job. Rev. Coe resigned in May after four years as pastor because, he believed, he had lost the confidence of his parishioners. Besides serving as chair of the Clergy Committee of the North Shore Summer Project last year, he has vocally and aggressively espoused civil rights and supported anti-poverty and anti-war causes. (Prediction: He'll return but he won't last long because, as he says, "Some members think I'm going too far while I myself don't think I'm going far enough.")

CHAPTER 10

★————————★

Notable Women

American society in 1872, the year of Wilmette's founding, severely limited the role of women. The rights and opportunities enjoyed by men were less available or totally denied to women: education, employment, and voting, for example. Wilmette was reflective of American society, and over the years, Wilmette women have actively participated in the movement that has successfully challenged those limits to their advancement.

Throughout this struggle, women have had at least as much influence as men in shaping the character of the village. They were the leaders and workers of an incredibly wide array of organizations that performed vast social and civic services. These organizations and the women who created and served them were the heart and soul of the village. They include the women's groups of the churches, the Woman's Club of Wilmette and the organizations it spawned, the garden clubs, the women's auxiliaries of the men's organizations, the PTAs, the Red Cross, and the volunteers who gave their time and talents in support of orphanages.

During the 1960s and 1970s, a group of women activists successfully pushed for transparency and democracy in local government and for housing availability on a non-discriminatory and affordable basis. They brought change to the political environment. This group included Thelma Brook Simon, Jean Cleland, Mimi Ryan, Rayna Miller, and Clarice Stetter—all members of the League of Women Voters of Wilmette.

The stories that follow in this chapter attempt to capture some of the experiences, struggles, and successes of Wilmette women. But first, a fictional discussion over the origin of the name Wilmette.

What Gender is "Wilmette"?

SHE: Wilmette is such a wonderful place. And it's so inspiring for all the little girls here to know that their hometown is named for a woman.

HE: That's nonsense. Wilmette isn't named for a woman. It's named for a man, just like most red-blooded American cities and towns.

SHE: I say that Wilmette was named for Archange Ouilmette, a woman of Pottawatomie descent. In 1829 she was granted 1,280 acres by the federal government as part of the Second Treaty of Prairie Du Chien. The boundaries of this land, in present-day terms, were Lake Michigan on the east, Elmwood Avenue on the north, 15th Street on the west, and Central Street in Evanston on the south. This grant was known as the "Ouilmette Reserve." Most of the land ended up in the Village of Wilmette when it was founded in 1872. I say the founders selected "Wilmette" (the phonetic version of "Ouilmette") as the village's name because of Archange and her reserve.

HE: I say that Wilmette was named for Antoine Ouilmette, Archange's husband. He was a French-Canadian fur trader employed by the American Fur Co. He came to this region in 1790 and was one of the very first white settlers of Chicago. He traded with the Indians and developed good relations with them. He married Archange, a member of a North Shore group of Pottawatomies. They had eight children. They initially lived in a small settlement near Fort Dearborn in Chicago. Antoine farmed, hunted, and ferried travelers across the Chicago River. They survived the Fort Dearborn massacre and remained in Chicago until 1826. Then they moved north. For about ten years, they lived on the Ouilmette Reserve, in a cabin on the bluff of Lake Michigan at present-day Lake Avenue. As between Antoine and Archange, I say *he* was the pioneering historical figure whom the founders honored in naming the new village.

SHE: Antoine and Archange left the State by the late 1830s. They died in Iowa in the early 1840s. Their children sold the land comprising the Ouilmette Reserve to investors shortly after their parents' death. By the time the founders got around to naming the village in 1872, the name "Ouilmette" undoubtedly came to their minds mainly because of the reserve, not because of Antoine. And the reserve got its name from Archange, not Antoine.

HE: Antoine deserves as much credit for the Ouilmette Reserve as Archange. He was directly involved in the negotiations leading up to the Second Treaty of Prairie du Chien. Under the Treaty, the Native Americans ceded large areas of western Illinois and southwestern Wisconsin to the U.S. In exchange, the U.S. paid them $16,000 annually. Antoine helped the parties reach agreement, but he was also looking out for himself and his family. The treaty included a few grants to individuals of Native American descent. Antoine made sure that Archange received one of these grants, 1,280 acres in the vicinity of the Ouilmette family home. The Ouilmette Reserve owed its existence as much to Antoine as to Archange.

SHE: Perhaps there's common ground. There's no definite proof that I'm right or you're right. We don't know for sure what the founders were thinking when they chose the name Wilmette. I'll stick to my opinion, and you can stick to yours. Let's agree, though, that the name Wilmette honors the first family known to have established a permanent home here; and that in adopting the first family's name for the new village, the founders hoped that a thriving community of many families would follow.

The Woman's Club of Wilmette

The Woman's Club of Wilmette is an organization that helped women find meaning in their lives and a role in the community. As former club president Debby Burdick explained a few years ago, "We were women who made a difference, not just in our community, but to each other. We were networking before the word came into being, not just to benefit others, but each other, too."

The club dates back to 1891 when two sisters, Ida and Anna Law, hosted 20 women at their home at 1137 Forest Avenue. This meeting produced an organization called the Reading Club, whose members met to read books and papers. Before long, the club adopted its current name and broadened its mission to include reading and discussing history, literature and art to promote the moral, intellectual, and social culture of its members.

Membership steadily increased, and the club needed a permanent home to accommodate its many activities. In 1910 member Blanche Freeman donated property at 930 Greenleaf Avenue in memory of her mother, Orrea Lansingh. The first clubhouse, a modest wood-frame structure, was built there in 1912. It was significantly enlarged and faced with limestone in 1929.

From its earliest days, the club contributed to the lives of Wilmette residents. In the late 1890s a library operated by the Elmwood Library Association (which predated the Wilmette Public Library) was damaged by fire. The club rescued the surviving books, added more books, rented space in a building on Central Avenue, and operated a library until Andrew Carnegie donated funds for a new public library that opened in 1905.

In the early 1900s the club petitioned the village board to place a drinking

Local Artist George Lusk painted his conception of Archange Ouilmette in 1934.
Courtesy of the Wilmette Historical Museum, where it can be seen today.

fountain for humans and horses in the Village Center. When the board declined, the club took on the project and installed an elaborate iron fountain at the intersection of Wilmette and Central avenues.

In 1913 an explosion west of the village exposed the uncoordinated nature of the village's welfare services. The club not only provided long-term care for an injured girl, but it organized the forerunner of the Family Service Center to coordinate welfare services in the future. Other offspring of the club were the Central-Laurel PTA (1915) and the League of Women Voters of Wilmette (1924).

During World War I, members of the club sold $87,000 in war bonds. And during World War II, they operated a Red Cross Production Unit which performed charitable works like sewing clothing for the needy, conducted blood drives and first aid classes, and ran a canning kitchen where victory garden produce was canned for a small fee.

During its long history, the club has raised money for charitable giving by operating a resale shop, holding annual rummage sales and antique shows, and renting its facility for parties and events. It has generously donated money to local organizations and causes and opened its facility free-of-charge to organizations serving the community, including New Trier Extension and Go Green Wilmette.

February 15, 2015 was a sad day in Wilmette, especially for the club's members. The clubhouse was virtually destroyed by fire. This came at a time when participation in women's clubs was declining. The club decided to rebuild, and it remains to be seen whether, even with a new clubhouse, the Wilmette women of today will choose the club as their vehicle for networking and serving the community.

Suffrage

In 1913 women in Illinois gained the right to vote in elections for U.S. president and local offices. The passage of the Municipal Voting Act of 1913 made Illinois the first state east of the Mississippi River to grant women the right to vote for U.S. president. Six years later, Illinois was among the first states to ratify the Constitution's 19th Amendment, guaranteeing full voting rights to women throughout the nation.

Even before 1913, Wilmette women had voted in local elections. They voted for the first time in the school election of 1896. While they were allowed to vote for school board members, they weren't allowed to vote on a proposal to establish a free kindergarten. Still, women had a major impact on the outcome of that election. The Woman's Club actively supported a slate consisting of John Skelton for school board president and Estella Pierson and Florence Taylor for school trustees, and urged approval of the free kindergarten. The club-endorsed slate and the kindergarten proposal both won easily.

Women were also key voters in a 1903 referendum to select a site for a new Wilmette public library. Andrew Carnegie, the American industrialist and philanthropist, offered to give the village $10,000 for a library building if the village would provide a site and support the library through annual taxes of at least $1,000. (Carnegie made more than 2,000 library grants during his lifetime, including 106 in Illinois.)

Selecting a site for the library stirred a big controversy. Three options emerged. One was a parcel on Green Bay Road between Washington and Central avenues. It was owned by a New Yorker, Alexander Howell, who offered to donate it to the village. (I haven't found any connection between Howell and the village, but a mere one-mile stroll across New York City's Central Park was all that separated Howell's home on 89th Street from Carnegie's home on 91st Street. Perhaps they were friends.) Proponents of the Howell option obviously liked the fact that the site would cost nothing. Opponents argued that the site "is in an undesirable part of town and is surrounded by coal yards and wood sheds."

The second option was the "village triangle," which was then and is now the site of the village hall. By 1903, the original village hall, only 13 years old, was too small. Under this option, a larger village hall would be built elsewhere, making the triangle available for the library. Proponents argued that the library should be located at the village's "center of activity," and a beautiful library near transportation lines would favorably advertise the village. Opponents argued that the site was unsuitable because of noise from the trains.

The third option was to purchase a centrally located site, not specifically identified, at a cost of $5,000 to $8,000. This option's drawbacks were its cost, vagueness, and uncertainty.

On July 25, 1903, the men and women of the village voted. The ballot directed them to X their choice and sign at the bottom. The ballots were tabulated by sex. The men cast 114 votes for the Howell site, 104 for the triangle, and 73 for a site to be purchased. The women cast 112 votes for the Howell site, 131 for the triangle, and 61 for a site to be purchased. Combining the votes, the triangle garnered the most. The men's first choice was the Howell site, but the women's votes determined the winner. Not surprisingly, given the times, some chauvinistic men protested vigorously.

As it turned out, neither the men's nor the women's choice prevailed. The

Village purchased two lots on Park Avenue for $4,000 at the current site of the library. The Carnegie grant was finalized. The new library opened its doors in 1905. The building served the community well until 1950, when it was torn down and replaced by the current building. Meanwhile, a new village hall was built on the village triangle in 1910.

Carnegie said that the phrase "Let There Be Light" would be an appropriate inscription above the entrances to his libraries. I wonder whether the men who sought to disallow the women's votes in the 1903 referendum ever *saw* the light.

Katherine Merrifield: First Woman Juror

One milestone in the long march of U.S. women toward gender equality was achieving equal treatment regarding jury service. This occurred many years after women won the right to vote. In Illinois, it occurred in 1939. Dr. Katherine Merrifield, of 1014 Elmwood Avenue, was part of this story.

Born in New Britain, Connecticut, she attended Vassar College and Cornell University Medical School and practiced medicine in New York. In the summer of 1924, she volunteered her services to a charitable organization that provided health care to fishermen in Newfoundland and Labrador. There, she met her future husband, Dr. Frederick Merrifield, also a volunteer. At the time, he was a practicing dentist and a teacher of dentistry at his alma mater, the Northwestern University Dental School.

The couple married in 1926 and started a family. She stopped practicing medicine. He completed an internship in oral surgery at St. Luke's Hospital in Chicago and joined the staff at several hospitals. He also became a professor of oral surgery at Northwestern University's Dental School. They moved to their Elmwood Avenue home in the early 1930s.

At that time, jury service in both state and federal courts was mostly a male obligation governed by state law. Although some states allowed women to serve, they were often excused upon request or not called at all. In Illinois, jury service was historically limited to men, but the issue of allowing or requiring women to serve was debated through the 1930s. In 1939 a new Illinois law stipulated that women would serve on the same basis as men. The federal courts in Illinois followed this new approach.

The first federal jury in Chicago that included women was impaneled in October 1939. The case was a will contest. Wheaton attorney Samuel Howe had disinherited his son and given his entire $70,000 estate (equivalent to about $1.3 million in 2020) to Northwestern University to establish a memorial for his wife. The son claimed his father was delusional.

The jury included six men and six women. Somehow, Katherine was selected, even though her husband was a Northwestern faculty member. While the subject of the case wasn't particularly newsworthy, the inclusion of women jurors received widespread press attention. Midway through the costly month-long trial, it was reported that the women prepared afternoon tea and pastries for the men, and the next day the men took the women out for lunch.

The case was submitted to the jury on a Friday afternoon. Deliberations continued into early Saturday morning. A growing majority favored the son. Katherine became the final holdout on Northwestern's side. Finally, at 1:15 AM, she capitulated and signed the unanimous verdict.

On Monday morning, the judge polled the jury. Katherine stunned the courtroom when she replied, "That was not and is not my verdict." She explained, "I signed through cowardice. I submitted to the will of the majority. I realize now that I shouldn't have signed the verdict."

The judge called Katherine's change-of-mind "shocking" but "not a reflection on women jurors." He ordered a new trial, and seven months later the case was settled, with the university receiving the bulk of the estate.

This incident reopened the debate about allowing women to serve as jurors and buttressed some folks' stereotype. As one of the men jurors commented, "You know how they are. They change their minds." Time healed the damage. In 1957 Congress passed legislation removing gender as a factor in jury service throughout the federal system, and in 1975 the U.S. Supreme Court ruled that states must treat men and women equally in assembling juries.

Katherine was no flake. It took great courage to admit her mistake in that austere federal courtroom. As she recognized, "I guess I'll have to be the goat. I was clearing my conscience."

First Women in Local Offices

Just as suffrage and jury service were denied to women at the turn of the 20th century, the opportunity to serve in elective and high appointive office was also denied, not as a matter of law, but because men ran things. That's just the way it was. The table below lists 19 important local offices and, so far as I can determine, the first women to hold them. A couple of important offices aren't listed, because either I couldn't identify the first woman officeholder or no woman has ever held them.

Years ago, before I knew anything about Estella Pierson, I was told that she "didn't really count" as the first woman village trustee because she was slated in 1917 as a sympathy gesture following the sudden death of her popular husband in 1916. Her husband was Louis Pierson, who served as village attorney (1892–1893), village president (1898–1899), and state representative (1907–1916). After learning more, I'm confident that Estella was slated based on merit, not sympathy.

She grew up in Iowa, the daughter of a Union Army soldier who died on his way home from the South after the Civil War. She graduated from Cornell College and taught school until 1882 when she married Louis, then a lawyer practicing in Iowa. The couple moved to Wilmette in 1888. She was a founding member and four-term president of the Wilmette Woman's Club. She was one of the first two women to serve as a board member of Wilmette School District 39, and she was a leader of the Ladies Aid Society of the Methodist Church. She studied law under her husband's tutelage, although she never practiced. In sum, as reported by the local press a quarter century after her death, she was "probably the most active woman civic leader in the village with her advice and cooperation almost constantly in demand when matters of community interest were in contemplation."

FIRST WOMEN IN LOCAL WILMETTE OFFICES

OFFICE	FIRST WOMAN	FROM–TO
Wilmette Village President	Nancy Canafax	1997–2005
Wilmette Village Trustee	Estella Pierson	1917–1919
Wilmette Village Manager	Heidi Voorhees	1990–2001
Wilmette Village Clerk	Mary Elizabeth Brush	1949–1964
Wilmette Park District President	Marilyn Malles	1981–1983
Wilmette Park District Commissioner	Mary Johnstone	1973–1975
Wilmette Public Library Trustee	Harriet Gallie Elsie Rippel	1914–1923 1914–1916
Wilmette Librarian (now Director)	Anna Law	1901–1920
Wilmette School District 39 President	Carola Minar McMullen	1977–1981
Wilmette School District 39 Member	Estella Pierson Florence Taylor	1896–1900 1896–1898
Wilmette School District 39 Superintendent	Dr. Joan Hochschild	1998–2002
Avoca School District 37 Superintendent	Marie Murphy	1943–1968

Sexual Harassment

As sexual harassment allegations continue to swirl around high-visibility men, the case of Edward Sieber, Wilmette's first police chief, shows that the problem has deep roots. Edward was born in New York in 1857. His parents had emigrated from Germany to Schenectady County, New York, where his father was a farmer. Edward left the farm and came to this area in 1881. He joined the police force of South Evanston, then a separate town. There, he met his future wife, Catherine. After nine years in South Evanston, he was hired as Wilmette's street commissioner. He and Catherine moved to Wilmette (1118 Lake Avenue) with their two daughters, Mary and Alice. Six years later, in 1896, he became Wilmette's first police officer. He also served as water-meter inspector and, during his off-duty hours, he milked the cows of Village President Henry Gates, morning and night.

Edward was accused in 1902 when he was 45 years old. As reported by a Chicago newspaper, complaints of "bold advances and clandestine flirtations" were made to the village board by "a half-dozen of the offended members of the feminine sex." The allegations involved Edward's "practice of flirting with the girls and young married women along his beat" and "stealing a sly hug or a kiss from a good-looking maiden on occasion."

The newspaper reported that Edward, acting as a water-meter inspector, allegedly entered the Wilmette Avenue home of Charles Miller and his wife Alvina (age 22) through the back door and "without preamble, began to hug and kiss the frightened young woman." Charles was present in an adjacent room and overheard the commotion. He "followed the policeman from the house, threatened to thrash him, but the offender ran."

Among the other victims were Village President Gates' cook and a 14-year-old school girl. The cook complained that when she went to the Gates stable to get some milk, "the milkman-policeman-inspector persisted in bothering her with his attentions until she grew out of patience and reported the matter to her employer." The newspaper added that "several more have filed charges of a similar nature against the village policeman, but [President] Gates refused to make these public."

Based on these complaints, the village board launched an investigation but declined to suspend Edward because, in President Gates' words, "that would leave Wilmette without police protection." Gates added, "The police force of Wilmette has heretofore been above suspicion, and we shall not believe the truth of the present charges until we are furnished with unassailable evidence."

At its next meeting, the board declared without explanation that "the matter be dropped and no further action taken."

Edward continued to serve as Wilmette's police officer, rounding up runaway horses, catching speeding motorists, shooting un-muzzled dogs, and stopping beach orgies. In 1910, when the Village added a second officer, Edward became the department's first chief. In 1920, reacting to a spate of nighttime assaults on women in Wilmette and Evanston, he suggested that women who were required to be out at night should contact the department, and officers would escort them to their destinations. By the time of his retirement in 1924, his command numbered eight patrolmen. When he died in 1928, his funeral was attended by "many residents," and Wilmette police officers acted as pall-bearers and honor guard. He was highly regarded in the community.

Sexual harassment isn't new. The Sieber case illustrates society's longtime unacceptable response: trivializing the conduct (as the original newspaper report did), requiring "unassailable evidence" (as Village President Gates did), and burying complaints in secrecy. But times are changing. Society is beginning to understand that women will and must protest, and when the evidence is convincing, the offender must suffer an appropriate penalty, regardless of position, popularity, and politics. Potential offenders must be made to think twice, and women who complain must be protected from retaliation.

Hilda Schroeder: Ponzi Mastermind

Hilda Schroeder lived at 515 Gregory Avenue from about 1924 to 1930. Her time in Wilmette ended when she was sentenced to prison after becoming known throughout the United States as "Mrs. Ponzi."

Hilda was born in 1884 and raised in Wisconsin. In 1908, she married Edwin Schroeder, and they had two children, Hortense and James. Shortly before 1920, they moved to Chicago. Edwin worked as a dry-goods salesman, and Hilda was a stay-at-home mom. In the early 1920s Edwin died. Hilda was suddenly faced with the challenge of raising and supporting her two school-age kids alone.

I don't know how Hilda connected with Chicagoan John Naghten, a World War I veteran, but in 1923 they teamed up in the business of buying and selling real estate and mortgage securities from an office in the Loop. Hilda was then about 39 and John was younger, about 27. It was at this time that she moved her family from Chicago to Wilmette.

Hilda and John attracted investors by advertising extensively, lulling investors into believing that their business was legit. But it wasn't. Some of their mortgage transactions had major "flaws." The pair were selling securities backed by mortgages that were totally fake and never recorded. So long as they were able to keep selling, they had sufficient revenue to pay the interest that kept their investors happy. They pocketed the rest. Hilda was reputed to be "the Feminine Financial Genius of LaSalle Street," but Black Tuesday (October 24, 1929) and its aftermath changed everything. The real estate market dried up, and investors stopped buying mortgage securities. Their Ponzi scheme collapsed. By this time, the relationship between Hilda and John appears to have been more than business. He had moved into her Wilmette home as a lodger.

A score of disgruntled investors came forward and complained to law enforcement. Losses were said to be $1 million. A Chicago widow, 55-year-old Rose Rosted, was the biggest loser. She later testified that Hilda and John "swindled her out of $333,000 in seven years by juggling mortgages," adding, "They're crooks, that's what they are." In July 1930, Hilda and John were charged with embezzlement, but they couldn't be found. Hilda's Wilmette house was unoccupied, and neighbors told investigators that she was in a sanitarium suffering from a nervous breakdown. John had disappeared.

In November 1930, five months after their disappearance, Hilda and John were arrested together in Philadelphia, extradited back to Illinois, and jailed. Her attorneys filed for bankruptcy on her behalf, and she claimed to have assets consisting of her Gregory Avenue home ($17,000), home furnishings ($50,000), pawned jewelry ($70,000), and other real estate ($650,000). In January 1931 she and John were indicted for embezzlement, and their bail bonds (totaling $370,000) were record highs.

The evidence against the pair was overwhelming, and both were convicted. Hilda was sentenced to one to ten years in the Oakdale Reformatory for Women near Dwight, Illinois, with a possibility of release in six years. John was sentenced to one to five years at the Joliet Correctional Center. Hilda couldn't cope with her plight. She had lost everything, and her children, 20 and 15, were left with no parental support. Before long, she was transferred to the Kankakee State Hospital for the insane, where she died in 1932 at the age of 47.

John fared better. After his release, he married and returned to the real estate and mortgage business in Chicago. Hilda's two children seem to have survived the trauma. Hortense attended college for one year and worked briefly at Wieboldt's department store in Evanston while living in the Patrick Butler household at 630 Linden Avenue. James went to live with an aunt in Milwaukee. They both lived long lives.

Elizabeth Dilling: Anti-Communist Crusader

Elizabeth Dilling was a prominent anti-communist crusader. She was born in Chicago in 1894. Her father, a physician, died when she was an infant, leaving his survivors with considerable wealth. She attended the University of Chicago and became a proficient harpist. In 1918 she married Albert Dilling, a civil engineer and lawyer. The couple moved to 1047 Linden Avenue, but three years later, Albert was appointed chief engineer of the Chicago Sanitary District, and they moved to the city for a short time. By 1924 they were back on the North Shore, at 545 Essex Road, Kenilworth, where they lived with their two children during their rocky marriage that ended in 1943.

Inherited wealth enabled the Dillings to travel extensively throughout Europe during the 1920s and 1930s. Elizabeth formed strong views based on what she saw during a month-long tour of the Soviet Union in 1931: people living in incredible misery because of poverty and disease and deprived of religious liberty. She was transformed into an ardent crusader against communism, which she believed was an imminent threat to American democracy.

Described as a beautiful woman and "an excellent speaker of great personal charm," Elizabeth quickly became a popular lecturer with a resonating message. She spoke to mainstream groups throughout the Chicago region, including the Women's Catholic Club of Wilmette, the Logan-Howard PTA, and the Women's Society of the Wilmette Congregational Church. She helped organize the "Paul Reveres," a national organization whose purpose was to expose radicals trying to subvert the U.S. government. She protested against groups she regarded as pro-communist and the churches that hosted their meetings, including the American Civil Liberties Union and the First Methodist Church of Evanston.

In 1934 she compiled excerpts from her lectures and pamphlets into a self-published book called *The Red Network, a "Who's Who" and Handbook of Radicalism for Patriots*. The book includes an attack on the New Deal and lists more than 500 organizations and 1,300 individuals alleged to have communist connections, including Bahá'í International, the League of Women Voters, the YMCA, Jane Addams, Clarence Darrow, Albert Einstein, Mahatma Gandhi, Eleanor Roosevelt, and officials of the Roosevelt administration. The book was highly influential, partly because it was endorsed by the American Legion and the Daughters of the American Revolution.

As World War II approached, Elizabeth wrote *The Roosevelt Red Record and Its Background* (1936), elaborating on her thesis that the New Deal was closely linked to communism. This was followed by *The Octopus* (1940), claiming a

In 1939, Elizabeth Dilling testified in opposition to the confirmation of Felix Frankfurter as Associate Justice of the U.S. Supreme Court. He was listed in her *Red Network* as a communist sympathizer. From the Harris & Ewing Collection, Library of Congress.

link between communism and Jews. As war clouds gathered, she became a leader of the mothers' movement that opposed American involvement. Her opposition was based not on pacifism, but on her belief that Germany and its Nazi allies stood as the only real deterrent to the spread of the greater evil: communism.

Elizabeth's anti-war efforts led to her indictment, along with 29 others, for conspiring to overthrow the U.S. government, set up a Nazi government, and undermine the morale of the U.S. armed forces. A circus trial in Washington, D.C. that lasted six months ended when the presiding judge died in November 1944, forcing a mistrial. The indictment was finally dismissed in 1946 by a judge who called the six-year proceeding a "travesty."

Alfred Haake and Lillian Brown, two Wilmette residents, deserve mention because they publicly criticized Elizabeth's guilt-by-association approach to the communist menace. _____

Margaret Abeles: Refugee Sponsor

Memorial Days come and go. Wilmette does a fine job of honoring local heroes and the hundreds of thousands of other Americans who sacrificed dearly to defend our country's highest values, but Memorial Day ceremonies are only a partial way to honor the lives of so many men and women who sacrificed so much. Individual actions throughout the year that further the values they fought for are the greatest respect that Americans can pay.

Margaret Abeles stands tall when measured by this standard. In 1939 the Abeles family moved to 726 9th Street and joined Wilmette's Congregational Church. They had two sons, the older boy being of high school age. He was called by his middle name, "Beecher" (his mother's maiden name). She was the great-granddaughter of Henry Ward Beecher, a famous Congregational preacher and abolitionist of the Civil War era. She was also the great-grand-niece of Harriet Beecher Stowe, author of *Uncle Tom's Cabin*.

Beecher graduated from New Trier in 1941 and entered Northwestern University to study chemical engineering. Within a few months, the U.S. was enmeshed in World War II. Beecher continued his studies for a time, but in 1943, as military service loomed in his future, he enlisted in the Army Air Forces. He received his wings and commission as a second lieutenant in April 1944. One month later he married 18-year-old Shirley Elling of 610 4th Street. Their marriage produced a baby daughter, Susan Gail.

Beecher completed his training as a P-38 fighter-bomber pilot in October 1944 and departed for the European Theater. On January 23, 1945, while on a strafing mission from Belgium to Bonn, Germany, his plane was hit by anti-aircraft fire. The aircraft struck the top of a tree, exploded, and fell ablaze into a forest near the German town of Euskirchen. Although the location of the crash was reported by a member of his squadron, Beecher's body was never recovered. The War Department initially said he was "missing in action," but in October 1945 it notified his wife that he had been killed. He was 21 years old.

A memorial service was held at the Congregational Church in November 1945. Beecher is also honored by a marker at the Arlington National Cemetery, by the inclusion of his name on the Wall of the Missing at the Henri-Chapelle American Cemetery in Belgium, on a bronze plaque at New Trier, and on Wilmette's War Memorial. The greatest memorial of them all, though, is the action taken by his parents, especially Margaret, to further an American value that he endorsed: compassion for displaced refugees.

During his short time in France and Belgium, Beecher wrote letters to his parents expressing concern over the plight of the young refugees he met. Margaret and Alfred decided to honor their son with a living memorial: They'd bring one of these refugees to live at their home and receive the education that Beecher had started but not completed. The Congregational Church and its members rallied around this idea, and the outcome was a program that provided housing, employment, and educational assistance for hundreds of refugees for more than 15 years, with Margaret spearheading the effort. The Abeles alone hosted 40 "adopted" refugees. In 1958 Margaret's role as "the mother of exiles" was honored on the popular TV show *This Is Your Life*.

What would America's fallen heroes think today? Would they be satisfied that we, the survivors, have done our share to defend America's highest values? Or would they be thinking, "We did our part. Can't you folks do a little more to promote freedom, equality, justice, compassion and all of the other values that sent us off to war?"

Eileen Johnston: the Environment's Guardian

As evidence mounts that human existence is threatened by what's happening to the environment, it's time for everyone to act. "What can I do?" you may ask.

For starters, be inspired by the example set by Eileen Johnston, who lived at 505 Maple Avenue from the 1940s until her death in 2000 at age 90. Eileen's life work was protecting the environment as a citizen-volunteer. She was an effective educator and advocate because she knew her stuff and pursued her goals with persistence, enthusiasm, and civility. She was also likeable—a stout, smart, spirited, grey-haired lady, often wearing her trademark red bandana.

Eileen acquired a love for nature as a child. A graduate of the University of Michigan with a master's degree in geography, she became concerned about the environment when, as a Scout leader, she took her troops on long walks along the Lake Michigan shoreline and noticed the degradation of the water quality.

In the mid-1960s, she attended a conference that laid out the alarming details of Lake Michigan's pollution, and she took a cruise on the lake and saw firsthand the damage to the ecosystem and its threat to public health. Over the next 30 years, she single-handedly organized and conducted 72 educational cruises along the region's shoreline and waterways (72 miles in length). "It's just amazing what you see. People dump all kinds of garbage into the canals, even refrigerators and picnic tables." She recruited experts to join these cruises and help point out the problems and explain the solutions to industrialists, environmental officials, teachers, students, and the general public—7,000 passengers in total.

Eileen Johnston never stopped working for the environment. "As long as I'm breathing, I'll be trying to do something. I'll just stick with it." Courtesy of the Wilmette Historical Museum.

Over the same 30-year-period, Eileen organized 44 conferences and seminars on subjects like solar energy, acid rain, climate change, waste management, and the ozone layer. "I try to hear all of the speakers before inviting them to attend a conference. Many environmentalists are excellent researchers, but not all are good speakers. So far, I've been very lucky; I seem to be able to get some of the top names."

As an advocate, she attended virtually every regional meeting conducted by agencies dealing with environmental issues, including the Illinois Pollution Control Board, the U.S. Environmental Protection Agency, and the Chicago Sanitary District (now the Metropolitan Water Reclamation District). She lobbied the Illinois legislature and spoke to civic groups. Although she belonged to several organizations dealing with environmental issues, including the League of Women Voters of Wilmette, she spoke in her individual capacity. "I don't always agree with a group's position. Most of what I do is as an individual. Then I can say what I damn please."

These efforts were a labor of love, not profit. Eileen wasn't a wealthy woman, and she self-funded the cruises and conferences, taking the risk of loss if co-sponsorships and fees failed to cover the cost. She earned the respect and even the affection of officials of the agencies she monitored, and she was treated cordially by them at hearings. She was the recipient of several prestigious awards for her work.

Very few of us can make the environment our life's work, but we can do something. We can educate ourselves about the risks to the environment. We can recycle carefully. We can consider hybrids or electric vehicles when re-placing gasoline-powered vehicles. We can ask state and federal regulators to adopt sensible and meaningful environmental regulations. We can ask local government to adopt zoning controls and a sewer fee structure that discourage property owners from covering their land with concrete and asphalt. The lives of our children and grandchildren depend upon everyone doing what they can.

Jane Page Hlavacek: Aviator

Jane Page was born in Montana in 1918 but spent her entire childhood in Peoria, Illinois, where her father and grandfather were prominent lawyers. After attending the University of Arizona, she became one of only 1,074 members of the Women Airforce Service Pilots (WASP) during World War II. The main function of WASP, a civilian organization, was to ferry planes from factories where they were built to points of embarkation. Utilizing women for this domestic task freed up male pilots for overseas combat. WASP pilots learned to fly all types of military airplanes. Jane flew at least five models.

After the War, Jane came to Wilmette. She worked as a charter pilot for Hlavacek Air Service at Pal-Waukee airport (now Chicago Executive). In 1946 she married Frank Hlavacek, son of the charter service's owner. Frank had learned to fly at age 14, taught by his father who began flying in 1921 as a barn-stormer and charter pilot. After serving in the Army Air Forces during the War, Frank joined his father's charter service and worked alongside Jane.

Jane and Frank lived in Wilmette for 13 years. Jane not only flew charter flights, but she competed in airplane races, including the widely-followed National Air Races held annually in Cleveland. Competitors flew surplus military planes that were souped-up to achieve top speeds. Jane drew the press's attention and the public's admiration not only for her racing prowess, but for her beauty and "Junoesque" stature, "a glamorous six foot 'air queen.'" In the 1946 National Air Races, she won second place in the Halle trophy race for women. In 1947 she finished fourth in the Halle event and, competing against male pilots, ninth in the Bendix trophy race from Van Nuys, California to Cleveland.

In 1950, Frank joined American Airlines. Unfortunately, the skies became hostile to this family of flyers. On February 3, 1959, Frank was co-pilot on Flight 320 from Chicago Midway to New York LaGuardia. The plane was a Lockheed Electra, recently placed in service. As the plane neared LaGuardia, it crashed into the East River, killing 65, including Joseph and Jean Kaye of Wilmette. Frank was one of eight souls who survived. The Civil Aeronautics Board blamed the crew's inattention to instruments, but Frank insisted that the instruments gave false readings.

August 28, 1960 brought a second tragedy. Frank's father and his close friend, Elmer Hassen, the owner of Wil-Shore Ford on Green Bay Road, were returning to Sky Harbor Airport (on Dundee Road one mile west of Waukegan Road) after an outing in Hassen's Beechcraft Bonanza. The plane inexplicably crashed near Waukon, Iowa, killing both men.

Jane Page Hlavacek was a pioneering woman pilot. Courtesy of the Wilmette Historical Museum.

Despite these tragedies, the Hlavacek family can be proud of its aviation history, especially the War service of Jane and Frank. In 2010 Jane (posthumously) and the other WASP pilots were awarded the Congressional Gold Medal, the top congressional award for civilian achievement.

Breaking News about Influential Women

- January 14, 1897: The Wilmette Woman's Club declared war on the widespread practice of smoking by schoolboys of the village. One Club member urged a boycott against any Wilmette merchant who sells cigarettes to the boys, but instead the Club created a committee to study the problem and recommend the best approach for stopping the sales.
- October 7, 1903: Alma Severson, 16, of Wilmette, a recent Swedish immigrant, left her mark on a "masher" whom she encountered on the North Shore Electric train in Evanston. The young man, sitting across the aisle, "glanced knowingly at the pretty Wilmette girl. Then he winked at her." She turned away. Undaunted, he crossed the aisle and sat next to her. She demanded that he "go right back where you belong!" He only smiled. "Well, then, take this," she replied, striking him in his winking eye. He jumped from the seat and she gave chase, demanding that the conductor "put this man off the car at once!" The conductor complied. The startled passengers "cheered the plucky girl." A newspaper columnist in Davenport, Iowa, cited this incident while blasting "mashers" as "contemptible human beings," "freaks," "fools," "poor specimens of manhood," "imbeciles," and "a disgrace to the male sex."
- September 23, 1909: Wilmette authorities shut down a euchre party scheduled for Jones Hall at 1217 Wilmette Avenue and turned away 125 disappointed women. The event was sponsored by Chicago artist Clara Miles Surquist, 29, operator of euchre games in Chicago, to accommodate her many North Shore players. Clara's plan was to charge 50 cents and give several pieces of her "valuable" hand-painted china as prizes. Meeting in special session, the village board decided that this arrangement amounted to illegal gambling. Edmond Dunshee, 56, a former Village official who initiated the shutdown, explained that he had no "particular objection" but felt that the village board should consider the matter before such games are allowed. Clara responded, "If they consider a social game of cards gambling they're old fogies. What would they call some of the features at church bazaars in that village?"

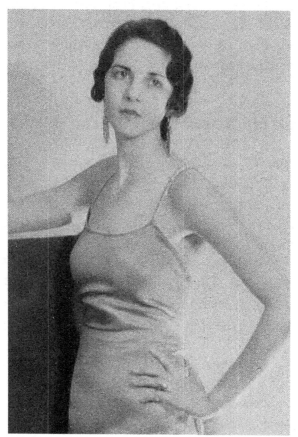

Wilmette's Ruth Wenter was Northwestern University's "most beautiful girl" in 1933.
See page 203. Courtesy of Northwestern University Syllabus Yearbook.

- March 8, 1911: Henry Mulford, 37, of 931 12th Street, shocked the Wilmette community, if not the world, by defeating all women-entrants and winning the blue ribbon for his strawberry shortcake in the Wilmette Woman's Club "domestic science exhibition." Mulford, an up-and-coming banker at Harris Bank, risked his career by taking the day off to shepherd his entry. (Observers compared his achievement to other ridiculously unlikely deviations from sexual stereotypes, like women becoming officers at his bank.)
- September 18, 1918: Marie Nelson, 26, made headlines because of her new job with a Wilmette dry cleaner as a delivery truck driver. Newspapers in Chicago and three other cities are praising her as a "deliveryette" and a "lady delivery boy" who's "keeping the home fires burning" by taking on this unusual job for her gender during the Great War.
- March 17, 1929: The Wilmette Woman's Club announced a major building project at its clubhouse site on Greenleaf Avenue. A Lannan stone structure,

designed by architects Granger & Bollenbacher, will expand the existing building. The new facility will feature an auditorium with a seating capacity of 650, a combination dining room/reception hall, and a large lounge. The facility will also have a lounge for men in the basement. The cost of the project will be $100,000.

- January 7, 1933: Ruth Wenter, 21, of 1204 Ashland Avenue, and Paul Cummins, 25, of Cedar Rapids, Iowa, were married at St. Augustine's Episcopal Church in Wilmette. The wedding was widely anticipated because the bride had been voted Northwestern University's "most beautiful girl" and the groom had been voted the university's "ideal man." The national press called them "the ideal couple." Shortly before the wedding, the couple received kidnap threats, and Wilmette police were stationed at the church as guards. Wayne King, 31, the popular orchestra leader, was the best man. The couple originally planned to honeymoon in St. Augustine, Florida but traveled instead to an undisclosed location in light of the threats.

- July 31, 1942: Mabel Ayres, 60, of 3035 Lake Avenue, pled guilty to official misfeasance and was fined $100 and removed from her position as New Trier Township's road commissioner. A longtime resident, she was the first president of the League of Women Voters of Wilmette. In 1938 she was appointed to the position of road commissioner following the death of her husband, Lloyd Ayres, who previously held the position. The most serious charge was diverting public funds and personally profiting through a truck-rental scheme involving her nephew, Benjamin McNaughton, 51, also of 3035 Lake Avenue. Her lawyer attributed her "technical violation of the law" to her "inexperience."

CHAPTER 11

★————————————————★

The Entertainment World

Throughout history, Wilmette residents have loved to entertain and be entertained. Be it by radio, TV, movies, theater, dance, or music, they've understood that entertainment lifts the human spirit and makes life more joyful.

From its founding in 1915 into the early 1980s, the Sunday Evening Club brought to Wilmette and the North Shore not only interesting and provocative speakers but also talented musicians. From its construction in 1937 as a WPA project, the Wallace Bowl in Gillson Park has been a popular venue for concerts, recitals, dance performances, and musical theater. New Trier High School and Northwestern University have outstanding performing arts programs that train and encourage young artists who, in turn, entertain the community with their concerts and shows. Small theater groups have performed the same function. Civic and business organizations and the Wilmette Public Library have sponsored concerts that bring talented performers to the community. Wilmette has been and continues to be a stimulating environment for learning and enjoying the performing arts.

Some of Wilmette's famous entertainers are profiled in this chapter, but there are many more who make the village proud: Bill Murray, actor; Ann-Margret Olsson, actor; Matthew Polenzani, opera tenor; Sarah Ruhl, playwright; Phil Ponce, TV host; Frank Mathie, TV news reporter; Brent Miller, TV meteorologist; Donnie Osmond, singer-actor; Clark Weber, radio personality; and Rainn Wilson, actor.

The Greatest Show on Earth

The traveling circus brought excitement to communities large and small across America long before other forms of entertainment arrived. Wilmette resident Henry Ringling was a member of the family that dominated this form of entertainment.

————

Henry was the youngest of the seven Ringling brothers who created a circus empire. He owned the house at 731 Elmwood Avenue from 1912 until his death in 1918. He, his wife Ida, and their son Henry lived there on a part-time basis.

Henry's parents, August and Saloma, came to the U.S. from Germany in the mid-19th century. Following their marriage here, they lived in several Midwestern states before finally settling for good in Baraboo, Wisconsin in the late 1870s. August was a harness-maker, and his four older sons initially followed in his footsteps.

But harness-making lacked the magic of the circus, a form of entertainment that was immensely popular in the 19th century. These spectacular traveling tent-shows featured entertaining performers and exotic animals. They fascinated young and old alike, and in the Ringling boys' case, they planted a seed that germinated a few years later in Baraboo.

In 1882, five of the brothers (Albert, Otto, Alfred, Charles, and John), ranging in age from 15 to 29, formed a song-and-dance troupe and went on the road. Two of the brothers (August, 26, and Henry, 13) weren't involved until later, and the only sister (Ida) was never involved. The brothers' dance troupe was soon transformed into a circus that saw decades of growth—new acts and more animals, bigger tents accommodating larger audiences and multiple "rings," and more wagons to transport the show from one town to another—until 1889 when railroad cars replaced the wagons.

Otto was the business manager. His obituary (1911) reports that he was "a ruthless, persistent, indefatigable competitor, possessed of a tremendous ambition and a tremendous capacity for profitable combination. As business director of the five Ringling brothers he added, one by one, to their possessions, like beads to a string, Forepaugh-Sells [major circus operators], Barnum & Bailey, Buffalo Bill, and by a process of pure weight, dozens of other smaller circuses. He made the Ringling brothers head of a combination, which, by its mere proportions, forestalled any chance of competition." By 1906, the Ringling Bros. and Barnum & Bailey Circus was the "Greatest Show on Earth," a virtual monopoly, and the brothers were wealthy.

Henry Ringling joined the enterprise in 1886 as an employee of his five brothers. His status changed from employee to co-owner in 1911, after Otto died and the surviving brother-owners divvied up his share. Henry had proved himself worthy by his able management of newly acquired circuses that the brothers continued to operate.

Henry was "fond of reading, and was, perhaps, the most home-loving of them all," according to his nephew, Henry North. His obituary emphasized his "quiet and reserved" nature, in contrast to the ballyhoo business in which he spent his entire adult life. "While Henry, as a manager, was exacting of his people, he was also kind, and no one ever appreciated good help more than did Henry Ringling. For two years he was manager of the Forepaugh and Sells and while he had but little to say, he managed the show in the same quiet manner that characterizes the man from his boyhood days."

The Ringling empire flourished through the 1920s but encountered a series of setbacks that eventually spelled doom: the Great Depression, World War II, a tragic 1944 fire in Hartford, Connecticut that took 167 lives, the advent of TV and other entertainment options, rising costs, and animal rights protests. On Sunday, May 21, 2017, the Greatest Show on Earth said goodbye to a sellout crowd in Uniondale, NY, leaving its vestiges at the Circus World Museum in Baraboo and the Ringling Museum Complex in Sarasota, Florida.

The Iroquois Theater Tragedy

On Wednesday, December 30, 1903, during the holiday week between Christmas and New Year's Day, schools were in recess, and moms were looking for ways to entertain the kids. A beautiful new venue, the Iroquois Theater in Chicago's Loop, was presenting the play *Mr. Bluebeard.* An audience of 2,000, mostly women and children, filled all 1,600 seats and overflowed into the aisles and standing room at the rear of the auditorium. Among the attendees was 30-year-old Florence Tobias of Wilmette.

The second act began at 3:00 PM. As the chorus performed the act's fourth musical number, "In the Pale Moonlight," a spark from a limelight (an early stage-illuminating device) ignited the fabric of a curtain. An attempt to extinguish the blaze with chemical spray failed, and the fire spread quickly, igniting scenery panels and dropping embers onto the stage. An asbestos curtain designed to protect the audience from a stage fire was lowered, but it failed to reach the floor, leaving a gap of several feet. A strong draft, created when performers fled outside through stage doors, swept the fire, heat, and smoke into the auditorium.

When the fire began, one of the actors, comedian Eddy Foy, tried to calm the audience, but as conditions worsened, panic erupted. People struggled to reach aisles, stairs, and exits, only to find aisles and stairs jammed and exit doors blocked or locked. Bodies began to pile up at the bottlenecks and exits, transforming the theater into a death chamber. In all, 600 victims, including more than 200 children, were trampled, suffocated, or burned to death. Many more were injured.

The following morning, the *Chicago Tribune* described the "anxiety" in North Shore towns (specifically Rogers Park, Evanston, and Wilmette) from which "the Iroquois drew heavily": "The telephone service from these points was kept busy all evening with inquiries," and "the Northwestern trains coming to Chicago after 6 o'clock were crowded with passengers who were hurrying in to get what information they could as to the fate of friends or relatives." Over the next few days, newspapers listed the dead, including Florence Tobias. At the time, she was probably living with her brother, George Tobias, at 1017 Central Avenue. He performed the grim task of identifying her mutilated body, and he later became president of the Iroquois Memorial Association.

Neighboring towns suffered devastating losses. Evanston's death toll was at least twelve. Three Evanston families lost two or more members. Winnetka's toll was at least nine, including Emilie Hoyt Fox and her three children: George, 15; Willis, twelve; and Emilie, nine. The following year, William Hoyt, the father and grandfather of these victims, donated funds to build the Episcopal Church at 784 Sheridan Road, Winnetka, in their memory.

In the aftermath of the tragedy, gloom settled over the entire nation. It was soon matched by angry calls for accountability. Three men associated with the theater company and two city officials were indicted for creating or ignoring dangerous conditions that contributed to the disaster. Hundreds of civil lawsuits were filed. Virtually all these proceedings came to naught.

Criticism was also directed at the theater's architect, 29-year-old Benjamin Marshall, whose "fire proof design" arguably included features that contributed to the disaster. His initial reaction was disbelief: "There were ample fire exits and they were available. The house could have been emptied in less than five minutes if they were all utilized…. I am completely upset by this disaster, more so because I have built many theaters and have studied every playhouse disaster in history to avoid errors." Marshall's career wasn't adversely affected. He went on to become one of Chicago's most prominent architects, and in 1921 he built for himself a magnificent mansion and studio in Wilmette just south of Wilmette Harbor.

Wilmette's Movie Theaters

The Iroquois Theater disaster had an impact beyond grief and anger. The tragedy occurred when the motion picture industry was just emerging as a popular form of entertainment. Theaters were springing up across the country. Some folks were skeptical about this new art form and how it might adversely affect the moral character of the community. The Iroquois disaster heightened the concern over safety. Highly flammable film and hot projection lights could be a lethal combination.

In Wilmette, the village board relied on both moral and safety grounds when it stubbornly rejected requests by some residents to allow movie theaters in the village. The Rev. Joseph Fogarty, Rector of St. Augustine's Church, spoke for many citizens when he urged the board to "suppress" movies in the village. The board obliged for several years.

In 1913 the board finally relented and set the stage for movie theaters, but only if they complied with ordinances that imposed strict safety standards, prohibited Sunday showings, and empowered the village president to censor their offerings. (Censorship was lawful, because First Amendment protection wasn't thought to apply to commercial movies.) Building permits were issued for two new theaters. Both opened in the spring of 1914.

The first was the 600-seat Central Theater in the new Metropolitan Block Building at 1122 Central Avenue (site of the current Wilmette Theater). The building was erected at a cost of $42,600, and the theater was managed by A.K. Brown, President of the American Theater Co., which also owned the Hinsdale Theater and the LaGrange Theater. On opening day, the Central Theater attracted 1,500 patrons.

Less than four weeks later, a second theater, the Village Theater, premiered in a new building at 1150 Wilmette Avenue (now called the Baker Building). It had 625 seats, a Kimball organ, and a grand piano; and it hosted 1,400 patrons at two showings on opening night. The owners were prominent Wilmette men, including Edward Kelley (President of Goelitz Confectionary Co.) and Frank Seng (President of the Seng Co., manufacturers of furniture hardware). They hired Myron Sparr, an experienced theater manager, to direct day-to-day operations.

Competition didn't work well for the Central Theater. The Village Theater had advantages: a nicer facility, more popular films, better management, and respected local owners. Less than four months after opening, the Central Theater's lease was taken over by the Village Theater, and Sparr managed both facilities in a coordinated way.

For a short time, the two theaters co-existed, but in 1916 the Central Theater closed. The Village Theater survived until 1927, when it also closed, a victim of competition from the new, luxurious Teatro del Lago in No Man's Land. Lying outside Wilmette, Teatro wasn't constrained by Wilmette's ban on Sunday showings, and its owner, Sam Meyer, had connections that enabled him to book the most popular attractions.

The Wilmette Fire Department visited the Village Theater shortly after
its 1914 opening. Courtesy of the Wilmette Historical Museum.

Wilmette residents reacted decisively. They wanted their own family-
friendly theater that would be subject to local control and local regulation.
They forced the village board to hold a referendum in 1928 to decide whether
the Village should allow Sunday showings to encourage the establishment of
a new Wilmette-based theater. Voters overwhelmingly approved this proposition. By then, though, the curtain had already fallen on the Village Theater.
The building was well on its way to becoming the new headquarters of the
First National Bank of Wilmette.

Teatro del Lago posed a huge competitive threat to any potential new Wilmette theater. Immediately after the referendum, its owner stated publicly
that he'd soon announce plans for a new theater in Wilmette. He hoped to
discourage competitors. This tactic didn't work. The former Central Theater,
shuttered for twelve years, was leased to Peter Kalleres and Phillip Adams,
theater operators from Gary, Indiana. They refurbished the theater, installed
modern sound equipment, and opened the Wilmette Theater in 1930 to capacity crowds. Their run was short. In 1934 they sold out to Sam Meyers.

Censorship continued. A Moving Picture Council—consisting of the Village's
social worker and representatives of the Woman's Club and PTAs—reviewed
the movies scheduled to be shown at the Wilmette Theater and Teatro. If the

theaters complied with the council's recommendations, everything was fine. If not, the council adopted a hostile attitude and, on one occasion, picketed the offending theater.

In 1946 a highly profitable exploitation film, *Mom and Dad,* was booked at the Wilmette Theater. This 97-minute film was designed to titillate without violating obscenity laws. It was heavily promoted wherever it was shown. It portrayed a teenage girl who became intimate with a pilot. Her mother rejected the girl's request for an educational "hygiene book" because the girl wasn't married. Weeks later the girl learned that she was pregnant, and the pilot had died in a crash. During a 20-minute intermission, an "eminent sexual hygiene commentator," Elliott Forbes, gave a speech. While Forbes was speaking, women in nurses' uniforms strolled the aisles, selling a pamphlet and two books. The movie resumed with scenes of childbirth and graphic charts of the female anatomy.

Turns out, "Elliott Forbes" was a fraud. At the Wilmette Theater, he was played by Charles Zimmerman, a Minneapolis undertaker. In a series of well attended showings, the film was presented to one gender at a time, although some men tried to sneak into the women's showings and vice versa. Many residents were outraged and complained to police. Sergeant Roger Sherman attended a mother/daughter showing and concluded that Zimmerman's talk "exceeded good taste." Zimmerman was arrested for presenting an indecent exhibition and selling indecent literature. The remaining showings were canceled. Zimmerman was fined $100, but he absconded without paying.

The era of unbridled censorship ended in 1952 when the U.S. Supreme Court ruled that movies are a constitutionally protected form of speech, but "obscenity," as determined by contemporary community standards, could be censored. Wilmette adopted a new obscenity ordinance implementing this new rule of law.

The Wilmette Theater closed in 1951. The building was taken over by Encyclopedia Britannica Films, the world's largest producer of educational films, for use as a studio. In 1965 Teatro del Lago also closed, leaving Wilmette with no theater. This created an opportunity for Richard Stern. His family operated the Cinema Theater in Chicago, which was known for showing art films. In 1966 he refurbished and reopened the Wilmette Theater, which had been vacated by Encyclopedia Britannica Films. From the beginning, business was tough. In 1967 Stern filed a lawsuit alleging that Balaban and Katz and movie distributors were conspiring to deny first run movies to the Wilmette Theater.

In the early 1970s Stern found a way to increase his audience: showing X-rated movies. During the summer of 1972 he presented a film called *Is There*

Sex After Death to capacity crowds. At the next village board meeting, a group of citizens vehemently protested and demanded that officials take action under the obscenity ordinance. Village President James Schwietert promised strict enforcement.

The issue festered as Stern continued to present a mixture of X-rated films and art films. In December 1974 he showed X-rated *The Cheerleaders,* prompting the village to issue citations under the obscenity ordinance. This action didn't stop Stern. In February 1975 he showed X-rated *Panorama Blue.* In attendance were Robert Mangler, village attorney; Donald Sternberg, police sergeant; and Harold Sullivan, circuit court judge. According to legend, the village treasury paid for their theater tickets but parsimoniously refused to pay for their popcorn. After viewing the film, Judge Sullivan ruled that it was obscene and ordered its confiscation. Stern promptly filed a lawsuit against the Village and the three officials for violating his constitutional rights.

The legal proceedings and public controversy gradually faded away. Stern was the ultimate winner of the legal wrangling. He continued to show X-rated films from time to time without challenge, including Russ Meyer's 1979 film, *Beyond the Valley of the Ultra Vixens.* It drew capacity crowds, mostly Wilmette residents. Stern retired in 2006 and sold the theater. Currently, the building is occupied by two not-for-profit organizations. One conducts a multi-arts and performance center in the spaces on the first floor. The other, called Actors Training Center, trains and educates performers of every age on the second floor.

Hans Spanuth, Motion Picture Pioneer

Hans Spanuth was a longtime resident at 229 6th Street and an important figure in the early motion picture industry. He was born in Bremen, Germany in 1884. His parents, August and Anna, came to New York City when Hans was an infant. The father was an acclaimed pianist, composer, and music critic. The mother was a dramatist and concert vocalist whose voice was praised as "a full mezzo soprano of noble tone." The couple divorced during Hans' childhood, and his mother took her talents and her son to Cincinnati, Indianapolis, and Chicago for several years before returning to New York City, where Hans attended Columbia University.

Hans spent his entire adult life in the motion picture industry. He began his career in 1907, showing films in New York City "nickelodeons," a term that originally referred to converted store fronts where movies were shown for a nickel. He went on to produce, distribute and exhibit movies. He sometimes worked with the industry's big players, and he sometimes worked independently.

In 1911 he produced America's first feature-length film, *Oliver Twist*. At the time, an adaptation of the Charles Dickens novel was being performed as a stage play on Broadway. Hans's film was based on that adaptation. In the lead role of Fagin, he cast Nat Goodwin, a distinguished Broadway actor who was playing the same role in the stage play. Although it was then considered degrading for a stage actor to appear in a motion picture, Hans convinced Goodwin "to preserve his performance for posterity." Exhibitors initially declined the film, believing (as Hans explained) that "no one would sit for over an hour looking at a picture." The exhibitors were quickly proved wrong. Hans licensed a theater and filled it night after night. Following this success, he was able to market the film quite profitably. Of the film's five reels, only four survive.

A few years later, Hans came to Chicago, which was then an important center for motion picture production. He engaged in a number of production and distribution ventures before founding his own production company, Commonwealth Pictures Corp. Commonwealth produced numerous films, but the most important were his *Spanuth's Original Vod-A-Vil Movies*, produced between 1918 and 1920.

This was the silent movie era. It was a time when the big movie houses in urban areas also offered live stage shows featuring Vaudeville acts. Smaller theaters in outlying areas couldn't afford live acts, so Hans came up with an idea: Film the acts and distribute the films for exhibition in the smaller theaters. Film them he did: hundreds of vaudeville acts, 77 reels, four acts to a reel. Among them were *The Kawana Trio* (foot jugglers), *Tom Tinker's Pony Patter, Jumbo, the Trained Elephant*, and *Observe Amazing Animals!* (featuring a fiddling baboon, a rope-jumping dog, and an ornery donkey). These films today are an important historic record of vaudeville.

Hans ended his career as television began to emerge. In the mid-1940s he produced a television series called *Woman Speaks,* documenting the activities and achievements of women. In 1949 he predicted "that in the not too distant future the major picture producers will present special televisions features. You will see first run special TV features, other than those shown in regular theaters, but equally as good if not better because of the close-up feature of television production."

On Location

Serving as a location for the filming of scenes in a motion picture has pluses and minuses. It can generate revenue for resident-hosts and businesses that assist the endeavor in one way or another. It's also fun and interesting to be present at the filming, watch the stars plying their craft at familiar hometown places, and later see the finished product. On the other hand, the tedious filming process can be disruptive to quiet neighborhoods invaded by film crews working late into the night.

Wilmette's first known filming experience occurred in 1917 when Selig Polyscope Co. came to the village to film *Pioneer Days,* a historical drama about the Fort Dearborn Battle. More than 60 years passed before Wilmette was visited again by filmmakers. That's when a scene from the Oscar-winning film, *Ordinary People* (1979), was filmed at Walker Bros. Pancake House on Green Bay Road.

The movie that made Tom Cruise a star, *Risky Business* (1983), came to Wilmette four years later. It includes a car chase on Sheridan Road past the Bahá'í House of Worship. Some interior scenes were filmed in the gymnasium of the old Howard School, which was converted into a temporary movie studio. The school had been closed in 1980 and was awaiting the wrecker's ball and the creation of Howard Park.

Michigan Shores Club was the site of the dance in *A Night in the Life of Jimmy Reardon* (1988), starring River Phoenix. *Home Alone* (1990), the Christmastime favorite, includes a scene in which the Macaulay Culkin character heads into Trinity United Methodist Church.

Margaret, the little girl in *Dennis the Menace* (1993), "lived" in a house in the 1200 block of Gregory Avenue. *Uncle Buck* (1998) includes scenes shot at Romona School. *The Trouble with Dee Dee* (2005) has scenes shot at the Wilmette Woman's Club and the Baker Building in the Village Center. *Derailed* (1995) includes scenes shot in the 1000 block of Chestnut Avenue.

Two sources report that *High Fidelity* (2000) contains a scene of a family wake that was filmed at a house on Greenleaf Avenue, just east of 10th Street. Scenes in *Contagion* (2011) were filmed at Central School and Scott Funeral Home, attracting hundreds of Wilmette movie fans hoping to catch a glimpse of Matt Damon and the film's other big-name stars.

Ralph Bellamy

Ralph Bellamy is the first of three homegrown actors profiled in this chapter, selected because they achieved stardom in long acting careers now ended. Others of equal distinction aren't profiled, because, fortunately, they're still among the living and adding credits to their careers.

Ralph was born in Chicago in 1904. His family soon moved: first to 1050 Linden Avenue in 1909 and then to 1214 Forest Avenue in 1916. His father made a decent living in the advertising business. Ralph attended Central School and New Trier (class of 1921) until he quit during his senior year while on suspension for smoking a cigarette on campus. He wasn't much of a student.

As a boy, Ralph worked a variety of odd jobs. He had a newspaper route. He delivered groceries for the Brinkman grocery store at 601 West Railroad Avenue. He ushered at a local movie theater and at Ravinia Park. He was a soda jerk at the Snider-Cazel drug store at the northeast corner of Wilmette and Central avenues. At home, his chores included beating the rugs, cutting the grass, and raking and burning the leaves.

His interest in acting may have started at age 11 when his mother took him to California for the summer, where he witnessed the making of a silent movie at Universal Studios. He returned to California four years later. There, he met Louise Lovely, a star of the silent screen. He told her he wanted to be an actor. She got him a one-day job as an extra in a film called *Wings of Morn*. He earned $5.

Back at New Trier, Ralph's interest in acting grew. He often went downtown to see plays. He joined the New Trier Dramatics Club and became its president, but its infrequent productions didn't satisfy his yearning to perform.

He was 17-years-old when the smoking incident led to his suspension. This was a turning point. He decided not to return to New Trier, and he began a twelve-year apprenticeship that included leading a company of North Shore actors and acting with various stock companies. He reached Broadway in October 1929 in *Town Boy*, which opened and closed after three performances. Between 1929 and his death in 1991 he appeared in almost 200 plays, movies, and TV shows. Here are a handful of highlights:

- On Broadway, he won a Tony Award and a New York Drama Critics Award as best dramatic actor for his role in the hit play *Sunrise at Campobello* (1958). Playing a young FDR fighting polio, he mastered the role by studying Roosevelt's life and the struggles of paraplegics.
- In the movies, he received an Oscar nomination for his supporting role in *The Awful Truth* (1937), a romantic comedy in which he lost the woman

played by Irene Dunne to her estranged husband played by Cary Grant. He also played the evil doctor in *Rosemary's Baby* (1968), the greedy co-owner of a commodity trading firm in *Trading Places* (1983), and the vulnerable businessman targeted by the Richard Gere character in *Pretty Woman* (1990). In 1987 he was awarded an honorary Oscar for his unique artistry and service to the acting profession. (He was a founder of the Screen Actors Guild and president of Actors Equity.)

- His TV credits include three Emmy nominations: for best supporting actor playing FDR in *Winds of War* (1983); for best supporting actor playing Adlai Stevenson in *The Missiles of October* (1974); and for best actor as Father in an episode of *The United States Steel Hour* called "The Fearful Decision" (1956).

Ralph Bellamy starred as Mike Barnett in the TV series *Man Against Crime* from 1949 to 1954. In the 1953 episode pictured here, he questions a gangster's wife, played by Gloria McGhee. Photo from Wikimedia Commons.

Charlton Heston

Charlton Heston was born John Charles Carter in 1923. He spent the first ten years of his life in St. Helen, Michigan, where his father operated a sawmill. He came to Wilmette in 1934, after his mother's divorce and second marriage. His took his stepfather's surname to avoid having to explain the divorce of his parents. The Heston family's home was at 325 Maple Avenue, and "Chuck" lived there from 1933 until 1943 when he enlisted in the Army Air Corps.

Charlton Heston and his mother, Lila Heston, were repeat customers of Wilmette's Crystal Cave. Pictured here with the store's proprietor, Josef Puehringer. The Crystal Cave relocated to Glenview in 2012 after 40 years in Wilmette. Courtesy of Wilmette Historical Museum and Josef Puehringer.

In 1995 he wrote his autobiography, *In the Arena,* which included detailed information about his time in Wilmette. He admitted to being unsophisticated and socially inept during his youth. He wasn't yet the handsome and commanding presence that movie-goers would come to admire. His family struggled financially during the Great Depression, and Chuck worked in various menial jobs (caddying, selling magazines, and laboring at a steel mill) to earn spending money. His stepfather was kind and helpful but distant and demanding. From these conditions emerged one of the biggest names and highest paid actors in motion pictures.

Charlton praised New Trier: "the kind of school that can ignite a kid." Despite what he saw as his personal shortcomings during this period, he thrived at New Trier, especially in its theater program. He loved the theater and acting.

His enthusiasm and talent drew the attention of the Winnetka Community Theatre, which awarded him a $300 scholarship that would pay his tuition at Northwestern University to pursue his interest in the theater.

During a 60-year acting career, he appeared in about 100 films. He was also active on stage and TV. Film critic Roger Ebert wrote that "Heston made at least three movies that almost everybody eventually sees": *The Ten Commandments* (1956), *Ben Hur* (1959), and *Planet of the Apes* (1968). He won the Oscar for Best Actor for his performance in *Ben Hur,* most remembered for the daring chariot race. He proudly rebuffed the suggestion that a double had driven the winning chariot. He had practiced for two months. "I couldn't drive it well, but that wasn't necessary. All I had to do was stay on board so they could shoot me there. I didn't have to worry; MGM guaranteed I would win the race."

He was a controversial figure in later life because of his conservative views and his strong and vocal support for gun rights. Overshadowed were his advocacy for civil rights and his strong support for Dr. Martin Luther King, Jr. during the 1960s. His lifetime body of work brought him the Jean Hersholt Humanitarian Award, the Kennedy Center Lifetime Achievement Award, and the Presidential Medal of Freedom.

He was married for 64 years to Lydia Clarke, a fellow drama student at Northwestern. He died in 2008.

Hugh O'Brian

Hugh O'Brian was a man whose philanthropic achievements arguably outshine his stellar acting career. He's best known for playing the title role in the popular ABC-TV series, *The Life and Legend of Wyatt Earp* (1955–1961).

O'Brian was born Hugh Krampe in Rochester, New York in 1925. His father, a mechanical engineer, was a sales manager for Armstrong Cork Co. During Hugh's childhood, the family moved often: from Rochester to Chicago to Lancaster, Pennsylvania, to Evanston and finally in 1935 to Wilmette—first to 700 Laurel Avenue and then to 808 Greenleaf Avenue.

Hugh attended Wilmette's District 39 schools, entering fourth grade at Central elementary school in 1935 and graduating from Stolp junior high school in 1939. He entered New Trier with the class of 1943. Unlike other Wilmette boys who achieved acting stardom, Hugh didn't pursue acting in his youth. Like Bellamy, he didn't finish high school at New Trier. Instead, he transferred to military school and then enrolled at the University of Cincinnati, aiming for a law career.

After one semester, Hugh enlisted in the Marines and served for four years. He was offered an appointment to the Naval Academy but declined after deciding to pursue law training at Yale. First though, he needed tuition money, and Los Angeles seemed like a good place to earn it. There, he became friendly with members of a theater group. When one of the actors became ill, he filled in. This led to more roles. One of his performances was seen by actress Ida Lupino, who was about to direct her first film, *Never Fear*. She launched his movie career by casting him in a significant part.

The Wyatt Earp role brought him to the attention of Dr. Albert Schweitzer, who invited him to his hospital in Lambarene, Gabon in 1958. The two men worked together for nine days. Hugh was inspired by Dr. Schweitzer and his strongly held belief that "the most important thing in education is to make young people think for themselves."

Soon after returning home, Hugh founded Hugh O'Brian Youth Leadership (HOBY). This not-for-profit organization conducts leadership development seminars, bringing together high school sophomores who have leadership potential and adult leaders in business, education, government, and the professions. Through a program of interaction, the students are taught to think and advocate for themselves and to work with and serve others. Hundreds of thousands of students have participated in HOBY over the years, including students from New Trier.

Hugh O'Brian gathered with student participants at the Lincoln Memorial for the HOBY World Leadership Conference in July 2003. Courtesy of HOBY and Virginia O'Brian.

Hugh often expressed his philosophy about individual freedom and service: "I do not believe we are all born equal. Created equal in the eyes of God, yes. But physical and emotional differences, parental guidance, varying environments, being in the right place at the right time, all play a role in enhancing or limiting an individual's development. But I do believe every man and woman, if given the opportunity and encouragement to recognize his or her potential, regardless of background, has the freedom to choose in our world. Will an individual be a taker or a giver in life? Will that person be satisfied merely to exist or seek a meaningful purpose? Will he or she dare to dream the impossible dream? I believe every person is created as the steward of his or her own destiny with great power for a specific purpose, to share with others, through service, a reverence for life in a spirit of love."

Hugh returned to New Trier on September 24, 1998 for the reunion of the Class of 1943. He spoke to a group of sophomores about HOBY and to several music classes about his experiences as an actor. He died in 2016.

Twelfth Night Festivities

For five years, 1952–1956, Wilmette held a huge Twelfth Night Festival. In 1955 four residents who were among Chicago's most popular radio and TV entertainers came together to excite the crowd. They were Mal Bellairs, Jack Brickhouse, Johnny Coons, and Frazier Thomas.

A Twelfth Night Festival wasn't unique to Wilmette. In one form or another, Twelfth Night has been observed for centuries. Falling on January 6, twelve days after Christmas, it celebrates the arrival of the Three Kings at the birthplace of Christ. Its customs include taking down Christmas decorations; holding feasts, balls, and carnivals; and crowning a king and queen (the man and woman who find a bean in their pieces of cake).

Wilmette's festival adopted these traditions. The centerpiece was a Christmas tree bonfire. Residents delivered their trees to collection points or took them directly to the site of the event, the Village Green (now Howard Park). The fire consumed 1,500 trees the first year and as many as 6,000 in later years. The festival also included clowns, magicians, and chorale groups singing Christmas carols. The boy and girl who found beans in their cake were crowned king and queen and were carried about on the shoulders of clowns. In 1956 the festival was televised by WBBM-TV.

Besides attracting a big crowd, the bonfire served two municipal interests. One was fire safety: The fire chief, who called dry trees "dynamite," supported the bonfire as a way to discourage residents from burning them on their own. The second was tree disposal: The Village had difficulty disposing of trees placed in the trash.

Wilmette's last festival was in 1956. Later that year, the Village built the state's first municipal outdoor artificial ice rink at the Village Green, taking up space needed for a safe bonfire. Roemer Park was thought to be an acceptable alternative for 1957, but at the last minute the event was canceled because of neighbors' concerns. Sponsors searched for an acceptable site for 1958, but the festival never resumed, probably for a combination of reasons: no site was found, outdoor burning was becoming an environmental issue, religious demographics were changing, and the Village purchased a chopper that facilitated tree disposal.

How exciting it must have been for adults and kids to see in person four giants of Chicago radio and television who lived in their hometown. Here's a brief introduction of each:

- Mal Bellairs joined WBBM in 1955 and for the next 15 years was the most popular radio personality in Chicago. He lived at 1424 Wilmette Avenue from 1950 to 1955 and at 720 Lake Avenue from 1955 to 1969.
- Jack Brickhouse was a radio and TV sports broadcaster, known primarily as the Chicago Cubs play-by-play announcer from 1948 to 1981. He lived at 806 Linden Avenue in the 1950s and later at 1100 Locust Road.

Jack Brickhouse calls the season opener between the Chicago White Sox and the Detroit Tigers from Comiskey Park on April 26, 1948. Photo from Wikimedia Commons.

Mal Bellairs (left). Courtesy of the Bellairs family. Frazier Thomas
(and friends, right). Courtesy of the Wilmette Historical Museum.

- Johnny Coons, known as Uncle Johnny by his young audience, hosted *Noon-time Comics* (featuring "Crusader Rabbit" cartoons) on Chicago's WNBQ-TV during the mid-1950s. For a time, he was the hottest performer on Chicago daytime TV except for *Howdy Doody*. He lived at 1031 Greenwood Avenue in the 1950s, before moving to California in 1959.
- Frazier Thomas was the longtime WGN-TV host of *Garfield Goose and Friends, Family Classics*, and *Bozo's Circus*. He lived at 1945 Wilmette Avenue in the 1950s and later at 1232 Greenwood Avenue until his death in 1985.

Some grey-haired folks fondly remember the excitement of Wilmette's Twelfth Night and the towering flames and distinctive odor of its roaring bonfire. Meanwhile, some younger folks may be wondering, "What's a bonfire?"

Milan Lusk, Violin Virtuoso

Born in 1893, Milan Lusk lived his entire short life (39 years) at 810 Michigan Avenue. He was an acclaimed violinist and toured the world in concert. His parents were born in Bohemia and immigrated to America as children. His father was a successful lawyer, his mother an accomplished painter. At age four, his musical talent began to show, first with the piano and soon with the violin. He studied under virtuoso Joseph Capek and at Northwestern's School of Music.

At age 20, he traveled to Pisek, Bohemia with the goal of perfecting his skills under Otakar Sevcik, a Czech who was recognized as the world's foremost violin teacher. Lusk remained in Europe more than three years, studying in Pisek and Vienna and performing as soloist with the Prague Philharmonic Orchestra and other ensembles. He gave concerts to benefit the Red Cross and received awards for this service. When relations between the U.S. and Austria deteriorated before U.S. entry into World War I, he attempted to leave Europe, only to be stopped at the Austrian border and jailed for 22 days.

Milan Lusk as drawn by his mother, Marie Koupal Lusk, an accomplished painter. Courtesy of the Wilmette Historical Museum.

His reputation as a virtuoso spread quickly to America. Over the next decade, he gave hundreds of concerts; was a popular radio performer (including Sunday mornings on WGN); cut records for Victor, Emerson, and Columbia recording companies; and gave private lessons to promising students. Critics were enthusiastic about his talent. Sevcik, his teacher, captured the essence of their accolades: "He possesses a brilliant technique, a beautiful tone, and his playing displays temperament." With his 6'4" stature, hazel eyes, thick black hair, and pleasing manner, he impressed audiences before playing his first note.

He returned to Europe frequently for concert tours. In 1924 he performed for

President Tomas Masaryk of Czechoslovakia and twice for Queen Marie of Romania, who became his patron. In 1927 King Ferdinand of Romania awarded him the Order of the Crown for outstanding service to the kingdom.

In July 1928 Benito Mussolini, Italy's Prime Minister, invited Milan to his office in Rome. Knowing that Mussolini had studied the violin seriously as a child and still played for diversion, Milan brought along his violin. Mussolini examined the instrument, recognized that it had been made in Cremona, Italy and said, "Ah! A fine Cremona make. No better workmen in the world. What wonderful low tones you must be able to get out of it." Milan offered to play, but Mussolini countered with an invitation to play at his summer residence, Villa Torlonia. "What will you play for me?" he asked. Milan replied, "Dawes and Dambrosia."

"Dawes" was Charles Dawes, then the U.S. vice president under Calvin Coolidge. A resident of Evanston before his election, Dawes was a self-taught pianist and composer. At Villa Torlonia, Milan played Dawes' composition, "Melody in A Major," a piece for piano and violin that was later transformed into the pop song, "It's All In The Game," a hit in 1958. Mussolini was impressed. "When you go back," he said, "tell him I admire him." During the recital, one of Milan's strings broke, and Mussolini helped replace it with one of his own. "Nothing like having a spare tire," he quipped. At the end, Mussolini thanked Milan by giving him an autographed photograph.

On his final European tour in 1932, Milan died suddenly in Prague following surgery for stomach cancer. Some of his recordings survive, but if you acquire one, you'll need a 78-rpm phonograph to play it.

Breaking News from the Entertainment World

- April 17, 1913: Annie Eggert, 49, of 914 Oakwood Avenue is highly offended by what she saw on stage at the Evanston Stock Company's production of the play *Old Heidelberg* at the Evanston Theater. She took her complaint to the box office: "That little miss [Isabel] Randolph kissed the hero just as though she liked it. She puckered up her mouth and stood on her toes during that long parting scene. I don't care to have my daughter see any such performance as that." (Eggert has two sons, no daughter.)
- March 19, 1962: Film star Ann-Margret, formerly of Wilmette, returned to her home town for a two-day visit. Her latest movie, *State Fair,* co-starring Pat Boone and Bobby Darin, is opening at Chicago's Oriental Theater on April 13, and she's appearing on the Ed Sullivan TV show on April 1.

Chicago's Isabel Randolph had a long and successful career as a character actor in theater, radio, TV, and film. One of her best known roles was Abigail Uppington on the *Fibber McGee and Molly* radio show. Photo from Wikimedia Commons.

Ann-Margret's talent as an artiste emerged at New Trier High School (class of 1959). As a senior, her steamy performance of the song "Tropical Heat Wave" in *Lagniappe*, the annual variety show, caused a stir among some parents. Photo from Wikimedia Commons.

Percy Faith's music was easy listening. Photo from Wikimedia Commons.

- February 9, 1976: Canadian-born Percy Faith, 67, who lived in Wilmette from 1940 to 1946, first at 901 Greenwood Avenue and later at 744 Sheridan Road, died of cancer. While living in Wilmette, Faith was composer, conductor, and arranger of the orchestra that entertained NBC's radio listeners on the *Contented Hour*, sponsored by the Carnation Milk Co. He went on to became internationally renowned during a long career highlighted by numerous gold records, seven Grammy Award nominations and two wins ("Love Theme from Romeo and Juliet" and "The Theme from a Summer Place"), and an Academy Award nomination for best musical score in 1955 (*Love Me or Leave Me*). His ingenious use of the violin in his compositions and arrangements made his music especially pleasing to the ear and popular with listeners.

CHAPTER 12

★————————————★

More of the Arts

Wilmette residents have contributed to the world of art in a variety of ways, ranging from street photography (Vivian Maier) to landscape design (Jens Jensen) with much in between.

Vivian Maier was a street photographer whose collection of negatives assembled over her lifetime (1926–2009) numbered more than 100,000. Neither the negatives nor Vivian's talent came to light until after her death. She was very private and eccentric, and perhaps even mentally ill. Despite this, or perhaps because of it, she had an uncanny ability to capture interesting subjects in natural and poignant moments. She spent many years working as a nanny on the North Shore, including a stint at the residence of Dr. Frederico Baylaender at 831 Michigan Avenue from 1989 to 1993. She has been the subject of numerous books and documentaries in recent years.

Jens Jensen achieved fame as a designer of parks in the Chicago park system. In 1920 he retired and started his own landscape architecture practice, designing private estates and public parks throughout the U.S. From 1920 to 1935, he lived in Wilmette at 1211 Elmwood Avenue. He was known for his use of native plants placed in natural settings. One of his favorite design features was called the "council ring," a circular limestone bench nestled into the landscape where visitors could connect with one another and nature. Locally, he designed Mahoney Park on Sheridan Road in Kenilworth and the landscaping for the estate of Perry Smithers at 711 Lake Avenue. (The Smithers estate no longer exists.)

Future historians will undoubtedly honor architects Carol Ross Barney and Martin Wolf, artists Jim Nutt and Gladys Nilsson, novelist Scott Turow, architectural critic Blair Kamin, and other creative Wilmette residents. The sketches that follow are limited to those whose careers and lives have ended.

Jens Jensen had the look of an artist. Photo by Helen Balfour Morrison, © The Morrison-Shearer Foundation, Northbrook, IL. Located at Newberry Library.

Eliel Saarinen's Proposed Tribune Tower

Eliel Saarinen, a native of Finland, became a world renowned architect and urban planner during a career spanning the first half of the 20th century. He lived in Wilmette during the early 1920s, after leaving Finland and before settling in Michigan. His residency was brief, but he enjoyed his time in the village. As he told a *Chicago Tribune* columnist, "Wilmette is the most beautiful of small and simple suburban communities. It is full of cozy, unpretentious little houses, each one conveniently designed so that the family can dispense with the almost unattainable 'hired help'. It is so modern that it has none of the shabbiness of older communities of its type." This was high praise, coming from the mouth of an architect and planner who was already acclaimed in Europe for designing the Finnish Pavilion at the 1900 Paris World's Fair and the Helsinki railroad station, and for planning future growth in the cities of Helsinki and Tallinn, among other projects.

Eliel Saarinen's second prize design was published
in the *Chicago Tribune* on December 3, 1922.

Saarinen came to Chicago in response to the *Tribune*'s contest to design "the most beautiful office building in the world." The winner would receive a prize of $50,000. Second place and third place finishers would receive $20,000 and $10,000, respectively. Ten prominent U.S. architectural firms were each paid $2,000 to participate. The competition drew tremendous international interest, with more than 260 architects from 23 countries submitting entries. The ideas presented by these architects influenced the design of high rise office buildings for many years.

Saarinen's design was Gothic in spirit but forward-looking. It incorporated "verticality as its primary principle." Its four setbacks thrust the building like a spear into the sky. But sadly for Saarinen, it was adjudged by the Jury of Award to be runner-up to a Gothic art-deco design by New York architects Raymond Hood and John Howells. Their design incorporated "architectural ideas borrowed from the past." It was built; Saarinen's was not.

Many critics, led by Chicago's Louis Sullivan, the "spiritual father of modern American architecture," favored Saarinen's design over the Hood/Howells design. Sullivan wrote, "[T]he second and first prize stand before us side by side. One glance of the trained eye, and instant judgment comes; that judgment which flashes from inner experience in recognition of a masterpiece. The verdict of the Jury of Award is at once reversed, and the second prize is placed first, where it belongs by virtue of its beautifully controlled and virile power. The first prize is demoted to the level of those works evolved of dying ideas, even as it sends forth a frantic cry to escape from the common bondage of those governed by ideas."

Basking in the glory of these plaudits, Saarinen came to the U.S. in 1923 to be honored by architectural and engineering societies and clubs. He decided to move to the Chicago area with his family, pursue his interest in designing high-rise buildings, and join the urban planning process then underway in Chicago. Soon, though, he altered his plans and moved to Ann Arbor to accept a visiting professorship in architectural design at the University of Michigan. In 1925 he moved again to Bloomfield Hills to oversee the architectural and landscape development of the Cranbrook Academy of Arts. He later became the Academy's president.

Saarinen's son, Eero, was also an accomplished architect, and the two men collaborated on projects until the father died in 1950. Both men were involved in designing Winnetka's Crow Island School (1940), recognized nationally as an icon of progressive school design.

Cartoonists Luther Bradley, William Schmedtgen, & Carey Orr

During the early years of the 20th century, the Wilmette Public School Art League worked to cultivate students' appreciation of art. It sponsored lectures, and it acquired works of art through purchases and donations and placed them in schools. Prominent women of the village led this organization that once boasted hundreds of members.

By 1924 the estimated value of the artwork displayed at the schools was $5,000. The collection included 15 hand-colored Copley prints of the Holy Grail series by Edwin Abbey and original cartoons by famous Chicago newspaper cartoonists John McCutcheon, Luther Bradley, and William Schmedtgen. Two of these artists, Bradley and Schmedtgen, were Wilmette residents.

Luther Bradley was born in Connecticut in 1853 and came to Evanston as a child. Early on, he showed artistic talent, but he found greater pleasure in outdoor activities like horseback riding through the Ouilmette Reserve and sailing a small boat on Lake Michigan. For college, he went east to Yale, but after one year, his father called him home to join his real estate firm. There, the young man labored for seven years.

In 1882 Bradley yielded to wanderlust. Eventually reaching Australia and being short on money, he answered an ad for a newspaper cartoonist. This led to eleven years of employment in Melbourne. His cartoons received international recognition. When he returned to Evanston on account of his father's illness and death in 1892, he easily found work at Chicago newspapers, spending the last 17 years of his career at the Chicago Daily News.

He married in 1901 and initially settled in Evanston. In 1909 the family moved to 822 Michigan Avenue, Wilmette. From his home near the Lake Michigan bluff with its expansive beach, he resumed the outdoor activities of his youth with his four children as companions.

He reached his creative peak at the close of his career during World War I. His cartoons depicting the devastation caused by militarism won him accolades as America's greatest cartoonist. *Just Another Little Fellow,* for example, showed Mother Europe cradling Child Romania who had just been run down by a speeding war tank. Its driver shouted back, "He ran right in the way!"

This Bradley cartoon appeared in the *Chicago Daily News,* November 28, 1916.

Bradley's contemporary, William Schmedtgen, was born in 1862 and raised in Chicago, the son of German immigrants. He studied at the Art Institute and in 1883 started his art career with a stint at the *Chicago Evening Mail* as an illustrator. After working briefly as a commercial artist in St. Louis and New York, he returned in 1886 and headed up the art department of the *Chicago Record.* When the *Record* merged into the *Chicago Record Herald* in 1901, he continued as a staff artist. He mastered the process of chalk-plating that revolutionized newspaper illustrating and cartooning. His subjects ranged from the execution of four men accused of inciting Chicago's Haymarket riots in 1886 to naval maneuvers in Cuba during the Spanish-American War.

The Schmedtgen family moved to 710 Greenleaf Avenue in 1909. Midway through his career, William became an accomplished landscape and wildlife artist, producing both fine art and commercial illustrations for outdoor magazines and advertising calendars. One of his watercolors, *Old Fort and Block House,* was a scene he recorded at Santiago, Cuba during the Spanish-American War. He donated it to the Public School Art League, and it hung at Stolp junior high school until it was destroyed by a fire in 1920. He generously replaced it two months later.

Not only is the Art League gone and forgotten, but so is the art it placed in the schools, including all of the original works by McCutcheon, Bradley, and Schmedtgen. No one seems to know what happened to them.

This 1912 Schmedtgen illustration of the sinking of the *Titanic* appeared in the *Chicago Record-Herald* and later on the cover of the sheet music for the popular song "Just as the Ship Went Down."

Carey Orr is another distinguished cartoonist who lived in Wilmette: first at 225 Woodbine Avenue from the early 1920s to the early 1940s, and later at 1630 Sheridan Road from about 1964 until his death in 1967. He was born in Ada, Ohio in 1890. His mother died during his infancy, and he was raised by his grandparents on their farm in Union County, Ohio. His interest in drawing was sparked at age 10 when a beggar came to the farm and thanked his grandmother for giving him some food by drawing a picture of Jesus for her. However, a career in art seemed doubtful for young Carey after he lost vision in his left eye after an accident. He tried to conceal this condition throughout his life.

When Orr reached adolescence, he moved to Spokane, Washington to live with his remarried father, a lumberman. There, he took correspondence courses in cartooning. Despite his impaired vision, he became a standout pitcher in high school and semi-pro baseball. After earning enough money (at the rate of $75 per game), he gave up a promising baseball career in 1911 and enrolled in the Chicago Academy of Fine Arts to study cartooning.

His first newspaper job was with the *Chicago Examiner,* followed in 1914 by a job as cartoonist for the *Nashville Tennessean.* His work at the *Tennessean* caught the attention of Robert McCormick, owner and publisher of the *Chicago Tribune,* who brought him to Chicago in 1917. At the time, John McCutcheon, another Pulitzer Prize winner, was the paper's chief cartoonist, but Orr's cartoons were often featured because McCutcheon traveled extensively. Orr succeeded McCutcheon in 1940. Besides drawing cartoons, Orr taught at his alma mater, the Chicago Academy of Fine Arts. In 1917 one of his students was Walt Disney, then a teenager and aspiring cartoonist.

For many years, into the 1960s, the *Tribune* displayed a cartoon on its front page, just above the fold. When advances in newspaper printing allowed, the cartoon was printed in color. Because of its prominent placement, it immediately drew readers' attention and was a popular feature. Orr's cartoons appeared there regularly.

It's difficult to summarize his thousands of cartoons drawn over a 50-year career, but sharing the conservative philosophy of the *Tribune* and its publisher, Orr often targeted FDR, the New Deal, Harry Truman, and other "liberal" subjects. He also took aim at communism, crime, Prohibition, and government waste and corruption. Shortly after his death, his colleagues, who knew his work best, said that "Carey's pen could be slashing, for he was no friend of corruption or political bombast, but his gentle nature was often expressed in human interest subjects, evocative, nostalgic, and homespun."

Orr won a Pulitzer Prize in 1961 for his cartoon, *The Kindly Tiger.* Just before its publication in 1960, the Congo (a major uranium supplier to the U.S.) had become independent from Belgium, and Patrice Lumumba had become its first prime minister. Some folks worried that Lumumba was too friendly to the Soviets. Orr's cartoon shows Africa on a "long trek to freedom" coming upon "Krushy's [Khrushchev's] Kat," a tiger kindly asking, "May I give you a ride?," but secretly salivating over the prospect of devouring Africa.

Shortly after receiving the Pulitzer, Orr was the honored guest on the popular TV show, *This Is Your Life*. Two years later, he ended his distinguished career by retiring at age 73. He died in 1967.

This Orr cartoon ridiculed William Jennings Brian for opposing science while acting as prosecutor in the "Scopes Monkey Trial." It appeared on page 1 of the *Chicago Tribune*, July 9, 1925.

Depression-Era Art

The federal government was deeply involved in local public works during the Great Depression. In Wilmette, federally funded or assisted projects included remodeling the second village hall, relaying the brick streets, revamping Washington (now Gillson) Park, and constructing the post office, the waterworks, and Vattman Park's tennis courts. The federal government also funded recreational activities at the Village Green (now Howard Park), educational programs at the library, and concerts in Washington Park. The idea was to put the unemployed to work, modernize and beautify infrastructure, and rally dispirited Americans.

Federal programs also promoted public artwork and provided work for artists. "After all," said New Dealer Harry Hopkins, "They've got to eat just like other people." The first federal art program was the Public Works of Art Project of the U.S. Treasury. Lasting only six months, PWAP employed artists to create paintings and sculptures depicting "the American Scene" for public buildings.

There are six PWAP paintings in Wilmette, all created by George Lusk. Born in 1902, Lusk was raised in Wilmette at 810 Michigan Avenue, son of a lawyer-father and a painter-mother, and brother of violinist Milan Lusk. He studied art in Chicago and Europe and taught in California before returning home in the 1930s to be a full-time painter. His six large works are on display at the Wilmette Historical Museum, but they first hung in the council chamber of the second village hall. Two are portraits, one of Archange Ouilmette (the Pottawatomie woman to whom the federal government granted the Ouilmette Reserve), the other of John Westerfield (Wilmette's first village president). The remaining four are large murals, two depicting 18th century scenes of the village and the other two depicting some of the village's more modern (1930s) features. PWAP ended in 1934 before Lusk finished the works, but he completed them anyway without pay.

PWAP was succeeded by another Treasury Department program in which artists competed for commissions to create site-specific murals or sculptures for new federal buildings, mostly post offices. One mural is at the Wilmette Post Office. Painted by artist Raymond Breinen in 1938, it's a brooding farm scene called *In the Soil Is Our Wealth*. Breinen was born in Russia in 1910 and fled with his family to America in 1922, settling in Chicago. He achieved national prominence in the late 1930s, but his popularity declined in the 1950s as contemporary art ascended. Breinen also painted a mural at Winnetka's Skokie School, but officials thought it was "communist in character" and covered it over.

Two other Depression-era works of art in Wilmette were created by Gustaf Dalstrom under the Work Progress Administration's Federal Art Project, the government's biggest art program. Applicants qualified for this program by showing that they were actively-working, impoverished artists. They received $24 per week to create artwork for non-federal public buildings like schools and libraries. Dalstrom was born in Sweden in 1893 and came to America in 1900, settling in Chicago. He studied art in Chicago and Europe and, like his wife Frances Foy, became a prominent Chicago muralist. His huge Wilmette murals are called *Farming* (a springtime farm scene) and *Gardening* (villagers working and relaxing in a garden setting). They were originally displayed at Laurel School (400 7th Street) in 1938, one in the kindergarten and the other in the first grade room, but they were moved to Harper School's auditorium when Laurel was demolished in 1973.

Edward Gorey, Author and Illustrator

Edward Gorey spent three years of his boyhood in Wilmette, living at 1506 Washington Avenue, attending Howard School from 1934 to 1936, and graduating from Stolp School in 1937. His father was a Chicago newspaper reporter and later administrative assistant to Cook County Assessor Parky Cullerton. At Stolp, Edward showed signs of his artistic future by contributing drawings for the yearbook, samples of which are in the possession of the Wilmette Historical Museum. After graduating from Stolp, Edward went on to four years of high school at the Francis W. Parker School in Chicago, followed by the School of the Art Institute, the U.S. Army, and Harvard University. The Gorey family moved frequently during Edward's childhood—twelve different addresses, mostly in Chicago.

These drawings by Edward Gorey appeared in Wilmette's Stolp Junior High yearbook and hinted at the artistic style and humor that would bloom in Gorey's adulthood. Courtesy of the Wilmette Historical Museum.

Edward was a man of many talents. He was an author and illustrator of at least 90 of his own books, and he illustrated at least 60 books of others, including authors Edward Lear, H.G. Wells, T.S. Elliot, Samuel Beckett and John Updike. He was a Tony Award winning costume designer for the Broadway production of *Dracula*. He created the animated illustrations that served as the opening sequence for the PBS series *Masterpiece Mystery!*

His books revealed his quirky sense of humor, complimented by the unique pen and ink style of his illustrations. Many of his early books were supposedly written for children, but the dark humor and macabre drawings probably appealed as much if not more to adult readers. In the *Gashlycrumb Tinies*, for example, he teaches the alphabet through a series of 26 misfortunes, one for each letter. "A is for Amy who fell down the stairs. B is for Basil, assaulted by bears." And so on.

He was described as "clever," "bizarre," "eccentric," "witty," and "peculiar." He once said, "For some reason, my mission in life is to make everybody as uneasy as possible, because that's what the world is like." And also, "To take my work seriously would be the height of folly."

Chester Gould and Dick Tracy

A profile drawing of cartoon character Dick Tracy adorns a basement wall at 230 17th Street. It was placed there by Chester Gould, who lived at the 17th Street house from 1926 to 1936.

Born on a farm in Oklahoma in 1900, Gould showed artistic talent from an early age. After high school, he enrolled at Oklahoma A&M. Despite his passion for cartooning, he took courses in business, not art. After two years, he headed to Chicago with $50 in his pocket, a few drawings in his portfolio, and a dream in his heart: to be a cartoonist for the *Chicago Tribune*.

His dream would elude him for ten years. He initially worked in the art departments of several Chicago newspapers, creating artwork used in display ads. In the evening he studied art at Northwestern University. After graduating, he worked for five years as a cartoonist for the *Chicago Evening American* and another three years as a cartoonist and advertising artist for the *Chicago Daily News*.

During this period, he met a young Wilmette woman, Edna Gauger. In 1926 they were married at the home of her parents, George and Emily Gauger, 229 Linden Avenue. After the wedding, they moved into the 17th Street house, described at the time as a five-room "Spanish bungalow" with a pink stucco exterior and a tile roof. It was built for them by Edna's father, a building contractor. The couple's only child, Jean, was born one year later.

All the while Gould pursued his dream. He submitted 60 different comic strip concepts to Joseph Patterson, head of the *Chicago Tribune–New York News* syndicate. Patterson rejected them all. Then, in 1931 Gould proposed a strip featuring Plainclothes Tracy, an intelligent, hard-nose, square-jawed detective wearing a yellow trench coat and fedora. Patterson liked the concept, except he preferred "Dick" (slang for detective) as Tracy's first name. Thus was born, at the 17th Street house in Wilmette, the comic strip character Dick Tracy, and thus began Gould's 46-year career at the *Chicago Tribune*.

The strip was unlike anything seen before. The panels were drawn with hard lines and bright colors. The stories were fast-paced, action-oriented, and graphically-violent. The villains were grotesquely caricatured and often had amusing descriptive names. "I usually start with a repulsive character and go on from there," said Gould. Tracy used his keen intelligence and futuristic crime-fighting techniques (like a two-way-radio wristwatch) to inevitably bring down his villains. The constant theme was "Crime doesn't pay."

Gould drew Tracy on his basement wall at 230 17th Street.
Courtesy of R. Hirai and M. Fuzimoto.

The strip was inaugurated during Prohibition when organized crime was thriving and police were chasing gangsters like Al Capone. The public hungered for someone like Tracy. "I decided that if the police couldn't catch the gangsters," said Gould, "I'd create a fellow who could." The strip became popular immediately. It appeared in hundreds of newspapers read by millions of readers. The *New York Daily News* published it on page one for 45 years. It accomplished its purpose: It drove up the circulation of the newspapers that carried it. It spawned a high-budget motion picture (starring Warren Beatty), comic books, radio and TV shows, and merchandise.

The Gould family moved from Wilmette to a farm near Woodstock in 1936. With a studio there and an office at the Tribune Tower, Gould continued to produce the strip until he retired in 1977. He never missed a deadline. Following his retirement, others took over, but unlike Gould, none of them created both the drawings and the story line.

Gould died in 1985. A comic strip pioneer, he created one of America's most enduring pop-culture icons and left his mark, including on a basement wall in Wilmette.

Barry Byrne and the Angels of St. Francis School

Architectural gems of bygone times may go unnoticed today because of regrettable but perhaps unavoidable modifications. St. Francis Xavier School is one example. The school's architect was Barry Byrne, who lived in Wilmette at 1027 Locust Road from 1929 to 1932.

Born in 1883, Byrne was raised in an Irish Catholic family in Chicago. After dropping out of grade school, he developed a strong interest in architecture and convinced Frank Lloyd Wright to employ him as an office boy and apprentice. He worked under Wright for five years.

Byrne was a modernist with his own unique style. He was also a devout Catholic who supported the liturgical reforms that wouldn't be achieved until Vatican II many years later. According to Byrne's biographer, Vincent Michael, the architect "attempted to bring the challenge of modernity in function, design, and construction to Catholicism." Unlike other modernists, Byrne didn't shun ornamentation so long as it affirmed a building's function and design. He often collaborated with Alfonso Iannelli, a sculptor whose work has been praised by The Art Institute of Chicago, among others.

Byrne received numerous commissions from the Catholic Church. St. Thomas the Apostle is a Chicago masterpiece that's on the National Register

St. Francis School as it appeared when new. Courtesy of Tim Samuelson.

of Historic Places. The exterior is reminiscent of the Gothic style, but the interior is revolutionary. Anticipating changes that would occur in the Catholic Church decades later, Byrne's design welcomes worshippers to the Mass. The nave is almost as wide as it is long, and it has no columns to obstruct sight lines. The sanctuary juts out into the nave, bringing worshippers close to the altar.

In the mid-1910s Byrne met Father Francis Clement Kelley, pastor at St. Francis from 1917 to 1924 and later bishop of Oklahoma. Father Kelley, a progressive Catholic like Byrne, brought the architect to St. Francis to design a new school building. Completed in 1923 the building was "a decorated box" according to Vincent Michael, "but the decoration was pressed into the box rather than laid on top of it." The ornamentation included two great Iannelli sculptures entitled *Angel With Flame*. They stood as the children's spiritual guardians at the corners of the school's parapet.

The angels were removed long ago when the school's principal feared they might fall. The building's zigzag cornice and the ornamentation at the base of the building's south facade are also gone, as is the terraced lawn immediately south of the building (replaced by asphalt). A large addition to the school in a much different architectural style detracts from Byrne's original design.

Besides his larger projects, Byrne also designed a number of single-family residences, including two in Indian Hill Estates: 2710 Iroquois Road and 1027

Angel With Flame, like this reproduction, adorned the cornices of St. Francis Xavier School. Courtesy of Tim Samuelson.

Locust Road. Byrne and his family lived in the Locust Road house from 1929 to 1932. Because his commissions dried up during the Depression, he was forced to sell this house in 1932.

On a December evening in 1967, Byrne, 84, was crossing Lake Avenue on foot on his way to Mass at St. Joseph Church. Tragically, he was struck and killed by a car driven by Will Harridge, the American League president described in Chapter 13.

Architect J. Marion Gutnayer

Marion Gutnayer, a longtime Wilmette resident, was born in 1910 in Warsaw, Poland, where his grandfather and father were prominent art dealers and collectors. As a young man, he studied and practiced architecture with his brother Henry in France. Marion was visiting Poland in 1939 when the Germans invaded. Along with his parents and two other brothers, he was sent to the Warsaw Ghetto, but his "Aryan appearance" and forged papers enabled him to pass as Jerzy Bielaszewski, a gentile. His father was killed in the ghetto in July 1942; the others were exterminated at the Treblinka death camp.

According to a letter written to his brother Henry after the war, Marion tried to make a living during the war as an art dealer. This endeavor took him to Krakow "where the great 19th century painters lived." On one occasion in 1942, he was given the opportunity to visit the villa of Pieter Menten, a native of Holland who lived in Krakow from 1923 to 1943 and became a wealthy industrialist and art collector. Marion described him as "a Dutchman who was gathering art works and art masterpieces for the German Nazi authorities."

Outside the villa was "a military protection against acts of the Polish underground." Inside, every room "was decorated with magnificent paintings and artwork of an international recognition and quality." Two or three rooms "were filled with paintings standing on the floor." Menten told Marion that these paintings were available for purchase "because they did not represent (on this continent) any value for his collectors." Marion glanced at "a few hundreds of paintings" and was shocked to see "paintings that were our late father's property and also some that were sold to Mr. [Mieczyslaw] Zagayski—our father's client." One of the paintings, by Polish artist Stanislaw Lentz, was a portrait of Marion's white-bearded grandfather that hung in his father's home before the war. Marion concealed his shock and made no purchases, but the visit was forever seared in his memory.

In 1943 Menten moved his art collection to his mansion near Amsterdam.

In 1946 Dutch authorities charged him with collaborating with the Germans and stealing a Polish professor's art collection. He was found guilty and spent eight months in prison. Meanwhile, Marion came to New York City, where brother Henry and collector-client Zagayski were already living. He told Zagayski about seeing his paintings in Menten's villa. During the period of Menten's imprisonment, Zagayski traveled to Amsterdam and recovered some of his artwork.

Marion worked briefly in New York until joining the architecture faculty of the University of Illinois at Chicago. In the mid-1950s he launched a successful five-decade career as an architect and builder of modernist 20th century homes, including a home for his own family at 1128 Sheridan Road, Wilmette. For 30 years, the Menten matter lay dormant. Then, in 1976 Menten tried to sell some of his art collection. Publication of his name brought new accusations of additional war crimes, including his complicity in the 1941 murder of 20–30 Polish Jews in the village of Podhoroce. For the first time, Marion told the press about his visit to Menten's villa, except the details somewhat changed from those laid out in the letter. He made the visit, he said, as an undercover investigator for the Polish underground to gather evidence of looted art. The revised version was widely reported throughout the world. Menten was eventually sentenced to ten years in prison for complicity in the murders. He served six years, was released in 1985, and died in 1987. Efforts of the Gutnayer family to recover their stolen art were unsuccessful.

Architect Myron Goldsmith

Myron Goldsmith was a big project architect and structural engineer. He lived at 503 Central Avenue from 1968 until his death in 1996.

Myron was born in 1918, the son of Russian immigrants Martin and Fannie Goldsmith. He grew up in Chicago's Humboldt Park and graduated from Crane Technical High School. A fascination with 1920s-era construction projects led him to the Armour Institute (now the Illinois Institute of Technology) to study architecture and engineering. He received a bachelor's degree in architecture, completed one year of graduate school, and was licensed as both a structural engineer and architect.

At that time, the U.S. was less than two years away from entering World War II. After working briefly in Chicago, Myron went to Washington, D.C. and worked for the Navy as a civilian engineer until he was drafted into the Army Corp of Engineers. After the war, he parlayed his military experience into a job with Mies van der Rohe, under whom he had studied at IIT. His starting pay was $1 per hour, but he felt that learning from Mies was "money in the bank." He spent seven years with Mies. A highlight was managing the construction of Mies's acclaimed Farnsworth House in suburban Plano.

During his military service and work at Mies's office, Myron's interest shifted to large construction projects. In 1953 he received a master's degree in architecture from IIT. His cutting-edge thesis, *The Tall Building, Effects of Scale*, examined ways to construct skyscrapers. It advanced the idea of "diagonally braced steel buildings" that was later used to build Chicago's John Hancock Building. He received a Fulbright Scholarship to continue his studies under Pier Luigi Nervi at the University of Rome. Nervi was renowned for his technical engineering skill and dramatic design creativity, manifested in large-span structures built of reinforced concrete.

Two years later, Myron returned to the U.S. and got a job at the San Francisco office of Skidmore, Owings, & Merrill. There, he designed two huge hangars for United Airlines—the first hangars capable of accommodating the new DC-8 jetliners. He stayed in San Francisco for three years before transferring to SOM's Chicago office.

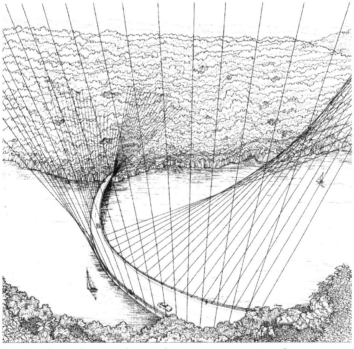

The Ruck-a-Chucky Bridge was designed to span a reservoir and connect two parallel roadways on opposites sides. The curved deck was supported by cables anchored into the mountainside and avoided the need to tunnel into the mountain at the bridge approaches. See page 244. Illustration © D. Hansen. Courtesy of Skidmore, Owings & Merrill.

Soon after his transfer, he met Robin Squier at a brunch. Afterwards, she commented to a friend, "I just met one of the finest people I have ever known." Myron was immersed in work at the time, so Robin took the initiative after waiting in vain for a call. She invited him to dinner. The invitation blossomed into marriage, family, and a Wilmette home.

Myron spent the rest of his career at SOM (1955–1983) while also serving as thesis advisor to graduate students at IIT (1961–1996). He excelled in both roles. Robin's "one-of-the-finest-people" assessment was shared by his colleagues and students.

At the end of his career, Myron summarized: "If I have a vision of architecture, it is that the majority of buildings should be a structural solution. The most modest solution for the problem, carefully executed and placed in its setting." He listed his favorite projects:

- McMath-Pierce Solar Telescope (Kitt Peak National Observatory, Arizona, 1962) ("for its beautiful form in the landscape" with "an enormous influence on modern sculpture").
- Brunswick Building (Chicago, 1965) ("for its boldness and clarity.")
- Republic Newspaper Plant (Columbus, Indiana, 1971) and St. Joseph Valley Bank (Elkhart, Indiana, 1974) ("very, very nice small buildings and very reasonable, very pleasant buildings, on very pleasant sites in a small town").
- Ruck-a-Chucky Bridge (over the middle fork of California's American River, 1978) ("a poetic bridge in the landscape" with "great originality"). The bridge was never funded and built.

CHAPTER 13

★————————————————★

Sports Stories

"Let's play two!" Chicago Cubs Hall of Famer Ernie Banks famously exclaimed. Folks in Wilmette have demonstrated similar enthusiasm for their chosen sports activity, whether it's engaging in athletic contests, maintaining health through physical exercise, or simply sitting on the sidelines, rooting on a favorite.

Over the decades, the Wilmette Park District and a long list of public and private entities have organized sporting activities of all kinds, including baseball, football, tennis, platform tennis, golf, biking, bowling, ice skating, hockey, running, lacrosse, curling, dancing, swimming, diving, sailing, gymnastics, soccer, and basketball. The village has excellent facilities, both public and private, for most of these activities. Roemer Park, a little league baseball field created in 1953 by the Wilmette Baseball Association, evokes fond memories for actor Bill Murray and thousands of other kids who competed there.

Many local kids achieve a high level of skill in a particular sport through play, practice, lessons, and coaching, usually with the strong support of parents. New Trier High School, Loyola Academy, Regina Dominican High School, and North Shore Country Day School have excellent intramural and interscholastic programs at the high school level. New Trier has won more state championships (120) than any other high school in Illinois, and Loyola is a perennial football powerhouse.

This chapter tells a few of Wilmette's sports stories, but first let's recognize some of the village's current and former top sports achievers: Mike Huff, MLB outfielder; Charlie Tilson, MLB outfielder; Bill Sharp, MLB outfielder; Pete Burnside, MLB pitcher; Alvin S. Culver, NFL offensive lineman; Jimmy Murray, NFL offensive lineman; Alvin H. Culver, Northwestern University's first full-time football coach; Emma Vlasic, NWHL center; Grant Golden, U.S. Davis Cup team member; Terry Brennan, University of Notre Dame football coach; Bill Carmody, Northwestern basketball coach; Randy Walker, Northwestern football coach; Jeremy Kipp, Northwestern swimming coach; Porter Moser,

Loyola University's basketball coach; Jack Brickhouse, TV sports broadcaster; Mark Giangreco, TV sports personality; Bill Jauss, Chicago sports reporter and TV personality; Tom, Todd, and Laura Ricketts, Chicago Cubs owners; and Howard Pizer, Senior Executive Vice President of the Chicago White Sox.

The Wilmette Golf Course

The Wilmette Golf Course at Lake Avenue and Harms Road occupies land that in 1920 was a truck farm owned by Peter Hoffman, who emigrated from Luxembourg in 1870 and settled in New Trier Township at the turn of the 20th century. In 1922 Hoffman sold 132 acres to a group of developers that included Joseph Roseman, a key figure in the early days of golf as a player, teacher, greenskeeper, course developer, and maintenance equipment inventor and manufacturer.

Joe learned the game as a child in Philadelphia and worked as a golf pro and greenskeeper at courses in New York, Iowa, and Wisconsin before coming to Westmoreland Country Club in 1913. He was Westmoreland's first pro and greenskeeper, positions he held until the mid-1920s when he left to concentrate on other golf-related enterprises. While working in Des Moines, Joe invented a hitch that allowed a horse to pull not just one mower, but a gang of three aligned mowers. At Westmoreland, he improved this technique by attaching the gang not to a horse, but to a modified Ford Model-T, affectionately called Henry. This combination moved along at seven mph. It could cut a swath 100 inches wide and mow a fairway in an hour.

Over the years, Joe enlarged the gangs, improved the tractors, and developed other innovations. One was a lightweight mowing roller that reduced turf damage. Another was underground irrigation. He founded the Roseman Tractor Mower Co. to manufacture golf maintenance equipment. He also was involved in designing and building more than 100 golf courses.

Roseman was heavily involved in the design and construction of the original 18-hole, 6,855-yard Wilmette course, initially called Playmore Golf Club. The principal designer was George O'Neil, also an investor in the project. O'Neil was one of America's foremost golf experts. The builder was Lewis & Valentine Co., the largest landscape contractor in America and specialists in golf course construction.

Work proceeded quickly, despite the need to cut down 3,298 trees and remove their stumps with dynamite. In less than two months during the fall of 1922, 14 holes were completed. While construction was underway, memberships for the upcoming 1923 season were offered to men for $50 and women for $35. After December 1, 1922, the fees jumped to $100 for men and $75 for women. During its first year of operation, non-members could play on a daily fee basis.

The club was immediately successful. Just one year after its opening—and in response to pressure from its regular players—it was converted to a private club, called Wilmette Country Club. Membership was capped at 400. In 1926 the territory that included the club was annexed by the Village of Wilmette.

The successful launching of the Playmore/Wilmette Club was just the beginning of Roseman's involvement. There was enough undeveloped space west of the 18-hole course for a lighted, nine-hole, par-3 course. In 1932 he designed and built that course, perhaps the first lighted course in the nation. The lighting, regarded as excellent, was supplied from towers like those that lighted railroad switch yards.

In 1933 the lighted course was the site of a tournament held during Chicago's Century of Progress Exposition. A star-studded field of golf pros participated. The tournament was won by Harry Cooper, a native of England who racked up 31 career wins on the PGA tour and was twice runner-up in both the Masters and the U.S. Open. Soon after, the lighted course was closed, the victim of the Depression and annoying bugs attracted by the lights.

One of the founding members of the original Playmore Club was Edward Zipf, a Chicago coal magnate and Wilmette's village president. Within months of the founding, he created a stir by resigning in a huff and urging his friends to resign, claiming that the club's finances were shrouded in secrecy and Evanstonians were "hogging" the organization. Evanston's Robert Cunningham, a car dealer, responded, "Zipf talks like a disappointed schoolboy. He wanted to invest a lot of money in the club, and when we wouldn't let him, he quit. And no one is sorry."

Playmore survived Zipf's departure, but Wilmette Country Club didn't survive the Great Depression. The club defaulted on its bank loan. In 1941 the Cook County Forest Preserve District tried to buy the land but no agreement was reached. Three years later, Northwestern University bought the property for use as a university golf course and the development of faculty housing.

In 1972 Northwestern tried to sell the course for residential development. The Wilmette community strongly objected. The Park District brought an eminent domain lawsuit and conducted a referendum to authorize the sale of $4.4 million in bonds to acquire the property for a public course. Voters approved overwhelmingly.

The Inside Story

Hello, former constituents. My name is John Sanderson, speaking to you from the great golf course in the sky. I was Wilmette's village president from 1957 to 1961. I'm here to supplement the information the author provided about the history of the Wilmette Golf Course.

I must say, I know a heck of a lot more about the subject than the author of this book. I'm familiar with it not because I was village president, but because I was Northwestern University's chief construction engineer and manager of its real estate department. In these roles, I was involved in saving the course from undesirable redevelopment in the 1940s.

During the Depression, the private club that rented the course from its original investors went belly up. Then, a syndicate acquired it and struggled to operate it on a daily fee basis. One of the members of the syndicate (holding a 40 percent interest) was the estate of Clara Abbott. She was the wealthy widow of Dr. Wallace Abbott, founder of Abbott Labs. She was also a generous benefactor of Northwestern University. In 1939 her estate gifted its 40 percent interest to the university.

After Northwestern acquired the Abbott interest, the course continued to struggle. By 1944 it wasn't making any money and couldn't even pay the property taxes. Its future was in doubt. That's when Northwestern bought out the holders of the other 60 percent interest at a bargain price: $113,732.

The university wanted to beef up its facilities in anticipation of the post-World War II enrollment boom that would see veterans flocking to colleges and universities. A new golf course was needed for the golf teams. The existing course was located in the Cook County Forest Preserve near Harms and Golf roads, but the relationship between the Forest Preserve District and the university was souring. The Wilmette property, with 132 acres, had space not just for golf, but for other athletic and recreational programs as well, and the clubhouse could be upgraded and used for student and faculty functions.

There was another potential benefit. Northwestern wanted to attract outstanding administrators and faculty members, but Evanston's wartime housing shortage presented an obstacle. The golf course property offered a solution. It included enough land to accommodate a significant residential development.

In 1945, I laid out the Northwestern University Golf Course Subdivision consisting of 78 single family home sites. Some were on the abandoned par-3, 9-hole lighted course. Under my direction, the university acted as architect and contractor. We intended to create a community of faculty, staff, and other close associates of the university by controlling the ownership of the homes, but the market soon forced us to abandon this narrow approach.

There were some early wrinkles: The post office refused to deliver mail to homes in the subdivision and would make deliveries only to rural-type boxes on Lake Avenue. The telephone company offered only rural service, requiring homeowners to pay an extra fee based on the distance from Hibbard Road. While the entire subdivision was situated within Wilmette's boundaries, the boundary line separating New Trier and Northfield townships cut through the subdivision, as did those of the elementary and secondary high school districts. The subdivision lay entirely within the Glenview Park District. Most of these complications were ironed out. (As you might suspect, the university had considerable influence.)

Despite my demise in 2003, I fondly remember leading the Wildcats to the wilds of western Wilmette in the 1940s and helping to save the Wilmette golf course for future generations of golfers. Incidentally, for many years, I resided at 4085 Bunker Lane, in the university enclave I laid out.

The Exploding Golf Ball Legend

An urban legend warns that golf balls are dangerous: They contain a poisonous substance, and they might explode. The legend's not true, at least not today, but it may have originated partly from an incident that occurred in 1912.

Nick Kalmes, a 12-year-old boy living at 127 Central Park Avenue, worked as a caddie at North Shore Golf Club west of the Kenilworth train station. He was a well known youngster in the small village of Wilmette (population 5,000). His father, Martin, was employed at a local coal and lumber company, and his grandfather, also Nicholas, was an early German settler of New Trier Township (1864).

It was a spring day when Nick found a golf ball on the grounds of the club. He was curious about the ball's innards: What caused it to jump off the club face when it was well struck? He decided to investigate, just as thousands of other red-blooded American boys have done since golf became popular in the U.S. at the turn of the 20th century.

The ball in question was manufactured by the St. Mungo Manufacturing Co. of America, a New Jersey branch of a Scottish firm that manufactured balls that were popular in Great Britain. (St. Mungo the Beloved is the founder and patron saint of Glasgow.) It was probably one called the Colonel. The core of the ball consisted of a small rubber bag about one inch in diameter filled with a zinc oxide solution. The bag was placed under great pressure by tightly winding rubber thread around it until the resulting sphere reached the desired size. A plastic covering called gutta percha was applied to complete the manufacturing process.

Nick held the ball in one hand and his trusty pocket knife in the other. He inserted the knife into the covering. Suddenly, the contents of the pressurized rubber bag inside squirted through the cut, striking Nick in the face, especially his right eye. He screamed in pain and ran home, more than a mile away. His mother immediately saw that his iris had already lost its brown color. She rushed him from one doctor to another, but the damage was done. Nick had lost all vision in his eye.

The Kalmes family wasn't wealthy or sophisticated regarding legal matters, but a local lawyer, Ralph Lounsbury, took Nick under his wing and found him a lawyer to sue St. Mango in New Jersey for manufacturing a hazardous product. The suit asked for $50,000 in damages. In May 1916 Judge Thomas Height ruled in Nick's favor and awarded him $2,400 (the equivalent of more than $62,000 in 2020).

Nick's misfortune had a silver lining. The incident was widely publicized in the national press. It was one of several cases at the time involving curious caddies and golfers who suffered eye injuries while cutting into balls to ascertain their contents. These cases drew the attention of government regulators and the U.S. Golf Association. Warnings were posted at club houses. Massachusetts passed legislation prohibiting the sale of balls containing pressurized caustic liquids. St. Mungo stopped manufacturing balls containing the zinc oxide solution.

Nick's injury undoubtedly explains why he didn't serve in the military during World War I. For the remainder of his life, he lived in Wilmette and Evanston and worked in a variety of jobs. He was briefly a member of the Wilmette Fire Department and the operator of a gas station at Wilmette Avenue and Ridge Road. In 1925 he married Marie Vettevogel, an Evanston resident and native of Holland. They had four daughters. He died in 1952.

Tug Wilson, Athlete and Sports Executive

Kenneth "Tug" Wilson, who lived at 36 Linden Avenue for 40 years, competed in the 1920 Olympics and later served the U.S. Olympic Committee as vice-president (1945–1953) and president (1953–1965). His service on the Olympic Committee was just one aspect of his long career as a sports executive.

Tug was born in 1896 in Atwood, a central Illinois farming community. As a youth, he played many sports. His high school coach saw great potential and urged him to set his sights on the Olympics. He attended the University of Illinois to learn the modern techniques that he would need as a farmer, his likely future career. He also starred in football, basketball and track. A new event was the javelin. Tug took to it naturally. He said it was like playing his childhood game of hurling cornstalks as spears. With the 1920 Olympics in Antwerp on the horizon, he tried out for the American team. He easily qualified but, in his words, "was completely outclassed" by the Swedes and Finns.

While at Illinois, Tug impressed George Huff, the athletic director. Huff offered him a job in the athletic department. Tug accepted and, within a year, moved on to the job of athletic director at Drake University. In four years there, he strengthened the athletic program, especially the Drake Relays. He also married his college sweetheart, Dorothy Shade.

At age 24, Tug Wilson competed in the javelin event in the 1920 Olympics in Antwerp. Photo from Wikimedia Commons.

In 1925, Northwestern offered him the job of athletic director. He accepted and became, at age 29, the youngest athletic director in Big Ten history. He soon learned that an alumni group was paying athletes in violation of Big Ten rules. He reported the matter to the commissioner and worked out a solution. Then, he took up the challenge of making Northwestern more competitive against other conference schools. In his second year, Dyche Stadium was opened. Northwestern won the dedication game against the University of Chicago and went undefeated in league play.

In 1933 the directors of the Century of Progress Exposition announced that they'd like to include a football game as one of the fair's events. Tug and two colleagues offered to sponsor an east-versus-west game involving players with no remaining college eligibility. Played at Soldier Field, the game was the forerunner of the once-popular College All-Star Game.

Tug left Northwestern in 1945 when he was appointed Big Ten commissioner. Among his achievements during his 17-year-tenure as commissioner were establishing a long-term Rose Bowl relationship; adding Michigan State to the conference; and adopting and enforcing strict rules governing financial assistance, eligibility, and recruiting.

Tug's service with the U.S. Olympic Committee began while he was Big Ten commissioner. After eight years as the committee's vice-president, he was elected president, succeeding Avery Brundage, who became president of the International Olympic Committee. Although Tug was a strong advocate for amateurism in college and Olympic athletics, he opposed Brundage's attempt in 1956 to require Olympic athletes to sign a pledge to remain amateurs forever. He thought this requirement went too far.

In 1956 and 1960 the U.S. Olympic teams underperformed. Some of the blame was laid at the feet of the National Collegiate Athletic Association and the Amateur Athletic Union, two organizations that fought for power over amateur athletics. With Tug's support, General Douglas MacArthur was brought in, and he successfully mediated the dispute.

In 1965, as Tug approached his 70th birthday, he was eased out of the Olympics. He died 14 years later, survived by his wife and two daughters, Nancy and Suzi. Famed sportswriter David Condon described him as "truly a gold medal man." The words "tactful," "ethical," "likeable," "effective," and "humble" are also accurate descriptors.

Skelton and Howell, Gold Medal Swimmers

Two Wilmette residents won gold medals in swimming events at the 1924 Paris Olympics. Both had connections to Northwestern University. One, Robert "Bob" Skelton, grew up in Wilmette; the other, Richard "Dick" Howell, lived in the village as an adult.

Bob was born in 1903. Until adulthood, he lived at 511 Railroad Avenue and then 511 Park Avenue with his brother, Earl, and his parents, Harold and Grace. Harold worked downtown as office manager at Bausch & Lomb, manufacturers of lenses and related products. Bob attended the local public schools, belonged to Troop 1 of the Boy Scouts, and was a drum major in the troop's 27-piece drum and bugle corps.

Bob was involved in a tragic accident while his family was boarding at the home of the Le Roy Rand family at 511 Park. Bob and Alfred Rand were buddies. On January 2, 1917, the two boys were target-practicing with a repeating rifle in the basement. Alfred's younger brother, 8-year-old Willis, got in the way and was shot and killed. After the accident, the boys were so hysterical that they couldn't give a coherent explanation of what happened.

Bob went on to New Trier High School, which had the country's first high school indoor swimming pool and dominated interscholastic swimming for years. During his junior year, Bob emerged as a top-notch breaststroke swimmer and was a member of the Dolphins, New Trier's expert male swimmers. The female experts were called the Goldfish.

Bob also swam for Chicago's Illinois Athletic Club and, by his junior year, was traveling around the country winning breaststroke events. As his high school career was ending in 1922, he won what was called "the greatest 220-yard breaststroke race ever witnessed" when he and the second-place-finisher both broke the world record.

In 1923, Bob entered Northwestern. Under Big Ten rules, he wasn't eligible for varsity competition until he finished his freshman year. When he was about to fulfill this requirement, the school's junior prom was held. After the event, Bob took his date to a dance hall not on the dean's approved list. Despite campus-wide protests, he was suspended for two weeks.

Bob chose not to return to Northwestern following his suspension. Swimming instead for the Illinois Athletic Club, he continued to win and set records. His coach was William Bachrach, who would soon coach the U.S. Olympic swim team. His teammate was Johnny Weissmuller, destined for Olympic glory and *Tarzan* stardom.

In March 1924, at a meet in Milwaukee, Bob broke the world record in the 200-meter breaststroke, previously held by Germany's Erich Rodemacher. Partial credit goes to Coach Bachrach, who taught Bob a new leg action, the "fish tail flip." Two weeks later, Rodemacher regained the world record. At the Olympic tryouts in Indianapolis in June 1924, Bob won the 200-meter event, breaking his own U.S. record but falling short of Rademacher's new world record.

Bob Skelton is sandwiched between his Olympic teammates, Ralph Breyer and Johnny Weismuller. Photo from Library of Congress.

Rodemacher wasn't at the 1924 Olympics because Germany wasn't invited. The field was clear for Bob. In the first heat, he broke the Olympic record by almost six seconds. The next day, he won his semifinal, four seconds off his record-setting pace. The following day, he won the final, almost matching his two-day-old record. The gold medal was ceremoniously hung from the neck of this 21-year-old Wilmette athlete with blue eyes, fair skin, and blond hair, standing only 5'3".

Bob was described as "a modest member of an extremely modest family" and praised as an athlete with a "passion for victory" but victory "built upon the principles of good sportsmanship and fair play." Speaking at the Rotary Club following his return to Wilmette, he insisted on "talking about everything but himself."

Bob continued to swim competitively but then, in August 1926, he became critically ill with typhoid fever. Whether due to this illness or something else, his competitive swimming stopped. In 1929 he married a Houston woman,

Helen Railton, and moved to Houston where he worked as a construction foreman. In 1942, at age 38, he enlisted in the Navy and served three years in the South Pacific, earning a silver star. Little else can be found about his life in Houston, where he died in 1977.

In 1994, 70 years after his Olympic triumph, Northwestern inducted Bob posthumously into its Athletic Hall of Fame. Incidentally, his Olympic record was 2 minutes, 56 seconds. The world record, set in 2019, is 2 minutes, 6.12 seconds.

Wilmette's other gold medalist, Richard Howell, also won his medal in the 1924 Olympics. Richard later lived in Wilmette at 1040 Forest Avenue (1939–1941) and 1023 Ashland Avenue (1941 until his death in 1967). He was born in Chicago in 1903. At Northwestern, he was a national champion, Big Ten champion, and all-American in 1924 and 1925. He won his gold medal in the 4 × 200 freestyle. His relay team included Johnny Weissmuller. His post-swimming career was in sales.

Cubs Player-Manager Phil Cavarretta

One of the biggest names in Cubs baseball history called Wilmette home for a short time. I'm referring to Phil Cavarretta, a Cubs star who was my favorite player until Ernie Banks debuted in 1953. Cavarretta lived at 2338 Greenwood Avenue from 1947 to 1949.

Unless you grew up in the Chicago area during the 1940s or 1950s, you may not recognize the Cavarretta name. I knew about him from watching the Cubs on TV. WGN-TV broadcast both Cubs and White Sox daytime home games starting in 1948, with longtime Wilmette resident Jack Brickhouse doing the play-by-play. (There were no Cubs/Sox scheduling conflicts.) I warmly remember rushing home from school to catch the end of a ballgame, or successfully claiming "I don't feel well" and being kept home on a game day, able to watch all nine innings.

The Cubs weren't very good. From 1947 to 1962, they didn't have a single winning season. Before 1954, the double-play combination of Eddie Miksis to Roy Smalley to Addison Street caused apoplexy among fans. The 1954 advent of a new double-play-combination—Gene Baker to Ernie Banks to Dee Fondy —offered a glimmer of hope.

Born in Chicago in 1916, Cavarretta grew up on the North Side and attended Lane Tech where he starred in baseball. In 1934 his high school coach took him to Wrigley Field for a tryout. At age 17 he signed with the Cubs. He won a spot on the big league roster in 1935 and remained with the team for 20 years. He was Mr. Hustle (long before Pete Rose) and was the most popular Cubs player of his day.

During his long career, he played first base and outfield. He batted lefty and racked up 1,977 hits for a lifetime .293 batting average. In 1945 he was the National League's MVP with a .355 average. (Some commentators downplayed this accomplishment because the "good players" were off serving in World War II. Cavarretta was exempt because of a perforated eardrum.) He was elected to the National League all-star team from 1944 through 1947.

Today, the concept of a player-manager is obsolete, but in baseball's earlier days there were several. Cavarretta served as player-manager for three seasons (1951–1953), leading the Cubs to 169 wins and 213 losses. During spring training in 1954, he bluntly (and correctly) told owner P.K. Wrigley that the team would again finish in the second division without better talent. He was summarily fired. He went on to play two more years with the White Sox.

Cavarretta left a permanent mark on Wrigley Field. In 1952 he was facing pitcher Curt Simmons of the Phillies. Simmons unleashed a fastball that sped toward the batter's head. Against the backdrop of white shirts in the center field bleachers, Cavarretta lost sight of the ball until, at the last split-second, he raised his hand in self-defense. The ball crushed his wrist. Since then, the offending bleacher section has been off-limits to spectators.

Everyone knows that the Cubs didn't win a World Series from 1908 to 2016. They came close seven times as National League champs, but they always lost the series, most recently in 1945. Cavarretta played on the last three teams that made it to the series before 2016. He was a deserving hero of many kids during his playing and managing days.

Will Harridge, American League President

Will Harridge was president of the American League from 1931 to 1959 and lived in Wilmette from 1910 until his death in 1971. His parents, David and Barbara, immigrated to Chicago from England in 1872 with Will's older sibling. The small family settled on the south side. David worked in unskilled jobs, and five more children were added to the family. Will, the fourth in age, graduated from Hyde Park High School and went to work as an office boy at the Wabash Railroad. He took business courses at night.

He advanced to the position of ticket agent. One of his duties was to book athletic groups, including American League umpires and teams. This brought him to the attention of the league's president, who hired him in 1911 as his personal secretary. At the time, Will knew nothing about baseball.

By 1910 Will, his mother Barbara, and a younger brother had moved to 1440 Forest Avenue, Wilmette. His father David continued to live in Chicago. After Barbara died in 1911, Will married Maude Hunter, and the couple bought the Forest Avenue house. Their only child, William Jr., was born in 1919. The family attended the Wilmette Methodist Church.

Will Harridge (center) throws out the first pitch on opening day at Roemer Park in June 1953. Courtesy of the Wilmette Historical Museum.

Will worked his way up the league's hierarchy and became its president in 1931. Here are six highlights of his 28-year tenure:

- Will's toughness was quickly tested. In 1932 Washington Senators outfielder Carl Reynolds angered New York Yankees star catcher Bill Dickey by sliding hard on a play at the plate. Dickey followed Reynolds toward the Senators' dugout and punched him in the face, breaking his jaw. The Yankees were in a tight pennant race, and the team's owner, Jacob Ruppert, was a powerful force who wanted his star player to receive no more than a slap on the wrist. Nevertheless, Will imposed a stiff penalty on Dickey: a $1,000 fine and a 30-day suspension. Ruppert responded by giving Will the cold shoulder for a year.
- Early in 1933 *Chicago Tribune* sports editor Arch Ward urged Will to support an all-star game between the National League and American League in connection with the Century of Progress World's Fair. Will liked the idea and

persuaded American League owners to participate. The first all-star game, intended to be a one-time event, was played at Comiskey Park that summer.

- In 1947 Larry Doby became the first African-American player in the American League, thanks to Cleveland Indians owner Bill Veeck. Doby's debut received less attention than Jackie Robinson's, but he suffered similar harassment. Will sent a clear message from the top: It's going to happen; we're going to accept it; and we're not going to let anyone abuse him.

- In 1951, Veeck (then owner of the St. Louis Browns) tried to generate interest in his awful team. He signed Eddie Gaedel, who stood 3'7", and sent him to the plate as a pinch hitter, wearing uniform number ⅛ and elf shoes. Gaedel walked on four pitches. The following day, Will voided Gaedel's contract and chastised Veeck for making a mockery of the game.

- In the mid-1950s, after five decades of stability, two American League franchises were sold and relocated: the St. Louis Browns to Baltimore and the Philadelphia Athletics to Kansas City. The two sales and relocations were highly controversial among owners. Will recognized that the moves were compelled by the teams' financial problems, and he was able to bring the owners together in support of the moves.

- In 1958, Will persuaded the owners to adopt a rule requiring batters to wear protective helmets, even though the players opposed it.

Will was a reserved gentleman who was widely regarded as a strong and fair leader and a capable administrator. He was elected to the Baseball Hall of Fame in 1972, the year after his death.

Chick Linster's 6,006 Pushups

Imagine doing 6,006 pushups, non-stop, in three hours and 54 minutes! This feat was accomplished in October 1965 by Charles (Chick) Linster of 633 Hibbard Road. It was reported in *Sports Illustrated,* Ripley's *Believe It Or Not!,* and numerous other publications; and in 1968 it was recognized as a record by the *Guinness Book of World Records.*

At the time, Chick was a 16-year-old junior at New Trier High School. He weighed 153 pounds and was 5'6". He was athletically gifted and pursued gymnastics in high school. As part of his training, he followed an increasingly rigorous daily regimen consisting of five callisthenic exercises, one of which was pushups. A childhood friend described his arm muscles as bigger than those of most adult men. A year before setting the record, he learned that a Marine had done 5,000 consecutive pushups, and he set his mind to beating that mark. After a year of arduous training, he decided he was ready. His goal was 6,006. He asked his New Trier coaches to witness his attempt and attest to the record he hoped to set. Each of his pushups was perfect. He could have done more, but his coaches feared he might injure himself and stopped him when he reached his goal. A small group of onlookers applauded.

Writing years later, Chick recognized that "in the greater scheme of things, it doesn't really matter who can do the most pushups. What is important is what I derived from the quest. I discovered and cultivated the virtues of discipline, sacrifice, and perseverance within me while pursuing a dream."

Little did Chick know when he set the record how much his future life would require those virtues. Only 69 days later, he was working on the parallel bars during gymnastics practice at New Trier when one of the bars came loose. He fell, broke his neck, and was permanently paralyzed. A lawsuit was filed on his behalf against New Trier and Porter Athletic Equipment Co., manufacturer of the parallel bars, charging the high school with failing to provide safety mats beneath the bars and Porter for selling defective equipment. Two years later, the suit was settled for $300,000.

Chick Linster set challenging goals for himself and
achieved them. Courtesy of the Linster family.

Meanwhile, Chick lay in a hospital bed and "saw only darkness. The body I had worked so long and hard to develop now failed to respond to my commands and imprisoned me. I worried that I would never be able to work or take care of myself and would be a burden on my family. Fears that I might die were replaced by the dread that I would live. But while my body was shattered, my spirit, although badly bruised, was still intact. I decided to fight back and redirected the effort that had made me a champion toward the arduous task I hoped would lead to my physical independence."

Following the same disciplined approach that made him a pushup champion, Chick went on to rehabilitate, complete high school at the Illinois Children's Hospital School, graduate from the University of Illinois, marry, be the father of two daughters, have a rewarding career as a federal civil servant, receive honors and recognition for his courage and accomplishments, and most important, achieve his goal of physical independence.

As for his pushup record, Chick said, "That one act proved to me what I was capable of if I set my mind, body, and spirit to it. It has fortified me to go on fighting battles. The experience has stood me in good stead, because the very essence of the independent life I fought so hard to regain is struggle."

Chick died in 2012. His consecutive push-ups record was broken in 1976 by Robert Knech, a 13-year-old professional acrobat, who racked up 7,026.

Breaking News from the Wide World of Sports

- August 19, 1895: The North End road race, featuring ten of the area's top cyclists, was held today. The course was supposed to start at Central Street in Evanston and proceed north on West Railroad Avenue, west on Wilmette Avenue to Ridge Road, north to Lake Avenue, west to Northfield Road, south to Wilmette Avenue, and back to the starting point. Unfortunately, the course had to be relocated to South Evanston, because heavy rains rendered Wilmette's unpaved roads too muddy. The fastest time for completing the six-mile South Evanston course was turned in by Christopher Arndt, 18, of South Evanston: 15 minutes and 45 seconds.

- June 11, 1899: Village Trustee Walter Faraday, 33, a cycling enthusiast, was arrested by Evanston police, along with 38 other bikers, for riding on the sidewalks of Evanston. The bikers claimed that riding on the sidewalks was necessitated by the impassable conditions of Evanston's unpaved roadways. Faraday should be embarrassed by his arrest, because one year ago, he spearheaded the passage of a Wilmette ordinance prohibiting sidewalk-riding, and he personally arrested twelve Evanstonians who similarly avoided Wilmette's impassable roadways by riding on the sidewalk. His apparent credo: "Do what I say, not what I do."

- July 20, 1931: Paul Bleser, 54, proprietor of the Bleser Bowling Academy at Schiller Avenue and Ridge Road, has finally received the village board's okay to operate his ten-lane bowling facility on Sundays, but only after 1:30 PM. Bleser, a barber, opened his bowling business in September 1927 and has occasionally been caught operating on Sundays despite the Village's blue law. In support of his request for a change in the law, the Chamber of Commerce argued that the blue law has been relaxed for movie theaters and golf facilities, and fairness requires that bowling facilities should receive the same consideration.

- March 16, 1937: The village board adopted an ordinance that prohibits bike riding on public streets and requires bikers to use the sidewalks. This action was prompted by a spate of accidents involving cars and bikes. The board seemingly ignored the hazard posed by bikers on the sidewalks. A few months ago, Guy Packard, 51, of 1240 Forest Avenue, was run down by a biker on the sidewalk in the 1100 block of Central Avenue.

- December 13, 1937: Herman Gersdorf, 53, a teamster with a stable on Happ Road between Winnetka and Lake avenues, captured a "wild horse that has been tearing up the Wilmette golf course" for weeks. Believing that he would receive a $100 reward if he captured the beast, Gersdorf used his mare Nellie to lure the animal into his barnyard. Neighbors helped him force the horse into a stall. Gersdorf's triumph was dimmed when he learned that no reward had actually been offered.

- July 13, 2003: The clubhouse at the Wilmette Golf Club was destroyed by fire. This is the third major fire at this location.

CHAPTER 14

★————————————————★

Local Tragedies

Traveling alone from Chicago to New York City to visit his grandparents, eleven-year-old Stevie Baltz was the lone survivor after his commercial airliner collided with another plane over Brooklyn, killing 133 passengers, crew, and people on the ground. What happened next confirms the reality that life isn't fair, especially when children are killed or injured. Stevie's story is told later in this chapter, along with the stories of other Wilmette tragedies.

1889: A Fatal Train Accident

Christmas of 1889 was going to be a happy time for the John Revell family of Wilmette. John, 41, his wife Hattie, 31, and their son Willie, 2, lived in a small cottage surrounded by a white picket fence at the corner of Central and West Railroad avenues. John was a coal dealer who also served as station agent for the C&NW. Shortly before Christmas, he had resigned as agent to begin a new career in manufacturing.

Christmas Eve was cold, snowy and windy. Braving the weather, John hitched up the horse to the buggy, and everyone bundled up for the short ride over to the Methodist Church at the northeast corner of Lake and Wilmette avenues. The church, organized 15 years earlier, had a growing congregation that gathered on Christmas Eve for fellowship.

Shortly before 9:30 PM, the time came to return home and put Willie to bed. John drove the buggy to the railroad crossing at Central Avenue. There were no gates or crossing guards, but he saw a northbound freight train rolling slowly through town, so he stopped and waited for it to clear. Then he whipped his horse forward.

John was oblivious to a southbound train bearing down from Wilmette's northern border at 50 mph. It was an express train from Milwaukee to Chicago scheduled to pass through town somewhat earlier but it had been delayed and was making up for lost time. Perhaps John didn't look to the north to see if the second set of tracks was clear. Or perhaps he looked to the north but the on-coming express train melted into the background of the departing freight train.

The tragedy that followed was reported in newspapers nationwide. At that time, newspapers often described accidents involving injury and death in gory detail, and the Revell tragedy was no exception. One of the milder newspaper accounts reported this: "The engine of the express struck the buggy containing the three people, scattering the splinters of the shattered vehicle far and wide, hurling the occupants quite a distance from the track and instantly killing the horse. Father, mother, and child were dead when picked up, the bodies of all three being more or less mutilated."

Grade-crossing accidents like the one that took the lives of the Revell family were all too common. One contemporaneous report states that 250 persons died in Chicago crossing accidents in 1889. Grade separation was a major political issue nationally and locally. As explained in Chapter 5, Wilmette officials considered grade-separation plans for decades but always deferred, mostly because of the cost.

1896: A Fireworks Factory Explosion

Fourth of July brings parades, picnics, patriotism, and pyrotechnics—but in the wrong hands, pyrotechnics bring pain. Here's a pyrotechnics story from almost seven score years ago. Its main characters are two children, Annie and Nick Borre, 16 and 14, residents of Gross Point.

Their parents, Nicholas and Gertrude (Schaefgen) Borre, were members of families that emigrated from Trier, Germany to the Gross Point farming community west of Ridge Road. Nicholas and Gertrude had six kids, including Annie and Nick. Nicholas also had two older children from a previous marriage. Life probably wasn't easy for a large Gross Point family like the Borres. Survival required the kids to pitch in.

Annie and Nick pitched in by going to work at the Gross Point factory of the Chicago Fireworks Co. This company was incorporated in 1891 with a not-insignificant capitalization of $100,000. Its proprietors probably considered its five-acre site in Gross Point to be an excellent location for a fireworks factory —close to Chicago but in an isolated area populated by industrious German-American farmers and laborers. Besides Annie and Nick, the company employed 33 other workers, including three girls and four boys under age 16.

Illinois had recently enacted a child labor law, called the Factory Law of 1893. It was a far cry from later state and federal protective laws. Its main feature was that it prohibited the employment of children under the age of 14 and, as to children between the ages of 14 and 16, it required their employer to obtain an affidavit, signed by their parents, attesting that the children were over 14. The law didn't limit the maximum hours of work per day or per week, or prescribe minimum wages. It defined no categories of dangerous work from which children were barred. Penalties for violations were modest.

At 8:00 AM on April 15, 1896, this unregulated environment proved tragic at the company's one-story factory building, measuring 60 feet by 24 feet. A partition divided the building into two sections. On one side, Annie and five other girls rolled and pasted small firecrackers. On the other side, Nick worked unsupervised. As he stuffed giant firecrackers with a mixture of potash and antimony, the material ignited and exploded. The blast hurled him through the roof. A second explosion dwarfed the first. Annie was killed immediately— "torn to pieces" and buried in debris. The demolished building was engulfed in flames. Other workers suffered gruesome but non-fatal injuries.

The father of Annie and Nick arrived at the scene to help rescue victims and douse the conflagration. He couldn't find Annie. Then, two hours after the first explosion, he saw Nick struggle for his final breath. "With tears coursing his cheeks and sobs that brought tears to the eyes of onlookers, he prayed piteously for the lives of his children."

An investigation showed that the factory's manager was "inexperienced" and "unacquainted with the nature of explosives", that the explosive material was "dangerously strong" and not safely stored, and that Nick wasn't adequately supervised. Moreover, the egress routes were obstructed, and there was no fire-fighting equipment, not even a bucket of water.

A coroner's jury censured the company "for not using proper precaution to protect the lives of its employees," but it didn't recommend any criminal charges. Eventually, the manager was charged with the minor offense of employing a girl under age 16 without obtaining a parental affidavit. Justice of the Peace George Kersten (later Chief Judge of the Circuit Court of Cook County) found him guilty and fined him $10.85. The Chicago Fireworks Co. continued in business.

1913: A Deadly House Fire

Fire isn't as big a threat as it once was. Major steps toward fire safety occurred when the Village installed the water distribution system in 1893 and extended it to the newly annexed Gross Point area in 1927. Fire safety has also been enhanced by smoke detectors, modern electrical and heating systems, fire-retardant building materials, sprinkler systems, artificial Christmas trees, and reduced cigarette smoking. It's possible that one or more of these modern safety enhancements might have saved the lives of Grafton and Virginia Stevens, but the biggest factor in their tragic deaths was their fatal decision to enter their burning house.

Grafton and Virginia Stevens both attended Armour Institute in Chicago. Afterwards, Grafton became an engineer at H.M. Byllesby & Co., a Chicago consulting firm. Virginia became head of the Domestic Science Department at Clarkson Memorial College in New York. Two years later, they were married. They established their home at 514 Linden Avenue. At the time of the tragedy, October 31, 1913, they were both 33. He was financially successful and had just started his own consulting firm. They were seven-year residents of Wilmette.

In other words, Grafton and Virginia were on top of the world that Thursday evening in October when they and Virginia's mother (visiting from Iowa) went out for the evening. The women walked to a neighbor's house to play bridge, and Grafton walked to another neighbor's house to meet up with the guys.

It was almost midnight when the parties broke up. Grafton stopped by the bridge game to escort Virginia home, and one of the women offered to drive Virginia's mother. Grafton and Virginia arrived first. They saw nothing amiss as they approached the front door, but when they opened it, they found the house ablaze from a fire that started in the cellar. They went inside and promptly fell through the weakened floor. Three hours after the fire was extinguished, their bodies were found, clasped in each other's arms, at the ruins of the cellar door, where Grafton's apparent effort to carry Virginia to safety had ended in failure.

Several theories were offered for the Stevens' inexplicable decision to enter the burning house: They wanted to call in an alarm from the telephone in the hallway; or they wanted to gather up some valuables and keepsakes; or they wanted to rescue the family dog; or they misjudged the fire's severity and thought they could extinguish it themselves.

The Stevens deaths are among at least ten caused by fires at Wilmette homes over the years, most recently in 2013 when an elderly woman died in an apartment fire in the 600 block of Ridge Road. There have also been fires in which lives were saved by the heroic actions of firefighters.

1919: The Crash of the *Wingfoot Express*

Little did Wilmette resident Josephine MacBeth know, when she left home at 121 Woodbine Avenue on the morning of July 21, 1919, that she was about to become a crash victim involving a lighter-than-air aircraft. It was America's worst accident of this type until the German dirigible *Hindenburg* caught fire and crashed in 1937.

Josephine, 48, was single. She lived with two older brothers at the Woodbine home. Canadian-born, she immigrated to the U.S. in 1898 and settled in Chicago. By 1910 she and her brothers had moved to Wilmette.

Josephine worked as a bookkeeper at Illinois Trust and Savings Bank at LaSalle and Jackson in Chicago. The bank's grand two-story edifice was designed by Daniel Burnham's firm. One of Josephine's longtime co-workers was George Cory, 30, an auditor. He was engaged to marry Josephine's niece.

July 21 was a Monday, usually a busy day at the bank. As 5:00 PM neared, the customers were gone, but Josephine and other employees were still at work in the ground-floor rotunda, surrounded by teller cages, beneath the building's gaping skylight.

On the same day, Goodyear Tire & Rubber Co. was test-flying an experimental blimp in Chicago. Goodyear's base of operations was a hangar previously used for building World War I airships. It was located at White City Amusement Park, 63rd Street and South Parkway. The park was a popular entertainment venue, rival to Riverview Park on the North Side.

Blimps were used successfully during World War I, and Goodyear hoped to launch a peace-time commercial operation. The experimental blimp was called *Wingfoot Express*. Its balloon was 158 feet long and 34 feet in diameter. It carried thousands of cubic feet of volatile hydrogen gas. The gondola, suspended from the balloon, was 34 feet long and was designed to carry two crew members and eight passengers. Two rotary gasoline engines affixed to the gondola drove the propellers.

During the morning, a three-man crew took *Wingfoot* aloft and followed a northward course paralleling Michigan Avenue to its first destination, the Grant Park airfield. The airfield was accustomed to spectacles of flight, having hosted competitions, including in 1911 the world's largest aeronautical meet up to that time. The second leg, early in the afternoon, was from Grant Park up the lakeshore to Diversey Avenue and back to the airfield. The third leg, late in the afternoon, was from Grant Park back to White City.

On this final leg, the crew was joined by White City's publicity manager and a newspaper photographer. The photographer convinced the pilot to fly over the Loop so he could take aerial pictures. All crew members and passengers were equipped with parachutes.

The blimp's maiden flight drew enormous public attention throughout the day. Shortly before 5:00 PM, with thousands of Loop spectators looking on, the balloon suddenly caught fire, 1,200 feet above ground. The crew and passengers bailed out as the blimp buckled and plunged downward. The balloon's skin, the gondola and one crew member plummeted through the bank's skylight and, along with glass and metal of the skylight, crashed onto the rotunda's marble floor. The craft's gasoline tanks exploded, and the rotunda became an inferno.

Josephine, in the rotunda with other employees, was engulfed in flames. There were only two exits from the area. George Cory, despite his own injuries, fought through the flames, wreckage, and pandemonium. He found Josephine and led her to safety. She suffered burns on her face and hands.

Thirteen people were killed—ten bank employees, the White City publicity manager, the newspaper photographer, and one crew member. The pilot and another crew member parachuted safely. Twenty-seven bank employees were injured. Miraculously, the bank was able to reopen the next morning. In a meager tribute to the dead and injured, silence was observed for five minutes.

Wingfoot Express takes flight minutes before the fatal
crash. Chicago History Museum, ICHi-034797.

Stores on West Railroad Avenue north of Wilmette Avenue suffered
heavy damage. Courtesy of the Wilmette Historical Museum.

1920: A Devastating Tornado

On Palm Sunday, March 28, 1920, four tornadoes touched down in the Chicago area. One of the four (estimated to be an "F4"—winds over 200 miles per hour) was first sighted eight miles southwest of Joliet at 12:15 PM. It skipped along a northwesterly path for 53 miles. It slammed into Maywood, Bellwood and Melrose Park and continued through northwest Chicago and Evanston into Wilmette and out over Lake Michigan. Along the way, it killed 20, injured 300, left 400 families homeless, and caused at least $2 million of property damage.

In Wilmette, sunny skies and unseasonably warm weather greeted 8,000 residents on Palm Sunday morning. At 1:00 PM, conditions drastically changed. As told by witnesses, the air was "still" and "vacuum-like." It became very dark. Then "egg-sized hailstones" pelted the ground, followed by a ferocious, deafening "death wind" and a "tremendous downpour." For six minutes, the tornado ripped a path of destruction several hundred feet wide from Gregory Avenue and 13th Street to Lake Michigan at Chestnut Avenue. The two main streets in the Village Center, Wilmette and Central avenues, suffered heavy blows.

West of the C&NW tracks, virtually all the businesses in the 600 block of West Railroad Avenue between Wilmette Avenue and Central Avenue suffered severe damage, as did St. John's Lutheran Church on Prairie Avenue and homes on Wilmette Avenue, Park Avenue, Prairie Avenue, Maple Avenue, and

Gregory Avenue. The windows of the William Brinkman Grocery Store and his second-floor residence at the northwest corner of West Railroad Avenue and Wilmette Avenue were blown in, and his merchandise soared to the heavens. Brinkman's wife Augusta was so frightened that when she died of heart failure seven months later, the cause was said to be "tornado shock."

As the winds crossed the railroad tracks, they took with them sections of the C&NW station, the depot and power lines of the North Shore Electric, and other railroad equipment. They also propelled the C&NW gateman's shanty at Central Avenue to a new location 50 feet away. Unfortunately, gateman George Mix was inside the shanty at the time. Police barely saved the severely injured man, who was pinned beneath the shanty that was set ablaze by its overturned stove.

Village Hall took a hit. Its roof was torn off and dumped near Ashland Avenue and 7th Street. The Wilmette State Bank, under construction at Central Avenue and 12th Street, was considerably damaged. Half of the roof of St. Augustine's Church on Wilmette Avenue was carried three blocks away, and all the windows were smashed. After leaving a trail of uprooted and stripped trees, damaged structures, and rubble, the tornado's last target was the Henry Gage mansion at Sheridan Road and Chestnut Avenue. By then, the mansion had been converted into a restaurant. The building successfully withstood the storm's blows with only minor damage, earning it the name Tornado Tavern.

1926: A Spectacular Train Crash

Just before noon on May 28, 1926, a southbound passenger train, speeding from Milwaukee to Chicago, was entering Wilmette from Kenilworth on the C&NW tracks. Simultaneously, a northbound passenger train, heading from Chicago to Minneapolis, was entering the village from Evanston.

Because of repair work on the east track, both trains were traveling on the west track. A dispatcher was on duty to direct trains through the repair zone safely. By throwing a switch located north of Lake Avenue, he could divert a southbound train from the west track to the east track. Aware that the trains were on a collision course, the dispatcher threw the switch to divert the southbound train and frantically signaled the engineer to slow down.

A string of freight cars was standing on the east track south of the switch. The southbound train hit the switch at high speed and plowed into the standing cars. The train's engine and tender left the track and overturned. Its baggage car and a coach also left the rails. Two hundred passengers were thrown from their seats. Four freight cars were demolished. Miraculously, no one was killed. Three trainmen and 15 passengers suffered minor injuries.

This event is described in the unpublished memoirs of William J. FitzPatrick, M.D. "Fitz" spent his boyhood at 1524 Lake Avenue. He didn't get the train story exactly right, but that's not surprising when an older man writes about events that occurred when he was a seven-year-old boy. From young Fitz's perspective, it all began with a non-stop shrieking train whistle. With other curious neighborhood kids, he ran to the tracks to investigate.

At the Lake Avenue crossing, he found utter devastation. To the south, the right-of-way was "piled high with a jumble of twisted and broken railroad cars. The track was ripped up and loops of rails stuck out of piles of splintered wood." To the north, the passenger train's locomotive and tender had left the tracks and "plowed into a heavy woods between the Northwestern and North Shore tracks" (where Wilmette's Fire Station 1 is now located).

"The engineer and firemen jumped and did not shut off the throttle. Surprisingly, the boiler did not explode—so the drive wheels continued to run. The engine rocked back and forth, like an elephant bedding down in a mud wallow, and all the time the wheels continued to turn and dug themselves deeper and deeper, with the whistle still blasting at full steam. After an eternity, some brave soul climbed up in the cab of this quivering locomotive and shut off the whistle and throttle. It was like suddenly being released from the bedlam of an asylum."

Amazingly, railroad employees were able to clear the wreckage from the tracks by the following morning, although the cleanup continued for several weeks.

Fitz describes how this event turned into one of those rare occasions when a community bonds. "That evening, everybody—I mean everybody in town turned out to watch…. Special lights had been set up for the work crews, and we all watched them through the flashing lights and shadows. Strangers were friends, and talked with intensity, clustered in small groups all along the block on Railroad Avenue."

Fitz envied those who had the foresight to pick up a piece of metal as a souvenir of the event. For him and other Wilmette youngsters of the 1920s, "this whole train-wreck incident was the highlight of my young life at the time."

1932: Desperate Parents, Desperate Action

Stories like this are sad and unsettling. I'm telling it as a reminder that folks in dire straits (like victims of natural disasters and crushing poverty) sometimes lose all hope and do the unimaginable.

In 1932, Walter and Grace Payne were a young couple (22 and 19) living in Plymouth, Wisconsin. He grew up in a large farm family. He quit school after eighth grade and tried his luck at the painting trade. He got into trouble with the law and was placed on probation for three years. Grace was the daughter of a Milwaukee factory worker. She quit school after ninth grade and worked as a laborer in a cheese factory. They found one another and were married too young—he 19 and she 17. They promptly had a daughter, Dorothy.

Life was hard in 1932 at the depth of the Great Depression, especially for a young couple in the Paynes' situation. Walter couldn't find work. Then the other shoe dropped. A second baby, Benjamin, was born on April 18, 1932. Within days, the couple panicked: We can't provide for two babies. We have nowhere to turn. Our first obligation is Dorothy. We must give Benjamin a chance for a decent life.

On Tuesday, May 3, 1932, they borrowed a car and, with heavy hearts, drove south. After three hours, they arrived in Wilmette. They scouted the upscale east side. They selected a prosperous-looking brick house at 1234 Ashland Avenue. Someone was inside. They pulled into the alley. Walter got out of the car with Benjamin, crept to the back door, set the baby on the steps, knocked on the door, and sprinted back to the car. After seeing that the baby had been found, they quietly departed.

The homeowner who responded to the knock was 59-year-old Judson Stone. He and his wife Estella had lived in Wilmette for 20 years and had raised two sons in the village. He was a prominent businessman who managed the McCormick Estate for many years. He eventually became chairman of the Harvester Co. and president of the Wilmette State Bank. Judson and Estella knew what they had to do: They took the baby to the Cradle Society on Ridge Avenue in Evanston and notified the Wilmette police. (Seven weeks later, Stone would deal with another crisis—a run on the Wilmette State Bank that ended when he assured depositors that the bank had ample money, and the directors would guarantee the security of deposits with their personal assets.)

The Cradle Society was founded in 1923. Its mission was to care for unwanted babies and find them loving adoptive families. In less than ten years, it built an outstanding reputation. The Depression had increased the number of babies available for adoption, but the supply never met the demand. When the economic recovery floundered in 1937, the Cradle had already cared for 3,100 babies and had found homes for 2,800. Its waiting list numbered 500 prospective families. Baby Benjamin was in a good place if, as likely, the Cradle would be asked to find him a home.

The case was publicized in the regional press. Neighbors of Walter and Grace put two and two together when the couple returned home without Benjamin. They notified authorities, and an investigation quickly disclosed the truth. The Paynes were charged with child abandonment.

The rest of the story is sketchy. Benjamin was never returned to Walter and Grace. The couple suffered little, if any, punishment at the hands of the law. They continued to live in Plymouth except for a brief period in Oregon, and they continued to struggle financially. They split up in the early 1940s. I don't know what happened to Grace, but Walter served in World War II and, afterwards, he had a new wife and two new sons. He died in 1995.

1960: Hope, then Grief

The holidays are a time for warm feelings and family cheer. But that's not the full story. The holidays are also a time when sad memories haunt. Here's one Wilmette family's story.

Stephen Baltz, son of William and Phyllis Baltz, was born in 1949. He had younger siblings, a sister Randee and a brother William Jr. William Sr. was a vice-president of Admiral Corp., and the family lived happily and comfortably at 110 Broadway Avenue.

At age 11, Stevie was a popular sixth grader at Central School—a good student, Boy Scout, little leaguer, and youth choir member. He fished off Wilmette pier. He built model airplanes. He and a friend raised hamsters, and on Northwestern football game days, they parked cars at his Broadway Avenue home for money to buy tickets to the game.

As Christmas 1960 approached, Phyllis planned a short visit to her parents in Yonkers, New York, with the two older children, Stevie and Randee. But Stevie came down with a cold and sore throat, so he was left behind. If he got better, maybe he'd fly to New York alone.

Stevie's condition improved, and he was booked on United flight 826 from O'Hare to Idlewild, departing on December 16. He was excited to go. He hadn't seen his grandparents in two years. William Sr. wasn't so excited. He was anxious about his son flying alone for the first time. Nevertheless, early that morning, he drove Stevie to O'Hare and took him to the gate. Along with seven crew members and 76 other passengers, Stevie boarded the DC-8. It departed at 8:11 AM. Phyllis would be waiting at Idlewild.

The plane was nearing its destination when tragedy struck at 10:33 AM. Flying in clouds 5,200 feet above The Narrows between Staten Island and Brooklyn, outside its assigned air space, the DC-8 collided with a TWA Lockheed Super Constellation, flight 266, en route from Dayton to LaGuardia with 39 passengers and five crew members aboard. The two planes plummeted to the ground eleven miles apart—at the time, the worst air disaster in U.S. history.

Six people on the ground were killed, along with everyone on the two planes —everyone, that is, except Stevie. When the DC-8 crashed into a crowded Brooklyn neighborhood, it exploded in flames. Stevie was thrown from the tail section onto a snow bank, his clothing ablaze. Bystanders rolled him in the snow and covered him with blankets. Conscious, he called for his parents. He was rushed to Brooklyn Methodist Hospital in critical condition suffering extensive burns, smoke inhalation, and broken bones.

Still conscious, Stevie told doctors, "I remember looking out the plane window at the snow below covering the city. It looked like a picture out of a fairy book. Then all of a sudden there was an explosion. The plane started to fall and people started to scream. I held on to my seat and then the plane crashed. That's all I remember until I woke up."

Americans were shocked by the tragedy, but the miracle of Stevie's survival offered a ray of hope. They took this brave child into their hearts and prayed for his recovery. But it wasn't to be. Twenty-six hours after the collision, with his parents at his bedside, Stevie died.

Stevie's sister Randee, a teacher in Park City, Utah, acknowledged that subsequent Christmases have had their ups and downs. "My hardest time is the actual date of December 17th," she said, "since my first born son died on the same day" 22 years later. But, she added, "I still love Christmas and do all the house decorating and tree."

1978: Another Fireworks Explosion

One of the biggest calamities in Wilmette's 150-year history occurred on St. Patrick's Day, March 17, 1978. Powerful explosions leveled the house at 1221 Cleveland Avenue where fireworks were illegally manufactured and stored. Responsibility for this calamity rests squarely on the shoulders of the homeowners, Grace and George Yule. (He was called Murray, his middle name.)

Murray was born in 1923 and raised in Evanston. His parents were Scots who came to the U.S. as children. His father was an accountant; his mother was a homemaker. He attended Evanston Township High School and served in the Marine Corps during World War II. He returned to Evanston following his military service and in 1948 was a student living in Evanston with his widowed mother. Grace was twelve years his senior. The couple married sometime after 1948 and moved to Wilmette in 1958. They had no children.

Murray had multiple brushes with the law. In 1942 he was charged with disorderly conduct after he and companions were found with revolvers, masks, and a fire axe in Glencoe. In 1950 he was arrested for auto theft in Evanston. In 1957 he was charged with manufacturing and storing fireworks at his Chicago home.

In 1959 Murray sold zinc and sulfur powder to a 14-year-old boy. It found its way into the hands of two other boys, both freshmen at Schurz High School. When they ignited some of the powder to kill a nest of ants, it exploded, blinding one boy and tearing off his left hand at the wrist, and blinding the second boy in one eye and inflicting bad cuts over his entire body.

When the warehouses of Worldwide Fireworks Co. in McHenry County exploded in June 1973, injuring seven and breaking windows three miles away, an investigator questioned Murray about the illegal storage of fireworks there. Murray claimed that he merely conducted displays for the company.

Murray retained the appearance of a legitimate tradesman while his illegal side-business grew. He joined an interstate network of manufacturers, distributers, and sellers of fireworks. He owned a 60-acre farm near Coon Valley, Wisconsin where 50 barrels of fireworks and chemicals were discovered following the Wilmette calamity. He was associated with another Wilmette resident, Richard Dunbar, in a Chicago business that owned warehouses where tons of volatile chemicals, miles of fuses, and four million paper tubes for firecrackers were found. It's estimated that Murray netted $250,000 to $500,000 annually from his illicit business—enough to allow a very comfortable life.

The Yules didn't associate or communicate with their neighbors. They didn't arouse much suspicion either, although with the benefit of hindsight, some neighbors saw signs of the trouble that would come.

While keeping to herself, Grace shared her strong opinions with Chicagoans through letters-to-the-editor. In these epistles, she complained that the state's attorney was ignoring corruption in government, that the U.S. was stupidly footing the bill to clear the Suez Canal, that the U.S. wasn't spending enough on national defense, that economic depression was imminent because of worthless foreign debt owed to the U.S., and that the U.S. was wastefully campaigning against cigarettes while ignoring the evils of alcohol.

The Yules knew that their fireworks activities were both illegal and an immense threat to public safety, but greed, like fireworks, can be a powerful force.

Friday, March 17, 1978 was a gloomy and unseasonably cold day in Wilmette. Nevertheless, it was a day that promised to be full of fun. It wasn't just TGIF. It was also St. Patrick's Day. It was corned-beef and cabbage, libations, Chicago's St. Pat's parade, and the dyed-green Chicago River. And there was another reason to be excited: The New Trier West boys basketball team was in Champaign, taking on Collinsville in the quarterfinals of the state tournament. (West lost, 71–56.) Those who weren't interested in either St. Patrick's Day or high school basketball could enjoy the final episode of the long-running and popular Carol Burnett show. Wilmette's mood was upbeat.

Everything changed at 11:40 AM. Murray Yule was working at his illegal fireworks factory in the attached garage at his Cleveland Street house. He was operating an electrically-powered, fuse-cutting machine. Suddenly, a spark from the machine ignited flammable material nearby and caused a small explosion. The Yules' longtime maid smelled smoke and ran from the house, injuring her knee as she escaped.

Wilmette's fire and police personnel arrived within minutes and helped Grace escape from the smoke-filled house. Then, two horrendous explosions lifted the house off its foundation, ripped the structure and its contents into shreds, and hurtled bodies through the air. In seconds the house became a pile of rubble.

Folks all around Wilmette and even shoppers at Old Orchard Shopping Center, two miles away, heard the thunderous blasts that were followed by smaller explosions. A mushroom cloud of dust and smoke rose over the area. Murray, severely burned, was found walking south on Cleveland Street in a daze.

The surrounding neighborhood suffered severe damage—walls and foundations were cracked, windows were broken, siding and shingles were dislodged, a water main was broken, branches were stripped from trees, and equipment of police officers and firefighters was damaged. The family room of the house to the south was destroyed and the rest of the house was severely damaged. The brick house to the north stood up better but many furnishings were destroyed.

At Harper School, two blocks away, the children heard the initial blast and ran to the windows to look, but the teachers wisely directed them to take cover. Students on the playground were brought into the building for safety. Then the major explosions erupted, breaking 160 windows in the school. The children were evacuated on foot to the east and then by bus to Locust Junior High.

No child was injured, but others weren't so lucky. Murray had burns over

60 to 70 percent of his body. Grace suffered chest wounds and an eye injury. One firefighter had a fractured jaw and another had an injured back. A police officer suffered a broken arm. Four other first responders were injured less seriously.

During the cleanup, investigators found large quantities of explosives in the debris, along with an arsenal of weapons and ammunition. Residents within a one-block radius were evacuated over the weekend while the hazardous material was removed. By Wednesday of the following week, all debris was gone, and 1221 Cleveland was an empty lot. The street reopened, and the gawkers arrived en masse.

Two weeks later, Murray died from his injuries.

Seven men and women were indicted on federal charges of illegally conspiring with Murray to manufacture and sell fireworks. One of the persons charged was Murray's friend and business associate, Richard Dunbar. He pled guilty and was fined $5,000 and placed on probation. Of the other six, three pled guilty, two were convicted, and one was acquitted. Grace was charged with state offenses, but the charges were dropped because she cooperated with federal prosecutors. She died less than two years after the explosion.

Tragic Breaking News

- May 27, 1979: Four members of Wilmette's Sutton family were among 273 people killed when an American Airlines DC-10 bound from O'Hare to Los Angeles crashed shortly after take-off. The accident is the deadliest in U.S. aviation history. It happened when the left engine and pylon separated from the wing and inflicted damage elsewhere on the aircraft. Stephen and Carolyn Sutton and their two boys, Colin, 9, and Chris, 7, lived in the 1400 block of Forest Avenue. Stephen was a senior editor at Rand McNally and edited Jeannie Morris's book about Chicago Bears star Brian Piccolo. Stephen was planning to attend a bookseller's convention in Los Angeles. The boys, students at McKenzie School, were excited about the prospect of visiting Disneyland.

CHAPTER 15

★────────────────────────────────★

Hometown Homicides

The legal definition of "homicide" is the killing of one person by another. It's not necessarily murder. It might be justified by self-defense or excused by insanity. It might be premeditated and severely punishable. It might be reckless and unintentional manslaughter, subject to a lesser penalty.

As best I can determine, 20 incidents within Wilmette's borders might be called homicides under this broad definition. Two "victims" were criminals in the process of committing serious crimes and were shot in self-defense. Only six involved a killer and a victim who didn't know each other at the time of the incident. Most of the rest involved relationships gone bad. Four were murder-suicides. What follows are details of seven of these incidents. A summary of all 20 appears in Appendix 3.

1893: Mary Cron

Mary Cron was born in Canada and lived most of her 55 years there. A widow of means, she came to Wilmette in the early 1890s to live in the home of her daughter and son-in-law, Mary and Frank Wheeler, 31 and 37 respectively. Frank was in the steam-fitting business. The Wheeler home was at Lake Avenue and 10th Street.

In the early morning hours of November 4, 1893, Frank Wheeler was awakened in his second floor bedroom by a noise in the hallway. His wife Mary was away visiting her sister in Colorado. With a loaded pistol in each hand, he stepped from his bedroom, looked in the open door of Cron's bedroom, and saw her lying motionless with blood on her face and neck.

Wheeler heard a noise on the back stairs. Investigating, he saw two men carrying a chest that had been in Cron's bedroom. He chased after them and fired his pistols. A bullet struck one burglar, who fell on the steps leading to the yard. As the burglar tried to rise, Wheeler repeatedly and fatally shot him again. The second burglar fled, joined by a third. Wheeler emptied his pistols in their direction and chased them into the darkness. Blood stains found later indicated that one or both had been struck. Returning to his house, Wheeler found it ablaze. The burglars had set it on fire, using kerosene as an accelerant. He was unable to reach Cron's bedroom, and her body was incinerated. A bloody knife was later found under her charred bones.

Wilmette's population was then under 2,000, and the little village was a hotbed of gossip: "Did you know that Mrs. Cron had $4,000 cash in her possession?" Actually, the cash was in a bank safety deposit box. The main target of the gossip was Wheeler. His story seemed dubious. Why would he chase a burglar outside while his mother-in-law lay bleeding to death? Some community leaders came to his defense.

The dead burglar was thought to be Paul Logan, an ex-convict from Louisville, Kentucky, based on an inscription in a Bible found on his body. Logan's identity wasn't confirmed until later. Meanwhile, his body was laid out in the undertaker's barn for all to come and see. Many did.

A suspect was later identified when bloody clothes and a razor were found in the cellar of Andrew Sherman's house at 1136 Greenleaf Avenue. (The house was the site where Village government was organized in 1872.) The clothes matched those that Charles Goodrich, 17, had been seen wearing shortly before the murder. Goodrich was the brother-in-law of Sherman's son Milton, 25, and had stayed at the Greenleaf house on occasion. When Goodrich was found and arrested six weeks later, he was wearing clothing belonging to Milton that had presumably been stolen from the Greenleaf house on the night of the murder to replace his own bloody clothes. He confessed to the crime and said the third burglar was a man named Schaefer.

At Goodrich's murder trial, his lawyers successfully argued that his confession couldn't be presented to the jury because it had been coerced. The defense attorneys then tried to shift the blame to Wheeler. They presented a witness, Dr. Rebecca Julia Ebert, who testified that months before the murder, Wheeler tried to enlist her in a conspiracy to murder Cron and steal her money. Wheeler denied this.

Despite these defense tactics, the jurors were convinced that Goodrich was involved in the crime. He was convicted of manslaughter and sentenced to five years in prison. Because of his youth, he was sent to the Pontiac Reform School. Eight months later, he died of natural causes.

"Schaefer" was never identified or apprehended.

Wheeler left Wilmette, driven away by the nasty rumors. He moved to Claremont, California, where he successfully engaged in real estate development and was a highly respected citizen. He died in 1939, still married to the murder victim's daughter.

1919: Fred Slokerman

On July 24, 1919 "Fred Slokerman" (one of many variations of his name) attempted to rob the Wilmette State Bank at Central Avenue and 12th Street. Slokerman, 28, handed a note to the bank's assistant cashier, William Leary, 37, of 430 10th Street. It demanded, "Pay to the bearer all you have." When Leary hesitated, Slokerman brandished a revolver and started shooting. Pandemonium broke out, and Slokerman fled. Leary ran outside and alerted Police Officer Sam Hoth, 48, of 724 12th Street, who was on duty at the village hall across the street.

Slokerman fled west on foot. Officer Hoth commandeered a taxicab, followed Slokerman, and overtook him at Walnut Avenue and 17th Street. There, Slokerman allegedly fired again. Officer Hoth returned fire, striking Slokerman in the chest multiple times. As Officer Hoth approached, Slokerman allegedly fired a bullet into his own chest.

Slokerman was a desperate man. He was born in Germany and came to the U.S. in 1906 as a teenager. Over the next dozen years, he bounced from coal mining in Rock Springs, Wyoming, to serving in the U.S. Army in the Philippines, to conducting a floral business near Joliet, to laboring in Clairton, Pennsylvania, to manufacturing patent medicine in Joliet.

He was drawn to Joliet because his parents lived in a small cottage at Harlowarden, the splendid Joliet estate of Harlow Higinbotham. (Higinbotham was a former partner of Marshall Field, president of the Columbian Exposition of 1893, and "one of the wealthiest and most prominent businessmen in Chicago." He died three months before the Wilmette robbery, and his son, also named Harlow, ascended as the new master of Harlowarden.)

While living in Joliet, Slokerman became romantically attached to a childhood acquaintance, Hattie Aldominowicz. As his patent medicine manufacturing business sputtered, he decided that his future happiness hinged on raising $3,000 so he could purchase a farm and settle down with "the most wonderful girl in Chicago." He closed his business and moved to the Wilmette home of a cousin, William Middendorf. He asked Middendorf for a loan but was turned down.

Assistant cashier Leary ran from the Wilmette State Bank (background) to alert police officer Hoth at the village hall (foreground) about Fred Slokerman's attempted robbery. Courtesy of the Wilmette Historical Museum.

Slokerman needed money and was crazy to get it. He targeted the younger Harlow Higinbotham, sending him a letter in early July 1919 that demanded $10,000 in small bills, outlined the method for making payment, and threatened the entire Higinbotham family if payment wasn't made. According to the letter, family members would be stabbed by a deadly "poison needle." The family was away from Harlowarden at the time, and the letter wasn't read until after the deadline had passed.

Seemingly ignored by Higinbotham, Slokerman opted to seek the needed funds from banks. In mid-July 1919 he walked into the First Trust and Savings Bank at Monroe and Dearborn streets, Chicago. He handed the teller a note, demanding $5,000 in small bills and threatening to blow up the bank with nitroglycerin if the demand wasn't met. When the teller refused, Slokerman departed, and the threat was exposed as empty.

Slokerman's fatal visit to the Wilmette State Bank occurred one week later. After being shot, he was rushed to Evanston Hospital, muttering his last words, "I did it all for the little girl in Chicago." Investigators later connected the Wilmette robbery to the earlier plots, based mainly on the similarity of the handwriting on the notes used in all three incidents.

1939: Dr. Gordon Mordoff

In 1930, Dr. Gordon Mordoff was a 47-year-old physician, living in Hettinger City, North Dakota, with his wife, Madge (43), and two children, Gordon Jr. (15) and Mary (11). The family moved to Wilmette in the early 1930s. Madge announced in January 1932 that she was pregnant. She immediately traveled to her family home in Minneapolis to spend her pregnancy and deliver the baby. She returned to Wilmette in late 1932 with a baby boy who, she said, was born on September 2. The Mordoffs named him Gordon III. He later became nationally known as "Sonny Boy."

The Mordoffs' marriage was troubled. The couple separated for a time. Then, in early 1936, Madge died. Upon learning about Madge's death, an Evanston woman, Margaret Mann, 24, came forward. She claimed that Sonny Boy was her child; that she had given birth to him in May 1932 at St. Vincent's Orphanage in Chicago; that she had named him Reginald Arthur Mann; that unable to care for him, she boarded him out to Madge; and that she never surrendered her parental rights. The custody hearing drew national attention.

Mann's version was supported by records and witnesses, including two of Madge's siblings. Madge's sister, Mary Fairchild, testified that Madge had written her a letter in 1931, saying she wanted to adopt a child. Mary added that Madge later told her that Sonny Boy wasn't her child. Madge's brother, John Quinn, testified that he accompanied Madge back to Wilmette from Minneapolis after the supposed birth, that she had no child, and that she visited three orphanages looking for a baby to adopt but was unsuccessful because her husband's signature was required.

Dr. Mordoff persisted. He may have actually believed that Madge had given birth to Sonny Boy. She had never said anything to the contrary, he said, and the "lad resembles me closely." He acknowledged that he found no record of the baby's birth in Minneapolis. The doctor who supposedly delivered the baby had died. Dr. Mordoff's version was supported by the testimony of his daughter, although she said that the baby's first appearance at the Mordoff home didn't coincide exactly with Madge's return from Minneapolis. She also mentioned that she "hated" her father.

Not surprisingly, the court awarded custody of Sonny Boy to Mann.

John Quinn, Madge's brother, also hated Dr. Mordoff. He believed that the doctor had caused Madge's death from worry, neglect, and a broken heart. Quinn was also angry that the doctor was pressing him to repay a debt. Being hated by Quinn, previously convicted of multiple violent crimes, wasn't a good thing.

On January 12, 1939, emboldened by heavy drinking and armed with a pistol, Quinn came to Wilmette, searching for the doctor. He found his prey at the doctor's office on the second floor of the Cox building at 1167 Wilmette Avenue. He shot repeatedly, killing his target.

Quinn was quickly apprehended. He confessed and was charged with murder. At trial, he claimed that he killed Dr. Mordoff in self-defense, only after the doctor made movements that made him apprehensive. The jury rejected this defense and found Quinn guilty. He was sentenced to 14 years in prison, the lightest possible sentence.

A battle quickly erupted between the Mordoff children over the doctor's estate, estimated to be worth $15,000. Mary and Gordon, Jr. each claimed that the other was not the Mordoffs' natural child, was not legally adopted, and was thus disqualified from inheriting.

1942: Leroy Race

Leroy Race was a bad dude. The life story of a man like Leroy isn't celebrated in obituaries with glowing testimonials. It has to be pieced together from newspaper accounts and public records. In Leroy's case, the newspapers and records tell the story of a boy born in Attleboro, Massachusetts in 1903, less than five months after the marriage of his teenage parents (George and Jessie). The marriage ended in divorce two years later. Growing up probably wasn't much fun for Leroy. At age 16, he lived as a boarder and worked as a machine operator in Attleboro's thriving jewelry industry. Neither parent was present to provide guidance during his formative years. His father remarried twice and finally settled in Springfield, Vermont. His mother just seemed to disappear.

Leroy first made headlines in 1930 at age 27. By then, he was hopping freight trains. In June he traveled to Vermont where his father was living. He went to the Springfield town office and, acting in a "peculiar manner," requested his birth records (which weren't there). He left the office and walked to Goulds Mill, a nearby village. He saw his father driving a truck and fired two shots in his direction. One shot shattered the windshield but missed its apparent target. He ran from the scene, fought off a pursuer, and disappeared by the time a posse was assembled to catch him. The local press called him "an armed madman."

One month later, Leroy was in Erie, Pennsylvania where he shot and killed a young African-American man because the victim was "a friend of an 18-year-old white girl." The crime wasn't immediately solved, and Leroy escaped to

Spokane, Washington. There his crime spree temporarily ended with his arrest for grand larceny. He was sentenced to 2–15 years in prison, but something about Leroy caused prison officials to transfer him to the Eastern State Hospital for the mentally ill near Spokane. There, he confessed to the Erie murder. Upon learning about the confession, the Erie district attorney announced that, in view of Leroy's "life sentence" in Washington, he wouldn't be prosecuted for the murder. Six months later, in November 1932, Leroy and two other inmates overpowered their guards and escaped.

Leroy next surfaced in the Midwest (August 1933), where he pulled off a violent store robbery in Granite City, Illinois and an express office robbery in Dover, Ohio. In Dover, he stole two revolvers, $1.36 in cash, and two old coins. A few days later, he was arrested in Ft. Wayne, Indiana for train hopping. Claiming to be "Roy Smith," he admitted the Dover theft when the stolen items were found in his possession. He broke out of jail but was recaptured two months later. He was tried in Dover, convicted of larceny, and sentenced to prison. In 1939 the Ohio parole board released him into the custody of Illinois authorities to answer for his Granite City crime.

By early 1941 Leroy was back in Massachusetts, working as a janitor in Boston. In April he traveled to Cumberland, Rhode Island. For some bizarre reason, he removed his clothes, approached two fishermen in the woods, and brandished a revolver. He was arrested a few hours later, fully clothed. He was charged with carrying a concealed weapon and assault with a dangerous weapon. Leroy shrugged off the incident as a "whim." The judge wondered, how can a naked man be charged with carrying a concealed weapon?

By his 38th birthday, Leroy had a lengthy record of violence and mental illness. He was a danger to society. His crimes crossed state lines, and law enforcement officials failed to put all the pieces together to protect the public from a menace (as they might today).

This background brings us to the period from November 1941 to January 1942. Leroy and an accomplice, Fred White, decided that Chicago's North Shore would be a fertile area for lucrative larceny. They targeted the affluent neighborhood just west of the Indian Hill Country Club that included parts of Wilmette, Winnetka, and unincorporated Cook County—Locust, Woodley, Ramona, and Indian Hill roads; and Fox and Meadow lanes. They traveled on foot at night and hid in shrubs whenever the lights of a vehicle approached, which was rare. White later estimated that he and Race committed 27 burglaries on the North Shore. Wilmette Police Chief Cloyd McGuire identified seven definite victims (including three in Wilmette) and six probable victims.

Race and White probably felt confident when, after a successful string of

North Shore burglaries, they decided to visit the Wilmette home of Walter and Nellie Hanna, 1224 Locust Road, on January 15, 1942. Inside were four sleeping occupants: Walter, Nellie, William Johnston Sr., and William Johnston Jr. ("Bill"). Walter and William Sr. were in the furniture business together. Nellie owned N.A. Hanna, Inc., a popular women's dress shop and wedding planner at Plaza del Lago. William Sr.'s wife, who was Nellie's sister, had died 15 years earlier, and the two households had merged to care for Bill, who was only seven-years-old at the time.

Bill attended New Trier High School and Lake Forest College. In December 1938 he married Virginia Brock of Kenilworth. They were both 19-years-old at most. The marriage lasted only a year. In January 1942 Bill was anticipating his second marriage, to Lois Wood of Evanston. The March wedding would be followed two weeks later by his induction into the Army Air Forces.

As Bill lay in bed at 5:00 AM on January 15, 1942, perhaps dreaming about these upcoming events, he heard someone whisper, "Here's a watch and some money. Let's see what we can find in the next room." Leroy Race and Fred White had entered the house through a first-floor window. Fully awakened, Bill remained motionless and waited for the intruders to depart. Then, he crept from his bed, grabbed two pistols from a drawer, followed the intruders to an adjoining bedroom, shielded himself behind a door, and shouted, "Raise your hands! I have you covered!" Armed with a .38 caliber revolver, Race fired five shots towards Bill, who responded with 17 shots in the intruders' direction. Race's shots missed, but several of Bill's shots struck the intruders, Race fatally and White superficially in the hip. Awakened by the commotion, Walter Hannah grabbed a baseball bat, turned on the lights, and found the two burglars lying on the floor of the guest room, groaning. Race died within minutes. White recovered and was prosecuted.

After this incident, Bill married Lois, served in the Army, became a plastics manufacturer's sales representative, and lived happily with Lois and four daughters in Highland Park. At the age of 34, he was diagnosed with multiple sclerosis and became wheelchair bound, but he bravely struggled on without complaint. He retired at the age of 46 and moved to Clearwater, Florida, where he died in 1987 at the age of 68.

1946: Otto Freund

The crime scene was a home on the 800 block of Michigan Avenue overlooking Gillson Park. For ten years, it had been the home of the Clarence Freund family. Besides Clarence and his wife Irene, the household included their daughter Irene, her husband Fred Popper, and their baby. Other household members were Otto Freund, Clarence's 84-year-old father, and Marie Held, a 52-year-old maid who had served the Freunds for 20 years.

Clarence was a partner in a printing firm. Fred was in the printing business, too. Otto, a widower, was a business executive who had retired in 1943. In better days, he was wealthy, but he lost everything in the Great Depression. He was described as friendly, good-natured, and gentle, with vibrancy belying his age.

On the afternoon of December 27, 1946 Clarence and Fred were at work in the city. Their spouses, with the baby in tow, were shopping locally for wallpaper. Otto and Marie were home alone. He was in the basement repairing a toy. She was in the kitchen washing dishes.

Shortly after 1:00 PM the doorbell rang. Marie opened it partway and saw two men, both wearing dark overcoats and hats, standing one in front of the other. She recognized neither. One asked if the lady of the house was home. When Marie responded that only she and an "old gent" were there, the men pushed their way in and told her to be quiet. Instead, she screamed, causing Otto to ascend the stairs from the basement. One of the men put his hand over her mouth. They drew revolvers, dragged her into the living room, and struck her on the head with their weapons. Her glasses, which she greatly needed, fell and broke.

The family dog, a German shepherd, initially barked over the commotion but then ran upstairs and hid under a bed, as was its habit during a thunderstorm. Marie ran toward the basement stairway, trying to escape, but the men pursued and pushed her down the stairs. She got up and staggered to a door leading from the basement to the back yard, but before she could unlock it, the men grabbed her and beat her unconscious.

During this melee Otto reached the dining room on the first floor, carrying a chisel he was using to repair the toy. The chisel had a five-inch wooden handle and a seven-inch steel blade, described by Clarence as "sharp as can be." One of the intruders grabbed the chisel and stabbed Otto nine times in the head.

Covered in the blood of their victims, the assailants ransacked the house, leaving blood stains throughout. They took only a few items. One was a platinum broach shaped like a bow knot, with a one carat diamond in the center surrounded by 40 smaller diamonds. Its value was about $1,000. Also stolen were a pair of gold earrings, a gold bracelet, and four silver bracelets.

Irene Freund called home at 1:30 PM to check in. No one answered. She made several follow-up calls until 2:00 PM. When no one answered these, both she and her daughter became alarmed. It was agreed that Irene Popper would go home and check.

Opening the front door, Irene saw Otto's body lying in the dining room in a pool of blood, with a bloodied and disarranged Marie approaching in the hallway. Believing that Marie had gone insane and killed Otto, she ran to a neighbor's house and called police. When the police arrived, they found Otto dead in the dining room, the victim of multiple stab wounds to the head. Marie sat near his body but was so badly injured that she couldn't respond to questions. She was rushed to Evanston Hospital.

Led by Chief Edwin Whiteside, the Police Department initiated an extensive investigation—searches, fingerprints, blood samples, interviews—everything a professional police department would do in that day and age. None of this produced a suspect.

At 6:50 PM on the evening of the crime, Marie regained consciousness and briefly told police what happened. She described the two assailants. Both, she said, were almost six feet tall and slender. She thought she would be able to recognize them if she saw them again. The first man wore rimless glasses, she said, and had brown hair and a dark complexion. She soon became exhausted, and the questioning stopped. At 10:15 PM, the interview resumed. She said she could describe the man with the rimless glasses "but I didn't see the other one very well." She estimated that both men were "35 years or near that." The man with the rimless glasses, she said, had a darker complexion than the other.

Marie was hospitalized for weeks, coming close to death. By February, she was able to give a formal statement. Her description of the assailants changed somewhat. The first man "didn't wear glasses" and was "about five feet three inches" and "unshaven." She said that she couldn't describe the second man at all.

Meanwhile, a possible witness came forward. Frank Elstad, a laundry truck driver, said that at about 1:15 PM on December 27, he was eastbound on Maple Avenue approaching Sheridan Road. As he stopped and then pulled forward, a southbound car whizzed by on Sheridan. Elstad shouted, "Where's the fire?" A man in the passenger seat turned and looked at Elstad, giving him a "good look." Elstad said he would recognize the man if he saw him again.

Identification of the assailants by Held and Elstad became the main hope for solving the crime. Over the ensuing months, police showed them photos of men charged with other crimes. Marie thought that some looked like her assailants. Elstad said that none were the man he saw. Then Chicago police arrested a gang of burglars for a series of currency exchange robberies. While incarcerated, one of the burglars, Harry Wagner, 49, allegedly told his cellmate that he was glad police hadn't investigated "the North Shore job." The cellmate reported this to authorities. In January 1948 Marie and Elstad were shown photos of the currency exchange robbers. Marie identified Nick Lococo, 37, as her first assailant and Wagner as the second. Elstad identified Wagner as the passenger in the car. They confirmed these identifications in police lineups.

Lococo and Wagner were charged with assault and murder. They denied the charges and were tried in June 1950, following their conviction for the currency exchange robberies and sentencing to 40–50 years in prison. Wagner was represented by Charles Bellows, a prominent criminal defense attorney. Bellows poked big holes in Marie's identification of the assailants, getting her to admit that she had erroneously identified three other suspects, and that her eyesight without her glasses (broken during the attack) was poor. Judge George Fisher directed the jury to find the defendants not guilty.

Despite the verdict, Wilmette's Police Chief Whiteside remained convinced that Lococo and Wagner were the assailants.

1965: The Crouse Family

It seems like a strange Christmas gift: a .22-calibre rifle from a husband to his wife. Maybe it wasn't so strange, given that the wife was a member of a North Shore gun club. Okay, not strange, but certainly unfortunate.

It was almost suppertime on Saturday, January 2, 1965 at the Crouse home on Oxford Lane. Morris Crouse, 48, was taking down Christmas decorations. His wife Norma, also 48, was preparing dinner. Their daughter, Sally, 16, was writing a letter in her bedroom. Their son Harrison, 18, home on Christmas break from the University of Illinois, should have been thinking about his double-date to the musical *Oliver* downtown. Morris had given him tickets for that evening's performance as a Christmas present. Instead, Harrison was thinking about killing his family.

He pointed his mother's rifle at the back of Sally's head and pulled the trigger, killing her instantly. Hearing the gunshot, Norma ran upstairs. Harrison aimed and pulled the trigger but missed. She darted into a bedroom and closed the door. Morris followed Norma upstairs and was fatally shot in the jaw. Norma emerged from the bedroom and was fatally shot between the eyes.

Harrison ran to a neighbor's house, shouting that Norma had gone berserk and killed Morris and Sally and tried to kill him. He said he escaped by locking himself in a bathroom and climbing out the window. Police confronted him with discrepancies. After several hours of questioning, he confessed. He said he placed the rifle in his room two days before the shootings. He offered no motive, saying, "I don't know." He showed no emotion and responded to police politely.

No one saw it coming. The family was upstanding. Harrison was described as quiet, studious, and ambitious. At New Trier High School, he had been active in theater, dance, and movies. He entered college as an art and drama student. Morris's brother, who lived in downstate Illinois, was notified and quickly lined up an attorney for Harrison. He and other family members remained supportive throughout the ordeal.

Harrison's mental state was an immediate concern. Jack Johnson, warden of the Cook County jail, ordered a psychiatric examination to see whether he had suicidal tendencies. The psychologist determined that he was "emotionally stable." Over the next few days, Harrison was reexamined, transferred to an isolation cell, and placed under surveillance. A funeral was held for Morris, Norma, and Sally at Wilmette's Presbyterian Church, with 200 mourners present, while Harrison remained in isolation, reading magazines.

Harrison was charged with three counts of murder. He pled not guilty. His attorney indicated that his defense would be insanity. Meanwhile, Morris's and Norma's wills were filed for probate. The estate was estimated to be $120,000. Harrison would inherit unless he was convicted.

More than five months later, a hearing was held to decide if Harrison was fit to stand trial. Two experts from Northwestern's medical school testified. One said that Harrison had severe brain damage shown by brain wave tests that could cause him to attack others. The other said that Harrison was highly intelligent but lacked emotion. Both agreed that he probably didn't understand what he was doing on the day of the killings. Harrison was found unfit to stand trial and was confined at Illinois Security Hospital in Chester, Illinois. After more than six years of confinement and treatment, he was ready for trial. Judge Saul Epton, known as a compassionate judge, presided over his 15-day bench trial in February 1972.

Between 1959 and 1969, Judge Epton presided over Boys' Court. This court dealt with male criminal defendants between the ages of 17–21. It recognized a "social responsibility" for crimes committed by boys in this age group and was committed to their rehabilitation. Critics thought the court was too lenient.

The sole issue at trial was whether Harrison was insane at the time of the killings. Under Illinois law, he wouldn't be criminally responsible if, as a result of mental disease or mental defect, he lacked capacity either to appreciate the criminality of his conduct or conform his conduct to requirements of law.

Harrison was represented by Herbert Barsy, a former assistant state's attorney. Barsy had an extensive criminal defense practice, including high-profile defendants like Judge Reginald Holzer (charged with accepting payments in return for appointments to receiverships) and Anthony Spilotro (charged with murdering two mob underlings).

Harrison's insanity defense was a magnet for dueling expert witnesses. The prosecution presented a psychiatrist, a physician, and several law enforcement officials who testified that, in their opinion, he was sane at the time of the killings. The defense presented five psychiatrists who testified to the contrary. Dr. Roy Grinker, director of psychiatry at Michael Reese Hospital, characterized Harrison as "schizophrenic" and the killings as a "psychotic episode." He testified that Harrison was insane at the time of the killings and was probably still insane. The disease, he said, is usually incurable. Dr. Benjamin Boshes, chairman of the neurology department at Northwestern's medical school, agreed with the diagnosis and added that Harrison should be regarded as dangerous.

Judge Epton ruled that Harrison was not guilty by reason of insanity. Because he was still "insane," Epton placed him in the custody of the Illinois Department of Mental Health. Harrison remained in the department's custody for only six months. Then he was released. He entered Southern Illinois University, completed a four-year course in two and one-half years, interned for Illinois Congressman David Sears, married, and adopted his new wife's surname (Cochran) as his own.

In 1976 Harrison moved to Denver and got a job as a reporter for a weekly newspaper. He quickly became its editor, general manager, and partial owner. In 1979 Cowles Media bought the newspaper. Harrison stayed on as publisher. In 1982 he became president of Cowles's *Sentinel* Publishing group, consisting of 13 suburban Denver-area weekly newspapers.

In 1985 word of Harrison's past spread to Denver. In January 1986 a Denver weekly reported it in detail. The writer suggested that the big Denver dailies were ignoring the story because of Harrison's stature in the publishing industry. Harrison responded in the *Sentinel*. He explained that doctors never disagreed about his incompetency or illness, although they offered several diagnoses. His treatment, he said, consisted of many hours of therapy that helped him regain the ability to feel emotion. "Only after being brought back through all the feeling about what I had done was it possible to begin rebuilding toward a normal life."

In 1991 Harrison and others bought the *Sentinel* group from Cowles. Twenty years later, they sold it to Aurora Media Group, and Harrison retired. A respected leader of the Suburban Newspapers of America, he was awarded its Lifetime Achievement Award in 2010.

Harrison's miraculous recovery, taken at face value, gives hope to families affected by the severe mental illness of one of their members. Not taken at face value, the case seems like it failed to deliver justice to the victims of Harrison's rampage.

1967: Robert Burghart

Bob Burghart and Dick Kay, both of Wilmette, were childhood friends and classmates in the class of 1967 at New Trier East. They lived less than a mile apart: Bob in the 100 block of 9th Street and Dick in the 700 block of 11th Street.

Bob's parents were separated. His dad, Robert Sr., lived in Northfield and worked as a buyer for Allis-Chalmers. His mom, Lorene, was Wilmette's village clerk. At the time, village clerk was an elected office, one she held from 1965 to 1969. Bob was the second oldest of four Burghart kids. He was a car enthusiast with a strong interest in mechanics and technology. He graduated from New Trier East in January 1967 with plans to enter Chicago's Mayfair College in the fall and study engineering. Meanwhile, he worked full time as a stock clerk at the National Tea grocery store in Edens Plaza.

Dick's mom, Sylvia, was a Latvian refugee whose family fled from the Soviets during World War II. After the war, she came to Wilmette with help from the Congregational Church. She took a job at Encyclopedia Britannica Films. Her husband, William, worked there as a film producer and director. Like Bob, Dick had three siblings.

Dick was an excellent soccer player at New Trier East. He had a high IQ and was a satisfactory student until his senior year. Then, his academic performance declined, and he eventually dropped out of school in May 1967. That's when the family of his girlfriend, Janet Gordon, moved to Long Island after briefly living in Wilmette. She was his first girlfriend, and he was distraught over her departure. After quitting school, he worked odd jobs, including as a dishwasher at San Pedro restaurant in Plaza del Lago.

Dick shared Bob's interest in cars, and the two boys spent considerable time fixing up the old cars that Bob bought. In other respects, they were quite different. Bob was outgoing, clean cut, and popular. Dick, on the other hand, was a loner with few friends. His girlfriend Janet said he had a "sensitive side" and was "hurt easily." He was a "kind person," she added, but he became angry at anyone who even slightly criticized her.

Dick didn't endear himself to either Janet's or Bob's parents. Janet's parents found him likeable, but they disapproved of his sloppy attire and grooming, "sort of a hippie type." They urged their daughter to stop seeing him, but she ignored their advice. No matter. The move to Long Island would probably end the relationship, they thought. But that didn't happen. After dropping out of New Trier East, Dick made several driving trips to Long Island to see Janet, prompting his parents to sell his car.

Bob's mother objected to Dick's "sloppy dress, surly manner, his long hair and unshaven face, and his tough talk." In June she drew a line. "I told him, in my son's presence, that he couldn't come back until he had cleaned himself up." Bob supported his mother: "Do you hear my mother? You'd better do that." This ended Dick's visits to the Burghart home, but it didn't end the boys' relationship.

Dick needed Bob's friendship, and Bob wouldn't turn his back on Dick during his time of need. Anyway, Bob enjoyed Dick's humor. He's "a barrel of laughs and harmless," Bob told his mother. And so, they continued to pal around.

The boys planned to meet on the evening of Monday, June 26, 1967 and go swimming. The previous weekend had been cool and rainy, but Monday was warm and sunny. Bob worked his job as stock clerk at National Tea until 6:30 PM. He was driving a car borrowed from a friend. He found Dick walking along Lake Avenue and picked him up. They headed out. Little did Bob know that Dick was carrying a loaded .22-caliber pistol, one he had stolen from a Wilmette home the previous night.

Bob believed that Dick's girlfriend, Janet Gordon, was a bad influence on Dick, and once again this subject came up. "You could be a pretty neat guy if you'd just stop messing around with Janet," he said. Dick was incensed. As the argument raged, Bob stopped in an alley in west Wilmette. The details of the ensuing events will never be known with certainty, but the outcome was tragic. Bob was dead, struck in the head with a blunt object and shot in the head by the pistol that Dick had brought along.

Now driving the borrowed car, Dick drove to Erickson Woods, just north of Willow Road, and dumped Bob's body in a clump of weeds about 200 yards east of Edens Expressway. Then he headed directly to Janet's new home on Long Island, a 14-hour trip. He stayed for several days. Janet later said that he seemed normal and didn't mention the killing.

After a few days, Bob's disappearance was reported to police, and a nationwide search was begun. When New York City police found Dick driving the borrowed car, they arrested him and turned him over to Wilmette police. He told the investigators that he expected Bob to pick him up on June 26, but Bob hadn't come. As to his possession of the borrowed car, he explained that Bob had given him permission to use it for the trip to Long island. In a phone conversation, he told Bob's mother that Bob may have run away to California, but she never believed this.

Three months went by. Police suspected Dick of foul play, but they had no proof. They interviewed more than 200 of Bob's friends and acquaintances. Dick passed a lie detector test as to whether Bob had picked him up on June 26. Unlike Lorene, the police gave credence to the possibility that Bob may have run away.

It was a horrible time for Lorene. She was not only distressed by her son's disappearance, but as village clerk, she had recently been named as a defendant in lawsuits challenging her handling of the local elections in April 1967. Believing that Bob had gone swimming, she arranged for one of his favorite swimming holes in McHenry County to be dredged. All these efforts produced no results. Meanwhile, Dick was suffering bad headaches, skipping meals, and taking lots of pills.

On Friday, September 29 the truth emerged. An animal control officer, while searching Erickson Woods for a monkey that had escaped from a nearby laboratory of Bio-Test Labs, discovered human remains. Police immediately suspected it was Bob, and the identification was confirmed by the clothing and dental records. That evening, Dick was arrested at his home. He initially denied any knowledge of the killing, but after two days of questioning, he finally confessed. He then went to a bathroom and drank a large quantity of detergent-laced water. He was rushed to Lutheran General Hospital where his stomach was pumped. He survived.

What follows is the forgiveness part of the story. After learning that Dick had confessed, Bob's mother and her two daughters visited the Kay home. "We told each other we were sorry," she said. Speaking later to the local press, she said, "I believe with all my heart that it was an accident, and I hold no malice for Richard or his mother. I feel sorry for them." She added, "I don't think Richard would consciously kill one of the few persons in the world who had befriended him."

On October 31 Dick was indicted for murder and two other offenses. On November 7 he pled not guilty. His family retained Emmet Byrne, a Chicago lawyer and former congressman, to represent him. In January 1968 a deal was struck with the prosecutor, and Dick pled guilty to the crime of voluntary manslaughter. He was sentenced to seven to 15 years in prison, with a possibility of parole after five and one-half to six years.

Lorene's forgiveness didn't fade. After Dick pled guilty, she offered to visit him in jail. She explained, "I will go to him and say 'I forgive you' if it will help him get back on the right track and live with himself. I bear no grudge against him. I feel sorry for him, and I believe the sentencing was fair and just." She acknowledged doubts about the veracity of his account but said that didn't matter. "I sincerely hope now he will get straightened out."

Lorene could have let it go at this point, but her love of Bob and her compassion for Dick led her to speak out again. In defense of Bob, she wanted the public to know that he and Dick weren't fighting over a girl, as local gossips had suggested, but that the conflict was based on Bob's unwelcomed advice about Dick's relationship with his girlfriend. She also wanted to answer speculation about the gun, explaining that it came to be in the car without Bob's knowledge. She added that Bob might still be alive if he had turned his back on Dick, but "that would not have been our Bob, as we, his family and friends, know him, and loved him."

Forgiveness was her main theme. "I don't believe Dick intended to use the gun on Bob," she said. "I do not believe it is for any of us to condemn and refuse to forgive any of what happened. We might, instead, pray for Dick and his family, that with the grace of God, young Kay will come out of prison some years from now straightened out, and that then only one life will have been lost because of this terrible tragedy."

Forgiveness is healing for victims who grant it and for offenders who truly repent. Yet, granting forgiveness is often difficult. In 1968 Lorene Burghart served as a role model for those of us who may sometimes have difficulty forgiving even minor transgressions.

Deadly Breaking News

- November 9, 1965: Albert Ritter was found shot to death in his rented car parked at 412 Wilshire Drive, one block from his home at 440 Cove Lane. The prime suspect in the murder is Gerald Covelli, a "former crime syndicate hijacker and triggerman" who has run afoul of the syndicate by testifying against several of its members. Ritter's wife Louise was at one time employed by Covelli at his Cafe Continental in Chicago and had dated him. Recently, Covelli called her several times, requesting a date, but she told him she was happily married and wasn't interested.

- November 11, 1965: The Wilmette Police Department assigned officers to guard the widow and three children of Albert Ritter while they search for his suspected killer, Gerald Covelli. Louise Ritter claims that Covelli is "extremely jealous," and she fears for her safety.
- March 3, 1966: Gerald Covelli and Louise Ritter were married in Las Vegas, Nevada.
- May 2, 1967: Louise Ritter Covelli was found dead at her home. She apparently overdosed on sleeping pills and fell down the stairs, resulting in bruises covering her body.
- June 18, 1967: Crime syndicate figure Gerald Covelli was killed when a bomb exploded under the driver's seat of the car he was driving from his Encino, California home. Police believe the bomb was triggered remotely from a nearby car, and that the bombing was in retaliation for Covelli's testimony against crime syndicate members.

CHAPTER 16

★────────────★

Other Crimes & Misdemeanors

It wasn't just the hometown homicides of Chapter 15 that brought nation-wide attention to Wilmette. Out-of-town homicides, kidnappings, arsons, and scams also made front page news nationwide. Perhaps it's not surprising that many of the crimes involved in these two chapters involve mental illness, a health issue that doesn't receive the attention it deserves.

1902: Imposter Visits Wilmette

In May 1902 James and Nannie Melville were newcomers to Wilmette, settling into their home at 1124 Greenwood Avenue. Like many contemporary families, the Melvilles had relocated from Chicago to partake in the village's friendly, peaceful lifestyle, but they may have second-guessed their move when, at 9:30 PM on May 7, they found what appeared to be a severely beaten and uncon-scious man, dressed in a U.S. Army uniform, lying on their front doorsteps. When the man regained consciousness, he told this tale, as paraphrased here:

"My name is H.E.H. King. I'm 26 years old and a lieutenant in the Army. My father is a retired brigadier general, living in Washington, D.C. Five years ago, in 1897, I was appointed to the U.S. Military Academy by Senator George Hoar of Massachusetts. A few days after enrolling, I was expelled from that vener-able institution when another cadet, a fellow named Ullchan, staged an inci-dent that made it appear as if I had insulted a superior officer. Ullchan's deceit was in retaliation for a thrashing I inflicted when he insulted a young lady.

"Following my expulsion, my family disowned me. I did everything in my power to clear my name. I persuaded the academy to readmit me. When the Spanish-American War broke out, I left the academy to serve in Cuba, but I became ill and was discharged. I took a position as a drill master in a military school in Cincinnati. Over the next five years, I scoured the country, searching for Ullchan. I was determined to get him to admit his malicious scheme.

"Last week, I found the villain in Cincinnati. Patiently awaiting my chance to gain an advantage, I followed him from Cincinnati to Pittsburgh, back to Cincinnati, and on to Chicago. I finally confronted him, at gunpoint, in his room at the Great Northern Hotel on South Dearborn Street. I forced him to write and sign a confession that my expulsion was due to his evil scheme. As I departed with his confession in hand, feeling euphoric about my upcoming exoneration, he vowed that he'd blind me with acid if he ever found me on the street.

"Today, May 7, I intended to visit Fort Sheridan to gather more evidence from a soldier stationed there. I boarded the electric line in Chicago. As I neared Wilmette, I noticed that Ullchan was on the train, apparently following me. Mindful of his earlier threat, I jumped from the train, hid in the woods, and slowly made my way to this neighborhood. To my great surprise, Ullchan suddenly leaped from the bushes and kicked me viciously in the abdomen, rendering me unconscious. When I awoke, my coat was ripped open, and the signed confession and $65 were missing from my pocket. I had been beaten mercilessly. I crawled to the door steps at 1124 Greenwood and fell unconscious again."

The public was outraged over this vicious assault on a member of America's armed forces. Sentiment soon changed, though. Senator Hoar and General King denied knowing H.E.H. King. The academy had no record of his registration. His bizarre tale shifted with each retelling. After enjoying the Melville's sympathetic hospitality for a couple of days, "Lieutenant" King disappeared.

In January 1904 King turned up in Vincennes, Indiana, supposedly searching for Army deserters. He partied with high society, amused the town's young women, and left without paying his hotel bill. In September 1904 he pulled a similar stunt in Albert Lea, Minnesota, but this time he was caught and prosecuted for stiffing the hotel and impersonating a military officer.

1912: Reckless Shooter Kills Chicken Thief

Is justice denied to a victim when mercy is shown to the offender? Take, for example, the case of Thomas Hagan, who was shot and killed by David Farnsworth, a onetime Wilmette resident.

David, the shooter, was born in 1860 and raised in Sycamore, Illinois, but he had deep roots in Massachusetts where his great-grandfather served in the Continental Army during the Revolutionary War. As a child, David lost a leg, but he learned to get around on crutches and, despite his disability, he had a long career at C&NW as a telegraph operator, inspector, and manager. He also contributed articles to farm journals about his favorite pastime, poultry raising.

From 1909 to 1911, David and his wife Margaret lived at 914 Oakwood Avenue. Then, poultry-raising became more than a pastime. David jumped at an opportunity to edit a farm journal out East. He took a leave of absence from C&NW and purchased a farm in Bridgewater, Massachusetts, home to his Farnsworth ancestry.

Thomas Hagan, the victim, was the son of Irish potato-famine refugees, drawn to Bridgewater by its iron works. In 1912 Thomas was 51-years-old, unmarried, living with his brother Joseph, and working odd jobs, one of which (allegedly) was stealing chickens, a lucrative pursuit that vexed poultry farmers nationwide.

David's poultry-raising and Thomas's chicken-stealing led to a fatal encounter on August 16, 1912. Days earlier, David had ignored the nighttime barking of his dog, and thieves had stolen 52 chickens from one of his henhouses. On the night of August 16, the dog again made "an awful noise." This time, according to David, "I jumped out of bed, grabbed my crutches and a revolver, and ran to a back window and fired a couple of shots, thinking to scare the thieves away." He and Margaret then went outside with lanterns to investigate. Switching to his rifle, David fired several more shots, still hoping to frighten the thieves. He and Margaret found the door of one henhouse propped open. In the darkness, they heard muffled voices and encountered a man. Margaret shouted, "Give me my chickens!" but the man denied having any chickens and escaped into the darkness. David fired one last warning shot.

Thomas's body was found the next morning a mile away, propped against a tree. He had bled to death from a bullet wound in the arm. The prosecutor contended that Thomas was the man David and Margaret encountered, and that David's final shot killed him. The Farnsworths insisted that the man they encountered didn't fit Thomas's description. (They weren't shown the dead man's body.) Nevertheless, David was charged with manslaughter, convicted, and sentenced to six months in jail, meaning he'd forfeit his employment and pension at C&NW, and his poultry business would fail.

The public was incensed. One editor said that "the poultryman had been too hasty in using his gun," and added, "He was in no danger himself, and it could not be shown that his victim was molesting the poultry. No one should keep a gun for protection unless he can judge calmly when to shoot." But poultrymen defended David for protecting his property when law enforcement was utterly failing to stop the thievery. His Illinois friends attested to his good character. Even the victim's brother sympathized, saying, "I would have done the same thing." Only 23 days after being jailed, David was pardoned by Massachusetts Governor Eugene Foss. He and Margaret returned to Illinois where he resumed his active employment with C&NW and died in 1923.

Was the outcome of this case "just"? Many folks would probably answer "yes." But who's to say that one offender deserves mercy while another doesn't, and that one victim receives strict justice while another doesn't? We depend on police, prosecutors, judges, juries, parole boards, governors, and presidents to dispense mercy and justice fairly. There are so many players with so much discretion. Who benefits from this system? Probably not the poor and the unpopular.

1916: Angry Contractor Kills Businessman

Dr. George Rider of Wilmette didn't go to Twin Lakes, Colorado (near Telluride) in February 1916 for skiing or hiking, as many folks do nowadays. He went there for business. He hardly expected what happened.

Rider was born in New York in 1868. He graduated from Albany Medical College in 1888 and practiced medicine at several locations, including the iron mining region of Ashland County, Wisconsin. There, he became interested in mining and metals. He eventually abandoned his medical practice and joined American Steel & Wire Co., the nation's dominant manufacturer of barbed wire. Later, he entered the fencing business in Chicago with partner Nelson Van Deventer. They achieved financial success and invested in mines. In 1907 Rider married Carrie Trinler. Their son, George Jr., was born in 1909, and the Rider family moved to 730 Central Avenue, Wilmette.

In 1915 Rider and his business partner joined an investment group that formed the Twin Lakes Mining & Milling Co. to buy, refurbish, and operate the Gordon-Bengal Tiger Mine, a defunct gold mine. The group contracted with Edward Sackett, a local foundry operator, to build an aerial tram 3,890 feet long connecting the mine and the mill. Construction was almost complete by year-end. Meanwhile, in January 1916, an avalanche crashed down the mountain, swept away the mine's surface buildings and killed two employees. Rider decided to personally inspect his investment property.

During his visit, mine officials learned that the validity of the company's title to the mine property was in doubt. Sackett, having just completed the tram, was expecting payment of $3,158. When he heard about the title problem, he became highly agitated. Would he be paid? He had been stiffed by mine operators before. He told one mine employee, "I'll have a settlement to-night, or I'll get the whole bunch of them. I'll fill one full of lead and the rest can't get away."

On the evening of February 9 Sackett borrowed a pistol, went to Rider's room at the Twin Lakes hotel, forced open the door, and demanded payment. Receiving no satisfaction, he fired two shots, fatally wounding Rider. A by-stander asked, "Ed, for God's sake, what have you done?" Sackett responded, "I killed the s.o.b."

Sackett, 41, was charged with murder. Little more than one month later, his four-day trial began. The prosecution easily proved that he had killed Rider. His attorney mounted an insanity defense and called numerous witnesses who described incidents of bizarre and violent behavior and extreme mood swings. They applied various labels to the defendant, like "peculiar," "depressed," "vicious," "high-strung," and "excitable." An alienist (psychiatrist) called by the defense testified that Sackett suffered from "hypo-mania," but two alien-ists called by the prosecution said he was "normal." After deliberating for five hours, the jury returned its verdict: Sackett was insane and not guilty. The judge ordered him confined to a sanitarium.

Was Sackett insane? Or did he receive favorable treatment by a jury more sympathetic to a local contractor than a rich out-of-towner who perhaps was reneging on a debt? Subsequent events vindicate the jury. After two years, Sackett was released from confinement. He returned to Telluride. Over the next eight years, he bounced around, plagued by mental illness that led to his recommitment in 1924 and a bizarre 1926 incident in Chicago and Berwyn: He hijacked a taxicab, kidnapped the driver and the driver's nine-year-old son at gunpoint, and forced the boy to play his violin during an hours-long police chase. Following a shootout with police, he was again hospitalized. Later that year, he committed suicide in Salt Lake City, explaining in a note that he was "a menace to society" and had "a duty to get out of the way."

1932: Sting Artist Snares Pigeon

Poor Joseph Kaszab. This unfortunate Wilmette resident—219 Central Avenue —was swindled out of $125,000 by a gang of con artists in the midst of the Great Depression. His loss was the equivalent of more than $2.3 million in 2020 dollars.

Until this incident, Joseph was an American success story. He and his wife Ethel were born in Budapest in 1878. They were married in 1897 and came to

Chicago in 1901 with their baby daughter. They had two more children and moved to Wilmette in 1927.

Joseph was a skilled woodworker. He worked as a manager in the furniture industry before going into business for himself as a manufacturer of ornamental woodwork and fixtures for large Loop office buildings, hotels, and stores like Walgreen. Joseph made a lot of money, which made him a target for the race track swindlers.

The swindlers used the good-faith-deposit sting on Joseph. It happened when he and Ethel went to Phoenix for his health in early 1932. There he met three men who identified themselves as tourists. One claimed to be an agent for a wealthy eastern manufacturer. He said that he had been using some of his principal's money to bet on "sure-thing" racing tips. Joseph was invited to join the men's sure-thing betting syndicate, and he accepted. He scored a series of "wins" that earned him $40,000 in "paper profits." Then, the men received a sure-thing tip that would yield them a big killing of $400,000. Joseph agreed to participate. What a surprise! They "won" again. Except for one thing: The men had to resolve a technical difficulty before they could collect the $400,000. The bookies with whom they were dealing required them to furnish proof, in the form of a cash deposit, that they could have paid the bet if they had lost. The men apologetically said that they could raise only part of the money, and Joseph would have to come up with $125,000.

Joseph took the bait. He and Ethel jumped on a train to Chicago, raised the funds, returned to Phoenix, and deposited the funds in a Phoenix bank. The men instructed him to convert the deposit into cash and meet them in the lobby of a local office building. As instructed, Joseph and Ethel took the cash to the building and delivered it. The men told them to wait in the lobby while they met with the bookies and made the good faith showing.

Joseph and Ethel waited. And they waited some more. When the men didn't return after an hour, they called the police. The men were nowhere to be found, and a criminal investigation was launched. Suspicion initially focused on a gang led by Joseph "Yellow Kid" Weil, the dean of Chicago's confidence men. Over a decades-long career, his schemes reaped about $8 million, but the investigation of his involvement in the Kaszab swindle hit a dead end. Then attention turned to the gang of Floyd Woodward. He began his career as a bunko artist in Atlanta in the early 1920s and moved around the country and world to avoid the clutches of the law. One of his classic cons was to persuade wealthy investors to buy phony stocks by claiming he had inside information that would produce quick profits. The investors eventually discovered that they had been fleeced, but they didn't complain to authorities, fearing legal problems for themselves as "inside traders." Woodward was brought to justice for some of his schemes and spent a few years in prison, but not for the Kaszab swindle.

Joseph died in December 1934. His estate, at $100,000, was considerably less than it was in 1932 when he met the race track swindlers.

1934: FBI's "Most Wanted" Dies in Wilmette

Notorious gangster "Baby Face" Nelson spent the last few hours of his life in Wilmette. He was born Lester Gillis and raised in Chicago. After changing his name to George Nelson, someone gave him the nickname "Baby Face," probably because of his diminutive stature and youthful look, and influenced by the 1926 hit song of the same name. In 1934, after committing a string of bank robberies and murders, some in collaboration with John Dillinger, Nelson became the FBI's "Public Enemy Number One" at age 25.

On November 27, 1934, the FBI tracked him down near Lake Geneva. Accompanied by his wife Helen, 23, and pal John Chase, 32, he tried to escape to Chicago, but FBI agents stopped him at Barrington and disabled his car. An ensuing gunfight left one FBI agent dead and another dying. Nelson was hit by multiple gunshots, but he managed to steal the agents' bullet-riddled car. With John Chase driving, Baby Face and Helen sped southeast to Wilmette.

Their first stop was at 1155 Mohawk Road. This was the home of Thomas Carney, 48, and his wife Marguerite, 40. Carney was an executive at Sears Roebuck and later became its president. His father and grandfather had been prominent Chicagoans. Also living at the Carney home was Marguerite's brother, the Rev. Philip Coughlan, 38, a Catholic priest. Father Coughlan had underworld ties, and he and Nelson were friends. Nelson hoped the priest would harbor him, but upon seeing the weak and bloody Nelson and the bullet-riddled car, Father Coughlan refused, explaining that the two Carney children were inside, and Marguerite was expected home soon. He said he would lead them to a safe place.

The second stop was at 1627 Walnut Avenue. It's uncertain whether Father Coughlan led the trio there. He claimed that he led them west, unsure where he was going, but they disappeared. The Walnut Avenue house was owned and occupied by Ray Henderson, 41, and his wife Marie, 37. Ray was born and raised in Wilmette, son of a livery owner. Marie grew up in Chicago, daughter of a city police officer. They married in the mid-1910s, and their first child was born in 1917, shortly before Ray enlisted in the Army. After World War I, they

"Baby Face" Nelson, the FBI's "most wanted," died in Wilmette from gunshot wounds in November, 1934. Photo from Wikimedia Commons.

lived in Chicago, and two more children were born. In 1931 they purchased the Walnut Avenue house and moved there, taking in boarders. During his working life, Ray worked sporadically as a truck driver and janitor.

Nelson was carried into the house where he died several hours later. The following day, his body was found at the fringe of St. Paul's Lutheran Cemetery in Skokie, and the FBI agents' car was found in a ditch alongside Winnetka Avenue in western Winnetka. Exactly what happened over the next few hours remains a mystery, but the Hendersons reputedly had connections to unsavory characters. Two years later, Marie Henderson told her friend, Kenilworth Police Sergeant William Sumner, that she knew details about the events of that night that were unknown to the FBI.

Ray Henderson died in 1936. Soon, Marie lost the Walnut Avenue house to foreclosure and moved to 1322 Forest Avenue as a tenant. In 1939 she married Edward Ward, a Wilmette fireman.

Neither Father Coughlan nor the Hendersons were prosecuted for harboring Baby Face. Helen Nelson was sentenced to a year and a day in prison for violating an earlier probation and, upon her release, was sentenced to a year of probation for aiding her husband. Getaway car driver Chase was convicted of murdering one of the FBI agents and was sentenced to life in prison. He served 32 years at Alcatraz and Leavenworth and was paroled in 1966.

1947: Dancer Kills Married Lover

At Jack Mee's funeral on April 22, 1947, Rev. Ross Cannon of Wilmette's Congregational Church didn't mention the circumstances surrounding the young man's death. "This is the Mee family's church," he said, "and this service is not related to the last days of John Lester Mee's life." He vaguely described Jack as a person "seeking to take that which is ideal and reduce it to pattern and rhythm" (whatever that means). Despite this disclaimer, the last days of Jack Mee's life were certainly on the minds of the 300 mourners.

Born on October 11, 1913, Jack spent his entire childhood in Wilmette. His family lived for many years at 1229 Chestnut Avenue. He attended public school in Wilmette and graduated from New Trier as an honor student in 1931. He participated in extracurricular activities at New Trier, especially sports. His father was a prominent doctor, and Jack grew up in a privileged environment. But everything wasn't rosy. According to his father, Jack was "something of a problem," a "restless child," and "inclined to impetuous decisions."

After New Trier, Jack went on to college and then tried his hand at various pursuits—poet, dancer, accountant, linguist, musician, and midway barker—until he finally entered John Marshall Law School at his father's urging. After law school, he briefly practiced law, married, promptly enlisted in the Navy (1942), served honorably as captain of a PT boat in the Pacific, and was discharged as a lieutenant (1945).

Jack's bride was Mary Dixon, a 24-year-old divorcee who came to Chicago from Missouri to perform as a nightclub "dancer" (euphemism for stripper). Jack frequented this type of establishment and was quite attracted to dancers. Mary worked under the stage name Marilyn Drake. Jack had little time for Mary before entering the Navy, and that didn't change much after his discharge. His family probably frowned on his marital choice, but it's unclear how much they knew. "Of course, we knew his wife was a dancer," said his father. "One of the ways she kept herself busy and made a little extra money while Jack was in the Navy was teaching at the Arthur Murray dancing school."

Before, during and after his marriage and military service, Jack had relationships with numerous other women, mostly dancers, documented in vivid detail throughout the sultry passages of his rambling diary. His favorite and the most prominent of these women was Lorraine De Wood. Described as a "black-haired, deep-voiced singer of Hollywood and Broadway," and billed as "sexotic" and "sextacular," Jack called her *La Tirana* (the tyrant). She described him as "brilliant, extremely intelligent—and nuts. Attractive? Don't ask."

Jack returned to Chicago after his naval service and tried to resume his fledgling law practice, but he couldn't settle into either the law or his marriage, and he couldn't stay away from the nightclubs. In April 1946 he met 21-year-old dancer Patricia Schmidt, who used the stage name *Satira* (saucy). A native of Toledo, Ohio, she was about to be divorced following a brief and stormy marriage. She took center stage in Jack's life. He promised to marry her. He didn't mention that he was already married.

In late 1946 Jack's wild impulses led him, in partnership with Chuck Jackson, a Navy buddy, to purchase a surplus 72-foot PT boat for $750. They intended to operate a fishing excursion business in the waters off Acapulco that winter. Jack named the boat La Tirana. In December 1946 they set out down the Mississippi River with some paying passengers, but they never reached Acapulco. Engine trouble (and an opportunity for Jack to connect with one of his lovers) took them in another direction—to Havana Harbor. Meanwhile, Jack's wife Mary remained in Chicago, pursuing her dancing career.

Jack arranged to meet his newest lover, Satira, in Havana. She was just finishing a Latin America dance tour. He said they would be married, but things didn't go well in Havana. Limited funds forced Jack, Chuck, and Satira to live on the "yacht" (renamed *Satira* for the rendezvous). In March Satira saw something in Jack's correspondence that revealed he was married. Their relationship started to crumble. The final blowup occurred on April 8, 1947. Versions differed, but it's undisputed that Satira, using a .22-caliber pistol she obtained from a drawer in Jack's stateroom, shot him in the neck, nearly severing his spinal cord.

Jack was taken to the Anglo-American Hospital in Havana, clinging to life. His father rushed to his side, and Jack pleaded, "Don't leave me alone with that woman. She shot me intentionally. I don't want to be alone with her in a room again. She wants to choke me. She's capable of anything." When interviewed by the investigating judge, Jack continued to insist that Satira had shot him "intentionally." Five days after the shooting, he died.

Satira's version of the incident changed seven times, but when questioned about this, she explained that, at various times, she was trying to protect Jack, to spare the Mee family, and to tell the truth. She also blamed her inconsistencies on her inability to understand and speak Spanish. She ultimately relied on a claim of self defense: The ongoing argument over Jack's marital status led him, on April 8, to strike her on the face and arms and order her off the boat. Then, in a rage, he threatened to kill her and blocked her exit from the stateroom. She said she was terrified, grabbed the pistol, brandished it to keep him at bay, and accidentally shot him.

Jack Mee and Mary Dixon were married shortly before he entered the Navy during World War II. Photo from *Life* magazine, May 5, 1947, p. 47.

Satira was charged with murder and manslaughter. These crimes carried maximum penalties of decades in prison. She was held without bail at Havana's Guanabacoa women's prison. Meanwhile, the case became a *cause célèbre* throughout the U.S. and Latin America, especially as Jack's perversions were revealed by the publication of his steamy diary and the kinky stories told by some of his lovers. Satira became a sympathetic victim in the minds of a growing fan club.

The trial in Cuba spanned three months and ended on December 22. Did Jack beat and terrify Satira and cause her to accidentally shoot him in self-defense? Was Jack mentally unstable and quick to anger? In the end, the three-judge tribunal sided with Jack, found Satira guilty of manslaughter, sentenced her to 15 years in prison, and ordered her to pay the Mee family $5,000 in indemnity.

Nine months later, Satira was back in the news. The outgoing president of Cuba, Grau San Martin, inexplicably granted her a pardon. She returned to Chicago and resumed her career as a dancer, more popular and profitable than ever. Mary Mee, Jack's widow, declined an offer to appear on stage with Satira. "This nightclub isn't big enough to hold both of us," said Mary. "I don't have any hard feelings for that girl. But, after all...."

1954: Pyromaniac Strikes Again

Stephen Posey's story ends in 2011 when he died in Port Townsend, Washington. But when does it begin? Perhaps it begins in 1935 when he entered this world, blessed with or burdened by a brilliant mind, as IQ tests would later reveal. Or perhaps it begins a few years later when his parents, Rollin and Elizabeth Posey, started to push their "boy genius" too hard. Or perhaps it begins in 1951 when, at age 16, he graduated from New Trier High School after only three years and headed off to Yale with a Ford scholarship, academically capable but immature and socially backward.

Things didn't go well for Stephen at Yale. He was caught stealing $400 from a classmate and was expelled. He returned home to 4025 Fairway Drive and went to work for a Chicago radio manufacturer while receiving psychiatric care.

Bear with me while I change course temporarily and mention two Wilmette fires that occurred in 1952. A June fire at the clubhouse of Northwestern University's golf course (later the Wilmette Golf Club) caused $50,000 in damage. A November fire at St. Augustine's Episcopal Church on Wilmette Avenue caused $85,000 in damage. The origin of both fires was undetermined.

Back to Stephen. His father was chairman of the Political Science Department at Northwestern University. His grandfather had been president of the University of Wisconsin. The family was well-connected in higher-education circles. That probably explains why Beloit College gave Stephen the benefit of the doubt in 1953 and accepted him as a freshman despite his Yale record.

Things didn't go well at Beloit, either. Stephen's few friends said he considered himself intellectually superior and couldn't bridge the gap socially. He cut numerous classes, although his academic performance was acceptable. In January 1954, he was arrested for stealing two students' billfolds and forging a student's signature on a check. While he was in custody, Beloit police received a call from Chicago police. They had been alerted by Stephen's psychiatrist that he had admitted setting fire to the Beloit College chapel and was dangerous: he might even set fire to his own home.

The chapel, a beloved campus building, had been destroyed by fire one month earlier. The loss amounted to $500,000. Investigators had originally blamed the fire on spontaneous combustion, but when questioned, Stephen admitted starting it by inserting a lit cigarette into a match book and placing the device in a closet near cleaning fluids. He said he didn't mean to cause so much damage.

Stephen was charged with arson and forgery. He entered a plea of not guilty by reason of insanity. At trial, two psychiatrists disagreed as to whether he knew the difference between right and wrong at the time of the crimes. The judge ruled in Stephen's favor and committed him to the state mental hospital. Four years later, in 1959, the judge found him sane and ordered his release.

Wilmette investigators wanted to interview Stephen about the 1952 fires. After all, the clubhouse was just down the street from the Posey home and was owned by Northwestern University, the employer of Stephen's father, and Stephen admitted to Beloit police that he had visited St. Augustine's on the day of its fire although he denied starting it. However, Stephen's attorney wouldn't let the investigators interview him. It was never proved that he was involved. But then, as the saying goes, where there's smoke, there's fire.

After 1959 Stephen apparently led a "normal" life. According to his obituary, he never finished college, but he worked in various science and technology jobs in Wisconsin, Illinois, Minnesota, Colorado, and Washington until his retirement. He was happily married for 33 years. After being diagnosed with terminal cancer, he took up tango dancing with a passion.

1960: Who Killed Rosie?

At 6:30 AM on January 10, 1960, a cold and foggy Sunday morning, a woman's body was found six miles south of Baton Rouge, Louisiana on a one-lane private roadway (and sometimes lover's lane) leading from a public highway to a levee on the Mississippi River. The body lay face down in a pool of blood, three feet behind the woman's parked car, a 1960 Renault Dauphine. Her head had been crushed by 13 blows from a blunt instrument. Her hand clutched a pack of cigarettes and a book of matches, and her purse was looped over her left arm. A pair of eyeglasses and a broken string of imitation pearls lay on the ground nearby. An overnight rain had obliterated any tracks left by the murderer, and there was no indication that the victim had struggled with her assailant. The murder weapon was nowhere to be found. The contents of the woman's purse were seemingly intact and revealed her identity to be Dr. Margaret Rosamond McMillan, 38, an assistant biology professor at the New Orleans branch of Louisiana State University. She lived at an apartment in New Orleans with two cats.

Rosie, as she was known, was born in 1921. She lived most of her 38 years at 617 Linden Avenue, Wilmette. Her dad was a mechanical engineer, and her mom was a stenographer. Rosie was their only child. She was raised in the Catholic faith at St. Francis Church. She attended public schools in Wilmette and was an honor student at New Trier High School. She studied piano and voice and was active in high school music groups. After graduating from New Trier in 1939, she continued her education at Mundelein College in Chicago where, again, she was an honor student. She received a BA degree in 1943 from Mundelein, and two years later, she received an MS degree from Northwestern University, concentrating on biology.

Rosie's training in biology led to her employment at Evanston Hospital as a laboratory technician and parasitologist (involving the relationship between parasites and their hosts). After a few years, she returned to Northwestern to continue her studies, aiming for a PhD. She was supervised by Dr. George Mickey, a pioneering geneticist who won awards, fellowships, and other recognition for his work in the emerging scientific field of genetics. He and Rosie worked together closely as she researched and wrote her thesis on "The Effects of Certain Metabolites on the Polymorphism of Some Chlorococcales."

After earning her PhD in 1955, Rosie took teaching jobs at Northwestern and later at Agnes Scott College in Decatur, Georgia. She began to study the reproduction of green algae, and her study drew NASA's attention because it might help to solve the problem of feeding astronauts on lengthy space missions. She became a well-established university teacher and scholar.

Meanwhile, in 1956, Dr. Mickey left Northwestern to accept a professorship of zoology at Louisiana State University. Over the next four years, he advanced to chairman of the Department of Zoology, Physiology and Entomology; dean of the graduate school; and preeminent authority on cytogenetics (the study of the relationship between chromosomes and cell behavior). In 1959, when LSU was opening a new branch at New Orleans, he helped Rosie obtain a position there as an assistant professor. And thus, Rosie moved to New Orleans.

What explanation could there be for the brutal murder of this promising young educator and scientist? Was it an abduction and robbery that went bad? Was it a crime of passion committed by a rejected lover? Was the assailant a deranged student fearing or receiving a bad grade? Or was Rosie simply in the wrong place at the wrong time?

Shortly after Rosie's body was found, investigators went to her New Orleans apartment and learned from the landlady that she had a date in Baton Rouge on Saturday night. Rosie didn't mention a name, said the landlady. "I just supposed it was the same one she goes up there to see occasionally—somebody who's on the faculty at LSU."

Dr. Mickey's contact information appeared on an emergency notification card found in Rosie's wallet. When contacted, he expressed shock and told investigators that he was unaware of any dating relationship. Meanwhile, the coroner opined that Rosie had died around midnight on Saturday but had been injured four to six hours earlier and bled to death while unconscious. He also reported that she consumed steak, potatoes, and beer between 6–7 PM.

Investigators visited the restaurant advertised on the matchbook clutched in Rosie's death grip. A waitress was certain that Rosie (whose photo appeared in newspapers) had dined there at 6 PM Saturday with a man who was "rather tall and distinguished looking"; they left shortly before 7 PM. Later, when shown a photo of Dr. Mickey, the waitress identified him as Rosie's companion. Investigators also canvassed local gas stations. At one, the manager recalled that Rosie had purchased gas there on Saturday evening. He insisted that she wasn't driving her Renault that was found at the murder scene. "It was an American-made car, and a man was with her." A more thorough search of Rosie's apartment revealed a batch of personal letters from Dr. Mickey and a will designating him as beneficiary of her estate.

Confronted with these facts, Dr. Mickey dismissed the letters as forgeries and expressed surprise at being Rosie's beneficiary, claiming their relationship was purely professional. He denied seeing her on Saturday and insisted that between 5–9 PM, he met with a federal education official. He explained that he and the official ate dinner (fried chicken) in the coffee shop of a Baton Rouge hotel, and afterwards he drove the official to the airport to catch a plane. He couldn't remember the official's name ("Silvery or Silby or something like that"). The federal agency later reported that no official was in the Baton Rouge vicinity on Saturday evening, and airport personnel reported that no person matching the description provided by Dr. Mickey had boarded a plane. The hotel coffee shop's personnel didn't know whether or not the two men had dined there, but they told investigators that fried chicken wasn't on the menu.

Dr. Mickey was arrested on January 14 and charged with murder. Investigators subsequently found blood matching Rosie's type on his car and mud matching the soil at the murder scene on the shoes he wore on Saturday.

The idea that Dr. Mickey committed a heinous crime was at odds with his impeccable reputation as a church-going husband and father, educator, and internationally known genetics expert. The grand jury refused to indict him, and the charges were dropped. Dr. Mickey and LSU severed ties, and he moved on to new teaching and research positions. He died in 1992 at the age of 82. Rosie's murder remains unsolved. Ironically, advanced techniques in genetics, Dr. Mickey's area of expertise, might well have solved the case if they had been available in 1960.

1968: Deranged Student Kills Former Girlfriend

We send our kids to college with the hope that they'll stay on track—learn, grow, and enjoy—and then graduate well-prepared for a rewarding adult life. For Robert and Dorothy Letsinger of 316 3rd Street, Wilmette, this hope for their daughter Louise became a nightmare.

Louise was born in 1944 and raised in Wilmette. She attended Central School and Howard Junior High. Her father was a distinguished chemistry professor at Northwestern, and her mother was a tutor in the Evanston school system. At age 11, she spent a year in Germany while her father was there on a fellowship. She learned the German language the hard way: by attending a German school. From this experience, she became interested in foreign languages, and at New Trier High School she studied both German and Russian. She was a shy and serious child with only a few good friends, a diligent student with little time for extracurricular activities. Her IQ was over 160, but her brilliance and lack of self-confidence made her feel isolated and depressed. After graduating from New Trier in 1962, she spent a year in an honors program at the University of Michigan, then transferred to Indiana University and spent another year in an intensive Russian program. In 1964, she transferred again to UCLA, where she concentrated on Russian. She hoped to work someday as an interpreter for a diplomatic agency, but as graduation approached, she realized that she was ill and "had to make a real positive effort." She had seen a psychiatrist and was considering intensive therapy.

At UCLA, Louise met Joe Gonzales, a graduate student in theater arts concentrating on filmmaking. Born in 1933, Joe had experienced little stability during his young life, with numerous changes in abode and schools. He spent his early years in Los Angeles. His father, an importer, died when he was six. His mother took him to Argentina when he was eleven. They returned to Los Angeles when he was 19. As an undergraduate, he produced a 14-minute film that was considered outstanding. It led to his admission into the graduate program. He also worked 15 hours per week in a work-study program, reading new plays and reporting on them to community theaters. One professor praised Joe: He was a "marvelous character" but "erratic"—"a highly articulate, brilliant, deeply sensitive young man with a very compelling personality. People simply were drawn to him." Another professor added that Joe was "a very charming, delightful sort of person to work with. He had a quick smile—a kind of warmth." He "laughed readily and seemed to get along with everybody" and was "a very promising film-maker." He showed no obvious sign of the psychosis for which he had been treated for six years.

Louise and Joe started dating in 1966. A few days after Christmas that year, the couple moved into married-students' quarters. That arrangement lasted only four months. Following the breakup, Louise moved into an apartment by herself and tried to avoid Joe, but he suffered an "acute psychotic breakdown," probably related to the recent death of his mother. Louise stood by him, helped him get treatment, and gave him money. On February 28, 1968 she moved again, into an apartment over a garage at 635 25th Street, Santa Monica, a ten-minute drive from campus. She tried to keep her new address secret, but Joe found out and, within a week, he had visited her three times.

There were qualities in Louise that attracted Joe, and vice versa. They were both highly intelligent achievers. His charm broke through her shyness, and her caring softened his anguish. They shared the pain of mental illness. Both had received psychiatric help from Dr. J. Allen Marshall at a local mental health center.

At 4 PM on March 6, 1968, Joe parked his car near Louise's above-garage apartment on 25th Street. He approached the fenced-in yard and summoned Mamie Flower, the landlady. She opened the gate while holding back the German shepherd that called the yard his home. Joe proceeded up to Louise's apartment. She knew that he was in crisis. He said that he was "haunted by the evil spirit of his dead mother." The previous day, Louise talked him into making an appointment to see Dr. Marshall, but the visit to her apartment occurred before the appointed time.

Joe was there for more than an hour. His description of the events during that period is so bizarre and grisly that I've chosen to omit the details. Let's just say that Joe stabbed Louise multiple times, believing in his demented mind that she was someone else.

Joe left and went to the Hollywood apartment of a friend. They called Dr. Marshall, who came and escorted Joe to the police. Joe then led the police to Louise's apartment where they found her body in the middle of the living room among upended furniture and scattered books. There were multiple stab wounds in her body and two bloody kitchen knives nearby. "She must have put up a terrific fight," said one veteran detective. "It's the most savage murder I've seen or heard of in my years of police work."

Joe was charged with murder and held without bail. He pleaded not guilty and raised an insanity defense. Meanwhile, a memorial service for Louise was held at Wilmette's Methodist Church. On June 17 a judge in Santa Monica, after reviewing psychiatric reports, ruled that Joe was unable to cooperate in presenting his defense. The judge committed him to a mental hospital until such time as he was fit to stand trial. The judge made no ruling regarding Joe's mental state at the time of the killing.

Less than one year later, Joe was released from the hospital and ordered to stand trial. On March 26, 1969 a judge ruled that he was insane at the time of the murder and thus was not guilty. The judge also ordered additional psychiatric evaluations to determine his current mental condition. These examinations led to a finding that Joe was still insane and would again be committed to a mental hospital. At this point, the trail becomes murky, but I'm reasonably certain that he didn't spend much time in the hospital.

1971: Desperate Gang Takes Banker's Wife Hostage

April Fools' Day 1971 began uneventfully for the Nortrup family of 2140 Thornwood Avenue. Larry Nortrup, president of Hartford Plaza Bank, was at his office in the Loop. Doreen, his wife, was at home, about to attend a bridge party. Their oldest child was away at college. Two younger children were at school.

Things changed at 11:30 AM. The doorbell rang. A man announced a delivery from Marshall Field's. Doreen opened the door. The man pushed his way in. Doreen tried to escape but fell. Brandishing a gun, the man subdued her. He bound her wrists and ankles to a chair. He repeatedly warned, "We're desperate."

The man phoned Larry. He threatened to kill Doreen unless Larry followed instructions. He put Doreen on the phone. She calmly confirmed that she was being held but was okay. The man ordered Larry to take $150,000 in cash to a Buick parked across from the bank within 15 minutes. When Larry responded that he didn't have $150,000, the man said "Richard can get it." (Richard was the bank's head teller.)

Larry had someone call the FBI and someone else gather the cash. The FBI instructed him to proceed with the payment but take all 15 minutes to give agents time to arrive. As time was expiring, Larry took two bags containing $119,000 outside. Unable to find the Buick, he returned to his office. Immediately, he received another call. A male voice gave him a precise location and one minute to get there. Returning outside, Larry found the Buick and placed the bags inside. He left without seeing anyone at the car. FBI agents watched as a woman entered the Buick and drove it to the parking lot of a nearby liquor store. She got out with a bundle and entered a Pontiac as a passenger. It drove off. To protect Doreen, the agents didn't intervene. The Pontiac was lost in traffic.

The man at the Nortrup home didn't stay long. Fifteen minutes after arriving, he received a phone call. After a brief conversation, he placed tape over Doreen's mouth, shoved her in a closet, ripped the phone from the wall, and left. Minutes later, Doreen's friend arrived to pick her up for the party. The front door was ajar. She heard muffled sounds. Finding Doreen in the closet, she removed the bindings and drove her to the Wilmette police station.

FBI agents had recorded the license numbers of the cars. The Buick was stolen and untraceable, but the Pontiac was quickly traced to Frederick Marschke, whose wife Lucille was identified as the woman collecting the cash. The driver of the Pontiac wasn't identified.

When confronted, Lucille pointed the finger at her former husband, Robert Manley, an insurance supervisor employed at the Hartford Building. Lucille claimed she drove the Pontiac to the Loop that morning, parked it near the building, gave the keys to Manley, and took the train home later. Manley denied involvement and claimed he had been at a restaurant from 11:45 AM to 1:15 PM with his co-worker, John Starble. Initially, Starble backed him up, but soon he admitted he had lied.

Five persons, most of whom were connected in one way or another to the Hartford Plaza Bank or the Hartford Building, were charged with bank robbery and related crimes. Plea bargaining led to a five-year prison sentence for Manley, three years' probation for Lucille, and their identification of Philip Justo as the hostage-taker. He also pled guilty. Most of the money wasn't recovered.

Some folks would suffer lifelong scars from this incident. Not the Nortrups. They quickly returned to their normal routine without serious loss of sleep. I spoke to Larry in 2012 when he and Doreen were in their 80s, retired, and enjoying life in Sarasota, Florida. He mentioned that Doreen believes he got a great bargain for $119,000.

Breaking Crime News

- November 7, 1914: Three sheriff's deputies raided a home at 1501 Wilmette Avenue, suspecting that the occupant, George Steffens, was operating a "blind pig" on the premises. When Steffins refused to allow the deputies inside, they forced their way in and found a group of men seated at tables with beer bottles in front of them. In an adjoining room, they also found two teapots containing whiskey. Steffins was arrested for violating Wilmette's strict prohibition ordinance. Immediately after his arrest, the unfortunate Mr. Steffins, only 32 years old, suffered a sudden and severe memory loss. He totally forgot when, how, and from whom he acquired the banned beverages.
- September 17, 1917: Fourteen male passengers on an early-morning C&NW commuter train to Chicago were arrested by three detectives for gambling. Two of the 14 arrestees were professional gamblers. The other twelve were

North Shore commuters, a.k.a pigeons, including three from Gross Point and Wilmette (John Bleser, John Huerter, and Frank Balmes). The men rode downtown in the baggage car, the most secluded location for their lively games of chance. The fun started two months before with a "little old pitch game" but it quickly grew into a high stakes dice game with the professional gamblers fleecing the North Shore dupes and sailors from Naval Station Great Lakes.

- June 12, 1918: Hugo Zeggel, 40, of 1326 Forest Avenue, was the victim of anti-German sentiment that's sweeping the nation as the Great War continues. Zeggel was born in Prussia and immigrated to the U.S. as a small child. Today, his garage was set ablaze and destroyed. A placard tacked to a nearby tree read: "Pro-Germans Beware—Zeggel you slacker, if you can keep a car you can buy a liberty bond." The "car" was presumably a reference to a vehicle in the garage that was also destroyed by the fire. The arsonists were apparently unaware that the car belonged to Thomas and Helen Cook, non-German neighbors, not to Zeggel.

- November 30, 1939: Josephine Pelikan, 41, was sentenced to five years in prison by a Michigan judge. She was convicted of fraudulently obtaining $460 from a gullible suitor by falsely promising to marry him. Investigators found that she was in the marriage business: securing grooms' assets and promptly vanishing. One of her victims was Gottlieb Holbik, 45, a gardener in Wilmette. He responded to Josephine's ad, published in a Polish matrimonial newspaper. This mistake led to their marriage, his opening a joint bank account, and her disappearance with the funds and his gold watch. Authorities in Illinois are awaiting their turn to prosecute Josephine for the Holbik caper.

CHAPTER 17

★————————————————★

It Takes All Kinds

Folks who live in Wilmette fit into no mold and bring a vast range of attributes and experiences to the table. What follows are stories of several onetime residents who further illustrate the adage that it takes all kinds of people to make an interesting community.

Mary Caspar, Uncertain in Love

Mary Caspar of Wilmette, described as a "pretty girl of 18," was pursued by two suitors at the turn of the 20th century. One was Joe Brucks, an 18-year-old Chicagoan who worked as a bicycle parts salesman. The other was Fred Willers, an 18-year-old Evanstonian who worked at an Evanston butcher shop. Mary's parents (Francis and Mary Caspar) lived at 157 Kline Avenue (now Prairie Avenue), but Mary lived and worked as a domestic servant in the Wilmette home of Edwin and Hannah Drury.

Joe was Mary's first serious suitor, but when their relationship cooled, Fred stepped in and won her affection. He soon proposed marriage; she accepted, and they planned to be wed in the fall of 1901. Joe learned about this plan and became distraught. He sent Mary letters, one declaring that he would have her, "dead or alive."

Matters came to a head on April 9, 1901. Joe came to the Drury house and talked to Mary for an hour. She afterwards told Hannah Drury that she was going to her parents' home and might not return that night. The couple then disappeared, leaving behind only a note from Joe to Mary's parents: "I am going away with Mary for a while. Will be back soon. Don't worry."

Mary's parents were convinced that she never would have gone with Joe voluntarily. "She disliked him too much," they explained. They obtained a warrant charging Joe with abducting her. But then they received a letter from

Mary: "Joe and I are married. The ceremony was performed at St. Joe [Michigan]. I am happy. After we visit Waukegan we are coming home. Hoping you will forgive us." Both sets of parents—the Caspars and the Brucks (Louis and Catherine)—were upset about this too-youthful elopement.

Two days after the wedding, Mary and Joe returned: she to her parents' home in Wilmette and he to his parents' home in Chicago. Meanwhile, Fred's ardor was undiminished. He threatened to kill Joe if he ever came to Wilmette to see Mary. Discretion being the better part of valor, Joe stayed away.

After a few months, Mary was no longer "happy." Her story changed. She claimed that Joe forced her to accompany him to St. Joseph at gunpoint, that he cowed her into compliance by constantly threatening her with death, that he drugged her with a drink that made her "senses become dull," and that she has only "a faint recollection of standing up and answering questions." She petitioned the circuit court to annul the marriage. Joe fought the annulment, claiming that Mary turned against him only because her family and Fred unduly influenced her. In the end, Joe lost both the lawsuit and his wife.

Epilogue: Mary and Fred were married in Evanston on January 25, 1902. They had one child, Raymond Frederick, and they enjoyed 52 years of marital bliss. Fred died in 1954 and Mary in 1969.

Joe wasn't so fortunate. Following the annulment, he was employed as a clerk by Hartford Fire Insurance Co. As the son of a wealthy and generous real estate and insurance dealer, Joe lived lavishly. In 1910, at the age of 29, he eloped again. The bride this time was a widow, Mary Freemantle, who was reported by the *Chicago Tribune* to be "nearly 20 years the senior of her husband." (Actually, the age difference was probably less than ten years.) She had a 19-year-old daughter and a one-year-old grandson. The Brucks family opposed the marriage. One week after the wedding, Joe died. The Brucks family was suspicious. Did Mary somehow cause her new husband's death for financial gain? No, Mary was innocent. The autopsy disclosed that the cause of Joe's death was pneumonia.

Western Starr, a Liberal Voice

What were James and Cynthia Starr thinking when they chose their firstborn child's given name? Did they foresee that their son, born in the "western" state of Iowa in 1854, would achieve fame in the "West"? Is that why they named him "Western Starr"?

Even if that's not the explanation, Western Starr did become a shining light while living in the Chicago area from 1889 to 1909, the last ten years at 1104 Forest Avenue, Wilmette. I was drawn to his story by a newspaper article concerning his opposition to Andrew Carnegie's offer to donate $10,000 for a public library in Wilmette. He spoke at a town hall meeting on April 3, 1903:

"I come here to plead with you for the honesty of your homes, the protection of your hearthstones—or whatever environment there is of your heating apparatus. No, I do not come to plead—I come to command! You must not accept this library from this man!" The question, he said, is simple: "Shall we take this blood money?" He emphatically answered, "No, I say, a thousand times, no, and more if necessary. Take this money, squeezed from the humble laborer in the field, the orphans, the slaves of toil, and even the widow's cruet! Never! Take this result of his grand larceny, and lay ourselves open to the charge of receiving stolen property? No, let me never have to say, in those moments of darkest despair, when I meet some friend on the trolley car, and he asks me about it, that such a thing is true; that Andrew Carnegie is guilty and Wilmette is particeps criminis" (partner in crime).

His plea was outvoted 242–2 by the residents gathered at the meeting. Wilmette accepted Carnegie's money and built the library. This wasn't the only defeat that Western Starr would suffer in a life devoted to liberal causes.

In 1882 he received a law degree from Columbia University where he was a friend and classmate of Theodore Roosevelt. He practiced law briefly in Chicago and then in North Dakota before returning to Chicago in 1889. As a lawyer, he represented ordinary folks like property owners challenging special assessments on their land and public employees fired from government jobs. As a political crusader, he promoted reforms that favored ordinary folks over the privileged few. He opposed the consolidation of utility companies and urged public ownership. He pushed for civil service systems with hiring and firing decisions based on merit, not connections. He opposed the expansion of Chicago to encompass all of Cook County. He favored municipal home rule and free trade. He joined the popular "Single Tax" movement that sought to finance all government operations through a tax on land. He railed against imperialists, corrupt politicians, and moguls like Andrew Carnegie and William Randolph Hearst.

He aligned himself with the Democratic Party and ran for the Illinois State Senate in 1902 and for Congress is 1908. He lost in heavily Republican districts but became quite popular as a lecturer—"a most interesting speaker, one of the best"—"not an orator" but "a forceful speaker nevertheless" who "pleased his audience."

Suddenly, in 1909, he stopped practicing law, pulled up stakes, moved to Maryland, took up farming, and became active in the Farmer-Labor Party. By 1919, he moved to Washington, D.C. and was associated with *The Searchlight*, a journal that claimed to report "the truth" about the U.S. government. His advocacy for social justice over the years led an agent of the Bureau of Investigation (now the FBI) to label him a "radical" in 1928. His light was dimmed by blindness in the 1930s and extinguished by his death in 1940.

Beatrice Engstedt, a Runaway

Fourteen-year-old Beatrice Engstedt made headlines in November 1905 when she mysteriously disappeared on her way to New Trier High School. When found the next day, she told a strange story. First I'll summarize the incident as reported at the time, and then I'll provide some important context that might cause you to see the incident somewhat differently.

Beatrice left her home at 1234 Wilmette Avenue on the morning of November 9, 1905, supposedly walking to school. The route took her through a lengthy stretch of woods. She failed to return home at the end of the day, and her "parents" (as mislabeled in numerous newspapers) notified police. Search parties, carrying lanterns, couldn't find her, but they did find footprints and a homework assignment thought to be hers. The fruitless search continued the next day. The "mother" was reportedly prostrated by her "daughter's" disappearance.

It turned out that Beatrice wasn't on her way to school at all. Instead, she sold her algebra book at a local book store, used the proceeds to travel to Chicago, and responded to an ad for a maid at the Chicago home of Joseph and Mary Cleverdon, 421 Pine Avenue. She was hired on the spot, but her employment came to a swift end the next day when Mary read a newspaper report about Beatrice's disappearance and notified Nilson Engstedt (now labeled as Beatrice's "uncle") in Wilmette. He came to the Cleverdon home to retrieve her. Between sobs, she explained, "Oh, uncle, I thought I was in the way there. I don't think auntie wants me to stay with you." She added that "auntie" had been "cross" with her. "I thought she was jealous because I stayed there and I could stand it no longer. I wanted to make my own way" and pursue my goal of becoming a teacher in the Chicago public schools.

Here's the rest of the story. Beatrice's parents, Henry and Augusta, were born in Sweden, 16 years apart: he in 1857 and she in 1873. After coming to the U.S. separately, they married in 1891 and lived most of the rest of their lives in Omaha, Nebraska. Beatrice was their only child, born soon after their marriage. Henry wasn't a good provider. He worked in unskilled jobs: porter, assistant county jailer, janitor, security guard. In 1898, when Beatrice was seven years old, Augusta was granted a divorce on grounds of cruelty and failure to support.

As her marriage was collapsing, Augusta entered the Creighton Medical College in Omaha. In 1899 she was one of the first women to graduate from that institution. She was licensed as a physician in Colorado and Nebraska and was probably an excellent role model for Beatrice.

But misfortune would test Beatrice's mettle. Henry died in 1900 at the age of 43. Three years later, Augusta died of complications following cancer surgery at the age of 29. Beatrice was placed in the care of Henry's brother, Nilson Engstedt, a plumber. Although he had once lived in Omaha, he had moved to Wilmette at the time of Beatrice's birth, and she barely knew him.

Nilson was a popular Wilmette bachelor. His time in Wilmette was interrupted by service in the Spanish–American War—Company G, First Illinois Infantry. The arrival of Beatrice in Wilmette in the early 1900s was followed quickly by Nilson's marriage to Vivian Griggs (a Chicago school teacher), the birth of their first child, and Beatrice's running away.

Nilson's family moved to California in 1909, leaving 18-year-old Beatrice behind in Chicago. I don't know how she did it, but she achieved her childhood dream of having a decades-long teaching career in the Chicago public schools. She married John Magnan in 1917, and they had one child, John Jr.

Frank Alles, in Absentia

Frank Alles was Wilmette's missing man. He was born in New Trier Township in 1846, long before any North Shore village was founded. He worked on his father's farm until shortly after his 17th birthday when he enlisted in the Union Army midway through the Civil War. After the war, he returned home and, a few years later, married Catherine Schaefer, a young woman who lived on a neighboring farm. Like him, she was a second-generation German-American. They eventually established their home at 1614 Wilmette Avenue. Over the next 15 years, they had six children. Frank worked at a lumber yard and at a gas manufacturing plant.

One morning in 1889, Frank left home with his lunch bucket and headed for work. He never arrived. He didn't come home that night, or the next, or the next. Days turned into weeks, weeks into months, and months into years.

There were no letters, telegrams or messages. Police investigated and found nothing. Catherine held steadfastly to the hope that he'd return, long after others had given up. Finally, in 1896, seven years after his disappearance, she accepted what seemed obvious and what the law presumed: Frank was the victim of foul play and was dead. She applied for a widow's pension based on his Civil War service, and she began to receive a small monthly stipend. She took in laundry and hired out by day to help support the six children ranging in age from infancy to twelve years old when Frank disappeared.

Frank Alles was a missing person from 1889 to 1909. Photo from Wilmette Public Library article "Civil War Veterans of Wilmette".

The years continued to pass. After 20 years, the six children had grown to adulthood. Catherine, a youthful woman of 37 when Frank disappeared, was 57, an "older woman" according to the standards of the day. The oldest son, John, a lad of seven when he last saw his father, was a man of 27. Frank himself would have been an "elderly" 63.

It's not clear what caused John Alles, the son, to travel to Whittier, California in March of 1909. One explanation is that he read a newspaper account about a man named Frank Alles working on an orange grove near Whittier, and because the name is highly unusual, he was intrigued. Another explanation is that this same newspaper account was brought to Catherine's attention, and she encouraged John to go to California and check it out. A third explanation is that the government raised a red flag when someone in California claiming to be Frank applied for a disability pension based on Frank's Civil War service.

No matter. John went to Whittier. Once there, he quickly located Frank working in an orange grove. He didn't recognized Frank, but Frank recognized him. Frank readily agreed to return to Wilmette. Catherine was undoubtedly made aware that he was on his way. When he arrived, she stood in the open doorway of the home he had abandoned 20 years earlier and said simply, "Come in, Frank. Dinner is ready." He replied, "I'm awful hungry."

Frank's explanation? "I got discouraged, that's all. I just thought I'd go west and see what I could do. I never succeeded much and so I didn't write. I felt it would be unmanly and cowardly for me to return without having anything to show for my absence. I was pretty glad to see John, though, I tell you."

Catherine died six years later, but Frank worked for a few years as a gardener and continued to live at the family's Wilmette Avenue home until his death in 1940 at age 93. He was Wilmette's last surviving veteran of the Civil War.

Betram Udell, a Colorful Conservative

One of Wilmette's colorful characters was Bertram B. Udell (1877–1956). He owned the Wilmette printing firm that preceded today's Mid-Central Printing, and he published *Wilmette Announcements,* a free weekly newspaper.

"B.B.," as he was called, was the son of a downstate printer and newspaper publisher. As a young man, he came to the North Shore and operated a commercial print shop at various sites, eventually at his home at 302 Park Avenue. He started publishing his newspaper in 1913 and continued until 1933. Only a few copies still exist, archived at the Wilmette Historical Museum. They contain mostly advertising, supplemented by a few local news items and an occasional opinion piece.

B.B. was politically conservative. In 1913 he campaigned against a new rule adopted by the Wilmette School Board requiring back-to-school physical exams to prevent the spread of disease. He called rules of this kind "paternalism contrary to fundamental principles of American government."

In the village election of 1923, he sided with Malcomb McKerchar, the candidate opposing popular incumbent President Edward Zipf. McKerchar was a spending hawk who promised to "retrench" the "unnecessarily expensive" village government. The day before the vote (won by Zipf), an anonymous pamphlet titled "The Ventilator" appeared around town. No copies are known to exist today, but *The Lake Shore News* said it contained a "scandalous" attack on Zipf. "Never before in Wilmette or on the North Shore has such filthy stuff been foisted on the public."

B.B., alleged to be the pamphlet's publisher, was indicted for violating an Illinois law prohibiting the anonymous publication of written material about a candidate. He provoked the wrath of local judges when he claimed they were all "prejudiced" and unfair. The case languished for months and then quietly disappeared. (Years later the Illinois Supreme Court declared the law unconstitutional.)

B.B. was renowned for feuding with local police departments. In the early 1900s, as automobile usage grew dramatically, "joy riders" were widely perceived as operating their "machines" recklessly. State and local officials responded by adopting new driving laws and equipping police with motorcycles to enforce them strictly. B.B., who probably opposed the laws on principle, accused the police of "grafting and fixing" and "persecuting motorists with unjustifiable arrests."

In Wilmette, the village board investigated these charges and found them "unsubstantiated," but this didn't stop B.B. He editorialized that police chiefs in Wilmette, Kenilworth and Winnetka had illegally adopted a 30 mph speed limit on Sheridan Road. It was illegal, he asserted, because state law prohibited local regulation of speed on state roadways like Sheridan Road.

B.B. had more than a journalistic interest in traffic enforcement. He and his sons had regular contact with the motorcycle police. In 1925 alone, the Udell family accounted for four arrests in Wilmette and Kenilworth. In 1928 B.B was stopped in Evanston for driving without a license. When told to go to the police station, he shouted, "Like hell I will!" He sped away and sought refuge in a shop from which he was dragged and jailed. In 1930 son Rutherford was seriously injured when his motorcycle crashed into a car. A news report mentioned 16 previous arrests for traffic offenses.

In 1932 *Wilmette Announcements* carried a series of controversial columns authored by Elizabeth Dilling, a former Wilmette resident who was about to become nationally prominent as an anti-communist crusader. Later that year, B.B. editorialized favorably on the creation of the Wilmette chapter of a new national organization called The Paul Reveres. Its purpose was to expose radicals

Bertram Udell's wacky personality may run in the family. He's the creepy-looking fellow on the far right, while his mother, sister, and three brothers also strike strange poses in this funny family photo, cir. 1920. Courtesy of the Udell family.

trying to subvert the government of the United States, especially communists and their sympathizers.

How did B.B.'s opinions and antics sit with residents? My only clue is that advertisers supported his newspaper for many years.

Edwin Dempsey, an Unrecognized War Hero

Victorious generals like General John Pershing, commander of the American Expeditionary Forces during World War I, become America's military heroes. He transformed America's unprepared armed forces into a skilled and disciplined fighting force over a period of 18 months. Other persons also contribute significantly to victories without recognition, like Edwin Dempsey of Wilmette, inventor of a coding system that revolutionized the transport of U.S. military personnel across the nation's railroads during World War I.

Edwin Dempsey and Mary Driscoll were second-generation Irish-Americans raised in large Catholic families in Chicago. They were married in 1907, came to Wilmette in about 1912, and raised their five children in the village. They lived first at 903 Elmwood Avenue and later at 607 Laurel Avenue. Edwin was a railroad man who started his career with the C&NW.

At the turn of the 20th century, U.S. railroads used telegrams to communicate and control the movement of trains carrying passengers and commerce. However, the high volume of lengthy telegraphic messages burdened the wires and imposed high costs in tolls paid by the railroads to the telegraph companies. In 1902, while working for C&NW, Edwin invented and patented a system of codes that enabled the railroad to transmit a large amount of information in short messages, thus reducing the burden and cost. He became a recognized cipher expert, and in the early decades of the 1900s, he worked successfully to extend his system to other railroads throughout the country.

During the 1916 Mexican Revolution and Pancho Villa's invasion of Columbus, New Mexico, the railroads had difficulty moving large numbers of U.S. troops to the border efficiently. Recognizing this deficiency, the U.S. Railroad Administration, headed by George Hodges, asked Edwin to devise a new system for the specific purpose of managing troop movements. Hodges said that Edwin was "conspicuously the most able man in this line in the nation."

The new system was described by Edwin as follows, "Of course I can't tell you the code, but this is an example. A train dispatcher might get a message, 'Take care of beans.' To him that would mean this: 'Companies C, F, and E of 122nd field artillery, bound from Camp Grant to Camp Logan; 48 officers, 221 men, due on my line at a certain time and to be delivered to the other line at a certain junction at a certain time.'" The codes were published in a small leather-bound volume and given to the appropriate officials of the nation's railroads. Edwin boasted that German spies were "never able to learn it, and the train dispatchers and those familiar with it really found it a new language. It is so simple that those familiar with it never need waste time decoding."

During World War I, millions of soldiers were moved long distances throughout the country, safely and efficiently, thanks to Edwin's codes. One source reported that "the total troop movement of the railroads from May 1917 to November 10, 1918 was 8,714,582," and between November 11, 1918 (the date of the armistice) and April 30, 1919, "a total of 3,389,665 soldiers were transported" as the troops returned home.

Edwin was pleased to contribute to the war effort by "loaning" the new system to the government, but he was annoyed that the government continued to use it after the armistice without a "by-your-leave." He felt that he should be compensated for half of the savings his system produced post-war, which he estimated to be "several millions." In September 1919 he traveled to Washington, D.C. to present his claim. He was accompanied by his attorney, Irving Herriott, who had previously worked as an attorney for C&NW. The outcome of that trip was not reported.

Edward Evers, *USS Wilmette* Commander

The *USS Wilmette* was a gunboat of the U.S. Navy from 1917 to 1945. The *Wilmette* never saw combat but served as a training ship on the Great Lakes for almost 30 years. Was she named *Wilmette* to honor our village? If so, why was our village honored in this way? The answer to the first question is yes, the *Wilmette* was named to honor the village. The answer to the second question is more complicated. It begins with Edward Evers, born in New York in 1878.

Evers was a young seaman on the *USS Indiana* during the Spanish-American War. The *Indiana* took part in the bombardment of San Juan, the blockade of Havana, and the destruction of Spanish ships at the Battle of Santiago. Following the war, Evers came to Chicago where his parents and siblings then lived. He worked as a clerk and then as a machinery salesman. In 1905 he married a Wilmette woman, Florence King, and the couple became longtime residents at 1020 Sheridan Road, the home of Florence's parents.

At about this time, Evers joined the Illinois Naval Militia with his father-in-law, Charles King. This organization was created in 1893 in response to the perceived lack of readiness of the U.S. Navy. While the federal government upgraded the fleet during the 1890s, it declined to create a naval reserve. This led several states, including Illinois, to create their own naval militias. Congress provided nominal funding for these reserve organizations.

By 1910 Evers advanced to the rank of captain and became commander of the militia, a job he held until his retirement as a rear admiral in 1942. His major problem as commander during the early years was the lack of a training ship. In 1915 he learned that a ship was available—a passenger steamer that had sunk earlier that year. It had been salvaged and was about to be auctioned to pay salvage costs.

Evers seized the opportunity. He assembled a dozen wealthy men, the pillars of Chicago business and society, who supported the Illinois Naval Militia's mission. The group put up the money needed to purchase the vessel, in anticipation of an appropriation by Congress to repay the group. The ship was purchased in late 1915 for $46,000. Evers laid plans to make it safe and suitable for its new use, but work was delayed because Congress failed to appropriate the funds needed to repay the group and modify the ship. Finally, six months into World War I, Congress approved the funds.

At this point, Evers wrote Navy officials, requesting that the ship be formally named *Wilmette* after the village where "a number of gentlemen interested in the financing of the original purchase of the *Wilmette* reside." (Evers didn't identify the members of the group.) The Navy promptly granted this request.

The *Wilmette* was formerly the *Eastland*. Courtesy of the Wilmette Historical Museum.

Evers seems to have exaggerated the involvement of Wilmette residents. So far as I can determine, the only Wilmette resident in the group, besides Evers himself, was Frank Baker, a wealthy executive in the business empire of Samuel Insull and owner of the Frank Lloyd Wright-designed house at 507 Lake Avenue.

Incidentally, before Evers purchased and renamed the *Wilmette*, it was the *Eastland,* the cruise ship that capsized in the Chicago River at Dearborn Street on July 24, 1915 as it was about to depart on a Lake Michigan excursion for Western Electric Co. employees. More than 800 lives were lost.

Jesse Grant, the President's Nephew

Jesse Grant, a nephew of Ulysses S. Grant, lived in obscurity at 1327 Washington Avenue from the mid-1910s until his death in 1939, but let's begin this story in the 1850s in Galena, Illinois. That's where Ulysses Grant's two younger brothers, Samuel and Orvil, operated a wholesale leather store owned by their father, an Ohio tanner. Ulysses joined them at the store in 1860 after resigning from the Army in 1856 and failing in his own business ventures. He lived in Galena only one year before reentering the Army at the outbreak of the Civil War.

Samuel died soon after the war began, but Orvil remained in Galena throughout. He and his wife Mary had four children, including Jesse, born in 1866. Meanwhile, Galena declined as a commercial center. In 1866 the Grants' leather business was sold. Orvil moved his family to Chicago, where he opened a "leather and saddlery hardware," while Ulysses became U.S. President.

Orvil's new business was abruptly ended by the Great Chicago Fire. Destitute, he moved his family again, this time to Elizabeth, New Jersey, home of his sister Virginia. Soon, Orvil scandalized his brother's presidency. In 1874 Congress appropriated money to survey the public lands in the Territory of Oklahoma. Orvil and two others persuaded the territory's surveyor-general to employ surveyors who would kickback a portion of their fee to the trio. In another scheme, Orville and Ulysses's secretary of war took kickbacks from the sale of franchises for western trading posts. In 1878 Orvil was committed to the New Jersey State Lunatic Asylum at Morristown. He died there in 1881 at age 46. Son Jesse was only 15 years old.

Like his father and grandfather, Jesse tried his hand at the leather business. He settled in La Crosse, Wisconsin and worked for a leather manufacturer with ties to the Grant family. He met and married Gertrude McDonald. Their only child, Ulysses, was born in 1892. Jesse quit the leather business and, for the balance of his working life, was a railroad accountant: first for the Chicago, Burlington & Quincy, and later for C&NW. This work brought him to Chicago and eventually to Wilmette.

The last few years of Jesse's life were sad. He retired in 1928. Gertrude died in 1929. Son Ulysses was injured and lost his bank teller job in 1931. Jesse and Ulysses lived frugally on a $9,000 legacy, but they ran out of money, and Jesse was too proud to ask for help. In 1937 their neighbors complained about their 14 cats. Jesse was charged with keeping a nuisance, found guilty, and fined $5. "These cats are just like children to me," he said. "If I have to give them up, I don't know what I'll do."

On February 5, 1939 Jesse was found unconscious on the basement floor of his unheated house, suffering from starvation and exposure. Four hungry cats wandered about the house, which was barren of food and furniture. Jesse was rushed to Cook County Hospital where he died as a charity patient. New Trier Township paid for his cremation. Only his son Ulysses and four others attended his funeral.

Daddy Hood

Greetings! My name is John Andrew Hood, but folks in Wilmette called me "Daddy Hood." I moved here in 1919 after my wife Amanda died, and I lived with my daughter, Lenoir Miller, at 106 6th Street for 20 years. Lenoir called me Daddy, and folks picked up on that. Everyone in town knew Daddy Hood when I died in 1939 at the age of 96.

I'm here to talk about my favorite holiday, Decoration Day. You call it Memorial Day. Before I begin, though, let me tell you about myself. I was born in 1842 on a plantation in North Carolina, one of 13 kids. Mother had a personal slave who helped bring us up. We called her Aunt Fanny. Her son was my best friend. When I was ten, my parents sold their property, including Aunt Fanny, and moved to Greencastle, Indiana for schooling. Mother was paid $1,100 in gold for Aunt Fanny, but she felt guilty and hid it away.

Eight years later, when the Civil War broke out, I joined the 51st Indiana Volunteers. I remember Shiloh, Chickamauga, Stone River, Lookout Mountain, and Sherman's march through Georgia. In 1863 I was captured and sent to Libby Prison in Richmond. It was a horrible place, but some of us were able to escape. Everything about the war was hell. I went in weighing 180 pounds and came out four years later weighing 98. But at least I came out alive. I loved what the North was fighting for, and I loved our president. I was grief stricken when he was assassinated. I became a loyal Republican.

After the war, I returned to Greencastle. With my saved-up military pay, I bought a fine horse and buggy to help me court my beautiful Amanda. It worked! After our marriage, I sold the horse and buggy and bought 80 acres of farmland near Glidden, Iowa. That's where we raised our family. We had nine kids, but the first five died young from diphtheria and scarlet fever. I made little wooden coffins and buried them right there on the farm.

In 1866, veterans of the war formed an organization called the Grand Army of the Republic. I was proud to join. In 1868 General John Logan, our commander, asked us to decorate the graves of our fallen comrades and conduct fitting services and testimonials of respect. This was the beginning of Decoration Day, as we called Memorial Day during my time.

To me, Decoration Day was the most important day of the year. I looked forward to it even more than my birthday. During my senior-citizen years, we celebrated Decoration Day by serving up ice cream to just about every Wilmette resident from the garbage man to the village president. In cities and towns across the country, GAR members led marches to cemeteries. Wearing my GAR uniform, I was among the marchers every year from 1868 until I died in 1939, whether I was living in Glidden or Wilmette.

Decoration Day started to change about the time I moved to Wilmette in 1919. The GAR died off, and a new organization, the American Legion, was created for veterans of World War I. Legion Post 46 took charge of the Memorial Day observance in Wilmette. At daybreak, wreaths were placed at the graves of fallen comrades in Memorial Park Cemetery just south of Wilmette on Gross Point Road. Later in the morning, a march through town was followed by a solemn service.

Here's the point I wish to make: The Memorial Day parade isn't supposed to be fun like a Santa or circus parade. It isn't supposed to be joyful and celebratory like a July 4 parade. Rather, it's a dignified, patriotic march of mourners to a monument where the ultimate sacrifices of more than 1.2 million American heroes are remembered, honored, and grieved. Thank you for listening.

John Andrew Hood was a patriotic Civil War veteran.
Courtesy of the Wilmette Historical Museum.

Mayor Richard J. Daley met Burton Kolman following his return from a trip to Israel. Daley was impressed by Kolman's ability to make the arduous journey alone. The following year, Kolman was appointed to the bench, undoubtedly with the mayor's support. Courtesy of the Kolman family.

Burton Kolman, Blind Man with a Vision

If you've driven along Glenview Road between Hunter Road and Edens Expressway during springtime, you've noticed the beautiful flowering trees that line the roadway on both sides. These honey locusts and crabapples are a labor of love.

Burton Kolman was 16 when he was struck in the head by a baseball. The blow caused him to lose his sight. His tough-love father told him, "You have a choice. You can get a tin cup and lead an unproductive life, or you can get on with the business of living in a harder but more rewarding way." Burton accepted the challenge. He continued his education. Unable to read, he learned by listening. He learned well. In 1954, he was graduated from De Paul University College of Law as valedictorian. There he met his future wife, Anita Harari, a foreign student from Israel.

Law firms weren't interested in blind lawyers, so Burton started his career as a law clerk. He later opened a successful law practice with his brother. He also participated in civic and professional activities. Meanwhile, in 1956, he and Anita moved to 527 Romona Road. They had three children: Bruce, Joe, and Carmella. Burton was a striking figure. Tall and handsome, he wore dark glasses and got around with the aid of a guide dog. He had a friendly, outgoing personality and was well liked and respected.

In 1966, at age 33, he was appointed magistrate judge of the Cook County Circuit Court. So far as anyone knows, he was the court's first blind judge. One year later, tragedy struck. Burton suffered a fatal heart attack while conducting a hearing in Arlington Heights.

Anita's grief was bottomless, but in her despair, she had an idea. She recalled driving along Glenview Road with Burton as passenger. As was her practice, she described what she saw. There were no homes fronting on the roadway; there were no trees; and no one maintained the right-of-way. Glenview Road was an unsightly, barren route through west Wilmette. Burton commented that the scene she described was sad. If only someone could do something about it, he said.

This memory sparked Anita's idea. She would create a living memorial. She would plant flowering trees and shrubs along the roadway, alternating the varieties to create a great burst of color in the spring. She maneuvered through the bureaucracy to get permission for the project.

With her personal funds, she purchased seedlings. She placed colored stakes (a different color for each variety) along the roadway where the seedlings were to be planted. They were all delivered at the same time. On Sunday, April 13, 1969, hundreds of family members and friends showed up with shovels and planted more than 1,000 trees and shrubs.

For the next two weeks there was no rain. Anxiety set in. Then, "the biggest thunderstorm you've ever seen," according to one observer, rained life-saving water. Even though some neighbors helped by watering the seedlings, Anita recognized their vulnerability. She convinced Cream Crest Dairy to donate an old milk truck so she and her helpers could water the trees on a regular basis. With a garden hose, it took a day and a half to fill the tank.

For several years, the Kolman family nurtured the trees and shrubs: watering them, placing mulch around them, replacing those that died, and mowing weeds along the right-of-way. From her personal funds, Anita paid kids to help. Finally, the village took over.

Anita moved from the village in 1979. In 1986, a plaque was placed at the east end of Glenview Road, commemorating the Judge Burton Kolman Tree Memorial.

_____

Vinton Bacon, Sanitary District Reformer

On August 22, 1966, Vinton Bacon left his Chicago office at 6:45 PM after a long day of work. He drove his employer-supplied 1966 powder-blue Ford, heading for his Wilmette home at 2206 Kenilworth Avenue. His wife Margaret was awaiting his arrival. He entered the village at 7:45 PM and noticed that his gas indicator was nearing empty. He stopped at Dale and Jack's service station at Lake Avenue and Green Bay Road to fill up.

At that time, full-service was the norm. Willie Maxwell, an Evanston resident, was one of three attendants who approached Vinton's car. While the other two filled the tank and washed the windows, Willie raised the hood to check the water and oil levels. Resting on the engine block were four sticks of dynamite. A hot wire, attached to the dynamite, had come loose from a spark plug.

Startled, Willie informed Vinton, "Sir, someone must be playing a joke on you. There's dynamite in your engine." Vinton calmly responded, "Oh? Well, take it out." No fool, Willie countered, "If you want it taken out, take it out yourself." Vinton paid for the gas with his credit card, walked across Lake Avenue to the Wilmette Police Station (located on Green Bay Road at the time), and reported the incident. Police and fire personnel rushed to the scene and cordoned off the area, awaiting bomb specialists from Chicago. The dynamite was removed, and no damage or injury was suffered. Undaunted, Vinton returned to work the next day, expressing contempt for the villains, whoever they were.

Why was a bomb planted in Vinton's car? The crime was never solved, so the motive remains unknown. However, the attempt on his life was undoubtedly related to his position as superintendent of the Metropolitan Sanitary District (now the Metropolitan Water Reclamation District). The district is the public agency responsible for safeguarding the Chicago area's drinking water.

In 1962 Vinton was the choice of a blue ribbon group to be the district's new superintendent, after the *Chicago Tribune* exposed massive corruption at the agency. A civil engineer, he built a reputation as an honest and effective administrator in the 1950s while working to clean up the polluted rivers of Tacoma, Washington.

With great intensity, Vinton began to reform the district, where jobs and contracts were traded for favors and kickbacks. He wielded power expansively to investigate and change the district's practices and policies and hold wrongdoers accountable. He stepped on the toes of the district's elected board members and entrenched staff. Tact wasn't his hallmark. He was a crusader, not a compromiser. He was also a strong proponent of the huge pollution-control project that became known as the Deep Tunnel.

Following the 1966 incident, Vinton continued to serve as superintendent until 1970, when he was summarily fired. Among those voting to oust him were trustees Valentine Janicki and Chester Majewski, both indicted in 1976 for taking bribes to award a sludge hauling contract to a Louisiana-based firm. Janicki was found guilty; Majewski was acquitted. An Illinois Senate subcommittee found that Vinton was illegally fired without good cause at an improperly convened meeting.

Vinton continued his public service at the University of Wisconsin, Milwaukee, as a professor of civil engineering. He died in Washington state in 1998.

Vinton Bacon was *Engineering News Record*'s Man of the Year, 1967. Reprinted courtesy of BNP Media, © 1967.

The Rev. Joseph Lauermann, Disrespected

My name is Joseph Lauermann and I'm a longtime Wilmette resident. For the last 82 years, I've been resting in peace in Lot 2, Block 2 of St. Joseph Cemetery, beneath a granite marker that says simply, "Rev. Joseph B. Lauermann, Soldier Priest."

I normally keep to myself, but I was aroused in 2007 when the Wilmette Park District named its newest park "Mallinckrodt Park" without giving serious consideration to another deserving option. Please let me expound.

My great-grandfather and my grandfather, both named Johann Lauermann, came to this area about 1840 from Trier, Germany. This was before New Trier Township and the villages of Gross Point and Wilmette were even figments of anyone's imagination. These Lauermann pioneers owned land in the vicinity of present-day Ridge Road and Forest Avenue. When New Trier Township was established in 1850, my great-grandfather was elected collector. He operated a tavern and store on the west side of Ridge Road opposite Forest Avenue and adjacent to the Mallinckrodt property. I can sense the site from here.

In 1857, my grandfather Lauermann drowned in a Chicago quarry. At the time, my father Joseph was just a child. Dad was a diligent young man. He worked as a clerk at grocery stores in Evanston and Chicago for a number of years, learning the business, before taking over the family's establishments on Ridge Road in 1872, after the Great Chicago Fire. For many years, you could find whatever you needed at dad's grocery and general store, including the latest gossip.

Dad married a Gross Point woman, Margaret Vollmann. They had eight children. They were devoted members of St. Joseph's Church. Besides operating the store and tavern, dad farmed his land, was a director of a fire insurance company, and dealt in real estate. He was also a public spirited citizen, holding several public offices, including Gross Point village trustee.

As for me, I began my life in 1884 at my parents' home at 832 Ridge Road. I attended St. Joseph's School, followed by St. Francis Seminary near Milwaukee and St. Paul Seminary in Minnesota. I was ordained in 1908 and was assistant pastor at St. Benedict's and St. Philomena, both in Chicago.

In 1918 I entered the Army. After finishing chaplain school, I received my commission as lieutenant and was shipped overseas with the 146th Infantry Regiment. I was with the 146th for the Ypres-Lys offensive. Later, I counseled our troops at St. Dizier, France and Coblenz, Germany.

After the war, I became pastor at St. Joseph's in Waukegan (a German national parish). Then I went on to St. William's, a new and rapidly growing Chicago parish. I inherited the task of raising money to pay for the parish's newly constructed buildings. I remained at St. William's until my final illness forced me into Sacred Heart Sanitarium in Milwaukee. My funeral mass at St. William's, in July 1930, was celebrated with full military honors. Afterwards, I was brought here, to rest near my parents and grandparents.

What name did I silently hope the Park District would pick for the new park in 2007? "Lauermann Park," of course. This name would have honored not just my family, but also the scores of German-American families who carved a community out of the Gross Point wilderness in the 19th century. Their contribution hasn't been honored by much "public naming," and in fact many of the original German-sounding names of Gross Point streets have been changed to Anglo names. The Gross Point community hasn't received the respect that it deserves. Shame on Wilmette!

It's said that good men (and women) may die, but their names live on forever. Maybe so, but attaching a name to a park assures its survival. I believe that Pauline von Mallinckrodt, founder of the Sisters of Christian Charity, who rests peacefully on another continent without ever visiting Wilmette, might acknowledge the merits of the Lauermann family's claim.

Arthur Howard, Honoree

Greetings from my grave at Memorial Park, Skokie! I'm Arthur Howard, the man honored by Wilmette in the naming of Howard School and later Howard Park. I'm here to assuage the feelings of Rev. Joseph Lauermann. I understand that he's sorely disappointed that Wilmette Park District failed to consider "Lauermann Park" as a worthy option when naming its newest park "Mallinckrodt Park." My message is simple: It's an honor to have a park, school, or other public facility named for you, but there's no disrespect when, despite being a deserving soul, you're overlooked.

Take my case. I was born and raised in Hyde Park, Massachusetts in 1876. I graduated from Harvard College, and I served briefly and without any particular distinction in the Spanish-American War. I married my beloved Emeline in 1899.

We moved to New York, where I worked as a book editor and salesman. In 1900 I joined American Sheet Steel Co. I served this industry in executive capacities until my death. After stints in New York, Pittsburgh, and St. Louis, I was transferred to Chicago in 1909. We rented on Lake Avenue until 1913 when we purchased the house at 1055 Wilmette Avenue. There I lived the remaining eleven years of my life. Emeline and I had three children.

Folks might think it strange that a man who lived in Wilmette only 15 years would have a major public facility named in his honor. I modestly acknowledge that I served the community well. During World War I, I held the rank of captain and was commander of Company D, 1st Regiment, Illinois Militia Reserve, a Wilmette-centered outfit. In those days, military command placed a man in a most favorable light. Through our unit's training and educational outreach, I became well known.

In 1922, I was elected president of the Wilmette District 39 School Board. During the next two years, I led the planning and approval process and monitored the construction of the new Ridge School on 17th street. I devoted much time and energy to this project. In recognition of my effectiveness, I was re-elected in 1924 without opposition.

Now, Father Lauermann, here's my point: There are many folks who have given valuable service or contributed greatly to our community. Only a combination of unusual circumstances caused my name, and not theirs, to be honored by a public naming.

First, I died suddenly (heart failure) at the youngish age of 48 while still in public office. Second, I was a leader in establishing a brand new school crying out for a more distinctive name than Ridge School. Third, the school district's superintendent pushed the idea of renaming the school in my honor. This was accomplished only four days after my death when folks were grieving and opposition would have been unseemly.

Fourth, if you want something named in your honor, educational service is the best path. McKenzie School was originally named for John Logan, a Civil War general and Illinois congressman and senator, but the name was changed in 1978 to honor Louise McKenzie, the school's principal from 1950 to 1978. Harper School is named for J. Robb Harper, superintendent of schools from 1908 to 1942. The former Bell School (now the Community Recreation Center) was named for Millard Bell, superintendent from 1942 to 1964. Mikaelian Education Center was named for Sam Mikaelian, superintendent from 1992 to 1998. Marie Murphy School honors her service as teacher and superintendent from 1932 to 1968. Baker School honors Clara Belle Baker, the school's founder and director from 1918 to 1952.

While I don't subscribe to Thomas Paine's opinion that "one good schoolmaster is of more use than a hundred priests," schoolmasters (and park officials) do have the inside track on public naming. That's just the way it is.

Meanwhile, if you think in retrospect that an unworthy name has been attached to a public facility, change it! There should be no such thing as perpetual immunity from analysis, evaluation, comparison, and justification of names honored by folks of the past.

CHAPTER 18

★————————★

House Talk

Hello! I'm the House Keeper, spokesman for HOW (Houses of Wilmette), an association whose members consist of Wilmette houses. You know nothing about HOW because our members are *private* residences. We don't share our *private* business with anyone. No way, no HOW! HOWever, we're making an exception because of your upcoming Sesquicentennial. Several of our members have been authorized to tell their life stories. We hope this is a valuable learning experience for you. By the way, we call you humans "visitors" because that's really what you are. You come, you stay, and you go. HOW members are much more permanent, although we do have a mortality rate of about 0.5 percent annually.

Before I introduce our talking houses, let me tell you about HOW. Our membership consists of almost 8,000 single-family homes. On average, each member provides housing to slightly fewer than three visitors. (I'm not saying that any specific house has a partial visitor). Each member contributes, on average, about $15,000 in property taxes to your local governmental units. We're very proud of our members. By and large, you visitors take good care of us. That's the way it should be. When you take good care, you enjoy us more, and your investment grows.

HOW members range from the modest to the over-the-top. Some are old-timers, others are in their infancy. Some are thought to be beautiful, while others are regarded as ordinary—which is an insult because every house, like every visitor, can be magnificent with loving care. We're a diverse group. That's a good thing. You visitors would benefit from a little more diversity.

To our visitors we say this: Every house has an interesting story. It just takes a little work to find it. If you want to learn the story of your house, visit the Wilmette Historical Museum. They're happy to help. Meanwhile, we houses are watching you. Maybe someday, perhaps at the village's bicentennial in

2072, more of us will tell our stories. Maybe one of us will talk about you. So mind your Ps and Qs.

I'm also presenting, later in this chapter, two humans who played an interesting role in the lives of several HOW members. For now, here's HOW:

716 Lake Avenue

Good day! I'm the house at 716 Lake Avenue. Folks walk by and say, "Look at that old house! If only those walls could talk!" Well, we old houses *can* talk. I'm going to talk about some highlights of the past.

I'll start with my site. I stand on two lots (with 100 feet of Lake Avenue frontage) that were originally part of the 1,280-acre Ouilmette Reserve granted to Archange Ouilmette in 1829. For the next 70 years, the reserve was forestland, gradually sold off by the Ouilmette family to investors.

My two lots were created when a portion of the reserve was purchased and subdivided by Henry Dingee, a New York investor, and added to Wilmette in 1873. For three more decades, my lots stayed in investors' hands. Finally, in 1904, my lots were purchased by Louis and Sadie Clark. They weren't investors. They wanted a home for their three sons. They built me with abundant space for themselves and the families that would follow—five bedrooms on the second floor and servants' quarters on the third. I was one of the first homes in Wilmette with electric lights.

I forget the name of the architect who conceived me. (Give me a break—I'm almost 120 years old!) I was pretty expensive for a young couple, but Louis worked for Sadie's daddy, Samuel Harris, a wealthy Chicago hardware merchant, so...well, you get the picture.

I suffered a major injury in 1924 while still hosting the Clark family. Faulty wiring in my attic sparked Wilmette's biggest fire in a couple of years. My roof, attic, and upper floors were badly damaged, along with valuable paintings, books and furnishings. The loss amounted to $30,000, the equivalent of $450,000 in 2020. I still bear a scar or two.

I was repaired, but in 1926 Louis and Sadie, getting on in years, moved to Evanston. My new visitors were Harvey and Elinor Craig and their six children. Harvey worked for his father, president of a Detroit meatpacking firm. By age 50, his occupation was what all you Wilmette folks aspire to: managing his own investments.

The Craigs and I suffered a huge sadness together. One of my favorite kids was their son Norman. As a teen, he scratched his initials on a windowpane

That's me: 716 Lake Avenue.

in his bedroom so I'd always remember him. Then came World War II. Norman, a second lieutenant, was co-pilot of a B-24 bomber. On his 26th combat mission, at age 22, he was killed in action near New Guinea. He was awarded, posthumously, the Air Medal for his meritorious achievement.

The next two families to receive my hospitality were the Wileses, Bradford and Elizabeth, from 1947 to 1957 and the Wollaegers, Frank and Janet, from 1957 to 1966. They were nice enough, even though Bradford and Frank were both Chicago lawyers. The Wollaegers left a bad taste in my mouth, though, when they disrespected me by "moving up" to fancier digs in Winnetka.

Then came Philip and Elizabeth Bockley. He was an HR exec at American Hospital Supply. The Bockleys were followed by Daniel and Nancy Mulvihill in 1980. He was an options trader. Finally, Frank and Joanne Weschler arrived in 1997. He's a physician, but more important, Frank and Joanne are loving and caring people.

I owe my longevity to the Weschlers. At a time when the word "teardown" was floating around Wilmette like cottonwood puffs in springtime, the Weschlers blew out my rear end and gave me a lifesaving kitchen and family room revival.

My walls could tell you more, but I'm not talking—not because I can't, mind you, but because the creed of us houses is to respect our visitors' privacy.

704 Lake Avenue

Greetings! I'm the house at 704 Lake Avenue. I feel compelled to participate in this forum, because my neighbor, the house at 716 Lake Avenue, considers itself to be superior to the rest of us HOW members. To put it bluntly, 716 isn't that special! Many houses in Wilmette have great stories. Take me for example.

I stand on two lots with 110 feet of Lake Avenue frontage. My lots were purchased by Edward and Harriet Scheidenhelm in 1903. They built me a few years later. Unlike 716 Lake, I haven't "forgotten" who conceived me. I come from superb stock: the firm of Tallmadge & Watson, famous for prairie-style houses. My Wilmette siblings include the Eastman house at 412 Central and the Andrews house at 411 Lake. I'm a spacious, three-story, brick abode.

My first visitors, the Scheidenhelms, were self-made folks. Edward's father was a blacksmith in Mendota, Illinois. Edward graduated from the University of Illinois in engineering and followed his older brother to Wilmette where in 1899 he married Harriet Joy, a Wilmette native. Edward became a successful construction contractor. One of his projects was building the superstructure of the Chicago Municipal Pier (now Navy Pier), completed in 1916. He left his mark on Wilmette as chairman of the panel that wrote the 1922 "Plan of Wilmette".

Edward was a superstitious fellow. When he moved in, he nailed a penny over my front door for good luck. It worked! The Scheidenhelms were my happy visitors for almost 40 years and raised three children here.

Here I am: 704 Lake Avenue.

After Edward and Harriet moved to Evanston in 1943, I entered a period of uncertainty. The Hodapps (George and Irene and their three kids) became my next visitors. George worked for Standard Cap and Seal Corp., Chicago. In 1945 I was sold to Frank and Adrienne Verbest. Frank was an executive at Keeley Brewing Co., Chicago. The Verbests never moved in, because he was named president of Blatz Brewing Co., the country's ninth largest brewer at the time. Off they went to Milwaukee.

My next three families stayed for only five years each. The first were the Carters (Burton and Irene). Raised in Wilmette, he worked for many years out-of-state as a salesman before returning to his hometown. The second were the Davenports (Haskell and Doris). He was president of John R. Thompson Co., a big food distributor and restaurant operator whose holdings included Henrici's restaurant. The third were the Leonards (Robert and Winifred). He was a Montgomery Ward exec.

In 1962, I laid out my welcome mat for Bud and Therese Hahn and their twelve kids. Bud was raised in Wilmette, and Therese in Kenilworth. Bud worked at Hahn Insurance Agency, founded by his father. For almost 20 years, I suffered the wear-and-tear that twelve kids can inflict.

Following Bud's death, Therese sold me in 1981 to the Pattersons (Russell and Hallee). They appreciated my grandeur and restored many of my finest features, like my wood floors, pocket doors, and stained glass windows. Russell and Hallee worked in her father's business, selling police and fire uniforms.

I nearly entered the rock music world in 1998 when the Pattersons sold me to James Iha, co-founder of the band Smashing Pumpkins. James planned to remodel me and use my basement as a recording studio. Thankfully, this plan never took off. My plaster can't stand vibration! In 2001 I was sold to James and Liz Van Horn. While preserving my historic virtues, they added a hearth room and remodeled my kitchen, bringing me to my current state of perfection.

720 Lake Avenue

Howdy! I'm the big yellow house of 720 Lake Avenue. I'm in the same block as the previous two participants. I'd like to make a point that they've overlooked. When a family lives in a house for a long time, say 20 years or more, the family's name becomes attached to the house, and it remains attached long after the family moves away. "That's the Smith house," neighbors say, even though the Smiths sold to the Joneses years ago.

I'm a special case, because I'm a celebrity house. In 2013, I became the home of the Reitz/Landwehr family (Eric and Elaine). For 18 years before that, I was the home of the Angley/O'Donnell family (John and Mary). And before that, I hosted the O'Brien family (Tom and Kathleen) for 19 years and the Grossman family (Herbert and Patricia) for seven years. You'd think that one of these family names might be attached to me.

Not so! Many folks still call me the Bellairs House. That's because Mal and Jo Bellairs and their seven children were my celebrity visitors for 14 years (1955–1969). If you're younger than 65 (like 80 percent of Wilmette's adult residents), or if you're a newcomer to the Chicago area, you may be wondering, who's Mal Bellairs?

Mal was born in 1919 and raised in Cheyenne, Wyoming. At age nine, he became interested in radio when he and schoolmates visited a Denver radio station. He attended the 1933 Century of Progress Exhibition with his family, fell in love with Chicago, and vowed to return some day. He studied dramatics at Colorado State and the Pasadena Playhouse (California). In 1941 he fulfilled his vow and moved to Chicago where he launched his acting and radio career.

Five years of Army service during World War II interrupted his fledgling career, but upon returning to Chicago, he joined WCFL as an announcer and then tried his hand at TV. In 1955 he moved to radio station WBBM, a CBS affiliate with a powerful clear channel signal that reached a large audience. In those days, radio was big, and for 15 years, Mal was the most popular radio personality in the Chicago area. Throughout this period, he was my visitor.

My visitor, Mal Bellairs, was Chicago's most popular
radio personality in the 1950s and 1960s.

He had a deep and resonating voice, perfect for radio, but his popularity was based on much more: his comfortable, kind, and gentlemanly style; and his ability to fill his broadcasts with material that his audience enjoyed. He was a class act, perfect for his era. In Wilmette he was an immensely popular friend and neighbor.

The Bellairs family left Wilmette when Mal decided to change the course of his career by becoming a station owner. He and Jo purchased and operated an AM station in Crystal Lake (renamed WIVS) and an FM station in Woodstock (WXRD).

Mal and Jo have passed away, but they left their mark on me. For many years, some of Mal's mementos adorned the walls of my entryway. My distinctive yellow siding dates back to Mal's time. My front-yard flagpole was where Mal hoisted messages like "Private Party, Can't Use Pool." This particular message told neighbors, who were generally welcome at my back-yard pool, to stay away.

For more than 110 years, I've hosted about a dozen wonderful families. Their average stay was almost ten years. They included, as already mentioned, Herbert and Patricia Grossman. He was a famous pediatric neurologist and professor at the University of Illinois medical school. In 1952 he participated in the pioneering surgery to separate Roger and Rodney Brodie, conjoined twins who were joined at the head.

Yet, when it came to house naming, Bellairs so far trumps all the others.

711 Lake Avenue

Salutations! I'm the former house at 711 Lake Avenue. Unfortunately, I met the wrecking ball in 2016, and my remains are scattered. I'm participating in this forum to remind you that nothing lasts forever, even good houses like me.

I was built in 1905 and, like 704 Lake Avenue, I was designed by architects Tallmadge & Watson. I was quite spacious inside, and my grounds included additional lots to the east and west. My first visitors were William and Blanche Freeman. William was a Chicago lawyer and a Colorado rancher, and he served on your village board from 1916 to 1918. Blanche belonged to the Wilmette Woman's Club and donated the land where the club built its clubhouse.

My second visitor was Perry Smithers. He bought me from Blanche Freeman in 1919, shortly after William died. Smithers occupied me for 20 years, along with his second wife Genevieve and their three children and servants. One of his first acts was to hire prominent landscape architect Jens Jensen to create a landscape plan. Jensen lived a few blocks away. Smithers had the big bucks needed to buy me and employ Jensen to spruce me up because of his success as an executive of Booth Fisheries Co.

It was during the Smithers' occupancy that I experienced the second most terrifying event in my life. (The first was 80 years later when the wreckers showed up.) In April 1937 the Smitherses were redecorating me. They hired a Chicago painting contractor, Gelden Co. While the work was underway, the family moved out. Shortly before 10:00 PM on Tuesday, April 20, a dynamite bomb crashed through my front window. An ear-piercing blast ripped my beams and flooring to shreds, tore plaster off my walls, broke windows, and wrecked furnishings. Fortunately, there was no fire. On the same day, four other bombings occurred in the Chicago area, and one more the next day.

Why? No one knows for sure, but the likely cause was labor unrest. Do you remember Judge Kenesaw Mountain Landis, the flamboyant federal judge and first baseball commissioner? Well, he was also famous for arbitrating a major construction industry dispute in the Chicago area in 1921. His award (like a court order) established wage scales and work rules for all the building trades. Arguably, the award was beneficial to both contractors and workers. While it reduced wage scales and liberalized work rules, it invigorated the floundering construction industry and spurred employment. But by 1937, the trade unions strongly opposed the award and battled the contractors who were sticking to its terms. The Smitherses' contractor, Gelden, was one of these contractors. Gelden was also performing work at Lake Shore Country Club in Glencoe, and minutes after the bomb sailed through my window, the clubhouse was also bombed.

Well, I was repaired, and my life went on. My next visitor, in 1939, was William Horsting, a dealer in oil leases, and also an inventor and hotel operator. The Horsting family occupied me for many years. I can't talk about my subsequent years of decline and, ultimately, demolition. It's just too sad.

2522 Iroquois Road

I object! I'm the house at 2522 Iroquois Road. So far, we've heard from only east side houses on Lake Avenue. Does anyone remember that Wilmette has other streets, including many on the west side of town? Let me tell you my story.

I was designed by Wilmette resident Maurice Spitzer. He lived at 604 Washington Avenue from 1922 until his death at age 72 in 1939. A Hungarian Jew, he immigrated to the U.S. in 1888 as a young man. He may not have been one of the architectural biggies of his day, but by the time he designed me, he had a solid record of accomplishment, concentrating on commercial and apartment buildings in Chicago.

Fearing that I might be lonely, Spitzer also designed a companion for me: the house immediately to the east (2512 Iroquois Road). He called me Charmant (charming) and my companion Cheri (beloved). We share the same style. He called it "French"; others called it "Tudor Revival"; I call it beautiful and unique. Originally, my companion and I also shared a circular driveway.

I'm Charmant in the background. My companion, Cheri, is on the right.

It's not just my design and surroundings that make me special. It's also my visitors. One fellow in particular deserves to be recognized: Jules Herbuveaux. He first crossed my threshold in 1929, and he graced my space until 1940 when he moved to 1042 Pawnee Road.

Jules is considered the Father of the Chicago School of Television. He took a roundabout path to this title. Born in New York, he came to Chicago as a child. In high school, he became a talented saxophone player. After serving as a Navy flier during World War I, he freelanced with various Chicago bands before settling with the band at the Paradise Ballroom. By 1921 he was the band's director. In 1922 the band was Chicago's first popular band to be broadcast on radio. Recording contracts and road tours followed. In 1925, his band moved to the Victorian Room of the Palmer House. In 1927 it became a studio band, first for radio station KYW and soon for the NBC radio network. NBC purchased radio station WMAQ from the *Chicago Daily News* in 1931, and Jules was given the job of producing musical shows for the station. By the late 1930s, he had worked his way up to the exalted position of station manager.

When WMAQ ventured into broadcast television in 1947, Jules was put in charge. The term Chicago School of Television refers to the relaxed, intimate, simple, low-budget, impromptu programming represented by shows that Jules introduced on WMAQ-TV: Burr Tillstom's *Kukla, Fran and Ollie;* Marlin Perkins' *Zoo Parade;* Studs Terkel's *Studs' Place;* Dr. Frances Horwich's *Ding Dong School; Quiz Kids;* Walt Durbahn's *Walt's Workshop;* Dave Garroway's *Garroway at Large; The Wayne King Show;* and Don Herbert's *Mr. Wizard.* Jules also produced the first 10:00 PM news show, *Five Star Final,* with Clifton Utley and Clint Youle. Under his leadership, WMAQ was the first station to broadcast 100 percent in color (1956). NBC recognized his enormous talent in 1955 when it made him a company vice-president.

Jules Herbuveaux brought Burr Tilstrom's *Kukla, Fran and Ollie* and other Chicago School programming to WMAQ-TV. Photo from Wikimedia Commons.

629 Park Avenue

Hi! I'm the beautiful craftsman-style house at 629 Park Avenue. In 2014 my visitors received a Historic Preservation Award for saving me from a life-threatening case of old age. The award exhilarated me. I'm now held in high esteem by other HOW members. Even the uppity houses in the CAGE (Chestnut, Ashland, Greenwood and Elwood avenues in east Wilmette) and their counterparts in Indian Hill Estates have taken notice.

Some of you have contributed to historic preservation, perhaps by restoring your vintage property or remodeling or adding to your house in a way that's sensitive to its original design or constructing a new house that's sympathetic to your neighborhood's historic character. If so, you too could win an award and receive the praise that's heaped on us winners.

After 107 years of devoted service, I was ingloriously placed on the market in 2013 as a teardown. How embarrassing and demeaning! But it was true. I was uninhabitable. I could almost feel the pounding of the wrecker's ball. Then a miracle happened! I was shown to Sarah and Craig Condry. Their reaction was startlingly different. Instead of "ugh," I heard hopeful comments: "It has good bones." "The space is good but it needs to be rearranged, restored, and updated." "What a great location—near the library, post office, and Village Center—in the heart of the community."

But the comment that touched me most deeply was this: "It has roots." Roots! This brought tears to my leaky faucets. Finally, someone realized that I'm more than just an expendable building. I provide context and perspective. I help define my neighborhood and its lifestyle. I safeguard the stories and spirit of the people I've hosted.

Even at my advanced age, I remember many of my visitors affectionately. Charles and Amy Kelley and their four children were my early favorites. They came in 1917 and stayed until 1924. They were fine teetotaling folks. Charles was a Methodist minister. In 1909, before he crossed my threshold for the first time, he was the pastor of a Chicago church, and he officiated at the wedding of Charlie Lew, a native of China, and Mabel Clark, a woman of European descent. Chicago officials regarded this interracial marriage as improper and arrested the couple. Although Illinois law didn't prohibit interracial marriage, Judge John Newcomer rebuked Rev. Kelley for performing the ceremony. Rev. Kelley responded publicly and firmly, "I do not see that a minister can do otherwise than marry properly authorized parties since the state and scripture declare their marriage to be legal. In Acts we read, 'God that hath made the world and all things therein hath made of one blood all nations of men.'" I say, Amen!

Margaret O'Keefe (widow of a Chicago physician) and her brother Daniel Rockwood (a conductor on the Northwestern Elevated) were my next visitors (1924–1946). They opened my doors to boarders—a gardener, music teacher, golf pro, grocery clerk, newspaper employee, salesman—mostly young single adults with diverse backgrounds. William and Rebecca Shiley (1946–1948) and Joseph and Rose Puize (1948–1966) followed. They continued the boarding house tradition, offering housing to Wilmette's less affluent residents. The

Here I am now, after my facelift. My internal organs are
also in good shape. Courtesy of the Condry family.

Puizes converted my third floor into a three-room in-law apartment and added
a three-car garage.

William and Ruth Randolph restored me to my original single-family status and graced my halls for many years (1966–2013). William served in the
Army Corps of Engineers in the Philippines during World War II. Afterward, he
founded his own construction business. He was a dedicated Boy Scout leader,
and his four sons were all Eagle Scouts.

So what are my roots? They include stories of decency, diversity, harmony,
achievement, service, and honor. If you look closely at your vintage house,
you may find inspiring messages in its roots, too.

The House that Wasn't

Like 629 Park Avenue, I'm an award-winning house. Well, not exactly. I'm actually an award-wining house *design*. I was supposed to be built at 1261 21st
Street in Kenilworth Gardens. I'm quite annoyed that it never happened.

My story begins with the 1933 Century of Progress Exposition in Chicago.
It was held in the depths of the Great Depression to celebrate Chicago's cen-
tennial and the phenomenal progress the city had made in its first 100 years.
Organizers wanted to inspire hope among Depression-weary Americans, and

they recruited exhibitors to display technological innovations that would make life better in the future.

In early 1933 the North Shore Real Estate Board held a contest in anticipation of the exhibition. Architects were invited to submit their designs for the "Ideal Average American Home" using "the latest in design, method and materials." Wilmette resident Arthur Lee, president of the North Shore Real Estate Board, explained that the goal was to design a house that would be a "yardstick of value." The cost of labor and materials would be fully disclosed, and thus the house would set a standard of quality and value that would enable nervous buyers to enter the market with greater confidence. The house would have a living room, dining room, kitchen, and lavatory on the first floor; three or four bedrooms and two bathrooms on the second floor; and a connected two-car garage, all within 28,000–30,000 cubic feet of space. The first-place winner would receive a $1,000 prize, and seven runners-up would receive smaller prizes. The winning design would be built on a lot at 1261 21st Street. Construction would be completed by June 30, 1933, one month after the exposition's opening day. President Lee estimated that 300,000 attendees and other interested folks would visit the house.

The contest's organizers expected to receive 1,000 entries from underutilized architects across the country, but they received only 100, mostly from the Chicago area. I was thrilled in March 1933 to be chosen the winning design. My creator was architect Robert Arnold of Winnetka. The judges described me as reflecting "that part of the Georgian period in England known as the Regency, particularly because of the segmental bays in my living room and dining room,

My highly symmetrical design features a stucco facade and a metal hip roof.
This rendering appeared in the *Chicago Tribune*, April 2, 1933, Part 1, p. 22.

my low-pitched hip roof, the detail of my entrance and porch, and my balanced facade." The second- and third-place houses were of similar design but, frankly, they were no match for me.

Construction began immediately, but not as originally planned. The idea of building me at 1261 21st Street was abandoned. I was forsaken and distraught. Instead of carrying out the Real Estate Board's promise, President Lee built models of me and the second- and third-place houses, using a scale of one-quarter inch to one foot. I was miniaturized. The models were displayed for several months on the seventh floor of Marshall Field's downtown store. Later, they were displayed at a Wilmette real estate office, where elevations and plans were given to anyone asking for them.

The lot where I was supposed to be built was purchased by George Roeddiger, an accountant. He built a house designed by prominent Chicago architect Clarence Lampe. The Roeddiger family moved there in 1936. Were the Roeddigers and Lampe influenced by my winning design, which they undoubtedly were aware of? I think so. In fact, I believe that many houses in Kenilworth Gardens were influenced by my design, even though I was never built.

16 Canterbury Court

Welcome! I'm the house at 16 Canterbury Court. I was one of the first houses built on this street. The year was 1929. My construction cost was $50,000 (not including my lot). My first visitors were Craig and Estella Hazelwood, formerly of the Englewood neighborhood in Chicago. They could easily afford me. Craig was a well-to-do banker: chairman of Lake Shore Trust and Savings Bank and executive vice-president of the First National Bank of Chicago. He hired Chicago architect Edwin Clark to design me. Clark did a terrific job. You would marvel at my beauty and functionality. Clark also designed Brookfield Zoo, Plaza del Lago, Winnetka Village Hall, and many luxury North Shore residences.

Craig, Estella, and their three kids enjoyed my friendly confines for six years, until Estella got sick and died in 1935. By then, the two older kids, Dorothy and Ora Jean, were in college, and the youngest, Craig Jr., would soon graduate from New Trier High School. In 1938 Craig sold me to Carl and Olga Wickman for $87,500. Carl was no slouch either: He founded Greyhound Bus Lines.

But the Hazelwoods were first in both my house and heart. The middle child, Jeanie (nickname for Ora Jean), was my favorite. She was a cute 12-year-old when she first crossed my threshold. She had a flair for the dramatic which she nurtured at New Trier. I vividly remember her practicing her lines for an amusing little play called *Charm School.*

I still saw Jeanie frequently after she graduated from New Trier in 1934. She entered Lake Forest College, not too far from home. She studied journalism and drama, and she appeared in at least two plays: *Street Scene* and *Ceiling Zero.* But the main subject of her attention was a student named Dick Widmark. She worked hard to get a date with him. They dated briefly, but then he stopped calling. Craig said it was all for the best: "Dick is a nothing. He can't think of anything to say. All he can do is clear his throat. He's a bumpkin." But Jeanie didn't agree. "My father was a Rotarian kind of banker," she explained. "He made a lot of speeches. He just didn't understand a man who didn't speak out."

They call me 16 Canterbury Court.

Jeanie remained smitten by Dick. She admired especially "the ambition that burned him up so intensely. A guy like that is irresistible." He graduated from Lake Forest College in 1936 but returned in the fall of 1937 as a speech and drama instructor. After a two-year hiatus, he and Jeanie crossed paths and started dating again. As both her instructor and boyfriend, he inspired her. "I just have to be an actress!" she declared. She graduated in 1938 and, with her recently retired father, moved to New York to study at the American Academy of Dramatic Arts. Dick followed and began his career as a radio and theater actor. The couple married in 1942.

Richard and Jean Widmark cut the rug in the 1950s. Photo from Wikimedia Commons.

I didn't have any contact with Jeanie after she and her father left Wilmette. All I know is what I read in the newspapers that were tossed aimlessly on my front steps. Bumpkin Dick Widmark became Richard Widmark, one of the longstanding bright stars of stage, screen, and TV; and Jeanie had some success as an actor and screenwriter. Most important, unlike many celebrity couples, the Widmarks had a loving marriage for 55 years that ended only when death did them part. Incidentally, baseball fans, their daughter Anne married pitcher Sandy Koufax.

The Conley House

Greetings, patrons of Wilmette's Village Center. I'm the house that once stood at 1113 Central Avenue. At one time, there were quite a few houses on Central and Wilmette avenues in the Village Center. All the others were relocated or demolished and replaced by commercial buildings. I was the last house standing. The Village demolished me in 1982. I hold no grudge. I had fallen into disrepair and was an eyesore. My site has since been put to a good use as pleasant little Veterans Park with public parking at the rear.

My memory begins in the early 1900s. That's when Dr. Montrose Conley and his new wife, Dr. Minnie Conley, became my visitors. He was a graduate of the

College of Medicine of the University of Illinois and taught neurology at the college. She was a graduate of the Women's Medical School of Northwestern University and worked as a psychiatrist at the Cook County Institution for the Insane at Dunning. She was probably the first woman psychiatrist in Illinois.

Montrose used my premises as his home and medical office. He headed the radiology department at St. Francis Hospital in Evanston and was a pioneer in the use of X-ray and radium to treat cancer. One of his favorite patients was Wilmette's beloved Father Edward Vattmann, the Army chaplain who was a close friend of Teddy Roosevelt. Father Vattmann officiated at the funerals of two Conley daughters who died young. Two other children, Susan and John, survived into adulthood.

After Dr. Minnie Conley died in 1939, Montrose rented one of my rooms to a younger woman, Elizabeth Fuller, a Wilmette librarian. They soon wed, retired to California, and became parents of a son. Their departure from Wilmette opened my doors to Montrose's older son John and his wife Natalie. John followed in his parents' footsteps and was a physician. Like Montrose, he used me as his medical office and home until 1974, when at age 62 he departed for Brownsville, Texas and started a medical practice there.

Things didn't go well in Brownsville. In early 1977 Natalie died. Later that year, the Brownsville Medical Center terminated John's staff privileges, and the Texas Board of Medical Examiners revoked his license, because "several of Conley's methods stood out as examples of very bad medicine." He was sued for malpractice involving a botched delivery that resulted in the baby's death.

Here in Wilmette, I sat vacant, deteriorating and casting a pall on my neighbors. The village board had long coveted my site for additional Village Center parking, but John had rejected all offers. Finally, in 1977, while John was struggling in Brownsville, the village board decided to exercise its power of eminent domain. John fought tooth and nail.

Perhaps John harbored the unrealistic idea of reopening his Wilmette office after putting his Brownsville problems behind him. He wasn't ready to retire. He didn't like the way his father had gracefully retired. He told the Texas Board of Medical Examiners that Montrose "accepted a briefcase and they thanked him for his many years of service and that was the end of it. I'm not that way. I saw what happened to my father. That's why I'm fighting [to keep my license]. Because I think he did it wrong."

The eminent domain battle dragged on for four years. Even after all proceedings ended in the Village's favor, John moved back in, locked my doors, and refused to leave—until he begrudgingly realized the futility of further resistance.

It was a fitting touch (even if unintended) for the Village to name my site

Veterans Park. Both Montrose and John were veterans. Montrose served in the infantry in the Spanish-American War and was a medical officer in World War I. John served in World War II, also as a medical officer. He was awarded the Bronze Star for heroic service in France.

The renovation of Hoffman House was completed in 2019. See page 355.

Hoffman House looked like this for more than a century.
Courtesy of the Wilmette Historical Museum.

Hoffman House

How do you do! I'm the oldest house speaking to you in this chapter. I'm now located at 1635 Lake Avenue, a prominent site one block east of St. Joseph Church. I don't look much like I did 100 or so years ago. I've been renovated and expanded.

Because of my age, I'm having trouble remembering some of my early history, but I date back to the mid-19th century. I was originally located west of Ridge Road in Gross Point and, at one point, I was used as a public schoolhouse. The bricks that make up my exterior walls were hand-made.

In the 1890s, the lot where I'm currently situated was part of a large parcel belonging to Hubbard Schwall, who operated a grocery store at the southwest corner of Lake Avenue and 15th Street. In 1899 Schwall paid off a debt owed to a Chicago butcher, John Maischaider, by transferring 165 feet of Lake Avenue frontage at the southeast corner of the 17th Street intersection to John and his wife Anna.

John was probably the person who moved me from Gross Point to my present location. A wood-frame kitchen was added. The Maischaider family visited here briefly before moving again to a farm in Northfield Township. At that time, John and Anna gave me as a wedding present to their daughter Anna and son-in-law Edward Hoffman. Edward was just starting a long career as a clerk with a gas utility company. Members of the Hoffman family would be my visitors for more than eight decades.

Anna and Edward Hoffman's first child, Esther, is the person closest to me, because she lived within these walls for her entire 84-year life (1897–1981). She once told a friend that she "had a very unhappy childhood because she lived west of the tracks," but I'm not sure about that. The west side has a lot going for it. Esther attended the local public schools and, after high school, she entered Lewis Institute in Chicago. Lewis was an engineering college for men, but it also offered women a degree in general science or household science. According to Lewis, "Womanly culture is no longer culture if it ignores science, and conversely science is daily becoming humanized."

Esther never married. For many years, she worked as a sales representative for Shaw-Walker Co., a manufacturer of office furniture and equipment. In 1928 she was president of the Club for Business and Professional Women of Wilmette. This club was part of a movement that began in 1919 when local clubs organized state and national federations that sought to advance the interests of women in the workplace. The Wilmette club was active in the 1920s and 1930s and usually met at the Congregational Church.

So back to me. Some folks dislike my recent renovation and expansion, which combines the original farmhouse style with a modern addition. I must admit that I myself had concerns while the project was underway, but now I'm quite satisfied with the finished product, which uses a grey exterior paint to link and harmonize the two styles. Aesthetics is a matter of personal taste—something that you probably don't want government to regulate in the case of single-family homes, even if aesthetics regulations were lawful (which is dubious). Fortunately, the vast majority of people who build or enlarge single-family homes, either for their own occupancy or as spec houses, choose a design that appeals to potential buyers upon resale.

The Seng Family Houses

I'm not a house, or even a visitor, but please allow me to introduce myself anyway. My name is Wendelin Seng. Although I normally rest in peace beneath a plain granite tombstone in Chicago's St. Boniface Cemetery, I'm temporarily aroused by the excitement surrounding Wilmette's upcoming Sesquicentennial. I've been here at St. Boniface Cemetery since 1896. I'm joined here by lots of other Seng family members. We Sengs also account for several houses in the village. Probably the most noteworthy are the twin houses on Chestnut Avenue in east Wilmette. Before I dangle a few tantalizing tidbits about these houses, let me tell you about me.

I was born in Germany in 1824. I learned the weaving trade, and in 1856 I immigrated to Chicago. I initially ran a grocery store with my brother, but after my marriage to Rose Baer in 1864, I entered the upholstery business. In the 1870s I began to mass produce the metal parts and fixtures used in furniture manufacturing, like platform rocker springs and jack-knife hinges for sofa beds. In 1894 the Seng Co. was incorporated by me and my two oldest sons, Julius and Frank. A third son (Wendelin) and two sons-in-law (Gerard Bichl and Edward Schager) later joined the company in executive positions.

For many years, the Seng Co. thrived as the world's largest manufacturer of metal furniture parts and fixtures. We had hundreds of patents and produced hundreds of different items, including frames for Hollywood beds, swivel chairs, recliner chairs, and a device that enables a person to pull a typewriter pedestal out from the side of a desk. The Seng family members who owned and ran the business became wealthy.

I don't recall ever visiting Wilmette, but after my death in 1896, the profits earned by the Seng Co. enabled six of my offspring to establish fine homes in your lovely village during the first quarter of the 20th century. Son Julius Seng and his wife Mathilda lived at 1222 Chestnut Avenue. Son Frank Seng and his wife Barbara lived at 435 Lake Avenue. Son Wendelin Seng and his wife Mary Jane lived at 401 Lake Avenue. Daughter Rose Seng and her husband Charles Barton lived at 1216 Chestnut Avenue.

Then there are the twin houses at 1050 and 1110 Chestnut. They were designed by prominent architect Philip Maher and built in 1923–1924 at a cost of $65,000 each. The house at 1050 Chestnut was built for my daughter Dorothea Seng and her husband Edward Schager. Its twin at 1100 Chestnut was built for another daughter, Helen Seng, and her husband Gerard Bichl.

The Seng Co.'s success made it possible for family members
to own at least six Wilmette houses, including the twin
structures at 1110 and 1050 Chestnut Avenue.

Separated by a gorgeous common garden, the twin houses are quite similar in appearance. Legend says they were once connected by an underground tunnel, but if so, that's no longer the case. Legend also says that the two houses had party rooms in their large basements with walk-in vaults for storing the alcoholic beverages served to guests at Prohibition-era parties. Most folks would call these twin houses mansions. Both have been designated local landmarks.

Incidentally, the Village's official designation of the twin houses as landmarks states that they were built for Dorothea and Helen "by their father," i.e., by yours truly. I had a good laugh at that. I died in 1896. The houses were built in 1922–1923, 26 years after my passing. By then, I wasn't building anything for anyone. I'll bet their husbands are spinning in their graves even now over the idea that I'm getting credit for sheltering their wives and children.

The Int-Hout home at 36 Crescent Place was demolished in 1996 and
replaced by a 2,800-sq. ft. house marketed at more than $1 million.
Photo appeared in *Popular Mechanics*, June 1911, p. 778.

From Innovator to *Persona Non Grata*

I'm Adam Int-Hout, the last participant of this chapter, and I'm also not a
house. In the early 1900s I achieved national recognition for designing two
affordable homes for my family: the first in Evanston at 2410 Hartrey Avenue
and the second in Wilmette at 36 Crescent Place. Then I became *persona non
grata* in Wilmette. Here's my story:

I was born in Thornton Township, Illinois in 1880, son of Dutch immigrants
who ran a grocery store. After eighth grade, I worked as a clerk in the store
until I joined Federal Pure Food Co. as a chemist and moved to Evanston. (In
those days, you didn't need a college degree to be called a chemist.) In 1907 I
married Gladys Melville. She was the daughter of a prominent Wilmette family.
When our first son was born two years later, I decided to build our first family
home.

I hope you won't think me immodest, but I was ingenious, frugal, and empa-
thetic for my new wife with her burdensome domestic duties. I desired to create
a spacious home within my limited means that Gladys could easily care for
without a servant. So, I designed and built our first house in Evanston at a cost
of $2,000, give or take. It was a very small bungalow (25-foot sides). Swinging
walls allowed the main floor to be configured into five fully furnished rooms

—living room, dining room, bedroom, guest room, and kitchen—but not all at the same time. An unfinished storage attic could be converted into two rooms at a later date. There was no basement. My design incorporated many space-saving features, like stairs to the attic that doubled as storage bins.

In March 1910, our Evanston house was featured in *Popular Mechanics* magazine. The national press called it The House of Many Wonders—a possible remedy for the shortage of affordable housing. It became a popular tourist attraction. Every Sunday, we had scores of visitors. To regain our privacy, Gladys and I decided to move on. Construction of our new Crescent Place home in Wilmette took six weeks, and we moved there in 1911.

My objectives for our new home were the same: spacious, low cost, and labor-saving. Having somewhat increased financial resources, I designed a slightly more expensive and larger home on two levels with no basement. It included an 8-by-8-foot living porch at the front and a small entrance porch at the side. The second floor had a 13-by-13-foot bedroom and two 6-by-9-foot sleeping porches on opposite sides of the bedroom, allowing cross-ventilation. I again used the swinging wall concept but I added some new space-saving features. For example, I placed kitchen cabinets at window-type openings on an exterior wall. Glass doors on the front and rear of the cabinets allowed natural light and air to pass through from outside and brighten and cool the interior space.

Once again, in June 1911, *Popular Mechanics* featured my ingenious Wonder Bungalow in a flattering article, and once again I was widely praised in the national media. I thought I was on to an idea that met a need. I planned a third house, also on Crescent Place. Then I encountered NIMBY. The wealthy neighbors on Crescent Place feared that more of my modest "2 by 4 dwellings" without basements would diminish their property values. They threatened legal action and ostracized my family. I surrendered. I agreed to abandon the project and sell them the lot.

Gladys and I moved from Wilmette, first back to Evanston and then to Thornton Township. I didn't build any more "doll houses," as they were called, and I eventually started a successful carton-manufacturing business. Here in my cramped quarters at Rosehill Cemetery, I often wonder whether Wilmette ever found it possible to accommodate affordable housing for folks of modest means.

CHAPTER 19

★——————————————★

"So What" Stories

Merriam-Webster offers the following as one of its principal definitions of the word *history:* "a chronological record of significant events (such as those affecting a nation or institution) often including an explanation of their causes." The stories in this chapter don't qualify as history under this definition. They describe unconnected events. In fact, they're almost frivolous, and you'll derive little benefit from reading them—unless you wish to be amused while gaining a greater appreciation for the rich history of Wilmette.

The Big Tree

How sad that we shall never see
Our hamlet's giant poplar tree.

Stretching limbs beyond the sky,
Marking trails for passersby,

Hosting crowds within its base.
Now it's gone without a trace.

Those who killed our tree shall pay
Quite dearly on their judgment day.

God's the One who makes Big Trees.
Only fools would mess with these.

The long life of Wilmette's Big Tree (more than 600 years) came to a sudden and tragic end on the night of November 5, 1901, but what a splendid run it enjoyed! The Big Tree took root in the Middle Ages, long before Columbus sailed on his first voyage to the New World. It avoided the hazards that threaten tree longevity and grew to become the biggest tree in Illinois—indeed, one of the biggest in North America. It was revered by Native Americans and later by the German settlers of New Trier and other folks who marveled at nature's awesome creation.

The Big Tree's home had become, by 1901, a Gross Point farm near present-day Hibbard and Glenview roads. (This area was annexed by Wilmette in 1926.) How big was the Big Tree? Estimates vary, and some were probably exaggerations, but here's what was reported in various sources: It was 130–170 feet tall. Its maximum diameter was 18–19 feet. Its circumference at a point three feet above ground was 31 feet. From 20 to 70 feet above ground, its trunk was uniformly five feet in diameter. Its lowest limb was 70–75 feet above ground. Its canopy covered 3,000 square feet. It was visible for miles around and served as a travelers' landmark.

At the base of the Big Tree was an opening almost five feet wide and more than eight feet high that provided access to a hollow chamber about twelve feet in diameter and more than 20 feet high. According to legend, the chamber was used for council meetings by the Pottawatomi, "who found room for forty persons." It also provided shelter, over the years, to a family of bears, a ring of thieves, a homeless human family, and a blind pig.

The identities of the adult and children aren't recorded, but they're likely Charles Kotz and his two youngest sons, John and Peter. Courtesy of the Wilmette Historical Museum.

Legend also claims that the Big Tree survived a fire in 1832 that wiped out every other tree in the grove. This miracle led Native Americans to believe that the Big Tree was protected by the Great Spirit, and its bark had medicinal powers. During the same year, Chief Black Hawk led members of the Sauk tribe across the Mississippi River from Iowa in an attempt to reclaim sacred tribal lands in Illinois that the U.S. government had confiscated. The chief supposedly used the Big Tree as "his principal point of assemblage" and led his braves in "a war dance around the big tree." (This Black Hawk legend is highly dubious.)

What killed the Big Tree on the night of November 5, 1901? A fire at the base of the tree sent flames roaring up the trunk with flares shooting from knot-holes 60 feet above ground. The blaze could be seen three miles away. What started the fire? Well, it wasn't lightning, as no storms occurred that night. It was probably vandals. The farm had recently changed hands from Charles and Gertrude Kotz to Michael and Louisa Kloepfer. (Charles and Louisa were siblings.) The Kloepfers started charging visitors ten cents to view the tree up close. It was rumored that "some soreheads" retaliated.

After the fire, the Big Tree was reduced to a 30-foot Big Stump and was used as a calf pen and a children's play house. In 1903 Richard Gloede, a noted land-scape architect and horticulturalist, purchased the Big Stump and moved it to his place of business and residence at 1405 Central Street, Evanston. Ironically, the Big Stump was almost destroyed by a huge house fire on that property in January 1930. It survived and continued to be displayed until the 1950s when the property became a Dyche Stadium parking lot.

H.H. Holmes, Grave Digger

Newlyweds Andrew and Sarah Parker, both in their early twenties, enjoyed visiting the dense woods between Wilmette and Evanston during the summer of 1896. This was before the forest gave way to the present-day rows of houses. The Parkers lived in Evanston at 2444 Evanston Avenue (now Pioneer Road), a short distance from the woods.

Not until September of 1896 did Sarah focus on something unusual. In a se-cluded area of the woods was a mound where the vegetation was sparse and newly grown, markedly different from its surroundings. She thought it looked like a recent burial plot. She pointed it out to Andrew, but he showed little interest.

Andrew was a member of a prominent Evanston family. His father, Dr. Arthur Parker, was president of the Common Sense Truss Co. Dr. Parker was such a

H.H. Holmes built this duplex at 727 John (11th) Street in 1891.
Courtesy of the Wilmette Historical Museum.

recognized expert in the treatment of hernias that the state granted him a medical license, even though he hadn't spent a single day in medical school. Young Andrew started his working life as a bookkeeper at the Evanston State Bank.

The image of the mound in the woods disturbed Sarah's sleep. She was haunted by nightmares that bodies were buried there. She begged Andrew to take a spade and investigate. To soothe his young bride, he reluctantly agreed. After two hours of digging, he found nothing and gave up. But Sarah's nightmares continued, and she insisted that he return and dig more. The second time, within a few minutes, his spade struck something hard. A little more digging exposed a leg bone, followed by two more bones. Andrew suspected that they were human bones, but he wasn't sure. He stopped digging and notified the police.

Further digging exposed a skull, several ribs, part of a spine, and several arm and leg bones. Police concluded that the bones were indeed human and probably came from at least two female bodies. There was no sign that the bodies were clothed when buried. The condition of the grave and remains indicated that the burial had occurred within the prior three years. There were no reports of any missing women in the area during that period, and there were no signs of violence.

The dearth of evidence didn't stop folks from speculating. You see, only four months earlier, Herman Webster Mudgett (alias H.H. Holmes) had been hanged in Philadelphia for the murder of Benjamin Pitezel. Holmes was the devil of *The Devil in the White City,* suspected of murdering scores of women at his "murder castle" in Chicago's Englewood neighborhood at the time of the Columbian Exposition of 1893. Reports of the horror wrought by Holmes filled the newspapers of the day.

It was widely believed that among Holmes's victims were sisters Minnie and Anna Williams. Holmes had a romantic relationship with Minnie. He conned her out of a substantial inheritance and "married" her (despite already having two other wives). He invited Anna to live with Minnie and him in a Chicago apartment. The two sisters disappeared in July 1893, leaving no trace. Holmes later told an interviewer that Minnie had killed Anna in a jealous rage; that he had helped Minnie dispose of Anna's body in Lake Michigan; and that she then fled Chicago to parts unknown.

Folks were convinced that the bodies found in the woods were the remains of the murdered Williams sisters, buried there by Holmes. What was the basis for this belief? The grave was close to the Wilmette duplex where Holmes had occasionally lived in the 1890s with his second wife, their infant child, and his wife's parents (727 John Street, now 11th Street). Moreover, only a monster like Holmes could so callously bury human bodies without clothing, coffin, and clergy. Besides, no local women were missing. What other explanation could there be?

Dr. Moore, Fly Foe

A momentous event occurred in August 1914. It was the adoption of Wilmette's Manure Ordinance. It happened at a time when villagers relied heavily on real horse power. There were several livery stables in the village, and many residents kept a horse or two at stables on their private property. Automobiles were ascending in popularity, but horses wouldn't be phased out for years.

With horses comes manure; with manure come flies; and with flies come contagious diseases: typhoid, cholera, and dysentery, to name a few. In 1913 the Village created a board of health. Edward Moore, a physician and surgeon, became the first health commissioner with immense power to protect residents from the spread of disease.

Upon taking office, Dr. Moore mounted a war against flies. "House flies are bred and born in filth—in the privy vaults, open garbage cans, and manure piles," he said. "The female house fly, which is really the only member of the family worth considering, has great perseverance and marvelous productive power. She can arise in the morning, knock the dust out of her eyes with her front legs, settle down to business, and by night be the mother of some seven million energetic children." (Whoa, Dr. Moore, your data just triggered the horse manure alarm!)

Based on Dr. Moore's recommendation, Wilmette adopted the Manure Ordinance. Anyone in charge of a barn or other structure housing livestock was required to provide, for each animal, an air-tight, cement-lined box with a heavy metal lid and a capacity of 25 cubic feet. During the fly season, the boxes had to be disinfected every-other-day.

Dr. Moore quickly discovered that the Manure Ordinance wouldn't solve the fly problem. Compliance was spotty. Even the Village itself ignored the ordinance at the Fire Department's horse stable. When Dr. Moore complained, the Village cleverly turned manure into gold and foul odor into sweet fragrance. It contracted with Paul Nanzig, a Ridge Road florist, to sell him a year's supply of the Fire Department's manure for $42, provided he must remove it strictly in compliance with the ordinance.

In 1915, Dr. Moore suggested an anti-fly program like one in Hutchinson, Kansas where the city gave weekly prizes ($2 for first place and $1 for second place) to kids who delivered the most dead flies to the board of health. The city's merchants offered additional prizes, like one movie ticket per 100 dead flies. According to Dr. Moore, the kids delivered 234.5 pounds of dead flies during the fly season. The flies' tiny smashed carcasses supposedly filled 37 bushel baskets—7,372,000 dead flies in all. (There goes the horse manure alarm again!) This success, he added, doesn't count the billions of potential descendants that never experienced the warmth of, well, you know what.

Dr. Moore next recommended fly traps. "To do effective work there should be at least 200 of these traps in operation throughout the town, and placed in every alleyway in the village there ought to be located three or four traps to the block." But alas, the Village lacked the resources to carry out this recommendation and to take other steps to eliminate the flies' breeding places. Villagers ignored the doctor's appeals to pitch in. It took years for sanitation improvements and other advances to transform house flies from the major disease spreaders they once were to the annoyances they are now.

Goldberg, War Hero

Goldberg arguably deserves to be honored as much as any other Wilmette resident. He excelled in his field of endeavor, achieved fame at a national level, performed his role with honor and distinction, and inspired and comforted his comrades in arms. Despite this, he's been largely forgotten, and this sketch may be the last hope for keeping his memory alive. You see, Goldberg was an Irish terrier.

In 1917, when Goldberg was a mere pup, he was found in Chicago by Jake O'Connor, a member of Battery B of the 122nd field artillery, and adopted by the unit while training for World War I. O'Connor named him "Goldberg." (Get it? Like *O'Connor and Goldberg,* the once-popular Midwest shoe store chain named *O'Connor & Goldberg.*) When the 122nd was shipped off to Europe, Goldberg went along, smuggled in the coat pocket of the bugler. He was spotted aboard ship by the commanding officer, Colonel Milton Foreman, but the colonel was a dog lover and overlooked the transgression. Goldberg ended up on the field of battle in France, where he experienced the rigors of war. He was gassed at Argonne. He was missing in action until discovered in the custody of another unit. He was at the battlefields of St. Mihiel, Toul Sector, and Meuse-Verdun. He was wounded and shell shocked. But all the while, he wagged his tail and uplifted the unit's morale. He returned to the U.S. in 1919 and was given an "honorable discharge" and other commendations.

Goldberg lives on at the Illinois State Military Museum. Courtesy of Justin Lutz.

His home for the next decade is unknown, but in 1930 veterans of B Battery tracked him down, purchased him, and placed him in the loving care of William McKeighan, a longtime resident at 1615 Walnut Avenue. McKeighan, a veteran of B Battery and a printer by trade, described him as "the ideal mascot, something to care for and protect. He was the expression of home ties—a binding link between civil and military life—a boy and his dog—two hundred boys and one dog." On August 2, 1932, the village board honored Goldberg, then 15 and one-half years old, by awarding him a free lifetime dog license.

Goldberg died in November 1933. The Illinois Pet Memorial Park in Hinsdale offered a free burial plot with all the trappings, but B Battery veterans turned the offer down. McKeighan announced that they would have Goldberg stuffed and displayed at the National Guard Armory in Chicago. And so it was. Goldberg was placed in a glass case and displayed there with his service record and awards. The armory is now gone, and Goldberg was moved to the Illinois State Military Museum in Springfield. Recently, he was refurbished.

Wilmette's "Too Good" Home

Donald Pressburger was born in 1939 to a single mother, 25-year-old Edith Pressburger. She worked as a telephone operator and hat check girl and lived in Chicago with her unemployed parents and another son, also born out of wedlock. Edith and her parents couldn't afford a second child, so Donald was entrusted to the care of the Children's Bureau of Jewish Charities of Chicago. The bureau placed him in foster care with Moses and Mable Kamerman at their Wilmette home, 220 Linden Avenue.

By all appearances, the placement was ideal. In early 1941, when these events occurred, Moses had a well-established law practice in Chicago. He and Mable, 47 and 43 respectively (an "elderly couple," according to the *Chicago Tribune),* had three children who were doing well: two in college and one at New Trier. They had previously served as foster parents for the bureau, so their child-care competence wasn't disputed. Their ten-room house had ample space for Donald, who had already lived with them for 19 months. They had come to love the little fellow so much so that they were willing to forego the $40 monthly stipend they were receiving as foster parents and adopt him as their own.

Things started to get sticky in February 1941. The Kamermans received a letter from the bureau asking them to return Donald because he "should live in a home where there is less educational and cultural stimulation." In other words, as Moses interpreted the letter, the bureau considered the Kamermans' home "culturally and educationally too good." The bureau disputed Moses' characterization but maintained that the Kamermans "might expect more of the child than the child could give," and added that Donald "would fit better in a different kind of a home."

The Kamermans responded by suing the bureau, and the case drew national attention. Moses explained, "I want to give him advantages so that he will get a better break than he would in a third floor tenement. I'm fighting to keep him. I will not have him kicked around from one home or institution to another at the whim of case workers."

The Kamermans initially asked only to be named as Donald's guardians, but the judge ordered the boy removed from their home and placed in foster care elsewhere, as requested by the bureau. Illinois law gave the bureau this right as the child's duly-appointed legal guardian. Then, another couple, Hans Albert Einstein II and his wife Frieda, offered to adopt Donald. The Kamermans countered by filing a second lawsuit, a petition to adopt Donald. This second suit caused the Einsteins to back off. They adopted, instead, a daughter (Evelyn) from The Cradle Society in Evanston. (Hans Albert Einstein was the son of Mr. E = mc². The adopted daughter, Evelyn, went on to live a tumultuous life that included multiple college degrees, periods of homelessness, and work as a dogcatcher, cult deprogrammer, and police officer.)

The Kamermans located Donald's birthmother, Edith, and received her enthusiastic support for their adoption petition. According to the *Chicago Tribune,* the bureau contended (in language that would be regarded today as highly offensive) that Donald was intellectually disabled and not suited for the Kamermans' care, but the Kamermans, with the support of psychiatrists, countered that the boy was "normal." Following a hectic hearing in which Edith "wept with wild abandon," Mable "screamed," and Moses "threatened to slap the charities' lawyer's face," the petition for adoption was denied.

I'd like to tell you that everything worked out well for Donald, but I can't. The records are sealed. Edith married in 1943 and had two additional children, but Donald never became part of that family. Moses died in 1949, when Donald would have been ten years old.

The Totem Pole's True Story

A few folks will remember the 12-foot totem pole that once stood on the west side of Hunter Road, in front of Highcrest School. Its tenure there was brief, only nine years, from 1986 to 1995, but it has a long and mysterious history.

For decades, the pole stood in the backyard of the home at 1025 Greenwood Avenue. In 1986 Theda Armstrong, the home's longtime owner, was moving away. She wanted to donate the pole for public display at an appropriate site. The Wilmette Park District agreed to display it at Highcrest, which the district was leasing from Wilmette School District 39 and using as its recreation center. The pole was erected in front of the school's oldest building, then occupied by the Wilmette Historical Museum.

At that time, Theda told this "true story" (she insisted) about the pole's origin—a story she heard from the home's previous owner. Supposedly, a beautiful young girl once lived there. She and her family spent their summers in the North Woods of Michigan near an Indian settlement. She fell in love with the tribe's handsome young chief, who proposed marriage. Her family wouldn't allow it. A few months after the girl returned to Wilmette, a truck carrying the pole arrived. It was a gift from the chief "as a token of his everlasting love." Many years after first hearing this story, Theda found an old woman in her back yard, gazing at the pole. The old woman said she was present when the pole was delivered and, at the time, she heard the same "true story."

Theda has now passed on. I'm sure she was a nice lady, and under the circumstances, I hesitate to use the term "gullible." But I thought to myself, "John, you're an amateur genealogist. You should be able to identify all the beautiful young girls who lived at 1025 Greenwood Avenue. Maybe that would shed some light."

Well, the house was built in the early 1900s. Its occupants were the Claude Brown family (until 1911), the Guy Morrison family (until 1919), and the Royal Buckman family (until the 1940s). All these families share a common characteristic: They were childless. There were no beautiful (or otherwise) young girls who might have endeared themselves to a handsome young Indian chief.

I have a theory about the origin of the pole. The original owners of the Greenwood Avenue house, Claude and Edith Brown, were natives of Michigan. Claude was a commercial artist and the art director of a firm that furnished illustrations and engravings to publishers. In other words, he was an artist in the art business who appreciated works of art. It was he who either purchased or created the pole and gave it to his young bride as "a token of his everlasting love." When they sold the Greenwood house and moved to Chicago in

This totem pole stood at Highcrest from 1986 to 1995.
Courtesy of the Wilmette Historical Museum.

1911, they left the pole behind but told the new owners a romantic story that would enhance its aura and chances of survival. I like my theoretical story better than the "true story."

In 1995 School District 39 repossessed Highcrest. It didn't want the pole, and no one else was interested in displaying it at another location. Supposedly, at Theda's direction, the Park District returned it to the tribe in Michigan from whence it came, but none of the Park District's old-timers seem to know anything about it. By the way, totem poles were made mainly by Native Americans living in the northwestern area from southern Alaska to northern California, not in Michigan.

A Stinging End to Halloween

On November 1, 1950, several Wilmette folks, including two police officers and five male juveniles described in the *Chicago Tribune* as "louts" and "oafs", were suffering pain in their posteriors. Fortunately for the juveniles, their identities weren't published. In 2022, they'd be about 87 years old, and if any of them were still hanging around with long-term memory intact, I'll bet his recollection of Halloween 1950 brings a guilty smile to his wrinkled face.

The five louts/oafs were wandering around Kenilworth Gardens on Halloween night with mischief on their minds. In those days, Kenilworth Gardens wasn't fully developed. Vacant lots awaited the houses that would become homes to future generations of young families. One of these vacant lots, near the Elmwood/Hunter intersection, featured weeds, grasshoppers, garden snakes, and a huge log, the remains of a fallen tree.

Adolescent louts/oafs in those days were similar to their modern-day counterparts. They act on impulse with no forethought, and they're amenable to the most dim-witted suggestion that a member of their crowd might offer up. In this case, the stupid idea was to move the huge log to the middle of the Elmwood/Hunter intersection. This, they believed, would be a hilarious way to block traffic. It might even lead to an unsuspecting motorist getting hung up on the log.

With the extreme muscular strength that only raging testosterone and youthful exuberance can muster, the louts/oafs managed to muscle the huge log into the intersection. Of course, their actions didn't go unnoticed. Witnesses to their shenanigans called the police while the deed was in progress. Young Wilmette police officers Harold Graf and Charles Taylor quickly responded.

In the years that followed, officers Graf and Taylor would become respected senior members of the Wilmette Police Department, advancing to the ranks of deputy chief and lieutenant, respectively. Taylor would also serve as an official of police organizations promoting progressive treatment of juvenile offenders. But on Halloween 1950, these young officers weren't prepared for what they'd encounter at the Elmwood/Hunter intersection.

Unbeknownst to the five louts/oafs and the two officers, a huge nest of highly temperamental wasps had taken up residence in the log. They regarded this space as their home-sweet-home, and they were more than slightly annoyed at the unexpected disturbance to their peace and quiet. As the louts/oafs dragged the log into the intersection, a tiny wasp bugler sounded the cavalry charge, and thousands of wasp bombers took their places in formation and launched an aerial assault on the louts/oafs' hind ends.

The juveniles took flight at the exact moment when officers Graf and Taylor arrived on the scene. The officers, erroneously believing that the juveniles were merely fleeing from the law, gave chase and grabbed the offenders. The wasp pilots, unschooled in distinguishing friends from foes, assumed that the officers were also louts/oafs. They dropped their buzz bombs indiscriminately on the posteriors of all.

With their captives in tow, the officers returned to their squad cars and summoned street department crews to deal with the infested log. For three hours, the crews and neighbors tried to lasso the log and drag it out of harm's way, all the while suffering additional posterior buzz bombs.

The bottom line, so to speak, was that the perpetrators and officers weren't able to perform any sitting activities on November 1. After a "rump session" at the police station, the louts/oafs were released, on the grounds that the prank was a very sore subject, and everyone involved had suffered enough.

A Message from The Moon

Hello Wilmette earthlings, it's me, the moon. I'm here to lodge a complaint. I believe that you're partially responsible for the trespass that occurred on July 20, 1969 when Neil Armstrong landed on my surface and took one small step. This intolerable intrusion into my privacy still sticks in my craw. It's been followed by other trespasses, and more are threatened. I don't like it one little bit.

Okay, I admit that you Wilmette earthlings played only a minor role. But you did host the wedding of said Neil Armstrong to Janet Shearon on January 26, 1956 at your Congregational Church. She was raised at 1221 Greenwood Avenue in your fair city and was a schoolmate of said Armstrong at Purdue University. Her father was a well-known doctor and a onetime president of your Shawnee Club, the one that later became Michigan Shores Club. I vividly remember folks at the reception babbling about how the newlyweds seemed to be "moonstruck" and "over the moon." This obviously planted the seed in said Armstrong's mind that he had the right to invade my space, and that's why I'm blaming everyone in Wilmette for playing a role in this trespass at my Sea of Tranquility (your name, not mine).

Janet Shearon and future astronaut Neil Armstrong were married at Wilmette's Congregational Church in 1956. Courtesy of Ohio History Connection.

My relationship with you earthlings has been deteriorating for centuries. There once was a time when you worshipped me. It was fun having folks worship me, and I didn't have to do anything in return. But then some smart guys finally figured out why I emit light, rise and set, change my shape, and occasionally disappear and reappear. That's when the worshipping stopped. Astronomers learned that I do all these miracles not because I'm a god, but because of the Big Bang and everything that happened afterwards. You know —Isaac Newton's gravity thing and all that stuff. I don't mean to stir up a controversy between science and religion. I know that the Bible says that God made me ("the lesser light") on the "fourth day." Maybe the Big Bang was the "first day." Hey, I'm no scientist or theologian. What do I know?

Anyway, even though most folks now realize that I'm not a god, I'm still an object of admiration, nostalgia, and mystery. Artists paint and sculpt me. Authors write about me. My favorite is *Goodnight Moon*. Poets and lyricist rhyme about me. If I mention a few song titles, a melody will surely pop into your head: "Fly Me to the Moon," "Moon River," "Harvest Moon," "Blue Moon," "Moonlight Sonata," "It's Only a Paper Moon," and "Twinkle Twinkle Little Star." (Oh wait, that last one may not be about me.) Michael Jackson named his best dance-move after me. Lovers go gaga in my presence. Navigators are guided by me. Tides are turned by me.

You earthlings might ask, "Why do you feel aggrieved when you're so admired?" Well, my grievances run deep. First, it was in 1610 that Galileo, the Italian guy, discovered that another planet, Jupiter, also has moons. In 1610 he saw four of Jupiter's moons and gave them wonderful names: Ganymede, Callisto, Io, and Europa. Later that century, some of Saturn's moons were seen and named: Titan, Iapetus, Rhea, Tethys, and Dione. Over a period of 400 years, astronomers discovered 350 moons in the solar system: 175 orbiting eight planets, nine orbiting dwarf planets, and the rest orbiting other bodies like asteroids. The planetary moons have fantastic names. I'd love to be called Titan, a name from Greek mythology that refers to the descendants of Uranus and Gaea (heaven and earth). It also means "extremely important person" (like me). But I'm simply called "moon," usually with no capital "m." My name "moon" is so generic. It gives me no unique identity. It's like naming one of your kids "kid" or calling your boy-child "bud." You folks creatively named a baseball stadium "Guaranteed Rate Field," but you can't come up with something better than "moon" for me? I'm also insulted by the meaning of the verb "to moon." Where did that come from?

I'm annoyed that I don't receive any royalties for use of my persona or payments for my services. My biggest beef, though, is your coming to visit me. You don't know how to treat us heavenly bodies. Look what you're doing to Earth: polluting the land, sea, and air and making your planet uninhabitable. I can see it coming. You'll do the same to me. In fact, you've already left a bunch of junk on my surface and stolen some of my rocks. As soon as you figure out how to make a profit off me, you'll come by the millions and ravage me. One of your nukes might even blast me out of orbit and cause me to crash into Earth. Stay away! You earthlings are unworthy of your intelligence!

This drawing of the "Traveling Tree" appeared in the *Chicago Tribune,* December 14, 1880.

Trivial Breaking News

- December 14, 1890: A gigantic 75-foot elm tree is slowly moving along Wilmette streets. The tree stands upright with its roots boxed by heavy planks set on top of rollers. It's being pulled by a team of horses with a crew of men holding guide ropes to maintain its upright position. It grew to its present size on a Gross Point farm west of Wilmette, and its destination is the grave of Jedediah Lathrop at Graceland Cemetery in Chicago. Lathrop, a wealthy businessman and investor, died in 1889. His will set aside $10,000 to place a majestic elm at his grave. Lathrop was a longtime resident of Elmhurst, so-named because he and other landowners in that village planted a large number of elm trees, his favorite variety, along a main thoroughfare there.

- June 22, 1905: A cow belonging to Wilmette farmer John Schwall terrorized Wilmette. Schwall, who noticed that the cow seemed distressed, headed to the pharmacist for a soothing nerve tonic. The animal then broke through a fence and charged east on Forest Avenue toward Lake Michigan, overturning wagons and threatening bystanders. Alarms were sounded, drawing police and fire personnel from Wilmette and Evanston. The hero of the day was Police Officer John McGuire. Like a gallant matador, he stepped into an open field and invited the cow to approach. The cow accepted the invitation. McGuire held his ground. Spectators in treetops and other havens held their breath. At the last instant, McGuire struck the cow with his club in a vulnerable spot. "She went down like a stone." The bells of Wilmette rang out "the joyful tidings that John Schwall's cow was stunned."

- August 25, 1911: Wilmette's nightly trysting place at Kline Street (now Prairie Avenue) and Wilmette Avenue has sparked more than amorous passion this week. On Monday, a ghost appeared and frightened away four spooning couples. It also frightened Anna Schaefer, 49, of 618 Kline Street, along with three of her children, Christina, 19, Frank, 15, and George, 13, causing them to beat a hasty retreat from their front porch into their house. Elizabeth Estes, 40, of 1622 Wilmette Avenue, was the next witness. "I'm not in the habit of seeing things, and I'm positively certain it was a real spook," she insisted. Since these sightings, Wilmette's two-man police force has patrolled the area, and 30 young men and women have camped there, hoping to see for themselves, but the ghost hasn't reappeared. Police suspect that the spirit is actually someone living in the neighborhood, intent on closing down the nightly revelry.

- September 22, 1932: Wilmette's village board dealt with a foul issue by adopting a chicken-noise ordinance. Neither roosters nor hens will be allowed to run at large and must be confined to enclosures. A rooster enclosure must be at least 300 feet from a neighbor's home, while a henhouse may be as close as 75 feet. No scientific basis was offered for this gender discrimination. Village President Carbon Dubbs assured citizens that the ordinance will be enforced only when a neighbor complains.

APPENDICES

Appendix 1: Wilmette Drownings

DATE	VICTIM	AGE	HOME	LOCATION
08/16/1875	George Ward	57	Wilmette	Shallow water at foot of Lake Ave.

Ward drove his wagon into the lake, intending to load gravel. When he dropped the reins and walked out on the wagon's tongue, he slipped and fell into the water, startling the horses and causing them to turn and head for shore. Ward never surfaced, even though the water was only three feet deep.

DATE	VICTIM	AGE	HOME	LOCATION
09/05/1893	John Brady	63	Wilmette	Unspecified Wilmette beach

Brady was a veteran of the Civil War, member of the GAR, alcohol abuser, itinerant worker, and colorful and popular local character. One of his stunts at picnics was to jump into the lake to amuse everyone. On this occasion, a strong undertow pulled him under.

DATE	VICTIM	AGE	HOME	LOCATION
08/24/1896	Zilfa Dunshee	12	Wilmette	Unspecified Wilmette beach

Dunshee went swimming with her father and brother. She was pulled under by an undertow and swept away. Her father tried unsuccessfully to rescue her.

DATE	VICTIM	AGE	HOME	LOCATION
10/23/1898	Louis LaBahn	22	Evanston	Eight miles off Wilmette
	William Schaffer	30	Evanston	
	Herman Pernitsky	?	Evanston	

LaBahn, Schaffer, and Pernitsky went duck hunting in a skiff from Gage's Pier at the foot of Chestnut Ave. in rough waters. The boat overturned, and the three men drowned.

DATE	VICTIM	AGE	HOME	LOCATION
09/07/1908	Joseph Reicnier	18	831 N. Halsted St., Chicago	Unspecified Wilmette beach

Reicnier took a break from fishing, went for a swim, suffered cramps, and drowned as his two younger brothers looked on.

DATE	VICTIM	AGE	HOME	LOCATION
07/30/1911	Arthur Brenner	10	3524 N. Ashland Ave., Chicago	Chestnut Ave. beach

At a family picnic, a group of children went onto Gage's Pier. Brenner dove off into 15 feet of water, mimicking the dives of other swimmers on the pier. He never surfaced.

| 06/14/1912 | Andrew Albert | 47 | 1846 Forest Ave., Wilmette | Chestnut Ave. beach |

Albert fell off Gage's Pier and drowned.

| 06/19/1913 | William Gaines | 8 | 2758 Woodbine Ave., Evanston | Chestnut Ave. beach |

While wading with a friend, Gaines stepped into a hole and panicked. A fisherman on Gage's Pier nearby, whose help was sought, yelled derisively that the boys deserved to sink if they couldn't swim and offered no assistance. Gaines drowned.

| 08/16/1914 | Charles Hansen | ? | 1838 N. Talman Ave., Chicago | North Shore Channel |

Hansen fell into the channel while fishing. His two companions tried to keep him above water by holding a fishing pole and a leg for him to grab, but he tired and slipped underwater.

| 08/20/1916 | Henry Metzer
John Kandyba | 18
30 | 2152 N. Claremont
2162 N. Irving Ave.; Chicago | Beach at the foot of Lake Ave. |

Wading in the lake at the foot of Lake Ave., south of the guarded beach, Metzer fell and called for help. He couldn't swim. Kandyba tried to help, but the two struggled in the water, and both sank. Metzer's brother, who couldn't swim, witnessed the tragedy. Five days later, the Park District banned swimming at that location.

| 08/11/1918 | Joseph Chroust | 17 | 4022 W. 31st St., Chicago | Chestnut Ave. beach |

Chroust stepped off a sandbar and fell into deep water.

DATE	VICTIM	AGE	HOME	LOCATION
07/19/1919	Gail Prim David Cameron	17 14	1829 Randolph St. 2132 Congress St.; Chicago	Chestnut Ave. beach

Prim and Cameron were on a Boy Scout outing. Cameron was in the water and called for help. Prim, who had heart disease, was the only person nearby. He called for help but no one responded, so he tried to rescue Cameron himself. Both died in the Lake. Cameron drowned. Prim's heart disease may have caused his death.

04/25/1921	William Gorman	26	2731 West 39th St., Chicago	North Shore Channel

Gorman, an electrician employed by the foundation contractor for the Bahá'í Temple, fell into the North Shore Channel while troubleshooting the lighting system used for night construction. He shouted for help, but his coworkers couldn't find him. Gorman was recently married.

05/21/1921	Mills Crawford	17	Winnetka	A mile off the Kenilworth shoreline

The sailing canoe in which Crawford and a companion were riding swamped. The companion swam safely to shore, but Crawford, a member of NT's swimming team, drowned. His body was recovered three weeks later at the mouth of the North Shore Channel.

06/12/1921	William Reinhold	19	1005 Ashland Ave., Wilmette	1.5 miles off the Wilmette shoreline

Reinhold and two Wilmette friends took a canoe into the Lake. It turned over. Reinhold was unable to hold onto the overturned canoe and slipped underwater. His companions tried in vain to rescue him. They were saved when a bird-watcher on shore spotted them and sent help.

08/27/1928	Fred Rummler	21	1015 Starr Rd., Winnetka	3 miles out of Wilmette Harbor

Rummler and three friends (one from Winnetka and two from Kenilworth) rented a catboat at Wilmette Harbor for an evening on the Lake. A gust of wind capsized the boat. The passengers hung on for hours, but Rummler's strength gave out and he drowned. The next day, air searchers found one passenger trying to swim ashore at 1:00 PM, and she led them to the other two, still clinging to the boat.

DATE	VICTIM	AGE	HOME	LOCATION
07/30/1931	Velma Johns	20	Esman Twp. IL	Chestnut Ave.
	Harold Parker	23	Morris, IL	beach

Johns and Parker were swimming off Gage's Pier with another couple when an undertow caught Johns. Parker tried to rescue her. Both drowned.

10/07/1931	Samuel Moore	53	707 Laurel Ave., Wilmette	North Shore Channel

Moore, a Peoples Gas executive, committed suicide by jumping into the channel at Maple Ave.

10/14/1944	John Hare	?	Both in the	0.75 miles off
	Jack Latimer	?	U.S. Navy	Hamilton St., Evanston

Hare, Latimer and Willard Bell, owner of the boat, sailed out of Wilmette Harbor despite high winds. The boat capsized. Bell kept Latimer afloat for 20 minutes, but Latimer panicked and struggled, and Bell was forced to release him.

06/28/1945	Jean Titus	22	9520 Monticello Ave., Skokie	5 miles from Wilmette Harbor
	Robert Hobart	23	U.S. Navy	

Titus and Hobart, who had met at a wedding the previous Saturday, went sailing in his 18-foot boat moored at Wilmette Harbor. It capsized in a squall, and Hobart's attempt to tow Titus to shore with a rope was unsuccessful. Both drowned.

07/29/1947	Virginia Wheelock	35	Golf Rd., Morton Grove	2 miles from Wilmette Harbor

Wheelock and her husband, Ralph, sailed their 18-foot sloop from Wilmette Harbor and anchored at the North Star racing buoy. After eating lunch, they went for a swim. Virginia disappeared while her husband was diving. He was unable to find her.

10/28/1951	Robert Sawyer	20	U.S. Coast Guard Station, Wilmette	20 miles east of Wilmette
	Max Wage	26		

Searching for three duck hunters missing on the Lake, Sawyer and Wage, guardsmen, went missing themselves in a 30-foot crash boat on rough water. A massive Coast Guard search found only a side board from an engine compartment and a wooden battery box cover from the crash boat. The duck hunters also perished.

DATE	VICTIM	AGE	HOME	LOCATION
08/16/1952	Peter Hernandez	10	1612 Wilmette Ave., Wilmette	At the pier north of Wilmette Harbor

Hernandez was washed off the pier while fishing with a companion, Thomas Nischan of Wilmette. His body was recovered by the Coast Guard.

04/02/1955	John O'Connor	5	1250 Chestnut Ave., Wilmette	Wilmette Harbor

O'Connor walked less than 0.2 mile from his grandfather's home in the 700 block of Michigan Ave. to the harbor, fell into the water, and drowned.

07/25/1963	Cindy Cooper	7	100 13th St., Wilmette	Gillson Beach, guarded section

Cooper's was the first drowning at Wilmette Park District's supervised bathing beach in its history, which dates back to 1916. The child's mother couldn't find her and hysterically sought help from the lifeguards. One eventually recovered the body from the water. A second girl, who was playing with the victim before the tragedy, explained that she had trouble getting back to shore because "there is a sand bar in the water and the ground was not level."

07/26/1978	Gerald Mariani	33	1814 Mura Lane, Mt. Prospect	South of Wilmette Harbor

Mariani was sailing in his 16-foot boat with his wife and two children when a storm forced them to beach the boat near the Bahá'í Temple. When the boat drifted away, Mariani pursued it in a plastic dinghy. The dinghy probably capsized, and Mariana's body was found one mile offshore.

07/17/1979	Michael Rebarchak	18	701 Linden Ave., Wilmette	Private Wilmette beach

Rebarchak, taking a break from work nearby as part of a house painting crew, entered the lake from a private beach. While swimming 200 feet from shore, he disappeared. The public beach had been closed earlier in the day because of a strong undertow along with four-foot waves and high winds.

DATE	VICTIM	AGE	HOME	LOCATION
10/07/1986	Kathy Mulvihill	29	1015 Chestnut Ave., Wilmette	Northwestern University beach

Mulvihill, an experienced windsurfer, was enjoying her sport before going to work as a United Airlines flight attendant. A massive search, begun when she failed to return home, was hampered by bad weather and rough waters. Her body was found two days later. Her searchers rescued a Northbrook man whose disabled boat was found 18 miles offshore.

08/27/2011	Tristan Shamblee	14	Evanston	Gillson Park near the Harbor pier

Shamblee was swimming in an unguarded section of the Gillson Park beach with friends when a wave pulled him under. Signs prohibited swimming in the area.

09/22/2012	Harsha Maddula	18	Evanston	Wilmette Harbor

Maddula, a Northwestern student, was last seen at a party on Ridge Ave. in Evanston. His body was found in Wilmette Harbor. There were no witnesses.

08/08/2020	Ankit Zutshi	31	424 W. Oakdale Ave., Chicago	Wilmette Beach

Zutshi was found in distress while swimming at Wilmette Park District's supervised bathing beach. Efforts by lifeguards and paramedics to revive him were unsuccessful.

Appendix 2: Village Center; Historically and/or Architecturally Significant Buildings

BUILDING NAME	LOCATION	YEAR	ORIGINAL OWNER	ARCHITECT
Second C&NW Depot	1139 Wilmette Ave. (since 1974)	1873	C&NW	Unknown
Schultz & Nord	1154 Central Ave.	c.1898	Unknown	Unknown
Wilmette Shoe Co.	1150 Central Ave.	c.1900	Unknown	Edgar Blake (1922 Remodel)
McGuire & Orr Block	Northwest corner, Wilmette and Central Aves.	1905	McGuire & Orr	Howard Hodgkins
Gold Medal	1123 Central Ave.	c.1905	Unknown	Unknown
Cox Building	Northeast corner, Wilmette and Central Aves.	1909	Albert Cox	Arthur Foster
Brown Building	1159 Wilmette Ave.	1912	J. Melville Brown	Unknown
Harding Building	Greenleaf Ave. and Poplar Dr.	1913	George Harding	Unknown
Baker Building	1150 Wilmette Ave.	1914	Edward Kelley, Frank Seng, others	Henry J. Schlacks (original); Hamilton, Fellows & Wilkinson (1928 Remodel)

BUILDING NAME	LOCATION	YEAR	ORIGINAL OWNER	ARCHITECT
Metropolitan Block	1120 Central Ave.	1914	American Theater Company	Unknown
Boulevard Building	1101–1107 Central Ave.	1916	J. Melville Brown	Howard Sturges (original); John Pridmore (1923 addition)
Post Office Building	1144–1146 Wilmette Ave.	1921	Frank Rockhold	Possibly Alfred Alschuler
Rockhold Building	Southeast Corner, Wilmette and Central Aves.	1923	Frank Rockhold	Alfred Alschuler
Nelson Building	1129 Central Ave.	1923	David Nelson	Andrew Sandegren
Wolff-Griffis Building	1119–1121 Wilmette Ave.	1928	Ernest Griffis & Alfred Wolff	Howard Bowen
Public Service Building	1220 Washington Ct.	1929	Public Service Co.	Herman von Holst
Sweet's Tin Shop	736 12th St.	1929	John Sweet	Robert Rae
Lad & Lassie Building	1115–1117 Central Ave.	1929	Unknown	Unknown
Corcoran Building	1109–1111 Wilmette Ave.	1930	Martin Corcoran	Anthony Quitsow
Prassas Building	1114–1118 Central Ave.	1949	George W. Prassas & Co.	Jens Jensen

WEST OF RAILROAD TRACKS

BUILDING NAME	LOCATION	YEAR	ORIGINAL OWNER	ARCHITECT
Mueller's General Store	601 Green Bay Rd.	1887	Max Mueller	Unknown
Hardware Store Building	605 Green Bay Rd.	c. 1890	Hansen & Hubbell	Unknown
Brethold Building	1209 Wilmette Ave.	1895	Charles Brethold	Unknown
Jones Hall	1211–1217 Wilmette Ave.	1901	Edward P. Jones	Unknown
Heffron Building	629 Green Bay Rd.	1912	Patrick Heffron	Unknown
Krauss Building	1215 Washington Ave.	1919	North Shore Construction	Frank Gathercoal (original)
Millen Hardware	1219 Wilmette Ave.	1923	John Millen	Unknown
Gathercoal Building	1211 Washington Ave.	1927	Frank Gathercoal	Unknown
National Tea Building	619 Green Bay Rd.	1927	George Rasmussen and National Tea Co.	Jean B. Rohm & Son

Appendix 3: Hometown Homicides

DATE	VICTIM	KILLER (ALLEGED)	LOCATION
03/13/1872	Michael Schaefer	Peter Schmidt, the victim's brother-in-law	An auction in Gross Point

Bad blood and drinking led to a scuffle and shooting.

05/21/1880	Willie Meyers	Willie's parents, Ernest and Anna, were accused.	Meyers' business and home at 603 Kline St. (Prairie Ave.)

Willie's body was found in a cistern under the kitchen. Foul play was suspected, and his parents were charged. The grand jury didn't indict, and the charges were dropped. Probably an accidental drowning.

11/04/1893	Mary Cron	Charles Franklin Goodrich, Paul Logan and "Schaefer"	Wheeler home at Lake Ave. and 10th St.

An apparent burglary. Cron was stabbed and her house was set afire. Goodrich was convicted and sentenced to five years in prison. Because of his youth, he was transferred to Pontiac reformatory, where he died in January 1895.

07/12/1915	George Maxwell	John Alfred Lee	"Oklahoma" district "blind pig"

Lee shot Maxwell during a bar-room brawl.

07/24/1919	Fred Slokerman	Possibly self-inflicted, possibly Officer Sam Hoth	Walnut Ave. and 17th St.

Slokerman attempted to rob the Wilmette State Bank and died after being struck by bullets during a shoot-out.

08/10/1931	Adolph Dumont	Three unidentified men	Main St. and Wilmette Ave.

Probably a gangland murder. No arrests.

DATE	VICTIM	KILLER (ALLEGED)	LOCATION
01/12/1939	Dr. Gordon Mordoff	John Quinn, the victim's brother-in-law	Victim's office at 1167 Wilmette Ave.

Quinn was angry over Mordoff's treatment of his sister, among other things. Quinn was sentenced to 14 years in prison.

DATE	VICTIM	KILLER (ALLEGED)	LOCATION
12/27/1946	Otto Freund	Two robbers, allegedly Harold J. Wagner and Nick LaCoco	Freund home at 819 Michigan Ave.

Home invasion and robbery. Freund was brutally assaulted with a chisel. Wagner and LaCoco were acquitted.

DATE	VICTIM	KILLER (ALLEGED)	LOCATION
01/02/1965	Morris Crouse, Norma Crouse, Sally Crouse	Harrison Crouse, son of Morris and Norma and brother of Sally	Crouse home at 917 Oxford Ln.

Found not guilty by reason of insanity on 02/25/1972. Hospitalized for seven years before trial. Released from mental institution and became successful local newspaper publisher in Denver area.

DATE	VICTIM	KILLER (ALLEGED)	LOCATION
11/09/1965	Albert A. Ritter	Gerald Covelli was suspected but never charged	412 Wilshire Dr., near Ritter's home at 440 Cove Ln.

Covelli married Ritter's former wife in 1966. She died under mysterious circumstances on 05/03/1967.

DATE	VICTIM	KILLER (ALLEGED)	LOCATION
06/26/1967	Robert Burghart	Richard Kay	Inside a car parked near forest preserve

Burghart and Kay, both teenagers, were best friends. Burghart supposedly disparaged Kay's girlfriend, and Kay retaliated. Burghart's body was dumped in the forest preserve and not found for four months.

DATE	VICTIM	KILLER (ALLEGED)	LOCATION
04/08/1970	Phyllis Adams	Dr. Richard W. Renn	Adams home at 108 17th St.

Murder-suicide. Less than one month before the murder, Adams had accused Renn of breaking into her home and raping her. Adams was separated from her husband. Renn was divorced. Adams and Renn had dated, but she tried to end the relationship.

DATE	VICTIM	KILLER (ALLEGED)	LOCATION
08/29/1983	Susan Lichtenstein	Eric Moses	Gas station at 133 Skokie Blvd.

Lichtenstein's body was found in her burned-out 1982 Honda Civic. Sexual assault was suspected.

| 08/06/1993 | Dr. Martin Sullivan | Jonathan Preston Haynes | Dr. Sullivan's office at 3612 Lake Ave. |

Haynes, a neo-Nazi, objected to Sullivan's using plastic surgery to create Aryan appearance. He was convicted and sentenced to death. The sentence was commuted on 01/12/2003 by Governor George Ryan to life in prison.

| 12/28/1993 | Suzanne Olds | Helmut Carsten Hofer, charged but acquitted | Olds home at 2832 Romona Ct. |

The victim's husband, Dean Olds, was also suspected. He and Hofer had a gay relationship.

| 10/15/1999 | Myung Hae Seo | Sang Hyun Seo, estranged husband | House at 527 Lavergne Ave. |

Murder-suicide. The estranged couple met at the house of friends who hoped they might reconcile. The husband shot the wife when the friends left them alone. The husband departed on foot and shot himself in the back yard of a nearby home.

| 06/10/2005 | Candice Sepehri | Richard Kahle | Outdoor seating at C.J. Arthur's restaurant, 1168 Wilmette Ave. |

Murder-suicide. Candice Sepehri, an employee at C.J. Arthur's, was shot by Kahle as she ate lunch with her two young daughters. Her four-year-old daughter was wounded. Police said only that the shooting was over a "domestic issue" involving Sepehri, Kahle, and the son of the restaurant's owner.

| 02/28/2009 | Kathryn Motes and her son, Christopher | Richard Wiley, husband of Kathryn | Wiley home at 826 Greenleaf Ave. |

Murder-suicide. Kathryn Motes was the second wife of Richard Wiley. Wiley had viciously murdered his first wife in 1985 and was released from prison for this crime in 2000, shortly before marrying Kathryn.

DATE	VICTIM	KILLER (ALLEGED)	LOCATION
07/06/2010	Veronica Rojas, 18, and Natalie Stygar, 17	Szymon Zawadzki	700 block of Sheridan Rd.

Zawdzki was under the influence of alcohol when he crashed his car, killing the two passengers and seriously injuring a third. He was charged with reckless homicide and other offenses, and he pled guilty to aggravated DUI resulting in an accident that caused death and injury. He was sentenced to ten years in prison. He served more than seven years and was paroled.

| 12/25/2010 | Nancee Rapoport | Anthony Rapoport, nephew of Nancee | Rapoport home at 3115 Hill Ln. |

Anthony was mentally ill and had serious drug problems and a history of violence. He beat his victim with a baseball bat following a domestic dispute. He pled guilty to murder and was sentenced to 30 years in prison.

Appendix 4: Famous Folks of the Past

NAME	WILMETTE RESIDENCE	RESIDENCY	LIFE SPAN	SOURCE OF FAME
	POLITICS AND GOVERNMENT			
Edward Evers	1020 Sheridan Rd.	1905–1942	1878–1954	Rear Admiral, Illinois Naval Reserve
Warren Orr	1415 Ashland Ln.	1940–1961	1886–1961	IL Supreme Court Justice
Elizabeth Dilling	1047 Linden Ave.	1918–1921	1894–1966	Anti-Communist Crusader
Thomas Kluczynski	35 Linden Ave.	Mid-1960s–early 1980s	1903–1994	IL Supreme Court Justice
Vinton Bacon	2206 Kenilworth Ave.	1962–1970	1916–1998	Superintendent, MSD
Charles Percy	1214 Lake Ave.	1935–1936	1919–2011	CEO, Bell & Howell U.S. Senator
	1517 Forest Ave.	1936–1937		
	415 Prairie Ave.	1937–early 1940s		
	2338 Elmwood Ave.	mid-1940s–1950		
	308 Linden Ave.	1967–1985		
	ARCHITECTS			
Jens Jensen	1211 Elmwood Ave.	1920–1935	1860–1951	Landscape Architect
Benjamin Marshall	612 Sheridan Rd.	1921–1936	1874–1944	Architect
Barry Byrne	1027 Locust Rd.	1929–1932	1883–1967	Architect
Myron Goldsmith	503 Central Ave.	1968–1996	1918–1996	Architect

APPENDIX 4: FAMOUS FOLKS OF THE PAST

NAME	WILMETTE RESIDENCE	RESIDENCY	LIFE SPAN	SOURCE OF FAME
		SPORTS		
Robert Skelton	511 Railroad Ave. 511 Park Ave.	1903 1917–mid 1920s	1903–1977	Olympic Swimmer
Richard Howell	1040 Forest Ave. 1023 Ashland Ave.	1939–1944 1944–1967	1903–1967	Olympic Swimmer
Will Harridge	1440 Walnut Ave.	1910–1971	1883–1971	American League President
Kenneth "Tug" Wilson	36 Linden Ave.	1939–1979	1896–1979	Big Ten Commissioner; President, U.S. Olympic Committee
Phil Cavarretta	2338 Greenwood Ave.	1947–1949	1916–2010	MLB Player and Manager
Jack Brickhouse	806 Linden Ave. 1100 Locust Rd.	1950–1956 1956–1978	1916–1998	Sports Broadcaster
Bill Jauss	246 Maple Ave.	1963–2012	1931–2012	Sportswriter, TV Personality
		AVIATION		
Jane Page Hlavacek	425 Prairie Ave. 2215 Schiller Ave.	1947–1953 1953–1960	1917–2006	WASP Member and Airplane Racer
Stephen (Stevie) Baltz	110 Broadway Ave.	1949–1960	1949–1960	Airplane Crash Victim
		BUSINESS LEADERS		
Benjamin Affleck	827 Greenwood Ave.	1911– at least 1919	1869–1944	President, Uni- versal Portland Cement Co.
James Kraft	17 Canterbury Ct.	Late 1930s– 1953	1875–1953	Founder, Kraft Foods

NAME	WILMETTE RESIDENCE	RESIDENCY	LIFE SPAN	SOURCE OF FAME
Fred Salerno	501 Lake Ave.	1927–1968	1877–1968	Master Baker and Biscuit Maker
Arthur Anderson	930 Chestnut Ave.	1924–1935	1885–1947	Founder, Accounting Firm
Carl Wickman	16 Canterbury Ct.	1938–1954	1887–1954	Founder, Greyhound Bus
Nathan Goldblatt	612 Sheridan Rd.	1936–1944	1895–1944	Department Store Proprietor
Mark Brown	32 Linden Ave.	1938–1963	1889–1968	President, Harris Bank
Kenneth Zwiener	610 Maple Ave.	1945–1956	1905–1997	Chairman and CEO, Harris Bank
Howard Reeder	1325 Gregory Ave. 1125 Sheridan Rd.	1930–1947 1947–1977	1906–1977	Chairman, CNA Financial Corp.

CARTOONISTS, ARTIST, ART PHOTOGRAPHER

NAME	WILMETTE RESIDENCE	RESIDENCY	LIFE SPAN	SOURCE OF FAME
Luther Bradley	822 Michigan Ave.	1909–1917	1853–1917	Newspaper Cartoonist
William Schmedtgen	710 Greenleaf Ave.	1909–1936	1862–1936	Illustrator, Cartoonist, Artist
Carey Orr	225 Woodbine Ave. 1630 Sheridan Rd.	Early 1920s–early 1940s 1964–1967	1890–1967	Newspaper Cartoonist
Chester Gould	230 17th St.	1926–1936	1900–1985	Dick Tracy Creator
Edward Gorey	1506 Washington Ave.	1934–1937	1925–2000	Book Illustrator and Author
Vivian Maier	831 Michigan Ave.	1989–1993	1926–2009	Street Photographer

APPENDIX 4: FAMOUS FOLKS OF THE PAST

NAME	WILMETTE RESIDENCE	RESIDENCY	LIFE SPAN	SOURCE OF FAME
MOTION PICTURES				
Hans Spanuth	121 3rd St. 1029 13th St. 229 6th St.	1917 1920 ≈1920–1976	1884–1976	Movie Producer
Ralph Bellamy	1050 Linden Ave. 1214 Forest Ave.	1909–1916 1916–1922	1904–1991	Actor
Charlton Heston	No Man's Land 325 Maple Ave.	1923 1934–1944	1923–2008	Actor
Hugh O'Brian	700 Laurel Ave. 808 Greenleaf Ave.	1935 1935–1948	1925–2016	Actor
RADIO AND TV				
Jules Herbuveaux	2522 Iroquois Rd.	1929–1945	1898–1990	TV Pioneer
Johnny Coons	1031 Greenwood Ave.	1953–late 1950s	1916–1975	Kids TV Show Host
Frazier Thomas	1945 Wilmette Ave. 1232 Greenwood Ave.	Mid-1950s– 1961 1961–1985	1918–1985	Kids TV Show Host
Mal Bellairs	1424 Wilmette Ave. 720 Lake Ave.	1950–1955 1955–1969	1919–2010	Radio Personality
WRITERS				
Robert Casey	934 Linden Ave.	1949–1962	1890–1962	Author, News- paper Reporter
Robert Remini	215 9th St.	≈1970–2013	1921–2013	Author, History
Lacey Baldwin Smith	243 Laurel Ave. 225 Laurel Ave.	≈1966–1969 1969–1993	1922–2013	Author, History
Jamie Gilson	777 Michigan Ave. 1500 Sheridan Rd.	1968–2014 2014–2020	1933–2020	Author, Chil- dren's Books

NAME	WILMETTE RESIDENCE	RESIDENCY	LIFE SPAN	SOURCE OF FAME
RESTAURATEURS AND CHEF				
Lewis Berghoff	1128 Greenwood Ave.	1936–1969	1891–1969	Restaurateur
Clement Berghoff	727 Laurel Ave. 640 Gregory Ave.	1932–1937 1937–1981	1894–1981	Restaurateur
Charlie Trotter	2822 Blackhawk Rd.	1959–1982	1959–2013	Chef/ Restaurateur
MISCELLANEOUS				
H.H. Holmes	726 11th St.	1890–1895	1861–1896	Serial Murderer
David Hall	809 Central Ave.	1913–1968	1875–1968	Hybridizer
Henry Cutler	407 Central Ave.	1921–1959	1879–1959	Lawyer
Milan Lusk	810 Michigan Ave.	1897–1932	1893–1932	Violinist
Percy Faith	901 Greenwood Ave. 744 Sheridan Rd.	1940–1946	1908–1976	Bandleader
Dale Mortensen	1420 Sheridan Rd.	2010–2014	1939–2014	Economist

ABOUT THE AUTHOR

John Jacoby has lived in Wilmette for almost 50 years. While practicing law with a Chicago firm, he actively participated in the civic life of the village, serving as Park District Commissioner (1979–1981), Village Trustee (1981–1989, 2004–2005), and Village President (1989–1997). In 1999 he was named Wilmette's Citizen of the Year. Recently, he served as chair of the Village's Minimum Wage and Paid Sick Leave Task Force, and he is currently co-chair of the Sesquicentennial Planning Committee. From 2010 to 2020 he was a contributing columnist for the *Wilmette Beacon*, writing a weekly column about local history and current issues.

Made in the USA
Monee, IL
21 December 2021

86739776R10221